S0-BKW-956

The International Series in

SECONDARY EDUCATION

Consulting Editor

JOHN E. SEARLES
Pennsylvania State University

Schools for the Middle Years: Readings

Schools for the Middle Years: Readings

Edited by

GEORGE C. STOUMBIS
University of Utah

ALVIN W. HOWARD
University of New Mexico

INTERNATIONAL TEXTBOOK COMPANY
Scranton, Pennsylvania

Standard Book Number 7002 2207 3

Printed in the United States of America by The Haddon Craftsmen, Inc., Scranton, Pennsylvania.

Library of Congress Catalog Card Number: 69-16619

Preface

The junior high school, from its beginning nearly sixty years ago, has had its share and more of controversy, strongly worded claims of potential, and sharp criticisms, which were often extreme and unwarranted. The movement for a reorganization of the public schools that developed in the late 1800's and culminated in the junior high school (which usually included grades 7, 8, and 9), was heralded by some as the answer to the majority of the problems besetting the public secondary schools of the times. College and university faculties were largely of the opinion that the new organizational pattern would do much for a better preparation of the pre-college student; industry hoped that the new schools would meet at least a part of the need for job training; public school personnel believed that the junior high school would reduce pupil dropout, improve retention, and furnish some pre-vocational training; and there was considerable expectation that the junior high school would provide a broader range of course offerings that would be of material value in the education of all youth.

Much of what was hoped for and promised came to pass. But changing social and economic conditions, expanded knowledge of the adolescent and the nature of learning, improved educational and teaching techniques and methods, earlier maturity and sophistication of American youth, and increased public interest in and critical scrutiny of education have produced criticism, controversy, and proposals markedly affecting the curriculum, organization, and administration of the junior high schools.

The readings in this anthology are a selected sampling of the debates, proposals, innovations, backgrounds, and practices of the junior high schools as they are to be seen today. Part I discusses the history of the junior high, the functions, administration, guidance, and today's adolescent. Part II is concerned with the proposals for the middle school with grades 6, 7, and 8 or 5 through 8, as opposed to the traditional junior high school with grades 7, 8, and 9, and includes the arguments for and against these organizational plans. Part III deals with the more common criticisms of the junior high schools and the controversies concerning such topics as interscholastic athletics; pupil conduct, dress, and grooming; junior high school activity programs; the Carnegie Unit; core programs; testing; study halls; grouping; and staffing. Part IV discusses the changing patterns of instruction as they affect the junior high schools, including team teaching, programed instruction, independent study, flexible scheduling, ungraded schools, and the use of paperback books. Part V focuses upon curricular areas and changes and trends in the curricula of the junior high schools.

We are sincerely and deeply grateful to the many authors, organizations, and publishers who have given permission to reprint their material in this anthology. The kindness, friendliness, and good wishes so often expressed were most gratifying. It is our hope that the final product warrants their interest and regards.

GEORGE C. STOUMBIS
ALVIN W. HOWARD

Salt Lake City, Utah
April 1969

Contents

Schools for the Middle Years: Readings

part 1

The Junior High School

The junior high school, brought into being in the early 1900's for a variety of reasons, has experienced a remarkable growth since Indianola Junior High School, Columbus, Ohio, and the Berkeley Junior High School, Berkeley, California, first opened their doors in the 1909-1910 school year. In some respects the junior high school owed its adoption to widespread dissatisfaction with the 8-4 system more than to any real reasoning or evidence that this was a better organizational pattern. College and university faculty wanted to begin academic education for adolescents at an earlier age, the student dropout from grades five to nine was incredibly high, there was a desire to provide prevocational education and a wider range of course offerings, and the work of psychologists, such as G. Stanley Hall in his studies of adolescence, all contributed to the feeling that the public schools should be reorganized for better curricular and administrative opportunities.

Changing times and conditions have resulted in changed concepts of the role and functions of the junior high school, a role that is still somewhat amorphous and undefined to many. There are too many school districts which have adopted the junior high organizational pattern from expediency, as a stop-gap measure, and too many junior high school teachers and principals who regard the junior high either as a little high school or an advanced elementary school. There is a real need for a clear definition, widely understood and accepted, of what the junior high school is and what its functions are.

How the Junior High School Came to Be*

JOHN H. LOUNSBURY

When Indianola Junior High School of Columbus, Ohio, opened in September of 1909, it was the first school to be specifically called a junior high school. Now, 51 years later, there are 5000 schools labeled junior high schools. Another 3000 are called senior high schools. Today, less than 6000 schools remain as traditional four-year high schools in 8-4 systems. The reorganized secondary schools, that is those that deviate from a four-year high school following an eight-year elementary school, now make up 76 percent of the 24,000 secondary schools and enroll 82 percent of the eleven million secondary pupils.[1]

The movement to reorganize secondary education has certainly come a long way since Charles W. Eliot first suggested the possibility of reorganization in 1888. Between that date and 1909-1910, the reorganization movement was confined primarily to the talking stage. Then the appearance of a number of new intermediate institutions moved reorganization into the experimental stage. During the 1920's the junior high school and its partners in the reorganization movement were rapidly growing educational innovations. In the 1930's the junior high school, the senior high school, and the combination junior-senior high school became accepted members of the American school family. By the close of the 1950's the separate junior high school, followed by the separate senior high school, had become the predominant pattern of secondary school

*Reprinted from *Educational Leadership* 18 (December 1960), 145-147, with permission of the Association for Supervision and Curriculum Development and John H. Lounsbury, Georgia College. Copyright © 1960 by the Association for Supervision and Curriculum Development.

[1]The figures given are 1959 estimates based on preliminary data as reported by the United States Office of Education in the May 1960 issue of *School Life,* p. 10-12.

organization in the United States. Together these institutions enrolled 50 percent of the secondary school population.

The movement centering around the junior high school, though already quite successful, is still a relatively young movement. Yet the span of this intermediate institution's existence is long enough so that the history of the junior high school movement can be viewed with reasonable objectivity. And it is appropriate to give some attention to the institution's historical development, for our understanding of the present and our vision for the future are incomplete without a knowledge of how and why the junior high school came to be.

Multiple Causes

As might be expected, a number of causes underlie the development and expansion of the junior high school movement. Things are seldom as simple as they seem at first glance. The glib quick answer of a pseudo-expert satisfies only those who know less. A scholar sees deeper, notes interrelationships, and only hesitantly draws conclusions. With reservation then, the factors which have helped to bring about the tremendous growth of the American junior high school can be considered.

"What is the present after all, but a growth out of the past?" asked Walt Whitman. His question with its built-in answer was well stated, for institutions and major events never spring up independent of time and place. They evolve from and are shaped by the ongoing society. The junior high school is a prime example, for it truly grew out of the times and has continued to shift with the times. The whole history of the junior high school movement is closely paralleled to the social, economic and political developments of the half-century which encompasses its life. The reader may be expecting some more spectacular statements regarding how the junior high came to be, but that is really the essence of it. The junior high school was initiated, developed and grew because a variety of factors, all of which related to the times, and existing educational theory and practice, supported it in one way or another.

The junior high school did not grow simply because college presidents in the 1890's wanted secondary schools to speed up and improve college preparation. Nor did the junior high school develop because several national committees issued influential reports which supported reorganization proposals in the period 1892 to 1918. The junior high school did not grow because educators were seeking a solution to the appallingly high rate of drop-outs and retardation as revealed by the pioneer studies of Ayers, Strayer and Thorndike. The junior high school did not come about simply because many educators were levying criticisms on the existing system with its all-too-evident ills and shortcomings. Nor did the junior high school start because psychologists, like

G. Stanley Hall, supported special insititutions as being better able to cope with the "new beings" early adolescents were thought to be.

The junior high school did not grow because educators aspired to put into practice more completely new understandings of individual differences which the psychologists were clarifying through their research in the 1910's. The junior high school did not grow simply because it afforded an outlet for the strong reaction against traditional education led by noted educational philosophers. The junior high school was not caused by the fact that the growing masses of immigrants and urban dwellers required a more extensive type of citizenship education. The junior high school was not created because the many who never reached the later years of high school needed vocational training. The junior high school did not come to its current position because it was a good solution to the school building shortage caused by World War I and again by World War II.

No, the junior high school did not develop, grow, and achieve its present status because of any *one* of the enumerated factors; rather, it grew because of *all* of them. The credit for the junior high school cannot be given to Eliot, Thorndike, Hall, or any other individual. Nor can the growth of the junior high school be written off simply because reorganization provided administrators with an expediency solution to the schoolhouse shortage problem. Many were the individuals who contributed to the development of the junior high school and many were the conditions which supported its growth. It was the interaction of the many conditions and factors which caused the successful growth of the movement.

In some instances, even the champions of the junior high school movement came from different philosophical camps. College men advocated reorganization for economy of time. Public school leaders were concerned over better meeting immediate needs and saw the junior high school as a means of doing this. Board of education members may have seen reorganization as an economy move, while teachers may have supported reorganization because it would bring about new and improved special facilities such as science laboratories.

A dominant factor, however, has undergirded the successful development of the junior high school movement over the long haul. This has been the desire of educators to provide an appropriate educational program for early adolescents. Such a desire was both an original impetus and a continuing concern. While certainly not denying the assistance of other factors in the development of junior high school education, we may note that the support of some of these factors has not been sustained. For instance, the original reason for reorganization, economy of time, was the movement's first fatality. The drop-out problem which motivated many early efforts to reorganize has largely been resolved at the junior high school level. The assistance which the junior high school received from the guidance movement is now given to other schools as well. But the attempt to provide an effective educational program based on the nature of young adolescents remains as the basic theme song of the junior high school movement.

Chronological Coincidences

"Nine-tenths of wisdom," said Teddy Roosevelt, "is being wise in time." And while we cannot credit an insititution, such as the junior high school, with wisdom, this statement may point up an important reason for the successful development of the American junior high school. Accidentally, coincidentally, and in some cases by design, the junior high school seems to have been wise in time. Its growth seems to have been assisted by many chronological coincidences. The way a variety of developments worked together to the advantage of the reorganization movement is at least a partial explanation for the notable success which the movement has enjoyed.

What if G. Stanley Hall had published his volumes on adolescence in 1925 instead of 1905? What if the school building shortage caused by World War I had come *before* the series of committee reports dealing with reorganization rather than *after?* What if the drop-out studies had been made in the 1880's rather than in 1907-1911? What if the movement to chart individual differences had come about before any mention of reorganization had been made? A number of similar questions might be posed, and probably would be equally difficult to answer with confidence. They are, perhaps, purely academic, yet they serve to point up how important the chronological convergence of numerous factors was to the growth and development of the junior high school.

In summary, many factors worked together to cause the inauguration and early success of the crusade to reorganize secondary education. The original impetus for reorganization came from the colleges and was concerned with economy of time and with college preparation. Discussions about reorganization then began to broaden their base. Proposals for reorganization became linked with other school problems, such as the high rate of elimination and retardation. From psychology came further justification. The culture provided fertile soil for the seeds of reorganization whether planted by college presidents, by public school administrators, by psychologists, or by professional educators. So the movement to reorganize secondary education, coming at a propitious time, prospered.

The junior high school may not have been all that many hoped it would be. It may never have proved itself on some counts, yet it has achieved marked success in its relatively brief history. Many new educational practices and ideas have been tested in the junior high school. More experimentation is in the offing, as glimpses of the future are beginning to come into clearer focus. The junior high school story is then an unfinished one; but its success to date augurs well for the future.

The Junior High School, A Product of Reform Values, 1890-1920*

W. RICHARD STEPHENS

It is difficult to describe with general terms, either presently or historically, the system of education in America inasmuch as there is not now, nor has there ever been, a single national system. There are as many different systems of education in America as there are states, and so the common attributes they share is primarily a function of extra-legal, nationwide agencies such as the N.E.A., accrediting agencies, commercial textbook and test publishers, and the like. This heterogeneity makes it particularly difficult to say when and under what conditions some educational program became a part of the American system, and the junior high school is but one focus of this problem.

The junior high school is, however, a vital part of the system of education in America and is often an arena of conflict regarding what its purposes, curriculum, methodology, and organization should be. Antagonists often appeal to what they presume it "has always been," its history, in order to support their proposals. It behooves us, therefore, to be as informed as possible about its history; not because we think we will find some inherent truth progressively working itself out into an ideal institution, but in order to learn what lessons there are for us and, thus, to be more intelligent in choosing its future course.

The effort in this article, therefore, will be to describe briefly some of the social conditions out of which the junior high school emerged around the turn of this century. It will be argued that the junior high school emerged in early twentieth century America not as a result of the new child study movement as

*Reprinted from *Indiana State University Teachers College Journal,* 39 (November 1967), 52-60, by permission of the publisher and Richard W. Stephens, Indiana State University.

some have argued, but primarily as a result of the progressive reform forces that honored the values of efficiency and economy. These values emerged in the schools in the form of more practical education for business and industrial efficiency.

By mid-nineteenth century the idea of an eight year elementary school had been developed and was well on its way to becoming a reality in various states. Its major purpose was the development of an enlightened citizenry which, it was argued, was necessary for the continued progress of a republican government based upon democratic values. It offered in its curriculum no vocational courses, but emphasized the intellectual skills necessary for literacy and computation.

Paralleling in several states the development of the elementary school, but not attached to it, was another institution of three or four years in length. It was variously called a high school, seminary, "peoples college" and in some cases an academy—not to be confused, however, with the private Franklin-type academy. The purpose of the high school was both the preparation of older boys, fourteen to eighteen, for civic and vocational competence, and in some cases admission to one of the classical liberal arts colleges. By 1880 the college preparatory goal became dominant in most of the high schools. It was not until the last quarter of the nineteenth century, however, that the high school became legally tax supported, and it was not until the second decade of the twentieth century that it would be considered as an extension upward of the elementary school.

By 1890 the high school had grown so spasmodically, and in such numbers, that it was becoming a problem for college admissions officers who were unable to tell what kind of education the high school certificate reflected. The high schools often varied greatly in the number of courses they offered, the amount of time allocated for teaching them, the number of years required for graduation, faculty training and the like.(1)[1] As a result colleges were unable to tell whether or not graduation from a high school qualified one for admission to college.

Not only were the colleges concerned about the substance and the lack of standardization of the high school, but industrial and business leaders were also concerned about its alleged overly academic curriculum, which seemed to make it irrelevant to their needs for industrial skills. Agriculturalists and laborers were also demanding that the high schools prepare their students for more vocational efficiency. And political leaders, sensing the rising pulse beat for more practical and efficient education to meet the growing social problems, began to criticize the academic high school. This reform sentiment would build to a peak in the first decade of the twentieth century and move the Nation's progressive President, Theodore Roosevelt, to say, "Our school system is gravely defective insofar as it puts a premium upon mere literacy training and tends, therefore, to train the boy away from the farm workshop."(2)

[1]Numbers in parentheses refer to reference at the end of the article.

In 1892 the N.E.A. responded to the demands for a standardized high school that would better prepare its graduates for admission to college and for practical life.(3) President Charles Eliot of Harvard, who was identified with more than 200 organized reform groups, was made chairman of a "Committee of Ten" college scholars whose purpose was to reorganize the high school elective curriculum comprised of four "programs" of study: Classical, Latin-Scientific, Modern Languages and English.(4)

The Committee was vigorously criticized because these courses of study did not contain any strictly vocational subjects even though some non-classical subjects were added such as English, history, modern languages, and the modern physical and biological sciences. In short, all four courses of study were college preparatory in that they all required a mastery of the classical studies. However, the Committee did make an innovative recommendation which is important for understanding the structural beginnings of the junior high school. What was the recommendation and what reform forces could have legitimatized it?

It was during the time when the factory was beginning to serve as a model for getting things produced faster, more efficiently and economically that Eliot proposed in two addresses, one in 1888 and one in 1892, that the elementary schools be both "shortened" and "enriched."(5) Eliot was clearly concerned about the upward trend in the age at which freshmen were being admitted to Harvard, and so he proposed that the "waste of time" in the elementary school be reduced two years in order to begin the students' college preparation sooner. The Committee of Ten gave evidence that it accepted Eliot's shorten, enrich, and economize thesis by recommending that either the elementary school begin to teach "several subjects now reserved for high schools—such as algebra, geometry, natural science, and foreign languages," or "the secondary school period should be made to begin two years earlier than at present, leaving six years instead of eight for the elementary school period." The Committee went on to say that "elementary subjects and elementary methods are . . . kept in use too long."(6) Throughout the remainder of the report there is an emphasis upon maintaining a four-year high school and making the seventh and eighth grades an intermediate organizational unit between it and a six year elementary school, in order to bridge the gap and more adequately introduce the student into the high school. Obviously, efficiency and economy would be honored and preparation for college begun earlier. As two scholars of the junior high school recently observed, "It is in this recommended framework that the organizational beginning of the junior high school is seriously suggested."(7)

A negative response to the Committee of Ten's suggestion that the seventh and eighth grades departmentalize and begin to teach college preparatory courses was made by the N.E.A. elementary education Committee of Fifteen in 1895.(8) It was the last N.E.A. committee to recommend an eight year elementary school. The direction of reform in America through economy and efficiency would not be diverted, however, by this recommendation and during the next decade,

1895-1905, many elementary and secondary schools were reorganized into two six year units.

The N.E.A. Committee on College Entrance Requirements, appointed in 1895 and reporting in 1899, sanctioned these reorganizations by urging that the "seventh and eighth grades" be made "parts of the high school under the immediate direction of the high school principal."(9) This Committee clearly continued the Committee of Ten's emphases on early preparation for college admission and efficiency. It also reflected the growing influence of the Child Study movement, which had been stimulated by Freud and led in America by G. S. Hall, by arguing that the "seventh grade rather then the ninth, is the natural turning point in the pupil's life."(10) But the organization and development of curriculum, based not on the disciplines but on the child's nature, designed to prepare for practical life, would not become dominant in American education until about 1918.(11)

Thus far, the case has been made that American educational leaders during the 1890's were stirred to committee action: 1)by the problems of articulation between the various organizational units, 2) by the forces of an infant reform movement which were responding to the dissolution of an agrarian society due to industrialism, the 1893-7 depression, the "status revolution,"(12) and the problems of city growth and immigration, and 3) by the emerging mechanisms of reform–economy and efficiency. It is now instructive to look at the specific changes which were made in response to these forces in the schools of Richmond, Indiana. This is one of several cities which is cited for having the first junior high school.

One of the first responses was a reform in educational reorganizations made in Richmond, Indiana in 1896, which some students assert was the first junior high school, although it did not go by that name. It was merely called the "Garfield School: Grades Seven and Eight." Gilbert Morrison, who was chairman of the N.E.A. Committee on Six-Year Course of Study, stated in his third report for this committee in 1909 that the Richmond school was in fact a six-year high school.(13) Morrison's assertion is corroborated by the fact that the Richmond reorganization resulted in high school courses being pushed down into grades seven and eight, a move which would certainly reduce the alleged waste in the elementary school. More specifically, the principal of the Richmond school reported that the departmental plan was introduced. "The curriculum was vitalized by the introduction of modified algebra, modified English, . . . and a more rigorous course in United States history. Elective choice could be made among Latin, French, English, music, art, and practical arts, available to both boys and girls. Subject specialists, promotion by subject, organization into homerooms with faculty advisers, . . . characterized this school."(14) This reorganization is clearly consistent with the 1893 recommendation of Eliot's Committee of Ten and the subsequent recommendation of the Committee on College Entrance Requirements. It was also a response to the mechanisms of reform—economy and efficiency. But, was it a junior high school? It seems warranted to conclude that it was *in the sense* that it mirrored the high school in its curriculum, organization, purpose, and teaching pattern. Further its term was half as long as the high school, lower in status, had younger students, and was, therefore, since identical in kind, its junior. However, it was not called a junior high school until 1916 when it was reorganized, in response to the forces of economy and social efficiency, into a three year unit.

Several other cities followed Richmond in effecting the 6-6 pattern of reorganization and the conservative college preparatory curriculum.(15) By 1910, however, the seventh and eighth grades in many of these six-year high schools would become separate organizational units. Also, these intermediate units, including the one at Richmond, would change their purposes and rationale in response to the forces of reform; this will be demonstrated in the remainder of the article.

It has been pointed out that educational reforms from 1892 to 1905 were essentially reorganizations of the structure of education. To be sure some curricular modifications were made by including some courses in the physical and life sciences. But from 1905 to 1918 educational reforms would again be urged not only in the structure of education but more radically in its substance. America would increasingly feel the unanticipated negative effects of the industrial movement and progressives would urge that the schools be reformed in order to curb these effects. Lawrence Cremin has commented succinctly on the variety of voices that demanded a reform of the schools so that they could help reform society.

> Business men and labor unions were insisting that the school assume the classical functions of apprenticeship. Settlement workers and municipal reformers were vigorously urging instruction in hygiene, domestic science, manual arts, and child care. Patriots of every stripe were calling for Americanization programs. And agrarian publicists were pressing for a new sort of training for country life that would give youngsters a sense of the joys and possibilities of farming ... the common implication running through these proposals is that educational functions traditionally carried on by family, neighborhood, or shop are no longer performed; somehow they must get done; like it or not, the school must take them on.(16)

An important direction, for understanding the origins of the junior high school, that this reform impulse took in the schools was a clamor for industrial and agricultural vocational education and a decrease in what President Roosevelt called "mere literacy training." The slogan around which this movement rallied was "social efficiency." (17)

Several educators added their voices to the cry for more vocational education as a result of their studies of school dropouts and retardation. E. L. Thorndike and George Strayer had made such studies, but Susan Kingsbury's and Leonard Ayers' were cited more often in the reform literature. The academic high school of the Committee of Ten, and the elementary school, it was argued by critics, were producing too many repeaters and dropouts who were ill-prepared for employment. In 1905, Kingsbury's study for the Massachusetts Douglas Commission reported finding 25,000 dropouts from the upper elementary grades. Her study was frequently referred to by the reformers and, according to Krug, it "laid the groundwork for the later advocacy of differentiated courses of study in the seventh and eighth grades." (18) In 1908 Leonard Ayers, a prototype of the efficiency expert, not only documented the high dropout curriculum by charging that it was "fitted not to the slow child or to the average child but to the unusually bright one," (19) but he also translated these data, using an "Index of Efficiency," into dollars and cents. Ayers then ignoring the overcrowded classes, poorly trained teachers, and the heterogeneous student body, told the cost-conscious public that their schools were inefficient to the tune of "about twenty-seven millions of dollars in our cities alone."(20) Raymond Callahan, a leading historian of education in the era of efficiency, cogently argues that:

> Ayers' book, together with the . . . dominance of businessmen and the acceptance of business values (especially the concern for efficiency and economy); the . . . critical, cost-conscious, reform-minded public led by profit-seeking journals; the alleged mismanagement of all American institutions; [strongly influenced] school administrators who were already under constant pressure to make education more practical in order to serve a business society better . . . (21)

In 1907 the findings of these dropout studies and the sentiment of reformers to vocationalize the schools resulted in the formation of the National Society for the Promotion of Industrial Education (NSPIE). This organization was a polyglot of progressive reformers, including bankers, industrialists, and labor leaders, which sensitized the Nation to the "need" for industrial education and set as its chief purpose: "To adapt public education to the real needs of American youth, nine-tenths of whom take up, directly or indirectly, industrial careers."(22) That it achieved its major goal is evidenced by its role in the drafting and passage of the Smith-Hughes Bill, 1917, and is a matter of record. That it significantly contributed to the development of the junior high school is demonstrable if less well known.

The annual meetings of the NSPIE were filled with arguments for teaching the fourteen to sixteen year olds vocational skills, and with reports of experiments in doing so.(23) In 1909 Charles De Garmo advocated a "junior industrial high school"(24) for this age group. At the 1910 meeting L. O. Harvey, Superintendent of Schools in Menomonie, Wisconsin, urged "more experiments" with the "intermediate industrial school" for the fourteen to sixteen year olds. He pointed out that the typical "trade school . . . is not the intermediate industrial school," and urged that industrial education be provided for in the grammar grades within the existing public school system.(25) At the same meeting Superintendent William H. Elson of Cleveland described with enthusiasm an experiment with an "intermediate industrial school" for fourteen to sixteen year olds in his system. He said that he "modified the curriculum from the usual literacy course for seventh and eighth grades" and added "shop work" for boys and "household arts" for girls. (26) Also in 1910 Superintendent Frank Bunker of Berkeley, California, developed a similar school, reputedly known as the first junior high school, out of grades seven through nine and called it an "introductory high school." (For a variety of other examples see Frank F. Bunker, *Reorganization of the Public School System* (Government Printing Office, 1916) Bureau of Ed., Bulletin No. 8, pp.75-95). Bunker described in detail the kinds of changes he made in the school's organization and purpose and the reason for the changes. He alluded briefly to the characteristics of adolescence and the need for a more "gradual transition" between the elementary school and the world of work.(27) However, among the more pressing reasons cited by Bunker for the reorganization were "congestion at the central schools owing to the growth of the city,"(28) "limited playground" space,(29) and improved "scholarship" at the lower and intermediate levels due to competition for promotion to succeeding levels.(30) Further, Bunker cited as reasons for the reorganization the studies by Ayers, Strayer, and Thorndike of retardation and the fourteen to sixteen year old dropouts. Bunker blamed the dropouts of the Berkeley schools on an overly academic curriculum and concluded that the occupational needs of these students required "radically changing the nature and the content of the course of study." (31) Bunker described in detail the industrializing of the content of study in the Berkeley school: he put "typewriting in the seventh, eighth, and ninth grades, bookkeeping and stenography in the eighth and ninth, and commercial law and 'elementary banking' in the ninth. Along with the special subjects, work in penmanship, in history, in geography, in manual training or domestic science, in drawing, and in music was continued." Further "To compete with the business-school interest," academic courses were modified to 'business arithmetic' and 'business English.' " The remaining academic courses were made optional for the few students who would go on to the upper high school.(32) Finally, Bunker had learned from the Ayers study that the dropouts meant not only social inefficiency but also *economic* inefficiency, so he argued that the reorganization of the "upper grades of the grammar schools" was the "only arrangement" that could be made "within reasonable limits of expense."(33)

This economic motive was also evident to the editor of the *Educational Review* when he commented on the Berkeley reorganization as follows: "Superintendent Bunker proposes a reorganization and a re-grouping of the several grades of the schools in the interest both of economy and of educational efficiency."(34)

Clearly these changes of both the substance and structure of the seventh, eighth, and ninth grades evidence the impact of the reform mechanism of social and economic efficiency as espoused by the NSPIE. That these changes were not limited to Berkeley, California, is evidenced by the fact that eleven out of 200 superintendents reported in 1911-1912 that they had reorganized grades seven, eight, and nine into separate units.(35) Also, during the next two years, 1912-1914, over one hundred and fifty city superintendents reorganized their grammar grades into junior high schools.(36)

It is instructive, for further understanding the relation of social and economic efficiency to the junior high, to look even more specifically than we have thus far at the role of the NSPIE in its efforts on the state and local level "To adapt public education to the real needs of American youth, nine-tenths of whom take up, directly or indirectly, industrial careers." The Society not only "propagandized" the Nation generally into an awareness of its "needs" for vocationalizing its schools, it also became directly involved in reorganizing them on the state and local level. The specific mechanism by which the Society became involved was the "school" and "industrial" survey. In 1914, Leonard Ayers directed the first survey sponsored by the NSPIE for the schools and industries of Richmond, Virginia. Ayers focused on the fourteen to sixteen year old dropouts and the relation of the curriculum of the schools to the needs of local industries. The pattern of conducting the Richmond survey was followed by Charles Prosser as he directed the Minneapolis survey in 1915; superintendent of schools Frank Spaulding, who was also an active member of the NSPIE, had requested the Society's sponsorship of the survey in April, 1915.(37) In both of these surveys the Society recommended that the curriculum of the schools, especially for the grammar grades, be "industrialized" to prepare the fourteen to sixteen year old youth for employment.

Inasmuch as we have already noted the junior high type of reorganization which took place at Richmond, Indiana, in 1896, and in view of the fact that the NSPIE sponsored the 1916 survey of its schools and industries, it will sharpen our understanding of the role of the NSPIE to look at its activities there.

In 1913 Indiana passed its Vocational Education Law. The law came out of the Indiana State Commission on Industrial and Agricultural Education whose secretary John A. Lapp was a leader in the NSPIE. Lapp reported to an NSPIE convention that the bill "reported by the commission had been enacted into law in the form proposed . . . with scarcely a dissenting vote."(38) After this law was passed Governor Ralston appointed to the State Board of Education Mr. P. A. Reid, who was a leading industrialist and secretary of the Elliott Reid Company of Richmond. Reid's appointment was made "on the basis of his interest in vocational education."(39) Inasmuch as Reid was a member of the Richmond Board of Education, his "enthusiasm for the newer (vocational) types of education was directly focused upon the Richmond situation."(40) State Superintendent Charles Greathouse observed that the Richmond superintendent, J. T. Giles, "supported by the board of education" led Richmond to the "conscious realization that the schools bore a direct responsibility for the training of boys and girls for industry, commerce, agriculture, and the household arts which," he said, "as yet had been but partly discharged." (41)

In May 1915 the Richmond board contracted Professor Robert Leonard, an active member of the NSPIE and recently appointed professor of vocational education by W. L. Bryan of Indiana University, to direct a survey of its schools and industries. This was the first of what were referred to as the "Indiana Surveys." The NSPIE "was invited . . .and urged to take a prominent part" in making the surveys, not only of Richmond, but also of Evansville and Indianapolis. "The Secretary of the National Society and two members of its Survey Committee, C. R. Richards and C. A. Prosser, were appointed on the Indiana State Survey Committee, Dr. Prosser being made Chairman of the Committee."(42) The Richmond board gave the Survey Committee a blank check by "obligat[ing] itself to carry out the recommendations for vocational education made by the State Board of Education. . .as rapidly as possible."(43)

It was recalled that Richmond effected a reorganization of its schools in 1896; the grammar grades, seven and eight, were separated from the elementary school and made more academic in their purposes. The general purpose of the 1915 survey, however, was radically different: it was to "outline an efficient and economic program of vocational training."(44) The specific purposes of the survey were, 1) "to suggest provisions which should be made in the reorganized junior high school for vocational preparatory and vocational education for industry, commerce, agriculture and household arts; and 2) "to devise a program for industrial, fine and household arts for the elementary schools."(45) It is obvious that these purposes honored the reformers' values of social and economic efficiency. It is further obvious that the leadership for the prospective educational innovation was coming from the powerful business and labor interests which had coalesced in the NSPIE.

To actually conduct the survey a Local Survey Committee was organized into sub-committees representing every facet of industrial, commercial, agricultural, and domestic activity carried on in Richmond. Members of these sub-committees were physicians, housewives, educators, social workers, industrialists, sales clerks, labor union leaders, Indiana University professors, the Earlham College President and students, but no farmers or ministers.(46) Each sub-committee studied in minute detail the tasks that each occupational group required, and then it recommended that the schools be changed in certain respects to provide students with opportunities to learn these tasks. For examples, the Metal Working Committee recommended that the Richmond schools "can be of real service to machine operators and to industry, by providing night school courses in machine operating and the general work of the machinist."(47) The Printing Committee recommended that a "trade preparatory" printing course "be provided in the senior high school." The Committee also recommended a "printing course . . . as a finding course . . . for the junior high school." (48) The Commercial Employment Committee recommended that a "general information course" emphasizing the "importance" of sales "to the entire community" be offered in the junior high school. It further recommended that the senior high school offer commercial courses that "deal largely with manufacturing processes, knowledge of stock and technique of store procedure, rather than generalities regarding the theory of selling."(49) The other sub-committees made similar recommendations occasionally referring to the relevant parts of the NSPIE surveys of Richmond, Virginia,(50) and Minneapolis.(51)

Upon the basis of the sub-committee recommendations the Survey Committee made the final recommendations per the prior agreement. The Committee commended the Richmond schools "for breaking away from the disciplinary, art craft" approach and for adopting the "life career" plan which called for vocationalizing the curriculum for all pupils " 'regardless of sex and future vocation.' "(52) The Survey Committee "heartily" approved the "platoon" experiment for one of the elementary schools.

In addition to these recommendations the Survey Committee approved the "proposal that the Garfield school (seventh and eighth grades) be developed into a junior high school, to include the pupils of the seventh, eighth and ninth grades." The Committee urged that the required courses for all junior high students be those which were of "general value" to all occupations, as well as providing some elements that make for practical efficiency." "Electives may be so chosen as to group the work about a life career motive in any one of the larger occupational fields; the professional or liberal arts group, the commercial, the industrial, or agricultural."(53) It seems clear that the NSPIE's major goal of "adapting" the schools to the vocational needs of the youth and community was being realized.

Finally, the Survey Committee recommended that the "character of the work in the several courses" be changed so as not to, as President Roosevelt said, "put a premium upon literacy training." The Committee urged that "civics" should deal with the practical "everyday problems of community life and the place of the citizen in sharing effectively the problems, local, state, and national . . . rather than with the mere machinery of government." "Science . . . should be approached from situations having immediate, appreciable problems," and "Mathematics . . . should be largely practical or economic arithmetic" with "most of the problems" growing out of the work in practical arts, "particularly as these are studied from the standpoint of the consumer." (54) The other courses, the Committee recommended, should also reflect the immediate social and economic conditions of Richmond.

References to psychological theories emphasizing individual uniqueness in growth and development are conspicuous by their absence in the Richmond Report. This is not strange inasmuch as these educational changes were the doing of reform minded practical men outside the school, not the doing of educators operating antiseptically with their theories. That educational decisions should have been made on educational grounds rather than on grounds of social and economic efficiency needs little defense, especially in view of the commonly observed anti-intellectual temper of much of American life.(55) However, it seems to me that Hofstader errs in placing the blame for this on Dewey's "vagueness," especially if we can assume that Richmond was but one instance of a general movement.(56) Neither can the blame be placed wholly at the door of the practical businesss man because many educators were also thoroughly committed to the values of social and economic efficiency.

Without doubt other significant reform forces, in addition to the NSPIE, played important roles in effecting these rapid reorganizations. Two of such were the muckrake journalists' attacks on the economic inefficiency of the schools in 1912,(57) and the report of the Committee on Economy of Time of the N.E.A. in 1913.(58) Both of these forces, however, articulated the same values of social and economic efficiency that characterized the NSPIE. In fact, the Committee on Economy in Time was staffed in part by key leaders in the NSPIE.

The Committee on Economy of Time had been thoroughly sensitized by the alleged economic and social inefficiencies in the public schools as was indicated by the number and character of articles and addresses upon which the report was based. Numerous writings by participants in the NSPIE were cited along with references to the retardation and dropouts studies by Ayers and others.(59) Also sensitizing the Committee were three of its members who were also active in the NSPIE: Frank Spaulding,(60) superintendent of schools, Newton, Massachusetts, Frank Thompson, professor of education, University of Colorado, and Frank L. Mc Vey, president of the University of North Dakota.

Echoing the sentiments of the NSPIE, the Committee of Economy of Time, argued that there was much "waste in education" which was "chargeable to the elementary" school. It was argued on the one hand that eight years of elementary education extended too high the age at which college graduates could begin productive work.(61) On the other hand, the alleged overly academic character of the elementary schools, especially in the seventh and eighth grammar grades, caused too many pupils to drop out at ages fourteen to sixteen, ill-prepared for employment in industry or agriculture.

Deliberately taking into account the "vocational movements" purposes, the Committee urged that the elementary school, "the period of general education, should be shortened at least two years."(62) They further recommended for the first time by this name "the organization of junior high schools out of the two upper grammar grades and the first-year high-school class" in the belief that this would give "those children who are more given to action than to abstraction" a chance to "begin vocational education, with its practical life-career appeal, at 12 rather than 14."(63) It was argued that this would "save many children from truancy and disinterest." Such a move, it was also argued, would give the bright high school and college bound student an opportunity to appreciate the "industrial" character of his society and give him an early start to college. It was further argued that it would reduce the waste of 16 years of general education, the "chief excuse" for which had been "culture."

It will be recalled that Eliot's Committee of Ten had recommended this shorten, enrich, and economize the elementary school thesis, but Eliot wanted to add the upper two grades to the high school and make them strictly precollegiate in subject matter. Threads of this recommendation are still evident in this 1913 Committee on Economy of Time's recommendation and the Richmond reorganization. But it is also evident that, in part through the efforts of the NSPIE, the progressive reformers had clearly vocationalized the content and focus of the grammar grades and bequeathed to American education the junior high school.

It is not within the scope of this paper to describe the spread and development of the junior high school from 1920 to the present. Suffice it to say that by 1920 three hundred and eighty-six cities reported 575 junior high schools to the Bureau of Education; and two years later four hundred and fifty six cities reported a total of 733.(64)

In conclusion, it seems altogether warranted to assert that the junior high school was one of many reform mechanisms which emerged during the first two decades of the twentieth century. That the NSPIE played an important role in its birth, and that the values of social and economic efficiency were more prominent reasons given for its birth than the psychological theories of G. S. Hall seems unquestionable. Clearly it was one of the first parts of the academic ladder to succumb to the onslaught of the practical, progressive, business dominated reformer. It was, however, but one leading edge of a host of educational innovations that would become a part of twentieth century American education including the vocational guidance movement, the profession of administration, and the process of curriculum making based on society's "needs."

References

(1) Charles W. Eliot, "Summary of Subject Offerings and Time Allotments in Forty High Schools," in the James B. Angell Papers of the Michigan Historical Collections of the University of Michigan, as presented in Edward A. Krug, *The Shaping of the American High School* (New York: Harper and Row, 1964) pp. 48-51.

(2) Theodore Roosevelt, "Annual Message, December 3, 1907." in *The Abridgements 1907,* Vol. 1, pp. 30-31.

(3) National Council of Education, Report of the Committee on Conference between Colleges and Secondary Schools, *N.E.A. Proceedings,* 1892, p. 754.

(4) National Education Association, *Report of the Committee of Ten on Secondary School Studies* (New York: American Book Company, 1894) pp. 46-47.

(5) Charles W. Eliot, *Educational Reform: Essays and Addresses* (New York: The Century Company, 1898), see Chapter VII, "Can School Programs be Shortened and Enriched?," and Chapter XI, "Shortening and Enriching the Grammar-School Course."

(6) *Report of the Committee of Ten*, p. 45.

(7) Nelson Bossing and Roscoe Cramer, *The Junior High School* (Boston: Houghton-Mifflin Co., 1965) p. 14. It should be pointed out that this interpretation of Eliot's addresses and the Committee's recommendations conflicts with that of Krug's: *The Shaping of the American High School,* p. 44.

(8) National Education Association, *Report of the Committee of Fifteen on Elementary Education* (New York: American Book Company, 1895).

(9) National Education Association, "Report of the Committee on College Entrance Requirements," *N.E.A. Proceedings,* 1899, pp. 659-660. This Committee's call for a "unified six-year high school course of study beginning with the seventh grade," was echoed by another N.E.A. Committee in its 1905, 1907, 1908, and 1909 reports.

(10) *Ibid.,* pp. 659-660.

(11) In 1918 Franklin Bobbit, the leading curriculum expert for the next fifteen years, published *The Curriculum,* and in 1919 the Progressive Education Association was organized.

(12) Richard Hofstader, *The Age of Reform,* (New York: Vintage Books of Random House, 1961), ch. IV.

(13) Gilbert B. Morrison, "Third Report of the Committee on Six-Year Course of Study," *N.E.A. Proceedings,* 1909, p. 409.

(14) Editorial in *The School Review* 47:564-566, October, 1939. Data based upon a statement prepared in 1935 by N. C. Herionimus, principal of this intermediate school in Richmond, Indiana, in 1896.

(15) National Education Association, "Report of the Committee on Six-Year Course of Study," *N.E.A. Proceedings,* 1908, pp. 625-628. Chairman Lyttle reported on ten cities where the 6-6 plan was in successful operation.

(16) Lawrence Cremin, *Transformation of the Schools* (New York: Alfred A. Knopf, 1962), pp. 116-117.

(17) William C. Bagley, *The Educative Process* (New York: MacMillian Co., 1905) p. 60. Bagley sensing the growing impact of this criterion, wrote critically in 1905 that, "Social efficiency is the standard by which the forces of education must select the experiences that are impressed upon the individual. Every subject of instruction . . . must be measured by this yardstick."

(18) Krug, *The Shaping of The American High School,* p. 223.

(19) Leonard Ayers, *Laggards in Our Schools* (New York: Russell Sage Foundation, 1909) p.5.

(20) *Ibid.,* p.90.

(21) Raymond Callahan, *Education and the Cult of Efficiency* (Chicago: University of Chicago Press, 1962) pp. 16-18. This study is a documentation of what happened to the administrators and the schools during the era of efficiency. Also see Raymond Callahan, "Leonard Ayers and the Educational Balance Sheet," *History of Education Quarterly*, Vol. I, Number I, March 1961, pp. 5-13. In this article Callahan cites the acceptance of Ayers dollar criteria for efficiency in the schools by the administrators.

(22) *NSPIE Proceedings* (1911) p. 11. Jane Addams had urged this path on the last day of the first meeting of the NSPIE, 1908, which was in opposition to Charles Eliot's keynote proposal for a dual system of trade and academic schools. She cautioned the educators to not let the "manufacturers . . . capture the public schools." She chided Eliot's proposal that teachers "sort" the children by saying that it would be a "very bold teacher who should attempt to decide definitely for a child of fourteen, especially if she had taught him for but one year and he was one out of a room full of thirty-five or fifty." She concluded the convention by challenging the educational reformers to "fit this trade education not only into the existing organization of the factories on the one hand, but into the existing organization of the schools on the other." Jane Addams, "Discussion." *NSPIE Proceedings,* Part II, (April 1908,) pp. 92-97. It is outside of the scope of this paper to give a detailed account of the formation and role of the NSPIE. For a brief study of it see Robert Ripley Clough, *National Society for the Promotion of Industrial Education: Case History of a Reform Organization,* 1906-1917 (unpublished Master's thesis, University of Wisconsin, 1957).

(23) For evidence of the overwhelming positive regard for industrial education in the "Grammar Grader" see the *NSPIE Proceedings,* 1907-1918, and the *N.E.A. Proceedings,* 1907-1915. One NEA speaker put it in 1909, "the program of this association bristles with the topic." p. 616.

(24) Charles DeGarmo, "Relation of Industrial to General Education," *School Review* (March 1909) pp. 150-153. DeGarmo also summoned the Douglas Commission Report of dropouts as a witness for his recommendation.

(25) *NSPIE Proceedings* (1910) pp. 195-199.

(26) *NSPIE Proceedings* (1910) pp. 172-179.

(27) Frank F. Bunker, *Reorganization of the Public School System* (Washington, D. C.: Government Printing Office, 1916) Bureau of Education Bulletin No. 8, p. 102.

(28) *Ibid.,* p. 105.

(29) *Ibid.,* p. 109.

(30) *Ibid.,* p. 108.

(31) *Ibid.,* p. 115.

(32) *Ibid.,* p. 146. For a fuller description of the effect of this reform on the courses, see chapter VIII.

(33) *Ibid.,* p. 110.

(34) *Educational Review* (February 1910) pp. 210-211. This statement plus Bunker's cited above make clearly suspect Krug's comment on the reorganization that "economy probably was not a motive for such reorganization in most communities." (Krug, *The Shaping of the American High School,* p. 328.) Further contradicting Krug's conclusion is the economic reason given by superintendent Clark of Somerville, Massachusetts, for the junior high reorganizations that he made in the fall of 1914. Confronted with the problem of overcrowding in all the elementary schools and the high school, Clark solved the problems "with the best regard for educational efficiency, of economy, and for convenience of pupils . . . by establishing four junior high schools . . . " Boston's Finance Committee also recommended establishing junior high schools "as a fundamental part of the city's school system . . . on the score of both educational efficiency and economy." For these citations as well as other Massachusetts reorganizations see Chester R. Stach, "The Junior High School Movement in Massachusetts," *Educational Administration and Supervision,* (June 1917), pp. 343-346.

(35) *Report of the Commissioner of Education,* 1912, Vol. I, p. 155. Similar reorganizations were made at Columbus, Ohio, Los Angeles, California, and others.

(36) *Report of the Commissioner of Education,* 1914, Vol. I, p. 147-151.

(37) C. A. Prosser, *Report of the Minneapolis Survey for Vocational Education* (NSPIE, 1916, Bulletin No. 21) p. 645.

(38) *NSPIE Proceedings* (1912) p. 6. Lapp said that even though separate trade schools had been set up in some states, most states were making vocational education "an integral part of the regular school system." The Indiana law followed Lapp's recommendation which he stated as follows: "The greater ease of modifying existing school courses to meet vocational needs and the greater harmoney resulting makes the plan seem advisable." Lapp further argued that this plan pleased the "American people" who are "jealous" of any system which separates different groups into classes." p. 8.

(39) Robert J. Leonard *Richmond Survey for Vocational Education* (Indianapolis: The Indiana State Board of Education, 1916) p. 4.

(40) *Ibid.*, p. 4.

(41) *Ibid.*, p. 4.

(42) *Ibid.*, pp. viii-ix.

(43) *Ibid.*, p. 6.

(44) *Ibid.*, p. *ix*.

(45) *Ibid.*, p. 7.

(46) *Ibid.*, pp. 9-13.

(47) *Ibid.*, p. 79.

(48) *Ibid.*, p. 175.

(49) *Ibid.*, p. 368.

(50) *Ibid.*, p. 124.

(51) *Ibid.*, p. 233.

(52) *Ibid.*, p. 545.

(53) *Ibid.*, pp. 545-548.

(54) *Ibid.*, pp. 551-554.

(55) Richard Hofstader, *Anti-intellectualism in American Life* (New York, Alfred A. Knopf, 1963) p. 375.

(56) Raymond Callahan, *Education and the Cult of Efficiency* (Chicago: Chicago University Press, 1962). This study clearly demonstrates that the business ethic was widespread.

(57) Raymond Callahan, *Education and the Cult of Efficiency* (Chicago, University of Chicago Press, 1962), ch. I.

(58) *Report of the Committee of the National Council of Education on Economy of Time in Education* (Government Printing Office, 1913) United States Bureau of Education, Bulletin No. 38.

(59) *Ibid.*, pp. 93-103.

(60) For an account of Spaulding's ideas and influences see Callahan, *Ibid.*, and W. Richard Stephens, *An Analysis of the Educational Ideas of Five Leaders in School Administration,* 1910-1930, (unpublished doctoral dissertation at Washington University, St. Louis, Missouri, 1964).

(61) *Report of Committee,* 1913, p. 9.

(62) *Ibid.*, p. 18.

(63) *Ibid.*, p. 23-25.

(64) Bureau of Education, *City School Leaflet* No. 12, September, 1923.

Junior High School, 1965*

PIERRE D. LAMBERT

Criticism of American education, with emphasis on teacher preparation, continues as one of the great national pastimes. A favorite target for the critic's dart is the junior high school—its purpose, program, and uncertain future. There is certainly less criticism of the junior high school in the literature than there is of teacher education; but there is no doubt that the junior high school is a source of much anxiety and a topic of heated conversation over a cup of coffee, whether in the faculty room of a school or college or in the neighborhood kitchen. Put together these two, the preparation of teachers and the status of the junior high school, and you have a problem of no small dimensions.

Many of us who are concerned with teacher education are sensitive to the fact that the preparation of the junior high school teacher has not been given the attention it presumably deserves.

However, a review of the literature would suggest that our concern be focused on that for which the student is preparing rather than on the preparation itself. Before one can talk meaningfully about improving the education of teachers for the junior high school, one must again ask certain basic questions about this level. The question, strangely enough, is not "What is the best way to prepare teachers for the junior high school in 1965?" so much as "What *is* the junior high school in 1965?" It would seem obvious that there must be at least substantial agreement on the answer to the latter question before any attempt is made to address oneself to the former.

Some will disagree, feeling perhaps that after more than half a century of the history of the junior high school in the United States, there is reasonable though possibly not universal consensus on its essential nature and purpose. Some may agree with Franklin Parker, who writes: "The wonder is not that the

*Reprinted from *The Clearing House*, 39 (February 1965), 323-328, by permission of the publisher and Pierre D. Lambert, Boston College.

junior high school exists, but that it came so late."[1] For every such statement, however, there are probably a dozen or more questioning the fundamental rationale, the very *raison d'être* of the junior high school. That such questioning is in order may be indicated by an analysis of some of the recent literature dealing with the subject. These comments are intended to show that while there may be general agreement on what *should be,* there is very little on what *is.*

The United States Office of Education, dedicated to the accumulation of vast arrays of bewildering statistics that probably gather dust on many an office shelf, published in 1963 a study of *The Junior High School* by Grace Wright and Edith Greer, based on a survey covering the academic year 1959-1960. In 50 years, the number of separate junior high schools has increased from one to approximately 5000, a figure which represents 21 per cent of all secondary schools, enrolling 25 per cent of all students at the secondary level. Since the year 1952, the number of such schools has increased by one half, the enrollment by one fourth. In addition there are today some 10,000 junior-senior high schools, representing 42 per cent of all secondary schools, a 36 per cent increase since 1952. To one who is interested in the history of education, it is interesting and rather disconcerting to note that a substantial proportion of principals could offer no reply to the question: "In what year were grades seven, eight, and nine in your school organized as a junior high school or as a part of a junior-senior high school?" The United States Office of Education writers seem undismayed, saying, "Understandably, the non-response was extremely high. One fifth of the junior high school principals and nearly two fifths of the junior-senior high school principals failed to report the years of establishment. Frequently, principals wrote that this information was available to them."[2] Reasons given for the failure to reply were "heavy staff turnover" and "lack of readily available records." One wonders, in passing, at the lack of sense of history among some administrators. But in spite of the incomplete nature of the data, it seems that 40 per cent of the junior high schools and 30 per cent of the junior-senior high schools were organized since 1950, while 19 per cent of the junior high schools and 11 per cent of the junior-senior high schools were organized before 1930. Thus the history of the junior high school is in a sense a 30-year or even 15-year history rather than a 50-year history—a fact which may have some bearing on the present confusion with regard to its status.

On the question of proposed changes over a two-year period, 34 per cent of 79 junior high schools replying hoped to add grade nine to the junior high school level, while 20 per cent expressed a desire to convert to some other plan.

[1]Franklin Parker, "Fifty Years of the Junior High School: Preface to a Bibliography of 131 Doctoral Dissertations," *The Bulletin of the National Association of Secondary School Principals,* XLVI (February 1962), 435.

[2]Grace S. Wright and Edith S. Greer, *The Junior High School.* U.S. Department of Health, Education and Welfare, Office of Education Bulletin 1963, No. 32, p.3.

Of 113 junior-senior high schools in the small-school category, 22 per cent would revert to an 8-4 plan, while 43 per cent intended to become separated from their senior division. These statistics, picturing simultaneous movement in all directions, certainly point up continuing dissatisfaction with the organizational set-up, whatever it may be, among a substantial minority of junior high schools.

The United States Office of Education grants but passing attention to the question, ultimately the most crucial, of the junior high school's purpose and function. The authors of the 96-page book quote, alas, from the Committee of Ten and the 1918 Commission on the Reorganization of the Secondary School, of happy memory. They add what is described as one of the most frequently quoted statements of objectives, that of Douglass and Gruhn, vintage 1956. The list,[3] comprising six objectives, is as follows (augmented with my own comments):

1. Integration of learnings into effective and wholesome pupil behavior (a concern of us all from kindergarten to graduate school).

2. Discovery and exploration of pupils' specialized interests, aptitudes, and abilities (admittedly one of the significant concerns of the junior high school, although not its exclusive prerogative).

3. Guidance to assist pupils in making wise choices educationally, vocationally, and in their personal and social living (one may add the same comment).

4. Differentiation of educational facilities and opportunities to care for the varied backgrounds and needs of pupils (probably one of the functions of the junior high school agreed upon by the majority, although still a subject for controversy).

5. Socialization, or the provision of learning experiences to prepare pupils to participate in the present social order and to contribute to future changes (again a praise-worthy objective, the responsibility for which is shared with the elementary and senior high schools).

6. Articulation through making possible a gradual transition from elementary to senior high schools (an ideal easier to state than to implement, as evidenced by the fact that 94 per cent of the junior high schools and 85 per cent of the junior-senior high schools reported that most effective technique to effect so-called articulation was the transfer of cumulative records, while in 70 per cent of junior high schools and 59 per cent of junior-senior high schools the most effective technique was simply described as making information available).

This list of objectives, then, brief and general as it is, will certainly not clarify the function of the junior high school for any one consulting this

[3]Wright and Greer, *op. cit.* pp. 5-6.

particular report. But the United States Office of Education is statistically and not philosophically oriented, so perhaps we should not look for too much here.

On a variety of practices and policies in the junior high school, the report suggests a wide range. For instance, the length of the school year may be less than 165 days or more than 180 days, the school day less than five hours or up to seven hours, a class period from 40 minutes to over one hour. Bases for homogeneous grouping in the junior high school include IQ's, school marks, reading levels, standardized tests, and teacher estimates, in that order. Departmentalization is found in 50 per cent of the seventh grades, 60 per cent of the eighth grades, and 80 per cent of the ninth grades. On library services, on the use of audiovisual equipment, again a wide range of practices is reported. In the field of testing, 69 to 87 per cent, depending on the size of the school, gave standardized achievement tests; 48 to 68 per cent gave tests of mental ability. Uniform standards as bases for marking were adopted in 48 per cent of the junior high schools, 53 per cent of the junior-senior high schools. Marking on the basis of individual pupil ability was preferred by 39 per cent of junior high schools, 36 per cent of junior-senior high schools. Uniformity in all of these practices is of course neither possible nor desirable; but one wonders at the complete absence of uniformity with regard to any of these policies and at the difficulty in identifying the character of the junior high school in the context of such wide-ranging practices.

In the area of the curriculum, to cite one or two more examples, the survey found a virtually uniform requirement for pupils in grades seven and eight in the language arts, math, and social studies; but in grade nine only in the language arts was the requirement universal. Math was required in 90 per cent of the schools at this grade level, social studies in 70 to 80 per cent. Among teachers in the junior high school, the majority were found to have done some graduate work but not to have attained the Master's degree. Again the range was broad, from less than a bachelor's degree to the doctorate.

The picture of the junior high school given by the United States Office of Education is, therefore, while statistically impressive, certainly not a clear picture of a well-defined school whose purposes and programs are explained to the satisfaction of the majority.

A more promising source of clarification would presumably be found in *The Bulletin of the National Association of Secondary School Principals,* particularly from the organization's committee on junior high school education. In recent years the *Bulletin* has devoted several issues to this area. But again here one finds some cause for concern as one reads the statements of presumably qualified leaders in the field. At a junior high school regional conference at Indiana University in 1962, Mauritz Johnson outlined some of the needs of the sixties which might serve as a guideline in the planning of a school program. Well and good—on the nature and crucial quality of these needs there is no argument. They include the unfinished business of democracy, the specifics of which we hardly need recall here; the impact of what he calls the third Industrial Revolution; the problem of bringing culture to the masses as opposed to the production of a mass culture; and the education of women, much discussed in recent popular as well as professional literature. But then Mr. Johnson offers some implications for the junior high school, which must be quoted verbatim so as not to lose any of the effect. He writes: "It is time now to turn to the schools, and particularly to the junior high schools, to consider some implications of the needs of the society and the individual in the sixties. I shall not attempt to arrive at a list bearing a one-to-one correspondence to the needs just discussed, nor will I suggest that the implications for the junior high school are unique to that level. If the junior high school differs from the adjacent levels, it is mainly in emphasis, and if it has any uniqueness, it is in sharing most of the characteristics and problems of the other levels."[4] We may well pause here and ponder the significance of that last statement–probably without much profit. What it says in effect is that each one of us is unique because we are all alike! And the whole passage certainly does not go far–does not go anywhere at all as far as delineating the specific role of the junior high school. In all fairness to the author, he does follow with some fairly concrete suggestions, but again few of them effectively specify the proper function of the junior high school. He suggests, for instance, that the junior high school teacher should guide the pupil in how to study. This is indeed a responsibility of the junior high school teacher, perhaps critically so because of the pupil's gradual assumption of independence at this stage, but certainly not a responsibility in an exclusive sense. Nor is it too rewarding to learn that the junior high school teacher should identify with the scholarly community. So should every teacher.

At the same conference, J. Lloyd Trump offered some thought-provoking suggestions, a review of which, however, again proves unrewarding in the quest for clarification of the role of the junior high school today. Mr. Trump in effect speaks of a sequential program, K-12, rather than of the specific responsibilities of the junior high school.

What then is the junior high school in 1965? What can be said of the preparation of teachers for the junior high school? At the Indiana Conference, Christian Jung contributed another list,[5] this one containing nine items, under the heading "What Kind of Teachers Do We Need?":

"1. We need mature persons recognizing their own abilities and weaknesses, sensitive to others and to their needs and aspirations." (Ditto, elementary schools, senior high schools, and colleges!)

"2. We need teachers with a sound, broad, and secure knowledge of their

[4] Mauritz Johnson, Jr., "Needs for the Sixties," *The Bulletin of the National Association of Secondary School Principals,* XLVII (February 1963), 7.

[5] Christian W. Jung, *loc. cit.,* p. 25.

teaching fields, who are able to see the relationships existing among the several subjects." (Who would have any teacher otherwise?)

"3. We need teachers with an understanding of child development who recognize the wide range of differences existing in grades 7,8, and 9: teachers able and willing to cope with the total development of the pupil in all aspects of growth." (Here, one may concede, is a point of direct relevance to the junior high school teacher.)

"4. We need teachers with a thorough understanding of the learning process; teachers who are able to teach pupils effectively at different levels of achievement; teachers who are acquainted with a multitude of resources and their use; and teachers who are able to use the various tools of learning to enhance the teaching-learning situation in the classroom." (Again, amen; but we need these teachers at all levels.)

"5. We need teachers with a sound general educational background." (Again one should certainly hope so, of the third grade or the sixteenth grade teacher.)

"6. We need teachers with enthusiasm for learning and teaching." (Hardly a unique requirement.)

"7. We need teachers with an abiding faith in the idea of an education for all." (Indeed we do.)

Finally, the author mentions one need that is peculiar to the junior high school, but in a negative way. This is the teacher we do not need. "For certain," he writes, "we do not need teachers who are using the junior high school primarily as a stepping stone or those who consider it an extension of the elementary grades or the lower grades of a senior high school. We do not want the junior high school to be the place for unhappy or unsuccessful teachers of other levels." (Sage counsel, again, but hardly enough on which to base a teacher-preparation program for prospective teachers in the junior high school.)

In one of the discussion sessions at the Midwestern meeting, it was agreed that such prospective teachers should have special material in the following areas: (1) the early adolescent, with emphasis on physical and emotional development; (2) the history, purposes, and functions of the junior high school: (3) guidance of the junior high school student; (4) particular methods best suited for teaching junior high school students; (5) teaching student how to study; (6) teaching reading; (7) discipline in the junior high school; (8) student teaching at the junior high school level. With the exception of the last of these recommendations, which is obviously a desideratum and creates no special problem, one is not sure what the reaction would be if we were to add substantially to our teacher-preparation program to include specialized courses dealing with the early adolescent, the history of the junior high school, and so on. It certainly would not help our rating with the Koerners and the Conants.

Other lists of qualities desirable in junior high school teachers were given at the Indiana Conference or at the Wisconsin Conference the same year. Again, while they provide interesting criteria of teacher effectiveness, they generally fail to pinpoint the problems at the junior high level, or the special needs in the education of teachers for this level.

Research on the education of teachers for the junior high school has been minimal. In the February, 1962, issue of *The Bulletin of the National Association of Secondary School Principals,* J. Lloyd Trump and his associates have provided a brief abstract of 174 doctoral dissertations dealing with some phase of the junior high school. Among these, 14 studies focused on some aspect of the teacher problem at that level. Conclusions drawn from these dissertations reinforce the view expressed here concerning the obscure status of the junior high school. One might cite Ackerman's[6] statement that in 246 collegiate institutions concerned with this area, only 36 provide some special curricula, while a number provide some special courses, most of which fall within the responsibility of elementary or senior-secondary teacher preparation programs. Maynard[7] pointed out that programs agreed upon as desirable are not the same as programs actually in effect in teacher-preparation institutions. Walker[8] found that 40 per cent of teachers questioned had stressed the junior high level in their preparation, and that approximately half of the group had been satisfied with their preparation.

The implications of such research seem evident. If one may add still another need to the already generous but often inadequate list of needs, it is the need for a careful, painstaking, rigorous attempt on the part of junior high school principals and teachers working with university personnel concerned with teacher preparation to spell out in detail the nature, the objectives, the functions of the junior high school, and then to discuss meaningfully the specific characteristics of teachers for this level and the specific requirements for a preparation program. There is a need for hacking away at the underbrush that obscures the true nature of the junior high school and makes any discussion of its problems difficult, if not impossible.

[6] Ralph E. Ackerman, "A Critical Analysis of Programs for Junior High School Teachers in Teacher Education Institutions of the United States." (1960) Unpublished Doctoral Dissertation, University of Connecticut.

[7] H. Glenn Maynard, "A Study of the Professional Preparation of Junior High School Teachers." (1960) Unpublished Doctoral Dissertation, Colorado State College.

[8] Benjamin F. Walker, "A Study of the Professional Preparation of Junior High School Teachers in Indiana." (1959) Unpublished Doctoral Dissertation, Indiana University.

Concerns of Contemporary Adolescents*

RICHARD SCHMUCK

In this paper, I will emphasize problems as seen by working and middle class adolescents with considerable economic security, little anxiety about survival, and generally healthy personalities. Youngsters of the working and middle-classes, though generally contented, healthy, and competent, do have realistic concerns which often keep them from fully realizing themselves intellectually and socially. These concerns are not focused on the tangible and the concrete, as they are for the impoverished youth of our inner cities and barren countryside. In contrast, working and middle-class youngsters are bothered by the complexities and conflicts in the interpersonal demands of the present and future—they are concerned with making sense out of the multiple demands of parents, teachers and peers while trying to become an autonomous and integrated individual.

Each of the adolescent concerns presented below was derived from questionnaires systematically collected from three groups of teenagers, 30 participants in a weekend human relations laboratory sponsored by the Institute for Social Research and YWCA,[1] about 200 youth of the Episcopalian church, and 15 Unitarian teenagers. The specific responses are grouped into more general categories of concern. In every case the listed concerns come directly from adolescents; they are not derived from a psychological theory. In the main, the concerns involve parents, teachers, and peers. Let us begin a description of the most common concerns with parents as viewed by the adolescent boy or girl.

*Reprinted from *The Bulletin of the National Association of Secondary School Principals,* 49 (April 1965), 19-28, by permission of the publisher and Richard Schmuck, University of Oregon.

[1]Hawkenshire, F. (ed.), *Parents, Teachers, and Youth: A Teenage Weekend Laboratory,* Document No. 9 of Inter-Center Program on Children, Youth, and Family Life, Institute for Social Research, The University of Michigan, Ann Arbor, Michigan, 1962.

Concerns with Parents

Adolescents view parents as the most significant figures in their lives. They usually refer to them whenever decisions they feel are important have to be made. Of all the concerns which the youngsters reported, over sixty-five per cent involved their parents. Although several hundred statements of problems with parents were collected, it was possible to organize almost all of them into four categories.

1. PARENTS NOT DISCUSSING WITH THE ADOLESCENT WHAT HE OR SHE CONSIDERS IMPORTANT

Some examples of statements about parents are: "They won't listen to me," "They think many of my wishes and fears are silly," "I often feel that I am not trusted and listened to by them," and "They treat me like a child, never listen to me." The adolescent who makes statements like these means that his parents and he are unable to communicate successfully; that the different generations cannot bridge the psychological gulf between them. These comments are seldom based on the youth's perceptions that his parents do not have enough time for him. Accurate communication and genuine empathy, not time spent, concern the adolescent.

Even a cursory analysis suggests that responsibility for unclear communication and an absence of empathy lies with both generations. On the one hand, parents often do not appreciate the importance to the adolescent of his own thoughts, feelings, and terminology; conversely adolescents have difficulty in perceiving the limits of their parents' knowledge about youth culture and become impatient with them too quickly. Often parents increase the gulf by failing to talk with the adolescent about values and personal controls. Because parents are looked to for guidance concerning important decisions, communication difficulties with them heighten the youth's anxieties about his autonomy. Adolescent anxieties over autonomy, as well as related fears of the parents concerning controls, complicate the youth's attempts to achieve individuality.

2. PARENTS DEMANDING THAT THE ADOLESCENT'S THOUGHTS AND ACTIVITIES BE PUBLIC

Some of the youth interviewed, mostly girls, were distressed about a lack of privacy. They said such things as, "My parents always want to know what I'm doing and thinking," "My mother sometimes picks up the extension phone and listens to my telephone conversations with boys," and "My father asks my girl friends about what I do on dates." Here the concern primarily is with clandestine parental observations of activities with peers. Often, of course, the youngster suspects his parents of doing more of this than is actually the case. Nevertheless, this fairly typical perception, represented by about twenty per cent of the youth interviewed, eighty-five per cent of whom were girls, is representative of a basic problem of trust.

Parents and teenagers find difficulty in achieving a comfortable balance in sharing their public and private lives. This difficulty in sharing often leads to distrust between the generations. Some parents try to develop trust by imitating the behaviors of their adolescent son or daughter. These parents feel that trust can be established by using teenage jargon, by joining the screaming over the latest theatrical or musical rage, or by dressing as though they were seventeen. In attempting to establish trust by imitating youth, parents forfeit their status leaving the adolescent without clarity in his search for attractive and reachable adult models. Without active parental guidance, the adolescent has little sense of where he is headed, experiences disorganization and discouragement, and is easily manipulated by the fads and fancies of the day. Parents tend to establish trust when they respect adolescent privacy while showing an honest and sincere adult interest in what the adolescent believes and feels.

3. PARENTS RESTRICTING DATING PATTERNS

Many of the girls (sixty per cent), but only a few of the boys (five per cent), discussed dating as a focus of conflict with parents. The girls mentioned such things as, "My mother doesn't allow me to date even though most of the other girls in my class date often" (a tenth grade girl), "My Dad gives me a hard time when I want to date a boy older than me," and "My father is always checking up on me when I'm out on a date." Comments like these demonstrate the importance of the adolescent girl's attempts to relate effectively to boys. In contrast to boys, for whom success in adult life depends largely on occupational adjustment, a satisfactory adulthood for girls depends much more on a healthy marriage. For adolescent girls, dating serves as a barometer of later happiness.

Although there is some pressure on girls to date early, the demands of the 1960's for specialized skills and advanced education increase the waiting period before marriage. One major consequence of this bind is that both parents and adolescent girls worry about the consequences of dating. The girl must date as a preparation for adulthood, but she must not go too far too soon with her dates. The anxieties raised by this dilemma manifest themselves often in a lessening of effective communication between the generations about romance and marriage.

Some parents unconsciously aggravate these adolescent concerns about dating and marriage. They dread the girl's eventual severance from home and respond by smothering her with affection and rigid controls. Fathers often react this way out of a fear that their daughter may be "ruined" by the "evil men" in the world. Some mothers fear that their child, male or female, will not be able to solve personal problems without parental guidance. In other families, the presence of an adolescent keeps the parents together. Such parents, out of anxiety over a loss of marital stability, work to keep the adolescent dependent on them. Parental over-control restrains the adolescent from doing what teachers and peers indirectly tell him to do—become an individual, rely on himself, become autonomous from his family, become competent on his own.

4. ADOLESCENT LACKING RESPECT FOR, AND TRUST IN, THEIR PARENTS

The most frequent concern for adolescent boys involves the integrity, trustworthiness, and forthrightness of their parents. Some boys say of their parents, "They say one thing and do another," "They are real phonies," and "They do not agree often on what they want me to do." Although comments like these occurred in only about twenty-five per cent of the boys interviewed, they were laden with feeling and must be considered as significant. The perceptions that parents are sometimes "phonies" leads to an alienation from adult modeling and often a destructive, extropunitive outpouring against adult society.

Some parents evoke such feelings through their own inconsistencies in decision-making about child-rearing. When one parent plays a minor role in the family *vis-a-vis* the youth, the adolescent becomes confused about parent expectations concerning his behavior. The adolescent learns about this power discrepancy and plays one parent against the other. The family without a united front and shared responsibility in deciding important matters with the youth tend to be manipulated by him. Moreover, given these family experiences, the youth often has difficulty in adjusting to others, especially teachers and peers who are not so easily manipulated.

Concerns with Teachers

Teachers were the second most common group of people with whom adolescents had major concerns. At least forty per cent of the youth remarked about problems they have had with their teachers. Some of these were:

1. TEACHERS NOT GETTING TO KNOW THE STUDENTS

The most frequent concern with teachers (about 20 per cent of the sample) had to do with a lack of intimacy and personal contact between the generations. Examples of comments which typified this concern were, "We get too little personal attention from our teachers," "Teachers don't care if they know you very well or not," and "Our teachers are like machines—you go to class and they 'spiel' out information." Adolescents making such statements are asking for some consideration and respect as persons.

Some teachers seemingly do not realize that an adolescent's perceptions of his own competence and effectiveness make up an integral part of his school motivation. Even where teachers are aware of this, they sometimes fail to appreciate that these self-perceptions can change from day to day, depending on the reflected appraisals received by the adolescent from important others. Since competence and achievement are valued so highly in contemporary society, the adolescent is especially sensitive to others' evaluations of his school performance. The teacher plays a special role in defining how competent or incompetent the adolescent is. Some teachers unknowingly deprive youth of their self-respect, confidence, and esteem. The more an adolescent is treated as incompetent, the more he will come to exhibit this prophecy; and, of course, conversely when he is given support and respect, he develops a more positive view of himself. The adolescent's concept of himself, especially in the areas of expertness and personal efficacy, is built up through the accumulated reflected appraisals of teachers with whom he comes in contact. A positive view of self facilitates high academic performance, while a negative view inhibits it.

2. TEACHERS LACKING INTEREST IN TEACHING AND YOUTH

About ten per cent of the adolescent boys and girls interviewed pointed to their teacher's lack of interest in teaching, and to their ineffectiveness in relating to students in the classroom. They said, "He always comes to class unprepared," "He doesn't seem to care if we learn," and "He isn't even interested in what he is teaching." Adolescent perceptions that the teacher does not care either about getting to know the student or about his subject matter encourage a lack of classroom involvement on the part of the student.

Moreover, some teachers treat adolescents as objects of manipulation rather than as human beings with which to relate honestly and sincerely. Such teachers are concerned that the adolescent not view their "seamy sides." For instance, the adolescent should not know that teachers smoke in the furnace room, that they drive cars rapidly, and that they enjoy sensational movies. The irony is that adolescents usually know these things about the teachers, and the teacher's inconsistencies lead to a feeling among youth that teachers are phony, distrustful, and not interested in youth. Teachers establish more respect from youth when they behave as adults and confront the adolescent directly with what their prerogatives are as adults and what the limitations are for the adolescent because he is young. To live by such a double standard, so long as both parties are aware of it, may be better than glaring inconsistencies between verbal platitudes and actual behaviors.

3. TEACHERS SHOWING PARTIALITY FOR OTHER STUDENTS

Here about five per cent of the interviewees, mostly boys, said about their teachers, "They have their pets," "Many girls get away with murder-simply because they are girls," and "You have to 'brown-up' the teacher to do well." Teachers, sometimes are not cognizant of the role they play in influencing a student's relationships with his peers. The teacher's own behaviors and feelings toward a student contribute toward the acceptance of that student by his peers. If the teacher himself accepts each student as an individual–understanding his limitations and giving him support to expand his strong points and help overcome his shortcomings–members of the peer group often will tend to follow a similar pattern. If, on the other hand, the teacher supports primarily the highly competent adolescents and shows rejecting or disapproving behavior to those who are not so successful, a competitive, non-supportive peer climate is likely to emerge in the classroom. Such atmospheres do not facilitate adolescent self-development. Adolescents who experience successful and secure relationships with their peers achieve more highly on academic tasks, have higher self-esteem, and more positive attitudes toward school than adolescents with poor peer relations.[2]

Concerns with Peers

Specific concerns over relationships with peers were brought up by about thirty per cent of the entire sample. Even though parents and teachers were mentioned more often, concerns with peers evoked a similar amount of strong feeling. Many different concerns were expressed but only two categories of responses occurred very frequently.

1. PERSONAL VALUES CLASHING WITH THOSE OF FRIENDS

The most typical concern dealt with discontinuities between one's own values and those of others. Comments expressing this problem were, "I don't always agree with them and it bothers me," "Sometimes you can't convince kids

[2]Schmuck, Richard, "Some Relationships of Peer Liking Patterns in the Classroom to Pupil Attitudes and Achievement," *The School Review,* Vol. 71, No. 3, Autumn, 1963, pps. 337-359.

that they're wrong," and "I don't agree with what some of the girls do on dates." These concerns demonstrate the tension which adolescents experience as they attempt to develop their own values and self-concepts.

2. DIFFICULTY IN RETAINING FRIENDS AND POPULARITY

Statements which were about as frequent as those on value conflicts had to do with friendship and popularity. Examples of statements in this category were, "It's hard to know what you have to do to be popular," "I'm very nervous about losing friends," and "I'm afraid that I won't be respected by other kids."

These two categories of concerns are closely interrelated. The adolescent begins to find out who he is and what his values are by intimately relating with others. Peers are the most available persons for intimate relationships. They have similar needs, conflicts, terminology, and interests. At the same time, conflicts naturally arise between peers as to the "right values and beliefs for me." Only through intimate sharing and introspection can the adolescent solve these conflicts for himself. His concern about being detached from friends stems from his fear that he will not be able to figure out who he is without assistance. Provided the adolescent has given up on adults in this regard, peers are the only relevant and available figures who remain.

Adolescent Concerns As the Social Psychologist Sees Them

My experiences with the working and middle-class adolescent of today indicate that he is not extremely rebellious and intransigent. His stated concerns involve relationships with other people, primarily parents, teachers, and peers. His problems center on integrating the simultaneous, and often inconsistent, demands of these three groups of people. The most basic issue for the adolescent is the attempt to achieve a sense of autonomy and individuality. Both this end of shaping an individuality and the means of reaching it, interacting with important others, are sources of concern.

In the junior and senior high school years, youngsters move through a developmental period of transition between childhood and adulthood. During this time, the adolescent structures his sense of who he is and how valuable he is; his self-concept and self-esteem take on a unique form. As the adolescent experiences this transition, the impressions he has of himself are tractable and his anxieties about how valuable he is are heightened. He is at the crossroads of developing an identity. At this point, he can become several selves, he can cherish several different goals for himself. The demands of parents, teachers, and peers somehow have to be joined and integrated to help in the development of a coherent self picture.

The interpersonal concerns of this period are heightened by the adolescent's physical development—biologically he is an adult during the high school years. He looks to parents and teachers as models for expectations about and ways of expressing his maturing urges. Adults often respond by being aloof and unsympathetic to these feelings. The adolescent then looks to peers as "safe objects" for trying out these new awarenesses. Perhaps the most outstanding feature which is easily visible during this period is the adolescent's self-consciousness about his clothing. If he does not feel properly dressed, or more importantly if he does not feel personally attractive, the adolescent feels inadequate. In fact, the conformity in dress, which is also widespread in adult culture, appears to stem in part from a fear of public criticism and loss of support and affection from others.

While the adolescent seeks security in his relations with peers, he also searches for a sense of competence and self efficacy. The achievement of competence and personal effectiveness becomes more difficult as the complexity of contemporary times increases. Indeed, in part at least, the adolescent's problems of becoming an integrated individual can be understood as a function of contemporary social changes. The most obvious change involves increased bureaucratization and the complexity of face to face relationships with various individuals and occupants of roles. One method of coping with the ever increasing sphere of interpersonal relationships that occur in the bureaucratic setting is psychological distance or impersonality. The adolescent who is trying to find intimacy and human affect with teachers and peers often finds superficiality and phoniness instead. Learning to be intimate with someone outside the family is a critical part of self-development. If satisfactory contacts are not available, the adolescent either withdraws or, more commonly, takes on the defensive aloofness and superficiality of his models.

While relationships with parents are very important for the adolescent, more and more I have come to the conclusion that relationships with teachers and peers also play a major part. In a recent study of junior and senior high school students, Van Egmond and I found that the perception of teacher emotional support was by far the most potent facilitator of academic performance in both sexes.[3] In fact, a high school pupil's relationships with his teacher was the most significant indicator of his school adjustment. The perception that one is respected by the peer group was the second most important facilitating variable. The perception that one's parents felt positive toward school was least important among these three variables, especially for boys. For girls, the perception of parental attitudinal support of school was, however, still significantly related to academic performance.

The most concise way of summing up the psychological basis of adolescent

[3]Schmuck, Richard and Van Egmond, Elmer, "Sex Differences in the Relationship of Interpersonal Perceptions to Academic Performance," *Psychology in the Schools* (in press).

concerns with parents, teachers, and peers is to point to the incessant attempt of the adolescent to establish a consistent picture of himself and to achieve a sense of self-esteem. Every adolescent makes use of the reactions of these other people in formulating his opinion of himself. He relies on them for the gratifications and rewards which make him feel worthwhile and esteemed, or for the punishments and disapproval which make him feel inadequate and worthless. It is primarily parents, teachers, and peers—in person or in the images the adolescent holds of them—who are able to make him feel secure and happy or lost and alienated. The adolescent strives to see himself as competent, respected, and effective in intimate interpersonal relations. If he sees himself this way—if he thinks others see him this way—he can continue the process of self-development and move toward a healthy level of personal esteem.

Conclusions

Observations and interviews collected over the last five years indicate that working and middle-class adolescents are not alienated from adults. They are not retreating from, or rebelling against, adult society; they are not against school achievement and the core values of the society. Adolescents are, however, struggling with the integration of interpersonal messages and appraisals from parents, teachers, and peers. They are attempting to pull these diverse inputs together into an autonomous and consistent picture of themselves.

The adolescent works out this integration through his intimacies with important others, most often peers in contemporary society. Teachers and peers can play a special part during this transitional period in assisting the adolescent in moving beyond the family. At the same time, the adolescent requires guidance from parental models. Parents and youth need to work more creatively to find ways of sharing their most meaningful and personal thoughts and experiences. The adolescent is in need of discussion with what he perceives to be trustworthy and forthright adults, whether they be teachers or parents. Moreover, the adolescent needs to be supported in his intimate sharing with peers and personal introspection about self. The contemporary adolescent builds a coherent picture of self with least pain and most satisfaction when he is allowed intimacy with peers within the context of mature and honest guidelines from both parents and teachers.

Social Change: Impact on the Adolescent*

JAMES S. COLEMAN

Adults have a special reason today to shake their heads and mutter, "the younger generation . . . ," as adults are wont to do. For today's adults and today's teenagers have special problems of communication that make it more and more difficult for each to understand what the other is up to. These communication problems arise not because teenagers are in some strange new way different than ever before, but because of changes in the structure of our society. These changes have produced a number of special problems in education and in the whole process of growing up, of which the communication gap is only one. I would like to indicate what some of these structural changes are, and some of their consequences for adolescents.

Societal Changes and Family Cohension

A number of changes have combined to make the family a less cohesive, less effective agent within which to raise children than ever before. One of these changes is the entry of large numbers of women into the labor force. Prior to World War II, in March 1940, 16.7 per cent of married women held jobs outside the home. By March 1961, this had doubled to 34.0 per cent. (In 1890, it was 4.5 per cent.) This change need not, of course, make a given family less tightly knit, nor give adolescent children a less rich "psychological home," but it tends to do so, and the overall social impact must be in this direction.

Another change is the smaller and smaller number of families that have

*Reprinted from *The Bulletin of the National Association of Secondary School Principals,* 49 (April 1965), 11-14 by permission of the National Association of Secondary School Principals and James S. Coleman, John Hopkins University.

relatives—aunts, uncles, grandparents—living in the household. This means that the typical family of today in America is parents and children, with nothing more. Thus the family's strength depends far more on the parents than ever before. The relatives are not there to provide adults for the children to model themselves after, or adults in whom they can confide.

A third change, which reinforces the preceding one, is the greater geographic mobility of families, particularly since World War II. An urban or suburban family today does not have a homestead that passes from one generation to another; nor does it even have a stable place of residence for a single generation. More and more, the typical "life cycle" of a family begins with a newly-married couple living in an apartment in the city; then with the first child comes a move to a suburb of families with young children; then later, as income and family grow, to a suburb of larger houses and older children; then finally, after the children are gone, back to an apartment in the city.

Such moves mean that the adult neighborhood, which was once an extension of the household itself, is hardly so now. Children make neighborhood friends quickly, but their parents do not; and perhaps most important, the children have few contacts and even fewer stable relationships with other adults in the neighborhood.

Finally, a change that has been going on for a long time is the shift of the father's work from the home or the neighborhood (e.g., the farmer or merchant) to a distant office or factory. Thus, the son knows only abstractly what his father does; and he can never enter into the father's work.

Consequences of Change

The effects of these changes on the adolescent are many. One of the most interesting indicators is the recent large increase in "going steady" among adolescents. This phenomenon, virtually unknown in Europe, can be explained only in terms of overall changes that have taken place in the teenager's life. Looking closely at the practice of going steady indicates that it is not (as some adults fear) principally a license for sexual freedom. Instead, its basis is more nearly in the kind of psychological security it provides, a psychological closeness that today's adolescents seem to need. When we ask why they need it, the answer is clear: the family no longer provides the closeness and security it once did. Because of the structural changes indicated above, the family fails to provide the kind of close, secure relationships that the adolescent had as a child and will once again have when he himself forms a family. His response comes by finding that close security in an attachment to another.

Going steady is only one of the consequences of these structural changes in society. Another is the greater and greater burden that falls on the school. The school was once a supplement to the activities of the family in making adults of its children. But the roles have reversed for today's adolescents: the home is more and more merely a supplement to the adolescent's life, which focuses more and more on the school. It may be, as some school adminstrators feel, that this places too great a responsibility on the school. Yet the condition exists, and many families, with their working parents, high mobility, and lack of other relatives in the household, are in no position to change the condition. The adolescents turn to one another, to the school, and to the entertainments of the larger society, for these are their only resources.

Another consequence of the family's weakness, one that stems from the same needs as does going steady, is the earlier age of dating and of interest in the opposite sex. The consequences of this for interest in schoolwork is particularly marked for girls. There is a sharp shift in early adolescence from a high evaluation of the bright girl to a much lower evaluation—for the girl who appears especially bright does not fare well in dates with boys. Among schools I studied a few years ago, this shift started slightly later in the rural schools than in the urban and suburban ones. In the former, the shift occurred during the ninth grade; in the latter, the shift had largely taken place before the ninth grade. In both sets of schools, the devaluation of brightness and the emphasis on good looks and popularity with boys was at its peak in middle adolescence. In the rural schools, it had sharply declined by the senior year in high school, while in the urban and suburban ones, the decline had already begun in the junior year. It appears that the most intense focus of adolescent girls on problems of popularity and dating, and the greatest devaluation of schoolwork occurs when the rating and dating system is still unsettled, and the uncertainty of who will ask whom for a date is at its height. These years, among modern adolescents, are earlier than ever before—in junior high school and early high school. The consequence for schools may be a peculiar one: to make the junior high school years more difficult ones than in the past, for adolescents and for teachers and school administrators, and to make the senior high school years (in three-year high schools) less difficult.

The earlier age of interest in the opposite sex, and the consequent earlier shift of adolescent values in this direction derives only in part from weakened family ties. It derives in part from all the changes in society that bring about early social sophistication among adolescents. Partly urban and suburban living, partly television and other mass media (for example, both popular music and movies have come to be more and more oriented to teenagers), partly the money they now have to spend, partly their better-educated parents, and partly the school itself, have made adolescents more wise in the ways of the world.

The Desire for Sophistication

In the schools I studied recently, the sharpest difference I found in the adolescents of the most rural schools and those of the most middle-class urban and suburban ones, was in the sophistication of the latter. The rural 9th graders were still children, obedient to teachers, and the middle-class suburban pupils were already disdainful of the ways of childhood. Such sophistication, and desire for sophistication, is a double-edged sword. It means that adolescents are more ready for new ideas, new experiences, quicker to grasp things. But it also makes them far less easy to teach, less willing to remain in the role of a learner, impatient with teachers, less likely to look at the teacher as a model or an authority. It need not make them more interested in school, but perhaps even less so. For the world whose sophistication they are taking on is one outside the school. Schoolwork, with its daily assignments and homework, they associate with childhood. Many of these children learn only years later, in college or after, that hard work and carrying out of assignments, attention to the demands of the teacher, become more important, rather than less, the farther they go in school.

Of all the recent changes in adolescents, this early desire for sophistication poses perhaps the greatest problem and the greatest challenge for secondary schools. Teenagers are less willing to respond to the teacher just because he is a teacher; less willing to "be taught." But they are more responsive *if* their imagination is captured, more able and willing to respond to a real challenge. It makes the school's task more difficult, for it cannot take the adolescent's interest for granted; it must find new ways of capturing this interest and energy. It has no other alternative but to accept these more sophisticated adolescents, and turn their sophistication to the advantage of education.

Altogether, recent changes in society have had a sharp impact on our adolescents. They present now, and they will present even more in the future, both difficulty and opportunity to the schools.

Causes of Conflict*

FRANCIS C. BAUER, M.D.

A comparison of today's adolescent with his counterpart of the 20's and 30's would certainly suggest that he has undergone considerable change. Whether this change is essential, however, or whether we are dealing primarily with a surface phenomenon seems a valid subject to debate.

To enumerate some of the apparent changes, today's adolescent is on the average slightly taller and enjoys better nutrition. He is physically healthier, perhaps more intelligent and certainly more sophisticated. He enjoys greater mobility, has more freedom and spends more money than any adolescent in history. But he is fundamentally the same adolescent struggling with the same basic problems that are characteristic of this somewhat disturbing phase of emotional development. Indeed his conflicts are greater today since not only is the adolescent expected to find himself, but he must do so in a world which refuses to remain the same for two consecutive weeks.

The basic conflict of adolescence is the struggle between his need to become independent on the one hand and his equally strong but opposite tendency to remain dependent on the other. Although present at birth and for some not resolved until death, this conflict is most disturbing during the adolescent period. Intellectual development enables the twelve to fifteen-year-old to see the future more clearly, and accordingly he yearns for independence and adult privilege. At the same time, however, he is reluctant to accept the responsibility of that state and desires for yet a little while the protective dependence of childhood. Since physical growth and development make it less appropriate to turn back than ever before in his experience, the conflict becomes intensified.

*Reprinted from *The Bulletin of the National Association of Secondary School Principals,* 49 (April 1965) 15-18 by permission of the National Association of Secondary School Principals and Francis C. Bauer, Board of Cooperative Educational Services, Third Supervisory District, Suffolk County, Huntington, New York. Coyright ©1965 by the National Association of Secondary School Principals.

Today's adolescent is fundamentally no different from the adolescent of previous generations. He is a child in the body of an adult, engaged in role playing, trying out emotions and assuming attitudes. He is confused, indecisive, insecure, self-conscious, and acutely in need of direction. He is fearful of his own inner impulses and more especially fearful of the consequences resulting from their satisfaction. Why then are his problems more numerous and more acute today? This question is more logically answered by examining today's radically different social structure than by postulating a change in the nature of the adolescent.

We have, in recent decades, made something of a fetish of progress. The need to change, often for its own sake, has embraced every aspect of our living including, unfortunately, our methods of infant and child care. As a result we have literally pushed our children out of infancy by weaning, toilet training, and sending them off to school before they are really ready for any of these events. We have robbed them of their childhood by organizing their games and structuring their play activity according to adult rules and standards. We have placed great significance on performance and achievement thereby encouraging the attempt of status conscious parents to accelerate the process of childhood development. We have indeed propelled our children toward maturity and independence and insisted that they assume responsibility sometime before they are ready for it. Excessive permissiveness and self-determination are two examples of these social trends. But in so doing, we have failed to indulge the dependency needs of children allowing them to persist into adolescence.

Having attempted to accelerate the natural development of childhood, it appears that society then reverses the process during adolescence and the weight of adult pressure become redirected toward retarding growth. Instead of strengthening the adolescent's striving for independence, we now deny him experience with practical problems, we indulge and overprotect him and in effect keep him in a dependent state of existence for ever-lengthening periods of time. The adolescent then is pressured from both directions and is told to, "Hurry up and wait!"

Money, mobility, and the use of goods have also had an effect on today's adolescent, making him appear quite different from his counterpart of a generation or more ago. It seems more reasonable, however, to assume that he is the same adolescent but that he is reacting to many more and radically different situations than were formerly found in his realm of activity. And it should be especially noted that today's adolescent is asked to react to some situations involving rapid change with which today's adults are themselves not familiar. It is probably for this reason that so many youngsters seem to have lost faith in adults and retreated to the more secure and highly structured society they have built themselves. It is always interesting to note, in this connection, that while adults seem fearful of setting limits on youngsters, the gang, the group, the club or whatever a particular segment of adolescent society may be called, set far more stringent limitations on its members and in place of rebellion receive cheerful compliance. The obvious conclusion is that children demand external controls.

Certainly money and the use of goods have increased the material advantages of our twelve to fifteen-year-old set. These can never realistically compensate, however, for the less tangible but more important advantages that have been replaced—consistent values, family unity, and the authority of the parent.

The contamination of a value system by unrealistic notions of democracy has had a significant influence on the inability of the adolescent to resolve his conflicts. Idealism predominates the emotional life of the adolescent and his need to believe in something is never stronger. If during his formative years, however, his parents were consistently indecisive regarding values, the twelve to fifteen-year-old has few resources to sustain him during the adolescent search for an ideal of his own. His parents may have disagreed on religion, for example, and rationalized their own inability to resolve the difficulty by allowing the child to develop without any religious influence and to choose for himself at sixteen. While this may be considered a mark of great sophistication and is certainly democratic, all that it means to the growing child is that neither parent cared enough to teach that child what he thought was right. How notions of democracy ever became involved in family living could well be the subject of a separate paper. Suffice it to say that if the family unit, the foundation of our social structure, becomes further eroded by commercialism and materialism, the adolescent of tomorrow will appear to have changed to even a greater degree than the early teenagers of today.

Adolescence has always been a time of conflict inasmuch as it hurts more than a little to grow up and to become involved with the reciprocal relationship between privilege and responsibility. The normally occurring conflicts are necessarily intensified when the youngster's childhood experiences provide a weak foundation upon which to build. And this is becoming rather more usual than extraordinary. When we reflect on the tired old statistic that in our society one of every four marriages terminates in divorce, thereby removing the most important source of stability in childhood, it becomes easier to appreciate why so many youngsters are overwhelmed by the challenge of adolescence. And if we recognize that in at least two of the three remaining marriages, the parents have abdicated their position of authority and have joined the adolescent they should be leading, we are still closer to an understanding of the problem.

Human nature is the one constant in an ever-changing universe. It has the unique capacity to effect change and to adapt to change without itself changing in the process. For this reason, if we are concerned with the adolescent today we must consider him not as essentially different from his predecessors. We must consider rather those changes which make him appear different from other adolescents at other times in other settings.

A Functional Junior High School Guidance Program*

WAYMAN R. F. GRANT, SR.

The complexity, multiplicity and depth of the personal, social, emotional and physical problems confronting early adolescents make it essential that the school offer organized guidance services. A pre-requisite to the development of an effective guidance program for the junior high school is to have a thorough understanding of educational aims for this level. The guidance program should be integrated with the total educational program and permeate the total school's program. Gruhn and Douglass state that—"The functions of the junior high school include guidance along with differentiation, integration, socialization, articulation, and exploration." A function, to these authors, is not an aim or objective as such, but "a condition which is instrumental in achieving the goals of the school."(1)[1]

Modern education is conceived of as the development of the individual in all aspects of his personality, not being restricted to the intellectual aspect. Basically, guidance functions are services rendered to assist children in making sound adjustments, choices, and plans. The caliber of guidance services afforded the junior high school students and their parents is a deciding factor in determining the degree to which the educational program is effectively focused on meeting the individual's needs.

Educators are being made increasingly aware of the importance of guidance services to acquaint them with the unique human characteristics discernible at the junior high school age level. In James B. Conant's pamphlet entitled, *Recommendations for Education in the Junior High School Years,* he described guidance as the "Keystone in the arch of education."(2)

*Reprinted from *The Journal of Secondary Education,* (October 1966), 255-259 by permission of the publisher and Wayman R.F. Grant, Sr., Booker T. Washington Junior High School, Mobile, Alabama.

1Numbers in parentheses refer to references at the end of the article.

To fulfill the democratic ideals of the American society, an educated citizenry is essential. It is believed that the most effective and productive people are those whose minds have been challenged through freedom to explore widely and creatively in terms of their individual capacities. This realization can be made possible through dynamic guidance services. According to Humphreys the fundamental aims of guidance services are:

"1. To help the individual, by his own efforts so far as possible: to achieve up to the level of his own capacity; to gain personal satisfactions in as many aspects of his life as possible; and to make his maximum contribution to society.

2. To help the individual meet and solve his own problems as they arise, make correct interpretations of facts, and make wise choices and adjustments.

3. To help the individual lay a permanent foundation for sound, mature adjustments.

4. To assist the individual to live a well-balanced life in all respects-physical, mental, emotional, and social."(3)

The Booker T. Washington Junior High School guidance program was formulated and implemented with the above goals in mind. The school's philosophy is predicated on the premise that each pupil is—and should be—treated as an unique individual. The guidance program had its inception in 1954, when a study of the community was conducted to ascertain the needs of pupils on the basis of the socio-economic groups represented. This study formed the base for the development and implementation of policies relative to curriculum and guidance practices. In-service meetings were conducted, and out of these action-research studies evolved the guidance program, philosophy, objectives, methods of grouping, types of lesson plans, and the ungraded activity program. These meetings enabled teachers to attain a higher degree of proficiency in fulfilling their roles and a clearer understanding of guidance and its implication in their work.

Guidance services at the Booker T. Washington Junior High School are executed through the homeroom, classroom and student activities. The homeroom constitutes the "heart" of the guidance program with greater significance being attributed to the services of the homeroom teacher. Efforts of homeroom teachers are augmented by the counselor and guidance specialist. However, students have the privilege of selecting any member of the school's staff when they desire a counseling session.

The homeroom is used for imparting information, discussing common problems, gathering information about pupils, group activities, individual counseling, pupil accounting, and planning educational and vocational programs. Teachers actively participate in the total guidance program.

A. ORIENTATION SERVICE

The junior high school as a whole constitutes a transitional stage for pupils. To maintain a continuity in the school's program, planned orientation services are performed to acquaint, not only the pupils, but their parents, with life in the junior high school, as they enter, and in the senior high school when they leave. The major objectives of our orientation program are to provide information relative to what pupils may expect, what will be expected of them, and to develop a wholesome attitude toward the school. Stress is placed on discussing similarities, as well as differences to be encountered in the new school environment.

B. INVENTORY SERVICES

The school has a systematic plan for recording important data about each pupil. Cumulative records for pupils are secured from the feeder school prior to the time incoming students enter. The records for new and returning students are kept up to date by the teachers and contain sufficient information to present a comprehensive picture of the pupil.

C. INFORMATION SERVICES

Information services include those activities in the school centered around securing and making available to the pupils facts about occupations, educational opportunities, school services, school activities, community services and organizations that may prove helpful to them.

D. COUNSELING SERVICE

To prepare students for their ultimate roles in society, the Booker T. Washington Junior High School incorporates in its counseling service the concept of values, the Golden Rule, and an interpretation of the school's philosophy, and the analysis of the qualities and characteristics of a "Plus-Plus" student. The concept of values is stressed in counseling because it is realized that values influence every aspect of our lives either advantageously or adversely.

In the lobby of the school, posters are on display depicting the Golden Rule as it is interpreted by the major religions of the world. This approach seems to be beneficial in promoting values and fostering introspection. If the nature of a counseling session so warrants, the student is encouraged to reflect upon his past actions in terms of the posters by asking, "Have I done unto my fellowman as I would wish him to do unto me?" This counseling technique allows the student to direct the session by examining, rejecting, reinforcing or modifying his past actions. This form of counseling provides the student with an opportunity to chart his own future in the light of his present, his past, his educational attainment and personal potentialities.

The technique of employing the philosophy of the guidance program in a counseling session allows the goals of the program to be constantly viewed. Another technique used in counseling which affords the student the opportunity to engage in self-appraisal is one which we refer to as the "Plus-Plus" student. The qualities and characteristics of a "Plus-Plus" student are discussed by students in their homeroom and also displayed in the school's lobby. Students are encouraged to examine their actions and future plans in terms of the desirable traits of a "Plus-Plus" student. The qualities and characteristics of a "Plus-Plus" student are listed under four major topics with a few of the subtopics being listed below:

Social Growth

Development of:

1. Respect for self and others
2. Emotional independence
3. Ethical character

Personal Growth

Development of:

1. Intellectual skills and understandings
2. Command of fundamental processes
3. The appreciation of aesthetic values
4. Rational and logical thinking

Economic Growth

Development of understanding and appreciation for:

1. The need for selecting and preparing for an occupation
2. Desirable work habits
3. Achievement of economic independence
4. Skills for intelligent counsumership

Civic Growth

Development of:

1. Civic responsibility in a democratic society
2. Respect for: law, property, authority
3. Loyalty to: home, school, country
4. Responsibility to: self, others, school, home, church, country

Counseling is just one of the services of the guidance program, but in regard to the individual student, it may well be considered the heart of the guidance program. It cannot be functional, however, in the absence of certain other guidance services. School counseling is concerned with the problem-solving issues that are common to all students. Examining lives, weighting decisions and planning futures are common procedures in the educational process.

E. FOLLOW-UP SERVICE

Follow-up services are an integral part of the guidance program and serve as an important technique for evaluating the school's guidance services. Results of these surveys help to determine the present needs of these individuals and permit appraisal of programs of study, method of teaching, guidance services, and co-curricular activities of the school.

The classroom teacher contributes to guidance by obtaining information about pupils, observing significant behavior, individualizing instruction, encouraging exploration, developing good study techniques and maintaining an atmosphere conducive to learning.

In all subject matter areas, vocational implications are made explicit by career posters, displays, learning to spell and define vocations, and by class discussions. In connection with various units in English, for example, students are given realistic information about the work of journalists, authors, librarians, actors, and other occupations and careers requiring a mastery of some aspects of the language arts. Teachers incorporate in long range lesson plans the correlation of course content with vocational implications of that subject area.

Each teacher helps pupils to develop and improve proper study habits by instilling the concept that the occasion for teaching how to study is when pupils are studying, and the place is in each classroom. The development of study skills is fostered by:

1. Providing every child with a study period and assigning each teacher the responsibility of teaching pupils how to study.
2. Using the block of time in scheduling classes except for specialized fields.
3. English teachers giving more detailed information about study skills and teaching pupils how to use the library.
4. Showing filmstrips and films, and films about proper study habits.
5. Having pupils create and dramatize skits in class, assembly, and P.T.A. meetings portraying desirable study skills as contrasted with poor study habits.

The activity program in the junior high school contributes unique guidance values. It affórds pupils opportunities to develop skills in oral expression, leadership skills, desirable citizenship qualities, ability to get along with others. At Booker T. Washington Junior High School, students are given opportunities to explore their interests and abilities, achieve social adjustments, and relieve physical tensions through the ungraded exploratory activity program.

The uniqueness of the school's ungraded exploratory activity program was acclaimed in the *NEA Journal,* Volume 52, Number 6 (September 1963), p.7.

Teachers contribute extra time at the end of the normal school day to help students explore broad areas of vocational and avocational experiences. The additional 50 minutes at the end of the normal day is referred to as the "ungraded activity period." Some 27 activities are offered during this period. They include such offerings as typing, medical self-help, dramatics, photography, conversational French, German, and Spanish.

One day each week this period is devoted to homeroom guidance sessions. On Thursday this period is set aside for service club activities.

The faculty of the Booker T. Washington Junior High School feels that guidance is concerned with helping pupils solve problems they encounter. As junior high school students, our children are confronted with problems involving development, relationship, the school situation, and planning for the future. Our guidance efforts are directed not only at improving present adjustments but also at the making of intelligent decisions relevant to the future. Helping pupils to adjust affords challenging experience, in that pupil's ambivalent feelings with respect to security and independence, being treated as children or adults, pleasing teachers or being accepted by peers, result in many perplexing situations.

The effective implementation of our guidance program is admittedly a challenging job. It requires us to use all the initiative, ingenuity, resourcefulness and intelligence at our command. However, the results are well worth it! Seeing a child develop into a truly mature and well-adjusted adult, one who is equal to life's demands, one who enjoys himself and contributes to his community, is a deeply satisfying experience, and it gives us the added pleasure of knowing that we have performed one of our most important and challenging functions, that of helping children grow successfully into worthy citizens in our American society.

References

(1) William T. Gruhn and Harl Douglass: *The Modern Junior High School,* 2nd. ed, Ronald, 1956, p. 32.

(2) James B. Conant, Recommendations for Education in the Junior High School Years, Educational Testing Service, 1960.

(3) J. Anthony Humphreys, Arthur Traxler and Robert D. North, *Guidance Services,* Science Research Associates, 1960, p. 79.

Bibliography

1. Conant, James B., *Recommendations for Education in the Junior High School Years,* Educational Testing Service, 1960.

2. Fullmer, Daniel W., and Bernard, Harold W., *Counseling: Contents and Process,* Science Research Associates, Inc., Chicago, 1964.
3. Gruhn, William T., and Douglass, Harl, *The Modern Junior High School,* Ronald Press, 1956.
4. Humphreys, J. Anthony, Traxler, Arthur E., and North, Robert D., *Guidance Services,* Science Research Associates, Inc., Chicago, 1960.
5. Johnson, Mauritz Jr., Busacker, William E., and Bowman, Fred Q., *Junior High School Guidance,* Harper & Brother, New York, 1961.
6. Miller, Frank W., *Guidance Principles and Services,* Columbus, Ohio: Charles E. Merrill, 1961.
7. Stoops, Emery, *Guidance Services: Organization and Administration,* New York: McGraw-Hill, 1955.
8. Zeran, Franklin R. and Riccio, Anthony C., *Organization and Administration of Guidance Services,* Chicago: Rand McNally, 1962.

Educational and Career Choices for the Junior High School Pupil*

GLEN N. PIERSON

Samuel Johnson once said, "To improve the golden moment of opportunity, and catch the good that is within our reach, is the great art of life." This art is one that young people must learn earlier in the game than did previous generations. Their preparation for living in this complex, technologically advanced society requires a longer sequence of planning than was required for the generation before them. Not only that, but the planning of learning experiences which will enhance these individuals' chances of leading meaningful, productive lives must be based on decision-making by the individuals themselves.

The project described in this article represented an effort to provide appropriate learning experiences for junior high school pupils. These pupils are on the threshold of making decisions concerning educational commitments and career aspirations, and the experiences and knowledge they gain at this level help them in making educational and career decisions.

The specific objectives of this project were to:

- Assist pupils to broaden their understanding of the world of work and of specific occupational areas
- Encourage pupils to make realistic self-appraisals by examining what they believe to be their interests and abilities in relation to relation to their abilities and interests as revealed by tests they have taken
- Assist pupils to develop aspirational levels that will result in educational and career commitments consistent with their attributes

*Reprinted from *California Education,* 2 (May 1965), 3–4, by permission of the publisher and Glen N. Pierson, Office of the San Diego County Superintendent of Schools.

- Assist pupils to gain greater understanding of high school course sequences, specific courses, and the relationship of these sequences and courses to ultimate occupational choices

The Grossmont Union High School District, nine elementary school districts located in the same area, and the office of the San Diego County Superintendent of Schools conducted the project. These districts had formed the Heartland Articulation Committee and the Heartland Guidance Council to facilitate intradistrict communication and coordination. Through a series of carefully prepared presentations by these groups on the nature of educational and career decisions, administrative support for the project was enlisted.

The Heartland Articulation Committee and the Heartland Guidance Council endorsed the general framework for the project and assisted in the selection of personnel to produce the learning materials. A request for NDEA Title V-A funds was endorsed by these two groups and submitted by La Mesa-Spring Valley City Elementary School District in behalf of the participating districts. The request was approved in July, 1964, and the first stage of the project was formally initiated.

All of the preparation for this project—from the initial presentation to the administrators, through the selection of personnel, the planning of the training of personnel, and finally the workshop period itself—follows the Brickell method of organizing for curricular change described by Henry M. Brickell in *Organizing New York State for Educational Change.* Dr. Brickell details three distinct phases essential for bringing about major curricular change: innovation, evaluation, and dissemination of curricular materials.

Four workshop teams, each of which was to work on a major unit of study, were selected to organize the learning experiences and prepare the materials. Each team was made as representative as possible of curricular staff members, administrators, counselors, and teachers so that the proposed experiences would be planned as a part of the total school program. The teams were highly motivated and competent. During the first week of the project the teams participated in a number of activities to become oriented to the spirit and intent of the project. Then the teams went to work examining existing materials in the four areas and adopting such materials when possible. As anticipated, however, material was lacking on many topics. Additional original materials were therefore prepared. The four units that were developed and the specific objectives of each follow:

History of Education and Work

Understand that the effective functioning of a democratic society requires that each individual be provided with full educational opportunity

Understand the role of education in the growth of the United States as a world power

Understand the need for an increase in the length and breadth of formal education as society has become more complex

Understand the changing educational requirements for entry into the world of work

Understand that education is a process which will continue throughout the lives of most individuals

Understand some reasons for differing educational aspiration levels among young people today

Understand the scope of educational opportunities available in California today

The World of Work

Understand how work enchances human life

Understand the relationship of some prevalent human needs and motives of occupational choice

Understand that the lack of a formal education can stand between an individual and a job

Understand that present choices affect future opportunities

Understand some significant economic aspects of past, present, and projected changes in the world of work

Be aware of the influence of social economic factors in the neighborhood on job choice

Understand the variety of intrinsic satisfactions derived from work

Self-Appraisal

Make a preliminary self-analysis of interests, aptitudes, achievements, personality, and physical characteristics

Cultivate the ability to relate personal attributes to education and to the world of work

Understand more fully those forces such as family, school, society, and personal drives which affect personal goal-setting

Appraise realistically one's personal strengths and weaknesses

My High School

Understand educational pathways in high school and the choices of jobs toward which they lead

Know specific course offerings and their requirements

Know the organization of the school such as the school personnel and student government

Know the cocurricular and extracurricular activities

Know the policies of the school relating to pupil behavior

Be aware of how freshmen feel during their first weeks in high school

A number of films, filmstrips, and other supplementary materials are recommended for use in each unit. In the unit on History of Education a case history approach is employed: conventional instructional methods are employed in the other units.

These materials have been developed in working form and are presently being field-tested in ten eighth-grade classrooms. The major purpose of field testing is to determine teacher reaction to the appropriateness and completeness of the materials. Teachers participating in the workshop teams were not included in the field testing groups, because it was felt that their close identification with the project might make it difficult for them to react objectively since they had helped produce the learning materials. At the termination of the field testing, the innovation phase of the project will conclude with revision of materials.

Next year a research study will be conducted to determine the effectiveness of the revised materials with respect to the specific objectives of the project. If the findings are favorable, efforts will be made to make the materials available to interested districts. This distribution would complete the third phase of Dr. Brickell's model of organizing for educational change: dissemination. Experience to date suggests that the steps he recommends hold great promise for curricular development in the area of educational and career planning for pupils.

Pressure on Disadvantaged Teenagers*

ARTHUR PEARL

The greatest pressure on the disadvantaged youth is caused not so much by his environmental deficit as by what he feels is his lack of a future. The truth of the matter is that our society provides little opportunity for a low-income youth to find a place in the world. As a result, most of his formal education and other kinds of social intervention are not only ineffective but often humiliating or debasing.

For example, he is compelled to go to school, but what he is presented with there has no meaning to him in terms of the way he sees the world. He is told to stay in school so that eventually he can get a better job, but in actuality being a high school graduate offers him little if any more in terms of access to the opportunity structure than being a high school dropout. He knows friends and relatives who have graduated from high school and are either unemployed or in some undignified, degrading, and debasing jobs. His real choice is often boiled down to becoming an unemployed high school graduate or an unemployed dropout.

Although society today is geared to favor the college graduate, a higher education is an impossible goal to most disadvantaged young people. Even if they could conceive of the possibility of going to college, there is little in their educational activity and nothing in their home background that prepares them for it. Many of them are in basic tracks that do not prepare for college. The slightly more fortunate are placed in a so-called general curriculum, which does not prepare them for college either.

What the schools need to do is to find some way to offer these disadvantaged youth the possibility of going to college or, at the very least, some hope for a future.

*Reprinted from *The NEA Journal,* 54 (February 1965) 19, 21, by permission of the publisher and Arthur Pearl, University of Oregon.

Another kind of pressure on the disadvantaged youth is exerted by love—the undiscriminating sort dispensed by well-meaning teachers. Not all of these kids are lovable, and they can see through any false posture.

Not long ago I heard the dean of a school of education say that the one thing disadvantaged children need is love. If we could only give them enough love, we could solve all of our problems, he implied. He became furious with me, however, when I tried to explain to him that love given so promiscuously is known in the streets as prostitution.

By trying to give universal love, the teacher actually punishes the disadvantaged student. In effect, the teacher is asking him to feel guilty for anything he does that displeases her because he is hurting or disappointing one who loves him.

For example, take the fifth grade teacher in a Chicago slum school who, shortly after the mass demonstrations against de facto segregation, found some salacious comments scrawled on her record book. Turning to the class, she asked, "After all I've done for you, why are you being so mean to me?"

After a long silence, one of the boys finally answered, "Because you're white."

The teacher, although she had just witnessed two racial school boycotts, was dumbfounded. With tears in her eyes, she told the class that she could not teach them any more that morning; she was too upset.

Her self-righteousness was the most excruciating punishment that she could have used against the boy. He had presented himself honestly and courageously and, if anything, should have been rewarded for his contribution. Instead, he was humiliated. Not suprisingly, at the end of class he walked up to the teacher and stamped as hard as he could on her feet.

The object lesson here is quite clear. The teacher had established a love relationship that no one had asked for. By failing to acknowledge the boy's honesty and by humiliating him, she drove him to the only kind of face-saving action he knew how to express. If she had handled the situation honestly, say by discussing this particular problem with the class, she could have built up this boy's self-respect and her own effectiveness as a teacher.

It is not love that disadvantaged children need so much as honest respect. Anything phony will force them to lash out against the teacher and whatever else the school imposes upon them.

Another pressure the schools have got to do away with if they are to deal effectively with the disadvantaged is the fiercesness of individual competition. Most disadvantaged children have nothing in their backgrounds to prepare them for school, and as a consequence they are unable to compete equally with most other children.

If the school continues to punish such children with failing grades and other forms of humiliation, these youngsters will be disaffected with the whole educational process. Even if they are not actually told they are stupid, the school implies it. They are asked to read when they can't read well; they have to stand at the board and face the laughter and ridicule of their friends. If they finally decide not to go to school, they are arrested as truants.

Admittedly, some of these children are not of high or even average intelligence—in the ways that we normally measure intelligence—but they can learn to do many useful things in society.

One of the interesting results of a recent experiment in programed learning reveals that IQ does not truly indicate how *much* a person can learn but how *fast* he can learn. Experiments with programed learning in physics and chemistry indicate that a person with an IQ of 80 can learn just as much as a person with an IQ of 140, although it may take the person with the low IQ a much longer time. (Incidentally, when tested a year later, the low IQ students, who had invested much more time in learning, scored higher than the high IQ students.)

Although their rate of learning is generally slower than that of the more fortunate children, disadvantaged students need not be placed in special groups. Homogeneous grouping, I believe, is done more often for the benefit of the teacher than for his students.

Instead of depending on such gimmicks, educators ought to be moving toward what I would call team learning. We have had team learning for a long time, but we have called it cheating. In the context I am speaking of, however, all students work together to help each other learn instead of working to beat the system. The effectiveness of this type of learning has been proven in scores of experiments, particularly some conducted by the Army.

In short, we have got to be less concerned with the outcomes of education and more concerned with the process of education.

Obviously, putting the right type of teacher in the classroom is a key to relieving many of the pressures on the disadvantaged child in school. Unfortunately, we have a lot of teachers in predominantly disadvantaged schools who should not be there. A lot of them are prejudiced, not necessarily because of their children's racial or ethnic background but because the values and mores of these children are opposed to the values and mores of the middle class from which most of their teachers come.

A teacher in a disadvantaged school should be nonjudgmental. He should recognize that his students may have a different approach to life, one perhaps more suitable to the kind of world they live in than the one in which he lives.

The teacher should also be attuned to the fact that while these children have many deficits, they have assets as well. The kinds of assets a child is likely to have will largely be in tune with the kind of world with which he has learned to deal.

The disadvantaged child lives in a very physical world, one which places little value on reflective thinking. His assets, therefore, are going to be largely physical—the ability to act out his emotions and feelings freely and honestly.

This is one reason why Frank Reissman and others place a great deal of emphasis on role playing as part of the learning experience of these children.

The teacher must recognize that children learn differently—that some learn by reading, some by listening, some by feeling, and some by acting out or projecting themselves.

Finally, the teacher should have a sense of humor. He should not take himself so seriously that he becomes outraged at a child's inability to respond in some preconceived way. A child should be able to come into a classroom knowing that he is going to have some fun. Even if the child looks upon learning as something incidental, it is surprising how much he learns in a relaxed atmosphere in which he is enjoying himself.

There is no reason why education has to be unenjoyable. If the teacher is nonjudgmental and free from prejudices, if he is willing to recognize the good qualities of his students, he can make of education what it is supposed to be—preparation for living in a democratic society where everyone has a chance to achieve dignity and status.

The Junior High-School Principalship*

H. RICHARD CONOVER

The study of the Junior High-School Principalship is the second part of the National Association of Secondary-School Principals' Committee on the Study of the Secondary-School Principalship, which contracted with the Educational Testing Service to complete two comprehensive studies of the high school principalship. The first part, the study of the High School Principalship, was presented at the National Convention in Chicago, 1964.

Since the inception of the junior high school in the early 1900's, there has been considerable controversy about education during the junior high school years. Through the use of an appropriate survey, the committee, composed of six representative members of the National Association of Secondary-School Principals, sought to derive further information which might more specifically describe problem areas as well as help to illuminate attitudes and opinions of junior high school administrators on educational issues and policies.

With these purposes in mind, the committee designed two different questionnaires that would permit a maximum of information and a minimum of respondents' time. In addition to the total responses, the questionnaires provided for subgroup responses in the following areas: location–urban or rural; region–northeast, southeast, west; per-pupil expenditure–$500 or more, $300-499, less than $300; size–1,000 or more, 500-999, less than 500; and school grade structure–6-3-3, 6-2-4, 5-3-4.

Approximately 6,800 junior high school principals were available for survey. Of this number 4,496, or 66 per cent responded. (This percentage figure should be kept in mind when interpreting responses throughout the report.)

*Reprinted from *The Bulletin of the National Association of Secondary School Principals,* 50 (April 1966), 132-139, by permission of the National Association of Secondary School Principals and H. Richard Conover, principal, Millburn Junior High School, Millburn, New Jersey.

In the near future, a copy of the complete report will be available for purchase by all members. The obvious bulk of questions or areas surveyed precludes a summary at this time. Therefore, it is the purpose of this report to comment on selected areas of particular interest.

The Principalship

As might be expected, the vast majority of junior high school principals (96%) are men. The median age of all principals surveyed is forty-four. Principals from rural areas and/or schools which are a part of a 5-3-4 grade structure tend to be somewhat younger.

There is a definite lack of mobility of junior high principals from one geographical region to another. Surprisingly enough 95 per cent of the principals remained in the area where they grew up.

Evidence suggests that the junior high school principal is characterized by considerable social mobility. Almost 70 per cent of the principals' fathers did not complete high school and the most frequently mentioned occupations were farmer, clerk, skilled, semi-skilled and unskilled labor.

Regarding educational preparation, most junior high principals did their undergraduate work at a public university or college, where their major fields were typically the liberal arts (57%), education (19%), and physical education (12%). Proof of extensive formal preparation is evidenced by the fact that 95 per cent have earned a master's degree or further advanced degree. Educational administration and supervision was the primary area of their graduate work.

Almost 70 per cent taught for seven or more years before principalships. The most frequent route to the principalship is not through teaching, but rather through an administrative post. Three-fifths of the junior high school principals were previously elementary or senior high school principals, while only thirty per cent were former teachers.

On this point, an interesting difference was noted—the person in a 5-3-4 or 6-2-4 type school was more likely to have moved from teacher to principal, while the person in the 6-3-3 type school was more likely to have been in another administrative capacity before his present position.

The median number of years of experience as a principal is 8-9 years, while the median years of experience in the current assignment is 4-5 years.

A majority of principals do not have tenure. However, principals from large city schools and/or 6-3-3 schools are much more likely to have tenure.

The Junior High School

Ninety-eight per cent of the junior high schools surveyed are public, with most of the remaining schools being religiously affiliated. About two-thirds of the schools have student bodies of 500 or more, while 15 per cent have less than 250 pupils. Most of the schools in this latter grouping are structured on a 6-2-4 grade plan and are located in rural areas. Fifty per cent of the schools have 750-1500 pupils, with an overall median enrollment of about 600 pupils.

The vast majority, three-fourths, of the schools are located in urban areas, where the population exceeds 5,000. Schools with 7-8 and 6-8 grade structures are usually located in small towns or rural areas.

Almost three-fourths of the principals surveyed reported that the average per-pupil expenditure for instructional purposes is over $300. Principals in the northeast and west reported expenditures in excess of $400 more frequently than did principals from the southeast.

In most cases (80%), the junior high building is physically separate from the local elementary or senior high schools. Again, principals in rural, 6-2-4 systems, are more likely to share their building facilities.

The vast majority of junior high schools have a gymnasium, library, industrial arts and homemaking lab, science lab and music room.

About three-fifths of the principals reported ratios of one teacher to 30 pupils; almost two-fifths reported a 1:20 ratio.

About one-half of the principals have one or more full-time assistants, a librarian, and clerks. However the majority do not have a full-time nurse or counselor.

The predominant grade structure includes grades seven through nine (67%); about 20 per cent utilize the seven and eight system, while 5 per cent include grades six through eight. Most of the schools in rural areas are geared to either the seven and eight or six through eight system.

What is the ideal junior high school grade organization? Responses break down as follows:

> 6–8 structure: most principals in this scheme considered it the ideal grade organization.
>
> 7–8 structure: half the principals involved in this plan considered a 7-9 structure as more desirable. Only one-fourth felt their present 7-8 structure was the best. There was pronounced dissatisfaction. Many would like to annex the sixth or ninth grade depending on their educational background and orientation.
>
> 7–9 structure: three-fourths of the principals thought their structure was the best.

Educational Issues

Having established a frame of reference, I would like now to share with you reactions to some of the long standing educational issues.

A primary concern has been identification of the valid functions of the junior high school. With the exception of independent school principals, acquisition of basic skills, closely followed by acquisition of basic knowledge, is rated as the most important goal of education. Due to the evolved change in the functions of the junior high, training in the technical skills is now considered the least important goal.

Ability grouping has become common practice as an effective procedure in compensating for individual differences. Almost 90 per cent of the principals advocate some type of ability grouping. Almost all who reported ability grouping use two or more criteria for such grouping, i.e., grades, I.Q. scores, teacher judgments, etc.

Another pertinent area—curriculum innovations—was surveyed in an attempt to evaluate frequency and impact. About three-fourths reported one of the "new" modern math programs and indicated satisfaction with it. Another thirteen per cent who do not have the program indicated they wished to implement such a course.

Many questions arise, concerning the contribution of foreign language study to the overall junior high program. About one-half feel that a foreign language should be part of the elective program for all grades. Surprisingly, one-fifth feel that foreign language study should only be offered as an elective in grades eight and nine.

In the past few years, several recommendations have been offered to reorganize the instructional program. Principals surveyed for this report were asked whether they approved or disapproved of the instructional organization in "the school of the future," as described by J. Lloyd Trump in *Guide to Better Schools: Focus on Change*. Almost one-half approved, while less than 10 per cent disapproved. The real surprise, however, was that one-fourth of the principals were unfamiliar with the Trump Plan.

One of the recommendations of the Commission on the Experimental Study of the Utilization of the Staff in the Secondary School was team teaching. What significant contributions are effected by team teaching? The largest group (62%) single out, as the most important contribution, allowance for students' capitalizing on the teachers' specific abilities. Increased scheduling, flexibility, and therein, provision for individual differences, is identified as the second most important contribution.

One of the major criticisms leveled at the departmental junior high school has been the lack of flexibility in the time schedule. Our survey indicates that over one-half of the schools maintain complete subject matter departmentalization with no "block of time." In response to which system of departmentalization is preferred, thirty-four per cent chose complete subject departmentalization with no "block of time." The data suggests that extensive departmentalization is here to stay; yet there is an indicated appreciation for and a desire to retain some "block of time."

What are the principals' views on federal aid to education and Supreme Court decisions?

About one-half of the principals favored federal aid to public schools only. One-fourth approved federal aid to both private and public schools. Less than one-half concur with the Supreme Court decision regarding compulsory prayer and Bible reading. The vast majority, four-fifths, agreed with the Supreme Court decision concerning racial segregation in the public schools. The practice of "bussing" students to schools outside the district as a means of facilitating integration was rejected by three-fourths of the principals.

Principals stressed adolescent development courses, practice teaching on the junior high level, and courses dealing with reading instruction, as the most valuable courses in the preparation of junior high school teachers. There is a definite feeling that course work should deal more with content and less with methods. Almost three-fourths felt that the degree program should be extended to five years and should incorporate more liberal arts courses.

In the much discussed area of accreditation, the greatest number of principals (36%) favor recognition and evaluation at the state level. Approximately one-third favor formal recognition or evaluation at the local level, while another one-fifth prefer regional accreditation. Principals from the southeast tended to favor regional accreditation, as might be expected, since the Southern Association of Secondary Schools and Colleges initiated accreditation of junior high schools in 1954.

The question of interscholastic athletic competition versus a well-constructed intramural program brought some interesting results. Approximately 86 per cent have some interscholastic competition, and most principals consider it appropriate in most sports, the limitation being football for ninth graders. However, more than half of the principals felt that a well-conducted after-school recreation and intramural program would be beneficial, and lead to a desired reduction, if not actual replacement, of the present interscholastic athletic program.

In the junior high school movement, the club or activity program was considered a strong point. What is its present status? The majority (almost 70%) of the 7-9 junior highs have service clubs, and principals consider them desirable. Somewhat less than half of the 6-2-4 and 5-3-4 schools have service clubs, but those that do, again, deem them desirable. Athletic clubs were present and suitable in all types of junior high schools. Absent, and considered undesirable by the vast majority of schools, were social clubs.

Duties and Activities of the Principal

A statement of fact—the principal's work week is lengthy, usually 50-54 hours.

Although about 70 per cent of the principals belong to State and National Associations of Secondary-School Principals, a significant percentage of this group are dissatisfied, on the whole, with the handling of their particular problems.

Certain activities seem to make greater demands of the principal's time; for example, administrative planning by himself or with subordinates, meetings and working with teachers regarding curriculum or instructional matters with groups of teachers. Approximately 10 per cent of the 6-2-4 and 5-3-4 principals spend one-fifth of their time in classroom teaching.

What are some of the major "roadblocks" which impede or deter the principals progress towards accomplishing school objectives? Among those most frequently cited are variations in the ability and dedication of teachers, insufficient space and physical facilities, time usurped by administrative detail, and teacher turnover.

Adding to the already complex scene is the pressure from outside groups. Chief among these major sources of pressure, according to the survey, are the local senior high schools, local newspapers, and P.T.A. groups.

Compensations

One of the more tangible compensations is money. The survey indicates that the median salary is slightly over $9,000. Slightly higher salaries are earned by principals in the northeast, 6-3-3, and large urban schools.

Other compensations lead to a greater understanding of the role itself. The study reveals that almost two-thirds of all principals describe themselves as deriving considerable self-satisfaction from the job.

One half of all surveyed principals felt that their position offers them a moderate amount of prestige in the community. Slightly over one-half of the principals reported that their long-range career objective is to be a junior high principal. A majority of the remaining principals are equally divided between aspiring for a district superintendent's job or "other".

In short, although the job of junior high school principal is characterized by long hours, "roadblocks," and pressures, the majority of principals would still elect educational administration as a career if they had the decision to make again.

I have attempted to report some survey highlights in an objective manner. As such, the data might be regarded as strictly informative, perhaps corroborating opinions already formulated from your background and experience. On the other hand, the report might well serve as a point of reference for any number and variety of subsequent steps and studies.

Ten Tenets of Junior-High-School Administration*

COUNCIL ON JUNIOR-HIGH-SCHOOL ADMINISTRATION

Foreword

Since 1951 a group of about 100 junior-high-school principals has been meeting annually in New York City for the purposes of exchanging ideas among themselves and stimulating and sponsoring research on–and professional study and investigation of–the junior-high-school program and its administration. This group of principals has come to be known as the "Long Group" in recognition of the leadership accorded it by Dr. Forrest E. Long, formerly of New York University.

At the thirteenth annual meeting (1963) Dr. Long recommended that the group adopt a more formal name. It was voted to continue designating the annual conference as the "Long Conference" and to adopt the formal name of Council on Junior-High-School Administration.

The Council on Junior-High-School Administration is affiliated with the Institute for Instructional Improvement. The Institute provides the Council with office space for its national headquarters and provides the facilities for caring for the details of administration of the organization.

At the 1961 conference a committee was appointed to draw up a statement of fundamental beliefs on junior-high-school administration. The committee, Mr. Harry B. Spencer (chairman),

*Reprinted from *The Clearing House,* 38 (February 1964), 329-333, by permission of the publisher and the Council on Junior High Administration, 22 East 72nd St., New York, N.Y.

Mr. Richard Conover, and Dr. L. Paul Miller, presented its report to the 1962 conference. The report was revised and presented again at the 1963 conference, at which time it was approved and its publication authorized.

This report is published by the Institute for Instructional Improvement, Inc., 22 East 72nd Street, New York 21, New York, for gratuitous distribution.

It is our belief that effective administrative attention should be given to each of the following concepts in any adequate junior high school:

I. The school must be organized for the benefit of all pupils who are able to profit from this type of education.

II. It is widely recognized that pupils of this age should have a broad program of general education.

III. Recognizing the differences among pupils of junior-high-school age, it is our belief that we should provide a wide variety of methods and materials for dealing with this range of differences.

IV. All who come in contact with pupils of junior-high-school age recognize the variations in their competency. To provide for these variations we believe that varying standards of accomplishment should be recognized.

V. Adequate administrative staffing can be justified in many ways. The costs of inadequate staffing may be high indeed.

VI. Exploration continues throughout life. We believe, however, that the junior-high-school age is an especially fruitful time for exploration, and that provision should be made in the junior high school for this type of experience.

VII. We believe that a vital guidance program should be provided—one that will assist each pupil to the fulfillment of his highest potential; lip service is not a substitute for a good program.

VIII. Personnel services for all ages are important in organized modern life. We believe, however, that the need is urgent at the junior-high-school age and that adequate services should be provided.

IX. A good junior high school cannot exist without a competent staff. We believe that our society can and should provide such a staff.

X. Finally, all that we attempt in the junior high school should be subjected to constant and careful evaluation. Testing in business and industry often prevents waste and spoilage. Sometimes there is waste and spoilage in education. Adequate evaluation will prevent the perpetuation of ill-conceived and ineffective procedures.

I. Organization

To organize the school for the benefit of all pupils who should profit from this type of education, we believe:

—that all educable young people between the ages of approximately 12 and 15 should participate in a junior-high-school program;

—that the junior high school should include three consecutive years, grades 7, 8, and 9;

—that the staff of the sending elementary school should decide when a pupil is to enter the junior high school;

—that the staff of the junior high school should decide when a pupil is ready to enter the senior high school;

—that the academic record made in the junior high school should not be a part of the requirement for senior-high-school graduation or a part of the requirement for college admission.

II. General Education

To provide a broad program of general education for all as a basis for living a full and productive life, we believe:

—that changing socio-economic conditions make it not only possible but also necessary to provide a relatively long period of general and comprehensive education;

—that these same conditions in society make it both feasible and economical to postpone specialization and curriculum differentiation until the pupils have received basic integrating education;

—that an acceptable program of general education will require not only the academic areas of language arts, social studies, mathematics, and science, but also health and physical education, the fine arts, and practical arts;

—that foreign languages, taught as a means of communication, should take their place in the broad language-arts program;

—that within the framework of these broad areas of general education we can serve individual differences through breadth and depth of learning;

—that we must continually redefine the content and methods of the several subject areas;

—that we must develop the library as a center for learning and self-fulfillment.

III. Individual Differences

To provide the variety of methods, materials, and experiences which will serve the differences found among pupils, we believe:

–that the spread of individual differences should be served largely through a variety of methods and materials;

–that we should recognize and provide for the degree of readiness of the learner and his potential for growth;

–that the junior high school should provide a well-organized program for the retardates of this age group;

–that special attention should be given to the potentially disturbed or mildly disturbed youth;

–that the educational needs of physically handicapped pupils should be met, whenever possible, through a program in the school; otherwise, in a homebound teaching situation.

IV. Competency

To provide a variety of standards of individual achievement based upon a recognition that people participate on various levels of competency in their several vocational, social, and civic activities, we believe:

–that we must define the various levels of competency observed in our society and establish standards of achievement accordingly.

V. Administration

To provide an administrative pattern based upon our knowledge and understanding of the learning process as well as the nature of the learner, we believe:

–that the principal is the key to the continuous success and improvement of the junior high school;

–that administrative acts must be in harmony with the purposes of the total school program;

–that the size of the school should be large enough to provide for efficient staffing and effective educational offering and services, suggesting a minimum administrative unit of 300 to 450 pupils;

–that large schools should be divided into internal units so that the individual identity of pupils and staff will be retained;

–that every pupil, at some time during his daily program, should be placed in at least one class–for example, language arts or social studies–that is composed of pupils fairly representative of his entire grade level;

–that instruction will be most effective when the scheduling of pupils has been in accord with the pupils' goals of learning, thus providing a compatible learning situation for all in the group;

–that where groups are formed to reduce the spread of differences within a class section, the purpose of the group should be well defined, and the criteria of selection should be consistent with the goals of the group and in harmony with the purpose of the total school program;

–that there should be one full-time administrator or supervisor to each 15 to 20 professional staff members, exclusive of the building principal;

–that balance in the program should be maintained through a supervisory organization that is general in nature rather than departmental;

–that the several subject areas and activities may require different time allotments and may be scheduled accordingly.

VI. Exploration

To provide the experiences and security, throughout the total school program, which will permit a pupil not only to explore the several subject fields but also to understand his personal strengths and weaknesses, we believe:

–that the interests of the early adolescent are in the formative stages;

–that exploration is an important function of the junior high school;

–that exploration is an integral part of all subjects and aspects of the junior-high-school program;

–that exploration is not only a part of the total program but should be incorporated into the teaching methods of the school;

–that inherent in the idea of exploration is the expectation that a pupil will do better in some experiences than in others;

–that if this function of exploration is to be served, it is necessary to plan for effective approaches and techniques to be used.

VII. Guidance

To provide the counseling and guidance necessary to assist each pupil in the discovery and fulfillment of his greatest potential, we believe:

–that guidance is a prime responsibility of the junior high school;

–that every pupil has a right to expect that some competent school adult will know him well;

–that the ratio of qualified personnel to pupils should be 75 counselees for each clock hour the counselor devotes exclusively to guidance, with a maximum fulltime load of 250 to 350 pupils;

–that the assignment of counselees to counselors should ensure continuity through the junior-high-school years;

–that the teaching staff should be scheduled in such a manner as to ensure that all teachers serving a particular group of pupils can be brought together regularly for case conferences and other guidance purposes;

—that full-time clerks should be assigned to the guidance office in the ratio of 1 for every 3 counselors.

VIII. Pupil Personnel Services

To provide those services appropriate to the school which will assist each pupil to attend regularly in such a state of mental and physical well-being as will permit him to profit most from instruction, we believe:

—that the services of the health team, including doctor, nurse, and dental hygienist, should be available to serve each junior high school;

—that the services of a psychological team, including psychologist, social worker, and psychiatrist, should be available to serve the junior-high-school age group;

—that the basic functions of these services should be prevention, diagnosis, and referral;

—that attendance services should be developed on a social casework concept;

—that the ratio of pupils to the pupil personnel staff should be in keeping with the recommendations of the appropriate professional associations.

IX. Staff

To provide a staff whose members have those patterns of preparation that will assure that each knows his subject thoroughly, understands the age group, and has the necessary attitudes toward the junior high school, we believe:

—that all professional staff members should have the basic preparation for teaching;

—that the junior-high-school teacher should be well prepared in the subjects he teaches;

—that a program of certification should be developed for junior-high-school staff members;

—that the junior high school is a professional level in education;

—that every member of the staff should be involved in self-improvement both in his area of specialization and in the total concept of the junior high school.

X. Evaluation

To provide the continual evaluation of both pupil development and the program of the school, we believe:

—that evaluation should be based on a sound philosophy and on clearly defined objectives;

—that a variety of techniques of evaluation should be used;

—that reports to parents must be more meaningful than is possible with a single symbol on a report card;

—that there is need for a reliable instrument designed specifically to guide in the evaluation of the modern junior high school;

—that each principal and his staff should assist in the development of the criteria necessary for the evaluation of their own school.

Flexible Design Matches Curriculum*

If flexible scheduling and team teaching set the learning pace for seven years at Lakeview High School, why not design its new feeder school—Jefferson Junior High—with the same instructional approach in mind? That's what planners of the 600-pupil, grade 7-8 school in Decatur, Ill., asked themselves, then did.

"We had ideas. We hadn't built a new junior high since 1932," explained Assistant Superintendent of Secondary Schools Norman J. Gore. "The district," he said, "was ready for the new building, and we wanted to tailor it to the educational program at Lakeview High, which most Jefferson pupils would attend. I think we got an outstanding building to meet our needs."

Before Jefferson was completed in September 1966, junior high pupils were housed at Lakeview, although the flexible scheduling, team-teaching concept didn't apply at the junior high level then. With major reshaping of the junior high curriculum in mind, architect E. E. Lohr of the Engineering Service Corporation in Decatur gave Jefferson the kind of flexibility that administration and faculty wanted. Examples:

Team Teaching. Space for teaching teams to work together, prepare lessons, construct materials, counsel pupils, and discuss instructional problems forms the core of the academic classroom area located on Jefferson's second floor. Adjacent to this space are the reading center and library areas, which are separate but close to each other.

Flexible Grouping. Instructional areas throughout Jefferson adjust to a variety of teaching approaches. Teachers can arrange large groups of 100 to 400 easily in the first floor instructional materials center where flexible partitions section the room into four separate areas. Elsewhere in classrooms, reading rooms, and science laboratories, groups of 5 to 50 can hold sessions. Individual study areas also are provided.

*Reprinted from *The American School Board Journal* (January 1968), 55-8, by permission of the publisher.

Flexible Scheduling. Because flexible scheduling is based, in part, upon multiples of small time modules, individual differences among pupils, and need for greater continuity in the study of some subjects, Architect Lohr grouped related instructional and space units together: Academic and library sections are by themselves on the second floor; shop and drafting, gym, band, science labs, home economics, and art areas are not so far from each other that pupils and staff have a long walk to get from place to place, but at the same time aren't close enough to distract each other by noise.

Teaching Aids. Provision was made in teaching areas for open and closed-circuit TV, teaching machines, video-tape equipment, and other electronic aids in use now and planned for the future.

Doing double service, the instructional materials center also is an auditorium and a center for community adult educational, recreational and cultural activities. Across the corridor and next to the kitchen is the cafeteria. Used for dining during part of the day, the cafeteria can convert to three classrooms the rest of the time when its two folding partitions are pulled out.

Jefferson's exterior of Norman face brick, porcelain enameled steel insulated panels around windows, and stone and aluminum trim reduce outside maintenance. Inside, maintenance is minimized through use of practical flooring: quarry tile in the kitchen, showers and locker rooms; sealed concrete in shops; resilient tile in instructional areas, and ceramic tile in washrooms. Acoustical formboard in shop and gym roofs absorbs noise. The hot water heating system was designed to take expansion of the school plant in stride and was sized for future air conditioning.

Besides providing a prime example of flexible school design, Jefferson also illustrates the school district's policy of cooperating with Decatur's park district on school site planning. Wherever possible, school sites are chosen close to city parks, and Jefferson's 10 acres are next to a 25 acre Decatur playground.

Construction Statistics. Cost of construction, including site work, parking lot, sidewalks and fixed equipment—but excluding architect fees—was \$1,374,078.52. Based on an enrollment of 600, per-pupil cost was \$2,290.13. With a total building area of 89,570 square feet, approximate area per pupil is 149 square feet.

Chattanooga Builds a Nongraded Junior High School*

JAMES D. McCULLOUGH

Decatur, Ill., got what it wanted when Jefferson was built: a feeder junior high that complements the high school.

The concept of nongraded programs of instruction is not new to Chattanooga public schools. Pilot programs in elementary schools have been in operation since 1959, but the junior and senior high schools followed the Carnegie one-grade-a-year approach until September, 1963. When it became apparent that a new junior high school was needed in North Brainerd, a rapidly growing suburban area east of Missionary Ridge, the instructional staff began studying the feasibility of extending the nongraded program to the junior high level. The Chattanooga board of eductation has always followed the philosophy of planning and building its schools in accordance with the needs of the community they are to serve. One nongraded-type elementary program had already proven itself in the Brainerd community. The idea of extending this program to the junior high school was presented to various groups in the community, and a preliminary nongraded curriculum was developed by the Division of Instruction for purposes of study.

Specialists Assist in Planning

For the past three years, the board has retained the services of the School Plant Planning Division of the University of Tennessee which operated under sponsorship of the Educational Facilities Laboratory. Specialists in school

*Reprinted from *The American School Board Journal*, 148 (February 1964), 71, 74 by permission of the publisher and James D. McCullough, Assistant Superintendent for Business, Chattanooga, Tenn.

construction and curriculum from the university worked with the instructional staff and teachers from the school system for a study of feasibility. After it was decided to construct a building flexible enough to accommodate a nongraded program and also to house the more traditional program, the consultants assisted in preparation of educational specifications. It was the desire of the board to design more efficient buildings than those previously constructed in this area. Therefore, the objective of the planning committees was a compact building providing the combination of a nongraded program and a building with minimum corridor space. Plans to air-condition also suggested the practicality of a compact building with reduced glass areas.

The services of Butler, Wilhoite & Hildebrand, a Chattanooga architectural firm, were retained by the board prior to preliminary planning of the building. This was consistent with board policy to employ its architects as soon as the need for a school becomes apparent in order that their advice will be available in selection of the site. The architects worked closely with the planning committee. They postponed developing preliminary plans for the building until they had thoroughly acquainted themselves with the concept of the nongraded program and with the philosophy of the board and staff as well as with the recommendation from the consultants representing EFL. The Dalewood building literally was planned from the inside out.

The first schemes that were developed were sketches of areas-science and mathematics, social studies, physical education, fine arts. Acceptable arrangements for these spaces were developed and were studied by the planning committees before an attempt was made to combine them into a building. After several weeks of planning, the staff developed comprehensive educational specifications which they transmitted to the architects for final study. Again the architects spent time studying and analyzing specifications. Only then did they begin to make line drawings which they felt would accommodate the program outlined in detail.

The final result of this approach to planning is shown in the floor plans. Statistics of the building reflect efficiency in the form of very little corridor and lobby space and a considerable amount of flexibility available to the staff in the form of folding partitions. The unusual shape of the classrooms originated from a sketch submitted by a group of teachers working on the mathematics area. These teachers suggested a small instructional materials center where a team of teachers could work and plan together, store materials, and share ideas as well as pupils. The proposal proved to be in keeping with the compact approach and was incorporated as a general arrangement for one side of the building.

The Educational Program

The language arts-social studies block of time is scheduled for all pupils during the first two hours of the day. Mathematics and science are scheduled during two hours in the afternoon, with half the pupils in mathematics and the other half in science; obviously, these groups exchange places midway of this block of time. All exploratory and enrichment courses are scheduled during the middle of the school day, with physical education receiving heavy emphasis during the seventh or last period.

The purpose of this type of schedule is to provide the flexibility required by a nongraded program. To clarify, pupils at varying instructional levels in the language arts-social studies field can be moved with little difficulty from one level to another as the need occurs. Similarly, pupils moving from one level to another in mathematics can do so without disturbing their time schedules.

Achievement of pupil mobility within an instructional area does not depend entirely upon such a schedule, but it is facilitated by a schedule involving the total student body—or half the student body—in the same area.

Natural questions arise as to teacher competency and building efficiency in such an arrangement. Leaders are those teachers with certificates in the instructional area, and their associates have completed more than the average amount of work in the area. Teachers of exploratory courses, all of whom have minors in other areas, are members of either the language arts-social studies teams or the mathematics and science teams. Individual teachers have the experience of taking leadership roles in one area and cooperating roles in another. Planning periods of team members are an essential part of the nongraded program.

The total building is used, though in what might be termed a decidedly nonconforming fashion.

The instructional program is designed for young adolescents of the usual junior high school age range and specifically provides for all boys and girls at whatever achievement levels they find themselves. The goal is continuous growth at the individual's best pace.

Classrooms in Cluster Arrangement

The four clusters of rooms at the north end of the building serve as the regular classrooms for what might be termed normal use in the core subjects of language arts-social studies, mathematics and science. These rooms circle the materials center which is immediately available to all of them. A wealth of instructional tools and their ready accessibility are essential features of the nongraded program. Small conference rooms and individual study spaces provide for special teaching-learning activities which are not "special" in this program.

The materials center and the adjacent commons, or cafeteria, are actually in the middle of the four incomplete-hexagon-shaped clusters of trapezoid classrooms. These two areas serve for large-group instruction for any of the core subjects. A recent afternoon visit to the school found half the student body—those taking science while the other half were studying mathematics—viewing an appropriate film which was to be discussed subsequently by the students grouped according to their varying levels of science sophistication. The students were comfortably seated in the gay-colored commons which had been speedily and easily converted from eating hall into viewing room. Promptly after the film, the students fanned out into classrooms in two nearby clusters.

The materials center serves as the heart of the educational program. Physically, it has the usual large room of any school library, with bookshelves around the walls and a limited number extending into the reading room. In addition to the main area, there is a rectangular area which can easily seat a class coming from any of the clusters; it provides amply for library research activities without interfering with other students working individually in the library. The study room and two conference rooms in the materials center enable small groups of students to do library research, view projected materials, plan special projects, and carry on other instructional activities under the supervision of the librarian. The audio-visual room is a well-organized storage space, not a viewing area; portable projectors and related equipment are handled by a group of pupils under direction of the librarian. A second storage room, for printed materials and smaller instructional tools, is a librarian's dream come true; it houses those expensive materials frequently needed in the classroom but not required at all times. An upstairs storage room accessible by means of a disappearing stairway expands the provisions for a multiplicity of instructional tools which can be protected when not required for immediate use. A preparation room available to all faculty members is located between the materials center and the commons: here teacher aids and teachers prepare all sorts of projecturals including transparencies for overhead projectors regularly used in large-group instruction

Pupils needing developmental reading instruction remain in the language arts-social studies block during the third hour, and these include the majority of boys and girls normally designated as seventh and eighth graders. Special grouping is provided for educable mentally retarded pupils. Pupils at the top of the "spiral" or in the upper levels of achievement in these areas have choices among many electives, including two modern foreign languages, vocal and instrumental music, art, mechanical drawing and shop, typewriting, and home economics.

Exploration is the emphasis at the fourth period. All pupils have experiences in the areas where electives are offered pupils have experiences in the areas where electives are offered spiral who have participated in similar courses during the preceding hour; they have physical education and health at this time.

Music Center

The music center, consisting of two main rooms, five individual practice rooms, a music library, and an office provides for general music, vocal and instrumental. It is in heavy use at third, fourth, and seventh periods and is also

Dalewood Junior High School
Statistics and Costs

Plot Area: 20.73 acres
Building Area: 79,494 sq. ft.
Units: 13 Classrooms
1 Outdoor classroom
4 Instructional material centers
1 Material center with audio-visual and teachers' workrooms
1 Staff lounge
1 Commons and kitchen
2 Science classrooms
1 Science laboratory with project room
1 Typing and business classroom with storage rooms
1 Home economics (multipurpose)
1 Choral room
1 Band room with music department office and library
4 Practice rooms and instrument storage
1 Art
1 Planning
1 Shop with finishing and project storage rooms
1 Exercise room
1 Weights room
1 Gymnasium with showers and locker rooms, first aid
1 Boiler room with heating and air-conditioning equipment
1 Administrative with health clinic, conference and offices

Auditorium to be constructed at a later date
Construction Cost:

General	$ 932,212
Kitchen	28,205
Architect's fees	57,625
Concrete testing	1,125
Insurance and legal fees	1,500
All equipment	98,000
Total cost of project as of October 31, 1963	$1,118,667

available for correlated activities at the language arts-social studies block in the morning. While music for all students receives major emphasis, performing groups come from pupils at the top of the fine arts spiral.

The home economics and industrial arts quarters provide for unit teaching in the former and general shop and mechanical drawing in the latter. Special teachers are in charge of the instructional program, and they also serve as members of teaching teams for language arts-social studies or for mathematics and science.

The seventh period, following the mathematics and science classes, finds most of the pupils in physical education and health, while those who have achieved high levels in the various instructional levels—the "Quest" group—are engaged in a variety of independent and special group activities, including work on the newspaper, participation in dramatics and a host of other clubs, and research in any of the subject-matter fields. Most of the staff members are necessarily engaged in physical education with the student body though certified personnel are in general charge of the instruction. An important by-product is the different type of relationship established between teachers and pupils when those teachers usually associated with so-called academic areas discover superior achievement among all levels of pupils. Much emphasis is placed on the health aspect of the physical education program, with unusual support coming from the competencies of these "other" teachers including a science teacher who is a registered nurse. The schedule is so arranged that about 75 boys and 75 girls at a maximum are on the gymnasium floor at any time, with three teachers assigned to each group of 75 pupils.

Courses of study as such are not equated with requirements for given grade levels. The sequence of skills, values, and concepts is identified, and pupils move upward in the various sequences at their own pace. The building accommodates this type of spiral mobility, and boys and girls "latch" on at the level where their maturity of understanding and achievement permits. Of particular significance to this type of continuous progress, as far as the physical plant is concerned, are the facilities of the materials center and the relationship of the four clusters of classrooms to each other and to the materials center and commons.

part **2**

The Middle School

Although the 7-8-9 pattern has been the most common in the junior high or intermediate school, this organization has never been universally accepted. Throughout the years a variety of patterns other than 6-3-3 have been adopted for the school in the middle, such as 6-2-4, 5-3-4, 4-4-4, 6-2-1-4, 6-2-2-2, 5-4-3, and 3-5-4. In many instances the grades included have been established because of the stresses of enrollment, finances, buildings, or community pressures. Recent years have seen an intensified interest in "middle schools" that include grades 6-7-8 or 5-6-7-8, and a recent survey indicated that there are probably over 1000 of these in existence in the United States as opposed to over 6000 of the 7-8-9 junior high schools. Reasons given for the change from the traditional junior high school to middle schools include the earlier sophistication and maturity of youth; criticism of high school-type activities in the junior high schools; changing curricula and innovations in education; and the need for a distinct middle unit in the public schools, between elementary and high school, with a status, curriculum, and staff specifically its own.

School in the Middle–Junior High: Education's Problem Child *

MAURITZ JOHNSON, JR.

Every so often some indignant or exasperated soul prescribes major surgery for the American educational enterprise, and more often than not the object of the incision and derision is the junior high school. While this operation has about as much chance of being pulled off as has the abolition of the income tax, such desperate proposals tend to divert attention from the very real needs for improvement at this school level. In an atmosphere of such dire threats, fervent supporters of the junior high school brook no criticism of their beloved institution, however valid it may be. But, while detractors who advocate decapitation to cure a headache are of scant help to the patient, neither are his well-intentioned friends who call the headache an illusion or a normal condition.

The junior high school is an American invention which dates from the first decade of this century. In 1920 there were fewer than 400 of them; in 1940 there were over 2,000; and now the number is probably close to 5,000. In quantitative terms the movement has been a distinct success.

Actually, it was an integral part of a larger movement which involved the downward extension of secondary education through the annexation of grades seven and eight from the elementary school. In large school systems, physically separate three-year junior and senior high schools were established, but in small ones a single six-year secondary school became the mode. In the latter, the old four-year high school usually persisted as a unit, with the two appended grades occupying an indefinite status. Rarely has the junior high school idea been a guiding force in the six-year high school.

What is the junior high school idea? In a word, asylum. The junior high school is supposed to be a bridge between the elementary school and the upper

*Reprinted from *Saturday Review*, 45 (July 21, 1962), 40-42, by permission of the publisher and Mauritz Johnson Jr., Cornell University.

secondary level and, indeed, a bridge between childhood and that attenuated near-adult stage we call adolescence. Within this "transition school for early adolescence," a very special environment is to be created in which pubescence can be experienced without trauma or trepidation. The forbearance of understanding teachers and the comfortable camouflage of the "peer group" (all of whom are in the same boat), facilitate the rapprochement of the sexes, the learning of new social skills, the exploration of bodily changes, and tolerant acceptance of ambivalent vacillation between childish dependence and brash assertiveness. At the same time, the right combination of wide "exploration" and wise guidance would assure that, when the metamorphosis was complete, the physically healthy, emotionally stable, socially adjusted, civic-minded specimen which emerged from the cocoon would be well prepared to take advantage of whatever opportunities later adolescence might offer.

If this description appears to be a caricature, such is not the intent. Realistic or not, defensible or not, these are the goals that junior high schools have sought to achieve. It is easy to extend our overly sentimental view of childhood too far, but it cannot be gainsaid that in the contemporary American culture the phenomenon of adolescence is characterized by a quest for heterosexual social relationships and emanicpation from adult control, and this phenomenon cannot be ignored. Apparently, the leap from childhood dependency to sophisticated individuality can rarely be accomplished in advanced Western societies without the intermediate use of the group of contemporaries as a transitory source of security. In a world in which adults expound one set of values and espouse another, in which schooling is prolonged and economic dependence is protracted, and in which social life is largely outside the family, the value of a haven the junior high school attempts to be is readily recognized by many parents of this in-between age group.

If this phase of development is often a difficult one for those passing through it, it is even more so for the adults around them. To establish and maintain a junior high school which fully exemplifies the idea underlying that institution is not easy, and many schools, it must be conceded, have been less than successful in this regard. And, as with the girl with the curl, a good junior high school can be very, very good, but a poor one can be horrid.

It is not difficult to find some teachers who view youngsters at this level as obnoxious nuisances, rather than as energetic, curious, fumbling individuals on the threshold of adulthood. Some junior high schools provide social activities as formal and sophisticated as those in which high school seniors engage. Some promote extensive interscholastic athletic programs which feature strenuous physical exertion, intense emotional involvement, and often late hours. In some, the break from grade six to seven is as abrupt as it ever was between grades eight and nine. But these are shortcomings in human performance and institutional arrangements, rather than inherent defects in the idea, which in many schools is faithfully and skilfully practiced.

But if the idea itself makes a certain amount of sense, it also gives disconcertingly little attention to the primary responsibility of any educational institution–intellectual development. Not that the intellectual aspect is completely ignored or that it is incompatible with the concern for transition, but simply that the emphasis on it is not explicit and its nature is not defined.

It was not ever thus. When the first junior high schools were established, there seems to have been greater concern about the downward extension of secondary education than about the separation of the secondary school into two components. The chief motive for extending downward stemmed from a dissatisfaction with the elementary school curriculum and methods in grades seven and eight. To a large extent these were "review" years, preparatory for eighth-grade graduation (or nongraduation). For many pupils this review was considered unnecessary, and it only delayed their beginning more advanced academic studies under teachers who were specialists in these subjects. For the many overage pupils who populated these grades, the steady diet of review of common branch subjects seemed, perhaps not entirely futile, but at least of less value for imminent entry into the world of work than one accompanied by some specific vocational training. It was through this combination of earlier academic instruction and terminal vocational training that the "needs" of the young (and not so young) adolescents were to be better met.

The separation of the junior high grades from the upper ones was not at that time so much for social and emotional reasons as to make the *academic* initiation at grade nine easier for pupils, since approximately half of all high school students were in the freshman classes of the conventional high schools, and that was as far as many of them ever got. It was *this* transition that was of greatest concern, not the one from grade six to seven or the one represented by pubescence. Indeed, if social and emotional considerations entered the picture at all, they revolved about protecting the younger children *from* the unwholesome influence of the young adolescents in the seventh and eighth grades within the elementary school, not providing a haven for the new junior high school group.

Again, this is not to deny the usefulness of a separate and special social setting for this transition period, but merely to emphasize that the early concern for more suitable intellectual fare has of late been obscured. We may grant that the earlier vocational emphasis is less appropriate today because of longer compulsory education, diminished overageness as a result of changed promotion policies, and increased importance of intellectual development in a technologically more complex economy. But precisely because more people do need to develop further than ever intellectually, it is all the more important that those who wish to improve the junior high schools again turn their attention to this central area of the school's responsibility.

It is in regard to intellectual training that those who are inclined toward abolition of the junior high school must also consider the consequences of such a step. To return grades seven and eight to an elementary school status is unthinkable. Pupils at this level must have the intellectual resources which a secondary school is better able to provide—teachers prepared in specific subject areas; laboratory, library, studio, and shop facilities; and a sufficient concentration of pupils for differentiation in the curriculum consistent with the extensive range of abilities among pupils at this level. The elementary school as we now know it cannot provide these conditions. If the junior high school were to be destroyed, the only other alternative would be to merge it with the senior high school in a single six-year unit. What advantage this would offer in strengthening the lower three grades intellectually is unclear.

Some communities, because of building considerations or sheer tradition, retain grade nine with the upper three and maintain a two-year middle unit. There is a feeling in some quarters that ninth graders fare better academically under such an arrangement. This is highly questionable, unless there is a great disparity in the qualifications of teachers at the two levels. Actually, when teachers are equally qualified, ninth graders in a junior high school setting appear to achieve as well or better than they do as freshmen in a four-year high school. Furthermore, a two-grade school lacks stability in that pupils enter one year and leave the next. Although it is better than no middle school at all, it has not been found to be as satisfactory as a three-year unit.

A legitimate question, however, is which three grades? While the seven-nine unit predominates today, there is increasing interest in a six-seven-eight combination, because it appeals to the four-year high school advocates, to the proponents of a three-year middle unit, and to those who want pupils introduced even earlier to teachers who are specialists in their subjects. It would be resisted by those who for several decades have introduced an elementary school philosophy into the junior high school to counteract what they consider to be too early departmentalization, too great an academic emphasis, and too much imitation of high school social and athletic practices. The wisdom of such a unit should not, however, be determined by how large a coalition can be mustered in its favor.

Since the middle school as a separate organization can be justified on social grounds only if it embraces the period during which the majority of pupils reach adolescence, the six-seven-eight unit would be valid only if it could be shown that large numbers of sixth graders are pubescent. There is some evidence that youngsters do mature earlier today than they did a generation or two ago, and certainly they acquire greater amounts of general information and social sophistication earlier. In some communities, however, this is not true, and it is senseless to argue for the same organizational pattern everywhere. But it does not follow that the matter of organization is, therefore, inconsequential. What is important is that we be clear as to why a middle school unit with identity of its own is desirable, and what it needs if it is to be a stable, visable unit.

Junior high schools can be eliminated or altered, but pupils of junior high school age will remain, and who will teach them and what they will be taught are the really significant questions. Their teachers need to be as well versed in their respective subject fields as possible, and in addition be cognizant and appreciative of the relative immaturity of these pupils, their transitional status, and their tremendous diversity. Junior high school teachers must be willing and able to help pupils become students, equipping them with the tools and procedures for a lifetime of study, rather than assuming that they are already so equipped or can acquire, on their own, the ability to study effectively and independently. If junior high schools would address themselves to this problem seriously, pupils, their parents, and all of their subsequent teachers would be grateful.

Good junior high school teachers are even harder to come by than good elementary or senior high school teachers. It would be an oversimplification to say that some teachers are attracted to the profession out of a desire to be with children and others from an urge to engage in the transmission of ideas, and that at the junior high school level the pupils aren't lovable enough for the one group and the ideas dealt with aren't complex enough for the other. Nevertheless, a recent study at Cornell showed that among some 600 teachers who were surveyed, those teaching grades seven and eight were markedly less satisfied with their level of assignment than were teachers in the grades below and above. When the reasons were analyzed, the nature of the curriculum (the ideas), rather than the nature of the pupils at this level, seemed to be predominant. Teachers who enjoy teaching many subject areas cannot do so in the junior high school, nor can those who enjoy teaching advanced content do that. Perhaps this is inevitable in an "in-between" school.

Yet, there is a clue here that the curriculum at this level needs some careful rethinking and perhaps a complete overhauling. Typically, all seventh and eighth graders are required to take some nine or ten subjects for the same length of time, despite considerable differences in their abilities, interests, and accomplishments. No matter that a pupil is tone deaf and has been taught music by a specialist throughout six elementary school years—he must still "explore" it, along with his friend who plays in both band and orchestra and practices an hour each evening. No matter that a pupil is weak in the fundamentals of arithmetic—his mathematics teacher, fresh from a course in partial differential equations, must teach him the types of life insurance and what enters into overhead in retailing, just as he must teach these topics to all the mathematically eager pupils awaiting the delights of algebra, geometry, and the infinity beyond.

In all fairness, it must be said that many program changes are currently being made in junior high schools—some eighth graders study algebra; foreign language, taught by the direct method, is offered in grade seven; set theory, Venn diagrams, and other modern mathematical topics have been introduced; and more science is being given. But these changes represent only creeping improvement, not the giant step that is needed. It is true that the quality of teaching makes or breaks any program, but a poor curriculum is a millstone around the neck of the best of teachers.

Take the bright young social studies teacher who did graduate work in comparative economics or American foreign policy. A complete stranger in the community, he must begin by teaching that one Silas Wright established the first local grist mill, and then recount for the nth time the story of the Indian tribes which inhabited the area and the great contribution they made to American culture, and spend the rest of the year in a provincial tribute to the greatness of the particular state. Or, consider the English teacher, a literature major, of course–primarily British literature, particularly poetry, especially the Lake poets–with no study of grammar since high school (the college English department didn't offer it) and only vaguely aware (from an education course) of the current controversy between proponents of structural linguistics and advocates of conventional grammar. What will be the major emphasis in her junior high school English classes? Grammar, of course, and what literature there is may consist of whatever novel is in the anthology, some short stories by Poe and O. Henry, and a long poem by Longfellow. The rest will be free reading of "adolescent literature" on romance and nursing for the girls, and war, sports, and automobiles for the boys.

Somewhere, at this very moment, an engineer, a doctor, and an AAUW member on a school board are doubtless fighting the good fight to employ a junior high school science teacher who has his master's degree in physics rather than education. The fact is, however, that most students who do graduate work in physics will be advised by their physics professors (and their common sense) to sell their valuable talents to some one other than a board of education. Those who actually become junior high school teachers may find that Ohm's law is the most advanced physics they teach, and that a large part of the time they must deal with such matters as testing food for starch with iodine, reading a weather map, and tracing the flow of blood through the heart.

Nevertheless, a curriculum must obviously be planned with the maturity and requirements of the learners in mind, not the strengths and desires of teachers. Yet, if the nature of the curriculum affects the availability and enthusiasm of teachers, so, too, the improvement of curriculum depends in the main upon the discontent and initiative of teachers. Administrators, laymen, and professors from both the scholarly disciplines and professional education can encourage and assist them, but in the final analysis, teachers, singly and in groups, must do the job. What deters them is not so much their own shortcomings as certain beliefs which are prevalent in many communities: that the problems in the junior high school are inevitable and unsolvable; that the junior high school must forever remain as it has been; that some outside authority really decides all the questions; that getting rid of the junior high school altogether will take care of the problem.

Many specific suggestions could be offered for the improvement of the curriculum at this level, but this is a matter on which those who are in a position to make the changes must work. It might be urged, though, that the changes be in the direction of greater emphasis on significant ideas as opposed to inert facts, greater continuity of intellectual development; greater flexibility of programming, particularly in the area of the "arts," for pupils who differ so greatly; and at least as much attention to independence in studying and thinking as in the social and emotional spheres. The fact that many junior high school pupils are so preoccupied with their adolescent developmental problems that they are distracted from learning may be, in part at least, of our own making. If we could provide a curriculum which would engross their attention more fully, they might then be distracted from many of their physical, social, and emotional problems.

One can insist that the curriculum of the middle school, and specifically its intellectual component, is in need of reexamination without implying that efforts to take into account the transition from childhood should be abandoned or neglected. Many problems, such as those relating to the grouping of pupils and the maintenance of standards, cannot be solved satisfactorily until the curriculum is reformed. For example, we currently form instructional groups, and then either fail to provide curricular differences or attempt to adapt the curriculum to each group. Instead, we should reverse the process by organizing the curriculum first and then forming the groups accordingly. We define junior high school courses in terms of grades, when we know there are greater differences among pupils *within* seventh grade than there are *between* an average seventh grader and an average senior. It is impossible to speak of standards without reference to relatively specific and stable curriculum elements, and the grade concept has lost its usefulness for this purpose.

To return to the opening metaphor, euthanasia is not the answer to the junior high school's malady, but a curricular lobotomy may be necessary. The present dosage of vitamins will not give us the kind of middle school we need.

Recommended Grades or Years in Junior High or Middle Schools*

A Statement by the Committee on Junior High School Education, National Association of Secondary School Principals

In terms of the number of schools involved, the most frequent pattern of grade organization today is the 6-6 arrangement, where the secondary school is an *undivided* six-year unit. In contrast, the 6-3-3 pattern—which enrolls a majority of all secondary school pupils—and the less common 6-2-4 organizational scheme each provides for a *separate* junior high school of two or three school years. Interest recently has focused on two other organizational forms, the 5-3-4 and the 4-4-4, both of which incorporate a modified junior high school typically called a *middle school.*

Analysis of these various organizations raises three questions: Why should there be a separate middle unit? How many grades or years belong in the middle unit? Which grades or years are most appropriate for each unit?

The Middle Unit

Three separate units—lower, middle, and upper—or, as they are usually called—elementary, junior high or middle, and senior high—are recommended. The separately organized and administered middle unit provides pupils with valuable opportunities to participate in and lead activities designed especially for their age group. Even in systems that provide K-12 or 7-12 programs in one unit, pupils in the middle years need specific identity with respect to administration, faculty, and student body activities.

*Reprinted from *The Bulletin of the National Association of Secondary School Principals* (February 1967), 51:68-70, by permission of the National Association of Secondary School Principals. Copyright: 1967 by the National Association of Secondary School Principals.

Three or Four Grades in the Middle Unit

The number of years that individual pupils spend in the middle school or junior high school will differ. Individual differences may produce variations in the rate of pupil progress through the school, especially in a nongraded format. The Committee believes that only two years or two grades are not enough to provide stability and to fulfill the stated educational goals of these schools because most pupils enter one year and leave the next. A one-year school is least desirable. At the other extreme, pupils who are five years apart in age have too little in common to function effectively together in the same unit. The best solution is a middle unit consisting of three or four grades or years. The Committee recommends three years as the better alternative.

Grades Seven (or Six) Through Nine

The onset of puberty is no respecter of grades. Nor is it possible to whisk pupils into another unit as soon as they enter pubescence. The goals, however, in selecting the middle-unit grades are to enroll most pubescents in them. Most studies indicate that the grades in which the greatest proportion of pupils are pubescent are seven, eight, and nine. Even greater program flexibility may increase that proportion by providing opportunities for pupils of diverse talents and past achievements to succeed educationally in each of the grades or years.

Anyone contemplating a grade combination other than 7-9 needs to have compelling reasons for making the change. There is some indication that pubescence now begins slightly earlier than previously. Furthermore, even before they become pubescent, children today adopt interests often associated with adolescence and engage in behavior indicative of conflicts between their dependency needs and the desire for independence. Their general level of information also is higher, due to the influence of mass communication media and to improved school instruction. Thus, the current sixth grader or eleven year old may be as ready for the junior high or middle school as the seventh grader was in former years.

Whether the school should aid and abet the trend toward earlier sophistication is another question. However, earlier assumption of increased independence and responsibility under the careful guidance and control of a middle or junior high school seems more appropriate for sixth graders than would the earlier introduction of ninth graders to the more advanced social atmosphere of the senior high school. The Committee sees greater merit in a middle school that encompasses grades 6 through 9 than one of grades 5 through 8. We believe that few fifth graders are ready for junior high or middle school activities and, therefore, are served better in a transitional fifth-grade program in an elementary school. We believe also that most ninth graders are not ready for the activities of the usual senior high school.

The Key

Administrative organization needs to be determined on educational grounds, rather than for such reasons as building expediency, economy, or racial imbalance. Nor is a special reorganization of units essential for encouraging needed educational reforms. Certainly, any three-year or four-year middle school or junior high school can and should engage in innovative teaching and learning programs.

The Committee urges the importance of research regarding such all-important matters as present levels of physical and social maturation of pupils, what determines quality in educational programs, and the special characteristics of existing grade organizations. In the meantime, every community that contemplates an organizational change is urged to obtain evidence regarding the maturation patterns of its children in deciding whether a 5-8, 6-8, or 6-9 school is likely to be as satisfactory an educational unit as the 7-9 school has been.

Are Junior High Schools the Answer?*

J. H. HULL

The junior high school, in my opinion, may be America's greatest educational blunder. It probably serves some children in some communities well. In others it fails perhaps in the way it is operated in a particular situation. One of its chief weaknesses is the blanket assumption that anything called a junior high school is the answer to all problems of early adolescent education. Junior high schools in practice are not what people dream about when they are organizing them; besides, they are expensive. They are not easy to put together and there are always loose ends.

In the first place, a junior high school is not a standard institution. It initially was an administrative device for controlling children in large groups rather than an organized effort to improve instruction. Some are called junior high schools and are only two-year institutions. They vary greatly in operation. Some are truly middle schools instead of junior high schools. To really say much, one has to be talking about a specific school. The criticism of being too general may apply to what follows, for there are not many objective facts to go on for either side of this argument.

Tests, research, experimentation, and evaluative devices of a so-called objective design lack sufficient comprehensiveness to match subjective judgment in measuring the value of anything as comprehensive as a junior high school program.

The seventh, eighth, and ninth grades are far from appropriate devices for grouping students together. Take a look at a group of seventh graders and at a group of ninth graders separately. If they have anything in common, it is that they are boys and girls with two eyes, two arms, and two legs; but there the similarity ends. Seventh- and ninth-grade interests are not the same, and their

*Reprinted from *Educational Leadership,* 23 (December 1965), 213-216, with permission of the Association for Supervision and Curriculum Development and J. H. Hull, Superintendent of Schools, Torrance Unified School District, Torrance, California.

growth and development are so far apart that they literally live in different worlds.

Many times one can observe maturing eighth-grade boys and girls completely drop their seventh-grade friends with whom they have been very chummy for several years until this physical change completely altered their interests and objectives. Maturing ninth-grade boys and girls have usually outgrown their former seventh-grade friends, and the seventh grade friends lose interest in them, also. To single out these youngsters and house them together in the same school appears to some to be illogical and poor educational design. Ninth-grade students have much more in common with high school students than they do with seventh graders.

A four-year high school transcript is much more meaningful than a three-year transcript of a three-year senior high school. Colleges prefer four-year transcripts.

High schools do not like to give full credit for junior high school subjects such as foreign language or typing. In fact they usually prefer not to give full credit even when the junior high school is a part of their own system.

Both high schools and colleges have much more confidence in a ninth-grade curriculum from the four-year high school. One reason for this may be that there is still no real source of training for the junior high school teacher. This makes most junior high school teachers either converted elementary teachers or high school teachers who too often are waiting for a senior high school job. This does not improve the morale of junior high school teachers or long-range thinking by the faculty.

Progress and Mobility

Today's society is fast moving. Subjects that once were studied in college are now studied in high school, and the elementary school teaches subjects that once were taught in high school. The trend is toward departmentalized upper elementary grades, semi-departmentalization, or what are coming to be called middle schools, including sixth, seventh, and eighth grades with the ninth grade back in the four-year high school where it belongs. The turnover in today's mobile population results in a two-year school being unstable and losing its identity. Every year the student body is 66 percent to 75 percent new. This gives pupils little chance to develop morale or anything else of a positive nature under these conditions.

In my opinion, the current trend to departmentalize the upper grades may be good. At least, this seems to fit the development patterns of some students better. Such an arrangement necessitates only one transition instead of two between schools to be achieved, and it tends to produce an institution that is sounder administratively and educationally. The seventh grader is not left dangling. Yet we must not ever assume that such a program is any easier to organize just because it is called upper elementary or intermediate. The problems still exist.

A subject formerly taught only in high school, such as science, which is not a standard elementary school subject, justifies the specialists who are being imported into elementary teaching, and one gradual change to high school rather than two changes make the arrangement worth while. How many teachers a day should young adolescents be expected to meet, and how many students should teachers be expected to teach per day is the key question.

The competitive athletics program that develops into too big a pattern of little high schools does not get out of hand in an elementary school setup. Such an arrangement would reduce the huge outlay for junior high gymnasiums and the whole competitive athletic show that the junior high school tries to carry. We have more important places for tax funds, and schools cannot be expected to do everything.

Anyone who has taught in a senior high school following a junior high that apes the high school knows the blasé junior high school student from the less sophisticated, or normal student who came up by way of the elementary school. It takes no great insight to spot such students immediately, but it does take a lot more know-how to get them to learn and take their schooling seriously.

The typical junior high school in the past decade has improved greatly in discipline, in curriculum, in organization, in counseling effort, and in attempting to be a responsible institution. However, it is still up against a lot of built-in problems that would not have to be overcome if we would avoid such an organizational pattern in the first place.

Teachers Make Schools

It is time parents, educators, and college professors went back to the fundamental truth that fancy organizations do not make good schools for young adolescents. Good schools are made by good teachers, regardless of level or organizational pattern. After a certain point, the fewer the number of students per day the teacher meets the better the job he is able to do with the ones he does work with. What is that number? We limit educationally handicapped classes to eleven. This is recognition of the problem and would improve the quality of education in the regular classes.

Simple, uncomplex organizations give students better relations and better contacts and better understanding between student and teacher. This is what we should be working toward. This is where elementary education excels.

The complex junior high with its huge enrollment, its frequent class changes, its teachers meeting 150 students a day, and its students being jostled about among all these strangers every forty minutes all day long is too often a six- or seven-ring circus instead of an educational institution.

Many parents with whom I talk do not want their children in one of these monstrosities. "It's difficult enough," they say, "to bring up children without adding all the problems a junior high school can provide a parent to cope with in addition to his child's normal early adolescent problems."

The junior high is one of America's educational blunders that was gone into for reasons that were not educationally sound. Because the existing system is not perfect and needs improvement is no sign that whatever is devised to overcome it (in this case the junior high school) is as good as or better than the thing it replaced. Why did many school systems never make the change? Neither is it a sign that the educational program could not have been improved better within the original organizational pattern, difficult though it may be, with the same effort and resources that were put into the junior high school movement.

A Service, Not a Product

The pattern of organization of the industrial revolution that produced a division of labor and specialized operations for the manufacturing of material things should not necessarily be applied to the design of educational services for early adolescents.

The fact is that there is mounting evidence that such an organization could possibly be all wrong because the raw materials upon which the services are applied are so unlike, so non-standard, and lack the uniformity of the raw materials for manufacturing a product. Nor can children be made uniform. We want intelligent, productive citizens, not sausages, when we complete the combined efforts of home, school and community in developing our future citizens.

We want to develop and recognize the variabilities of our future citizens. Mass production education will perhaps tend to develop the likenesses we want, but perhaps it may fail the recognition that is needed in the development of diversity. It is possible the junior high school can be made to meet this test, or any other kind of organization, if the right goals are set up to achieve it supported by adequate resources. Yet some educators still prefer to work toward the idea of taking a more gradual, less sophisticated step in the upper elementary school as a transition to the high school program. This is not an argument for holding children back, it is an argument for a little less pushing, less aping of the high school, and more appropriate tailoring of the program to the particular students.

Which Years in Junior High?*

ALVIN W. HOWARD

The intermediate school has proved its worth, but what grades may be included in it?

There is considerable variation throughout the United States in organization of the intermediate or junior high school. The 6-3-3 plan is not in sole use; variations include 6-2-4, 5-3-4, 7-5, 7-2-3, and 6-6 plans of organization. According to one writer, "The purposes and goals [of the intermediate school] tend to be based upon overcoming the deficiencies of the 8-4 plan rather than upon any sound thesis that a 6-3-3 arrangement has advantages. . . . This school [the junior high] is in the developmental stage; we must caution against standardization."[1]

The conditions which originally gave impetus to the junior high school movement either no longer exist or are considerably changed. Probably the first junior high school was a Kansas City school established for grades seven and eight in 1867. In 1896 Richmond, Indiana, set up a 6-2-4 plan. It was in 1909, in Columbus, Ohio, that a definite effort was made to revise the traditional 8-4 plan of organization, and a three-year intermediate school was established which included grades 7, 8, and 9.

Such reorganization was to a considerable extent based upon recommendations made by committees of the National Education Association and attempted to solve two primary problems: to reduce the high percentage of dropout, keeping youngsters in school for another year and providing terminal courses of a vocational or prevocational nature for those who left school at this point, and to provide for an earlier study of foreign languages, elementary algebra, constructive geometry, science, and history.

*Reprinted from *The Clearing House*, 33 (March 1959), 227-230, by permission of the publisher and A. W. Howard, University of New Mexico.

[1]Donald W. Lentz, "History and Development of the Junior High," *Teachers College Record,* LVII (May, 1956), 522-30.

Currently junior-high objectives are broadly stated to include four major functions: (1) Integration of subject matter areas, skills, interests, and abilities. (2) Exploration of interests, abilities, and aptitudes. (3) Social and educational guidance. (4) Articulation, transitional stage to high school.[2]

Many present-day junior high schools throughout the country have become obsolete, at least in their thinking, in that "they have failed to recognize that the purposes of junior high school are different from those of the high school and that changes in organization are needed if it is to funciton more effectively."[3] Too often the junior "high school" becomes just that, imitating the colleges and senior high schools, with all the accessories on a somewhat smaller scale—and occasionally on the same or a grander scale. Night games, night dances, cheer squads, "varsity teams", sophistication, result in its becoming only a watered-down version of the senior high school and not the distinctly different kind of school which young people at this stage of development need.

State and college requirements have become so many and so rigid as to render many junior high schools virtually bound to the ninth-grade program—a program which requires the ninth grader to earn such subject-matter credits as he may need for college entrance or to satisfy a state requirement. Possibilities for varied programs in the seventh and eighth grades are hedged in scheduling by the need to establish the pattern for the ninth grade and to fit the lower grades around this as can best be done. Usually this results in a tail wagging the dog arrangement, where desperate administrators attempt such expedients as operating a six-period day within an eight-period day or conclude by gearing and twisting the seventh-grade and eighth-grade programs to fit the needs of the ninth-grade requirements. For all practical purposes we frequently find that the ninth grade is attached to our building for rations and quarters only.

There is a real need for an intermediate school to deal with the problems of early adolescents. Children of this age need a developing opportunity to participate in student government and community projects and to accept increased responsibility. The intermediate school provides a more gentle shift to departmentalization, guidance functions are available, and more attention is given to individual differences. But what grade groupings are best?

"Research on a functional operational level is needed to determine whether there is any justification for a 6-3-3 organization other than to provide adequate housing."[4]

"There will be modifications in the present educational plan to meet future needs. Some of these will be 6-4-2, 6-4-4, 6-2-5."[5]

[2]Harry J. Merigis, "Junior High School Dilemma," *The Clearing House,* XXXI, No. 2 (October, 1956), 87.

[3]Adeline Hood, "A Junior High Division in the Elementary Schools," *The Clearing House,* XXIX, No. 8 (April, 1955), 462-5.

[4]Lentz, *op cit.*

[5]Walter H. Gaumnitz, "Strengths and Weaknesses of the Junior High School," Report

The junior high is still in the formative stage. The National Educational Association published in February of 1949 a research bulletin entitled, "Trends in City-School Organization 1938 to 1948," which is a study of organizational patterns in 1,372 city school systems and listed the following organizational plans of secondary schools: 6-3-3, 35 per cent; 8-4, 23 per cent; 6-6, 16 per cent; 6-2-4, 12 per cent; 5-3-4, 2 per cent; others, 12 per cent.

The study reported: "In these cities the 6-3-3 plan is the type which prevails more frequently than any other. Nevertheless, this plan prevails in only about one-third of the city systems. The diversity of plans demonstrates rather clearly that variation and experimentation is the order of the day in the matter of school organization and that as yet no single pattern has become clearly the dominant type."[6] The study went on to state that the choice should be made on the basis of the program to be carried out and the pupils to be served; the trend of practice alone cannot properly answer this. Whatever dividing lines and grade divisions are finally established should be set in terms of pupil need and good educational thought, not tradition.

In 1955 the United States Office of Education published a bulletin (Misc. No. 21), "Junior High School Facts–a Graphic Analysis," by Gaumnitz and others, which disclosed that of the 3,227 junior high schools in the United States in 1952, 2,395 (74.2 per cent) were grades seven, eight, and nine; 627 schools (19.4 per cent) were of grades seven and eight; 6.4 per cent were of other types. Four states had all of their junior high schools consisting of grades seven, eight, nine: Maine, Nevada, Rhode Island, and South Dakota.

The *Bulletin* of the National Association of Secondary-School Principals for September, 1957, carried an article by Tompkins and Roe, "The Two Year Junior High School," which debated the advantages and disadvantages of the two-year plan. According to the survey the authors made, the two-year junior high is the second most common type of junior high in the United States, appearing in a ratio of 1: 3½ to the three-year junior high. Some states have a high percentage of two-year junior high schools: Montana, 79 per cent; Wyoming, 78 per cent; New Hampshire, 75 per cent; Illinois, 66 per cent; Idaho, 65 per cent; Iowa, 60 per cent; Indiana, 58 per cent; and Oregon, 50 per cent.

In answer to the question, "Is your junior high contemplating a change to another type of school organization, and if so, what type?" 60 per cent of those reporting said no change was planned, 40 per cent stated possibility of change from 7-8 to 6-7-8, 6-7 to 8-9, 7-8 to 8-9, 8-9 to 7-8, and 6-8 to 7-8, "giving the impression of organization fitted to heavy grade enrollments."

---

of the National Conference on Junior High Schools, Washington, D.C., February 24-26, 1955, United States Office of Education Circular No. 441, p. 2.

[6]National Education Association *Research Bulletin,* "Trends in City-School Organization 1938 to 1948," XXVII, No. 1 (February, 1949), 11.

Asked if there are any special advantages or disadvantages to the two-year plan, 196 principals reported that there is an advantage, two say the two-year school is inferior, and 100 say there is no advantage.

Advantages listed include: (1) closer age group, better basis for common learnings and interests; (2) better attention to individual needs; (3) better opportunities for ability groupings; (4) better transition to high school; (5) more effective scheduling and programing procedures; (6) ninth grade better off in high school; (7) easier to administer; (8) fewer disciplinary problems; (9) closer pupil-faculty relationships; (10) freedom from college and high-school requirements.

Disadvantages mentioned: (1) belief that ninth grade belongs in junior high; (2) 6-3-3 plan best bridges elementary–senior-high gap; (3) ninth graders have social problems and developmental phases more in common with grades seven and eight; (4) school loses one-half of student body every year; (5) two years are not long enough to get to know a student.

In stating what type of intermediate school organization they preferred, 64 per cent of the two-year school principals said that they would choose a three-year junior high if they could change, some few stating that the three-year school should be grades 6-7-8. The two-year junior high was preferred by 32.9 per cent of the principals. These figures are interesting when compared with the previous question in which almost two-thirds of the principals said that they felt the two-year junior high possessed special advantages over the three-year plan. Also, since so many of these two-year schools are in states where this type is far in the majority, one wonders how many of those principals who wish for a three-year junior high have ever operated in one.

So, at this point, there seems to be little, if any, evidence to prove that one type of organization is superior to another. The philosophy of the intermediate school has changed and the reasons which gave rise in the early 1900's to its original plan, 6-3-3, are no longer valid, although one writer feels that "...some administrative thought is not too far from the 1910 conception of junior high schools."[7]

Mounting requirements by states and colleges are increasing the restrictions on ninth grades and warping the entire junior-high course of study. Some districts believe that the ninth grade belongs in the high school, where the entire four-year course of study can be cohesively planned and carried out. This situation, combined with the problem of the junior high's aping of the high school in everything from courses to activities, has caused many people to feel that more satisfactory results might be obtained with an intermediate school composed of grades seven and eight or six, seven, and eight.

Selection of the type of school organization must depend, it would appear,

[7]Nelson L. Bossing, "A Junior High School Designed for Tomorrow," *The Clearing House*, XXIX, No. 1 (September, 1954), 3-7.

upon what best suits the needs of the individual district. There is nothing which compels adoption of 6-3-3; even the authorities have not agreed upon the best type of intermediate school. The point upon which there is the most agreement is the need for some type of intermediate school, which type you must select to fit your own particular needs. Dealer's choice. There is plenty of precedent.

What Educational Plan for the In-Between-Ager?*

WILLIAM M. ALEXANDER

The junior high school was created some fifty years ago—usually by taking grades 7 and 8 from the elementary school and combining them with grade 9 from the high school. Although its original purpose was to provide a bridge between childhood and adolescence, opinions differ as to whether it still does perform this function. Critics of the present junior high school organization point to research which shows that children reach adolescence much earlier than children did fifty years ago; girls may be pubescent before grade 7, and boys have generally reached full-blown adolescence by the time they have reached grade 9.

Another factor which bothers the critics is what the label "junior" implies. It has become all too descriptive of an activity program (including interscholastic athletics), a departmentalized schedule, and a social system that look very much like those in the senior high school.

Education Editor Paul Woodring wrote in a recent issue of the *Saturday Review*: "It now appears that the 6-3-3 plan, with its junior high school, is on its way out." Whatever the accuracy of Woodring's statement, it is doubtful that school boards and other responsible agencies will want to revert to the 8-4 plan. If anything replaces the junior high school, it will probably be a "middle school."

Several of these schools have been organized in recent years to serve the bridging function that the junior high school was set up to do. Although the number of these middle schools is too small to substantiate Woodring's prediction, their existence does indicate some dissatisfaction with the present junior high school organization.

*Reprinted from *The NEA Journal*, 55 (March 1966), 30-32, by permission of the publisher and William M. Alexander, University of Florida.

Many of the middle school reorganizations include grades 6, 7, and 8, a practice of long standing in some districts. Grade 6 is simply moved from elementary to junior high and grade 9 is returned to the high school.

Such a grade reorganization does not necessarily involve any change in the instructional program or methods of instruction. The departmentalized schedule and the same program of activities may carry over into the new school, or grade 6 may be left on a self-contained basis and instruction for grades 7 and 8 departmentalized.

A few districts are making a more radical shift by setting up a middle school to serve children usually enrolled in grades 5 to 8—roughly those about 10 to 14 years of age. Such a school will take boys and girls from the years of upper childhood and see some 85 percent of them through to early adolescence. Unlike the tendency of the junior high school to precipitate adolescent behavior, this kind of middle school will prepare children over a period of years to meet the crises of adolescence.

A few school districts have reorganized along these lines, usually in conjunction with new building programs. Such schools have also been proposed in large cities as a way of ending de facto segregation in some neighborhood elementary schools. Whether this 4-4-4 plan would do this on a permanent basis is a matter of opinion. Nevertheless, such a plan, with its complete middle division of the school program, promises to span the years between childhood and adolescence better than the predominant 6-3-3 setup.

Whatever the faults of the present junior high school, American communities cannot be expected to move overnight into some new pattern of school organization—nor should they. Our nation's 6,500 junior high schools represent a large investment in facilities and employ many persons whose careers are intertwined with the present organization.

Furthermore, the junior high school represents a significant improvement over the old eight-year elementary school. It has enriched the educational diet of the preadolescent youngster and has frequently encouraged useful educational experimentation. It might still serve as a point of departure for experimentation in new forms of school organization.

As school authorities and others debate the value of retaining the junior high school or replacing it with some other kind of middle school, they will have to resolve many tough issues such as the following:

WHAT GRADES SHOULD BE INCLUDED?

As already indicated, the new middle schools usually include either grades 5 through 8 or, more frequently, 6 through 8. The middle school, however, may be ideally suited for a nongraded organization because of the wide differences in children in its age groups. Programs of diagnostic services, frequent teacher-student conferences, and much individualized instruction would help children achieve optimum progress without arbitrary grade level expectancies. Some pupils might move through the middle school in three years and others might need a fourth year.

SHOULD THE PROGRAM DIFFER FOR BOYS AND FOR GIRLS?

Since, on the average, girls reach adolescence earlier than boys, some of them may be encouraged to move through the middle school at least a year ahead of the average boy. This might help take care of the typical discrepancy in the interests of boys and girls in the 10 to 14-year-old age range.

HOW COULD THE PROGRAM BE MADE INTELLECTUALLY STIMULATING?

Both the self-contained classroom organization of the elementary school and the departmentalized junior high school have been criticized for their lack of intellectual stimulation. The weaknesses of these organizations should be avoided in the middle school, where new patterns of organization can be carefully tested.

For example, the middle school could try a team teaching arrangement in which four homeroom groups of about twenty-five pupils each share the same four teachers. Each teacher would serve as a homeroom teacher-counselor and each would have a different field of specialization (language arts, social studies, science, or mathematics).

Such a plan would facilitate planning for individual pupils and also utilize teachers in their area of greatest interest and competence. Rather than having a routine rotation of pupils through departmentalized schedules, such sharing of instruction and flexibility of learning groups would permit pupils and teachers to know each other well and would ensure that each curriculum area is taught in an intellectually stimulating manner. In addition, the flexibility of this plan would make possible extensive use of individualized instruction, including independent study.

HOW SHOULD LEARNING SKILLS BE TAUGHT AND EMPHASIZED?

Emphasis should, of course, be given to learning skills in all studies. But the middle school might be the strategic point at which to provide extensive use of many library and other learning resources. Special learning centers could provide individualized instruction in reading, viewing and listening, writing (including typing), interviewing, problem-solving, and other skills.

WHAT COMMON OR GENERAL STUDIES OUGHT TO BE PROVIDED?

The basic subjects of the elementary and junior high schools would undoubtedly be retained in the middle school: language arts, mathematics, science, and social studies. Some schools would include the fine arts and a second language as common subjects; others would make one or both an exploratory, individualized-choice area.

The content of the common areas would be planned with reference to the programs of the elementary and high schools so that there would be as much continuity as possible throughout the school program. A specific plan of scope and sequence in the general studies would assist teacher teamwork and also permit variations in pupil progress.

WHAT EXPLORATORY EXPERIENCES SHOULD BE PROVIDED?

The exploratory program of the junior high school has been one of its strengths; a major reason for moving children into a middle school earlier is to offer them increased opportunity for exploring many interests. In addition to exploratory experiences in such customary areas as foreign languages, the fine arts, industrial arts, and home economics, a range of interests might be served by other experiences such as in acting, photography, personal grooming, creative writing, and in assisting in library, laboratory, lunchroom, and office.

Many students could explore their leadership and vocational aptitudes by participating in various student-managed enterprises such as assembly programs, exhibits, school stores and banks, lost-and-found departments, school publications, and student government organizations.

WHAT TYPE OF AN ACTIVITY PROGRAM SHOULD BE PROVIDED?

A major criticism of the junior high school is its copying of the high school activity program. Many regard the need to eliminate this program as a justification for the middle school. The middle school could probably do without an organized activity program other than the student-managed enterprises already suggested. Perhaps each instructional unit (that is, a group of four homerooms involving approximately 100 pupils) could be left to develop its own activities, at least until and if enough common interests are discovered to justify schoolwide projects.

In larger middle schools, a "school within a school" organization might be desirable, grouping four instructional units to constitute a "little school" of 400 pupils encompassing the full age range of the school. These units could develop intramural activities for themselves and cooperate on some activities with other units within the middle school. Interscholastic athletic competition between middle schools would certainly not be permitted.

WHAT WOULD BE THE BEST WAY TO PROMOTE SOUND PERSONAL DEVELOPMENT?

With the perils of adolescence looming just ahead for most pupils, the middle school can give continued and direct attention to the formation of personal values and standards of behavior. In addition to many curriculum opportunities, the homeroom organization could help greatly in individual development. The homeroom teacher-counselor would be continually alert to the potentialities and problems of each of his advisees.

The school would seek maximum interaction with interested parents, as well as opportunities to plan with representatives of other community institutions and agencies.

Many other issues will undoubtedly arise as existing faculty groups plan reorganizations of educational programs in order to do a better job of bridging childhood and adolescence.

Two criteria may help to ensure the success of these plans: (a) The reorganization should provide such varied and excellent learning opportunities that each pupil, whether 10 or 14 years old, boy or girl, advantaged or disadvantaged, can find some success and challenge that will stimulate further learning; and (b) the plan should include instruments for rigorous evaluation of results.

This second criterion will help educational researchers answer with more certainty troublesome questions which they can now answer only with guesses.

What Type of Organization of Schools? *

HARL R. DOUGLASS

When one looks back over the history of the organization of schools in the United States, he may well think of one or both of the two following things: the motto of the Denver Post, to-wit: "There is no hope for the satisified man," and the silly limerick

"As a rule a man's a fool
When its hot he wants it cool;
When its cool he wants it hot,
Always wanting what is not."

It seems that as soon as we get a type of organization for which we have been working, we immediately develop a desire for some other form of organization.

Throughout the 19th century there was a growing desire to bring about articulation between elementary and secondary education in the form of an eight year elementary school, followed by a four year high school (except in the south where the elementary schools only were seven years in length), and in the latter decades of the century this goal was achieved. Early in the 20th century, and indeed a little bit before the turn of the century, there was growing dissatisfaction with the 8-4 plan which, after all, was a marriage of convenience of the elementary and the secondary schools, with a trend towards six years of elementary education and six years of secondary education, which in the actual organization took the form of 6-6, 6-3-3, and 6-2-4 plans. Now more than two thirds of the districts are now organized in either the 6-6 or the 6-3-3 plan and enroll nearly three fifths of the students in grades 7 through 12. More than ten thousand secondary schools are of the six-year type, an increase of nearly 40 per cent since 1950.

*Reprinted from *The Journal of Secondary Education*, 41 (December 1966), 358-364, by permission of the publisher and Harl R. Douglass.

In fifty years, the number of separate junior high schools has increased less than a dozen to more than 5,000. Since 1950, the number of such schools has increased more than 50 per cent and the enrollments in them by more than 30 per cent.

In a very recent study not as yet published, by Professor William T. Gruhn of the University of Connecticut, and the author of this article, of the opinions of a carefully selected representative sample of the junior high school principals, with grades 6, 7, and 8 or grades 7 and 8, approximately one-half said that they thought including grades 7, 8 and 9 would be better and 84 per cent of the principals of schools including grades 7, 8 and 9.

A summary of the responses to the check list sent out to junior high school principals relative to the organization of junior high schools revealed the following: that of the principals who replied of the three-year junior high schools including grades 7, 8, and 9, approximately 84 per cent of them preferred the organization including grades 7, 8, and 9; less than 10 per cent of them preferred the organization including grades 6, 7, and 8. The large majority felt that the three-year junior high school is able to attract and obtain more competent counselors and to develop a superior organization of academic studies, to attract and obtain competent teachers of science and mathematics and to develop a superior program in industrial arts and home economics, to attract and retain competent teachers of foreign language and to develop a good sports program. A somewhat smaller group, but still a fairly large majority, believed that it enables the school to develop a program of extra-curricular activities and to provide better experiences and leadership for early adolescents.

As reported by Lambert on the question of proposed changes over a two-year period, 34 per cent of 79 junior high schools of grades 7 and 8 replying hoped to add grade 9, while 20 per cent would revert to an 8-4 plan, and 43 per cent intended to become separated from their senior division, preferably on a 6-3-3 plan. (1)[1]

For various reasons some educators in this country have been opposed to "the organized" schools, or at best lukewarm. They have been seeking reduction in school expenditures and questioning the superior effectiveness of the junior high schools. The results of investigations did not uniformly show that, as judged by scores on standard achievement tests, the junior high school students learned of whatever was measured in those tests rather than in the traditional 8-4 form of organization.

However, there was general recognition that in three year junior high schools, boys and girls received better counseling service and they had more opportunities to participate in clubs and other valuable extra-subject activities. It was also recognized that having libraries, gymnasiums, cafeterias, and other desirable housing and equipment in elementary schools was expensive and this advantage of the junior high school form of organization contributed to the 6-3-3 plan becoming the standard form of organization.

[1]Numbers in parentheses refer to references at the end of the article.

The continuance of four year high schools in Illinois townships is for important financial reasons. In Illinois a constitutional limit for tax rates and bond issues applies to school districts in such a manner that a secondary school district and each of the elementary school districts which are within the secondary school districts in whole or part, may each vote tax rates or bond issues up to the maximum for the state, whereas, if they were in one unified district for grades kindergarten through the 12th grade, they would be held to the same limit. In California a somewhat similar, but not so important, situation exists—a definite trend toward the unified district and the 6-3-3 plan.

More recently, however, questions have been raised on a different basis and have come from different sources. In various parts of the country, there have been demands for the return to the 8-4 plan. These arise out of different situations and for different reasons. For example, in the New York city schools a committee has been studying the educational organization in that city in relationship to the problems of desegregation.(2) This committee favors a plan which involves a four-year high school. The same phenomenon has appeared in a small number of Eastern cities. Whatever may be said of the plan as appropriate and desirable for the purposes of desegregation, there are few elements in the situation in New York City which are present in other cities, especially in those districts in which the problem of desegregation is not important.

It is somewhat depressing to careful students of the problem of preparation for college, that out of the hysteria resulting from the college admission squeeze there has developed some feeling on the part of a considerable minority of parents that their children might be better prepared for college if they took their 9th grade subjects in the four-year high school; rather that they be taught by teachers with greater specialization in the subjects and of probable higher academic standards. There is nothing in the studies of the factors related to college success that would support this theory. It is one of a number of unsupportable theories or suggested practices that have come from parents who have been over-motivated by the desire to have their children accepted by and succeed in colleges or universities of a high status.

There is a very important argument against the four-year plan today which is a matter of very great concern to most parents, and, indeed, one which is considered to be a very important factor by students of child growth and development, particularly those interested in the moral and social development and problems of juvenile delinquency. There are many who feel that it is unfortunate for boys and girls in the 9th grade to be housed in and associated with the very sophisticated young men and young women of the 11th and 12th grades, with the increased tendencies of these older youngsters to consume alcoholic drinks, to drive fast, and with the modern ideas of sexual morality. It is clearly not good for the 7th and 8th graders to be housed and associated with 9th graders who are "chomping at the bit" to take on the social habits and vices of the older adolescents.

It has also been pointed out that many of the very outstanding secondary schools in the United States are four-year secondary schools, especially those of Evanstown Township, and the J. Sterling-Morton Township, Blue Island Township and Niles Township, near Chicago, as well as a considerable number elsewhere, especially in California. This argument loses much of its strength when one realizes that most of these schools are four-year high schools, not because the administrators and boards of education wish them to be, but for other reasons, e.g., greater freedom in tax levies in Illinois.

In a number of schools that have had the four-year high schools there has been in recent years a new development which deserves very careful attention. Realizing the serious dangers involved in having 9th grades, particularly 9th grade girls and 12th grade boys, so close to the 11th and 12th grades, a small but increasing number of districts apparently "stuck with" four year high schools. The last four years of secondary education are divided into units of two years each and of having what might be called the lower secondary school and the upper secondary school, both housed separately. The pioneer in this movement has been the Dwight Eisenhower High School of Blue Island, Illinois, developed under the leadership of Dr. Harold Richards, Superintendent. From one school for all four grades, there have developed since 1950 two upper schools with grades 11 and 12 and five lower feeder schools with grades 9 and 10. The plan has also been adopted in a number of schools in various parts of the country, possibly a hundred by now. Carlsbad, New Mexico; Medford, Oregon and Abington, Pennsylvania report very favorable results along a number of lines. Testimony from the districts employing it is universally favorable. From the beginning there has been the question of planning for the inter-scholastic athletic teams which came from two or more schools of different levels. A little experimentation with this problem, even in the Blue Island District with several feeder schools to each upper school, has proven that there need be no serious difficulty. There are two varsity squads, one each for the two upper schools with players from the upper school and its feeder low schools. The lower schools have their own teams for inter-school competition in the districts. On the other hand, many advantages seem to have been achieved from this type of organization. Among the more important of these are the following:

1. The 2-2 plan separates the younger students and thereby protects them, individually and collectively from the domination of the aggressive older students. Related to this advantage is the discipline of opportunities for younger people to get practice and skills in leadership through holding offices that would ordinarily be preempted by the older students.

2. Keeps the future size of schools smaller so that there are better personal relationships among the students and between individual students and individual teachers.

3. The lower division schools can be established in smaller areas and bring the school closer to the home, providing better home and school

relationships and public and community relationships in general. The lower school serves as a transition school between elementary and secondary education. In districts where the K-6, 2-2-2 plan is in operation, the transition from the self-contained classroom and elementary school subjects and the methods of the human relation units, working out human relationships between teachers and students may be stepped up gradually as the student moves from one of these four units to the next.

4. The social program and social life of school and the students may be developed in graduated steps so that the 9th and the 10th grade students are not pushed too rapidly into the more sophisticated social life of the older students.

5. The "upper school" schools may serve an entire district. The lower schools will serve the smaller areas with respect to various types of educational, recreational and civic activities making available, for example, athletic fields, gymnasiums, libraries, cafeteria, auditoriums, and other additional rooms.

6. Teachers in the lower schools can be selected on the degree of adaptation of their personality towards youngsters of 14 and 15 years of age and are not likely to be, consciously or unconsciously, comparing them with the achievements of 16 and 17 year old students in the 11th and 12th grades as they would do if they taught classes of the four-year level.

7. Standards of scholarship and social maturation can be set for the older students in the upper division.

8. Intramural athletic competition may be better developed in schools of both levels.

9. A broader range of subjects may be offered in the upper division schools—especially in electives such as vocation fields and foreign languages.

10. Discipline and behavior problems are reduced to a narrower age span (student driven cars are usually not permitted at the lower division level).

11. For reasons that are obvious, there will be many more opportunities for students in the lower school to participate in various types of extra class activities, probably because of the closer contact with the homes, and better knowledge of teachers and counselors of each of the students. The quality of counseling is reported to be much better in the lower schools for 9th and 10th graders in separate schools than in larger four-year schools, and the problems of discipline less serious and easier to deal with.

Over the years a large majority of the teachers at the Blue Island School have expressed themselves as being very much in favor of the 2-2 division. The large majority of them prefer to teach on a two grade level. Similar words come from Hobbs, New Mexico; Medford, Oregon, and other places where the 2-2 plan has been in operation for several years. In addition to the advantages mentioned above, Dr. Robert J. Letson, Director of Instruction, Carlsbad, New Mexico schools, reported the following additional advantages: (a) Relief of the traffic and parking problems because few of the 9th and 10th graders would be old enough to drive a car (probably there should be a Board of Education rule that no cars could be driven to the lower school by students): (b) By not establishing so many four-year high schools, but having a smaller number of schools for 11th and 12th graders, the curriculum may be offered in a four-year high school: (c) It would be possible to obtain better athletic teams and to put on better performances in such things as dramatics.

While, no doubt, all of these advantages pertain to some degree in the 2-2 plan, the author of this article is of a definite opinion that the outstanding advantage, and a very important one, is avoiding associating the pubescent 9th graders with the sophisticated adolescent in the upper school. The danger and bad results occurring from educating 9th and 12th graders in one building and one student body are not only becoming more obvious, but are becoming greater as there is an increase in adolescent drinking and a looseness of sex morals, and in great increased independence, if not class antipathy for adults.

In many districts which operate a four-year high school—divided or not—some form of "junior high school," probably better called "intermediate school," has been developed, including grades 7 and 8, or grades 6, 7, and 8, and grades 5, 6, 7 and 8 that in districts committed, for one reason or another to an 8-4 plan or an 8-2-2 plan, the best available choice is a semi-departmentalized school with grades 6,7, and 8, with a library, gymnasium facilities, shop and home economics facilities.

To the author of this article, it seems crystal clear that in such schools, transition from almost completely self-contained classrooms in grades 7 and 8 to a four-year high school or 2-2 plan, departmentalization should not involve more than half of the subjects taken by individual students. It is very likely that much experimentation with favorable results will be given a platoon type of organization for grades 7 through 10. Platoon teachers will be assigned two groups of students for approximately 40 to 45 per cent of the student programs, the other subjects being taught on a departmentalized basis.

The same reasons that have prompted a number of administrators where they have four-year high schools, to divide them into units of two years each, prompted a few schools to establish a separate school for ninth graders. In the fall of 1963 at Warsaw, Indiana, there opened a 9th grade high school, and apparently it was very successful, particularly in the area of reducing the discipline problems. As reported in the July, 1965 issue of *The Nation's Schools*, Vol. 76, No. 1, pages 27 and 28, administrators of Warsaw schools report as follows:

"As any school man knows, there is no crazier time in the youngster's life than the early teens when the conglomeration of psychological, physiological, and sociological factors create situations like the one which took place in our community: A young lady student in a junior high had arrived home one night from a school party. 'Did you have a good time?' her mother asked. 'Sure did, Mom,' she said, stifling a yawn. 'The girls danced and the boys wrestled.' "

"But what we thought most rewarding is the fact that serious discipline problems almost didn't exist in the new freshman high school. Last year, reluctantly, we asked the 9th graders to state in English reports what they thought of their arrangement. We expected they'd express a preference to be with the senior high school students. They didn't. 'It's our school, and we can run it without help from juniors or seniors,' was a typical comment. Another wrote, 'We aren't looked down upon by upper classmen, and we feel more at home with our own group.'

"Best of all from a boy, 'As I look back on some of the things that I did as a 7th grader, they seem pretty juvenile.' "

(This report was made by Superintendent Carl W. Burt of the Warsaw, Indiana Community Schools.)

While many schools have re-organized on one of the half-dozen new plans, it is quite evident that the 6-3-3, as the 6-6 plan, will continue for several decades to be predominantly prevalent, continuing to gain in number of schools and number of students as the ephemeral vogue of specialism and departmentalization continues to fade and give rise to new and different whims of the hour.

Fundamentally sound and certain to gain ground are the platoon plan of semi-departmentalization, and the 2-2 plan, or the 1-3 plan based on some form of organization of the lower eight grades: 8 year, 6-2, 5-3, 4-4 or K-12, 3-5, 6-7-8.

References

(1) Pierre D. Lambert, "Junior High Schools, 1965," *The Clearing House,* Vol. 39, No. 6 (February, 1965), p. 324.

(2) See "Four-Year High May Return as 'Giant Step' to Integration in New York." News item in *The Nation's Schools,* Vol. 75, No. 4 (April, 1965), p. 24.

What Do Principals Believe About Grade Organization?*

WILLIAM T. GRUHN

1. Purpose of the Study

There is more interest today in the grades that should be included in the junior high school than at any time since the beginning of the reorganization movement before 1900. This is due largely to the rapidly increasing enrollments in the elementary and secondary schools, leading to an unprecedented demand for new school buildings. The purpose of the present study was to find out what principals of junior high schools and representatives of state departments of education responsible for secondary education believe to be the best grade organization for junior high schools.

This study was part of a comprehensive survey of junior high school education in the United States which included all schools listed in the most recent state directory available for each of the 50 states and the District of Columbia. Schools were included only if they had a separate administrative organization, an enrollment of 300 or more pupils, and consisted of grades 6-7-8, grades 7-8, or grades 7-8-9. This study included "junior high schools," "middle schools," "intermediate schools," and any other schools which consisted of grades 6-7-8, grades 7-8, or grades 7-8-9.

The study was made through questionnaires sent to principals of the schools. For part of the study, questionnaires requesting opinions about grade organization were sent to the person responsible for secondary education in each of the state departments of education.

*Reprinted from *The Journal of Secondary Education*, 42 (April 1967), 169-174, by permission of the publisher and William T. Gruhn, University of Connecticut.

2. Grades and Buildings

Questionnaires sent to principals of junior high schools in the spring semester, 1964, requested information about the grade organization of schools as follows: (1) the numbers of schools of three types—grades 6-7-8, grades 7-8, and grades 7-8-9; (2)the year the schools were established; (3) the types of schools for which the buildings presently occupied were originally built; (4) plans to continue their present grade organization; and (5) reasons for establishing schools with their present grade organization. Questionnaires which included questions (1) and (2) were sent to principals of all schools in the state directories which met criteria for the study given above. Replies were received from 3368 schools as follows: (1) schools with grades 6-7-8—92% replied, 138 usable; (2) grades 7-8—91% replied, 442 usable; and (3) grades 7-8-9—84% replied, 2788 usable. Questionnaires which included questions (3), (4), and (5) were likewise sent to all schools with grades 6-7-8 or grades 7-8, with the replies as indicated above, but these questions were sent to only one in seven of the schools with grades 7-8-9, selected at random from the total file, with replies from 87%, with 402 usable. Information about the grades included in these schools, the year when the schools were established, the buildings in which they were housed, and their plans to continue with their present organization is summarized as follows:

1. The most common of the three types of schools in 1964 among the 3368 from which replies were received were those with grades 7-8-9. For the 3368 schools in the study, the percentage of each type was as follows: (1) grades 7-8-9—83%; (2) grades 7-8—13%; and (3) grades 6-7-8—4%. More than half the schools with grades 6-7-8 were in three states—Illinois, Michigan, and Texas. More than half the schools with grades 7-8 were in six states—California, Illinois, Indiana, Massachusetts, Michigan, and Texas.

2. The numbers of new schools of all three types established each year has been increasing, with more new schools established during the three years 1961-1964 than during any similar previous period. Among the 3368 schools in the study, the percentage of the total established by years was as follows: Before 1951—32%; from 1951-1961—45%; from 1961-1964—16%; no reply—7%.

3. Most of the schools were located in buildings originally intended for junior high schools. Only a small percentage of the schools were located in former senior or four-year high school buildings. For example, schools with grades 7-8-9 were located in buildings originally built for use as follows: (1) for junior high schools—69%; (2) for combined elementary-junior or junior-senior high schools—4%; (3) for senior high or high schools—16%; (4) for elementary schools—6%; (5) for other schools or no reply—5%. Schools with grades 7-8, as compared with grades 7-8-9, were less frequently located in buildings originally

built for junior high schools, as indicated by the following: (1) for junior high schools–51%; (2) for senior high and high schools–24%; (3) for other schools or no reply–25%. Schools with grades 6-7-8, as compared with the other two types, were least often located in buildings originally intended for junior high schools, as the following reveals: (1) for junior high schools–41%; (2) for senior high and high schools–33%; (3) for other schools or no reply–26%.

4. Schools with grades 7-8-9 more often than the other types of schools had plans to continue indefinitely with their present grade organization, while quite a few schools with grades 7-8 or 6-7-8 had plans to change to another grade organization, most frequently to grades 7-8-9. The percentages of the three types of schools planning to continue indefinitely with their present grades were: (1) grades 7-8-9–91%; (2) grades 6-7-8–64%; and (3) grades 7-8–51%.

5. More than half the schools with grades 6-7-8 and those with grades 7-8 were established with their present grade plan primarily because of school buildings or the school district organization. The percentage of each type of schools established with their present grade plan for these reasons was as follows: (1) grades 6-7-8–54%; (2) grades 7-8–57%. Only a few schools with grades 6-7-8 or grades 7-8 were established with these plans, rather than with grades 7-8-9, primarily because it was considered to be better for the educational program, with the percentages of schools giving this reason as follows: (1) grades 6-7-8–14%; (2) grades 7-8–12%. The principals of quite a few schools, however, replied that there was a combination of reasons for having their present grade organization, with almost all of them indicating that administrative reasons were among them.

3. Best Grades for the Junior High School

Opinions were requested through questionnaires in the spring semester, 1964, from principals of the three types of schools and from representatives of state departments of education on the grades that they considered best for the junior high school to achieve each of the following: (1) to provide the best total school program, (2) to attract and retain competent counselors, (3) to attract and retain competent teachers of science, mathematics, and foreign languages, (4) to develop a superior academic program, (5) to develop a superior program in industrial arts, music, home economics, art, and physical education, (6) to develop programs of sports and other extra-class activities, (7) to provide experiences in leadership, and (8) to provide the best age group.

Questionnaires were sent to all principals of two types of junior high schools, those with grades 6-7-8 and those with grades 7-8. Questionnaires were also sent to principals of one in seven of the schools with grades 7-8-9. Replies were received as follows: (1) grades 6-7-8–92% replied, 138 usable; (2) grades 7-8–91% replied, 442 usable; and (3) grades 7-8-9–87% replied, 402 usable. Similar questionnaires were sent in the summer of 1963 to directors of secondary education in the 50 state departments of education, with 100% replies from the director or some other state department representative. The opinions of principals and representatives of state departments of education concerning the grades that are best for the junior high school may be summarized as follows:

1. The "total program" for the junior high school can be provided best with grades 7-8-9, in the opinion of most of the principals (80%) of schools with grades 7-8-9, most of the principals (62%) with experience as principal of more than one type of school, and almost all (92%) of the state department representatives.

Principals of schools with grade 6-7-8 and those with grades 7-8 were divided in their preferences for the grades they considered best for the "total program." Principals with grades 6-7-8 indicated the grades best for the "total program" as follows: (1) grades 6-7-8–40%; (2) grades 7-8-9–39%; (3) grades 7-8–16% (4) no difference or no reply–5%. Principals with grades 7-8 indicated these preferences: (1) grades 7-8-9–43%; (2) grades 7-8–35%; (3) grades 6-7-8–11%; (4) no difference or no reply–11%.

2. Competent counselors and teachers of foreign languages, mathematics, and science can best be attracted and retained by schools with grades 7-8-9, according to a high percentage of the principals of all three types of schools and state department representatives. Only a few principals considered grades 6-7-8 or grades 7-8 to be best to attract and retain competent counselors and teachers of these subjects. Quite a few principals indicated that, in their opinion, the grades made "no difference" in attracting and retaining such staff members.

3. A superior program in industrial arts, home economics, music, art, and physical education can be best developed in a school with grades 7-8-9, in the opinion of a substantial percentage of principals of the three types of schools and state department representatives. Only a few principals of any group considered either grades 6-7-8 or grades 7-8 best for developing programs in these subjects, although quite a few principals indicated that the grades made "no difference."

4. Leadership experiences for early adolescents can be best provided with grades 7-8-9, according to a high percentage of principals of schools with grades 7-8-9, those with grades 7-8, those with experience as principal of more than one type of school, and state department representatives. Only principals of schools with grades 6-7-8 were substantially divided on this question, with preferences as follows: (1) grades 7-8-9–38%; (2) grades 6-7-8–36%; (3) grades 7-8–9%; (4) no difference or no reply–17%.

5. A sports program and other extra-class activities can be developed best

with grades 7-8-9, according to a substantial percentage of principals of all three types of schools and state department representatives. In fact, only a few of the principals of any group replied that, in their opinion, schools with either grades 6-7-8 or grades 7-8 were best for developing such programs.

6. A superior academic program can be developed best with grades 7-8-9, in the opinion of a substantial percentage of the following: (1) principals of schools with grades 7-8-9 (74%); (2) principals with experience as principal of more than one type of school (53%); and (3) representatives of state departments of education (82%). Principals of schools with grades 6-7-8 were quite divided on this question as follows: (1) grades 6-7-8–33%; (2) grades 7-8-9–29%; (3) grades 7-8–11%; (4) no difference or no reply–27%. Principals with grades 7-8 likewise were divided on the best grades for a superior academic program as follows: (1) grades 7-8-9–38%; (2) grades 7-8–22%; (3) grades 6-7-8–8%; (4) no difference or no reply–32%.

7. Principals differed more on the grades that "provide the best age group" for the junior high school than on any other question. Grades 7-8-9 were considered to provide the best age group by most of the principals of schools with grades 7-8-9 (71%), those with experience as principal of more than one type of school (57%), and state department representatives (86%). Principals of schools with grades 7-8 were divided on this question as follows: (1) grades 7-8-9–39%; (2) grades 7-8–38%; (3) grades 6-7-8–13%; (4) no difference or no reply–10%. Principals with grades 6-7-8 were likewise divided as follows: (1) grades 6-7-8–40%; (2) grades 7-8-9–32%; (3) grades 7-8–19%; (4) no difference or no reply–9%.

4. Best Place for the Ninth Grade

Opinions were requested in the spring semester 1965 from principals concerning the best place for the ninth grade–the junior high school (grades 7-8-9), the four-year high school (grades 9-12), or the six-year high school (grades 7-12)–to provide for each of the following: (1) the best experience in leadership and citizenship, (2) the best opportunity to develop wholesome boy-girl relationships, (3) the least likely to lead to undesirable early social sophistication for ninth grade girls and boys, (4) the least likely to lead to steady dating by ninth grade pupils, (5) the least likely to lead to dating by ninth grade girls and older boys (grades 11-12), (6) the best opportunity for the ninth grade in academic studies, and (7) the best total educational experience for ninth grade pupils.

Questionnaires were sent to all principals of two types of schools–those with grades 6-7-8 and those with grades 7-8, and to principals of one in seven of the schools with grades 7-8-9. Replies were received from principals, by types of schools, as follows: (1) grades 6-7-8–72% replied, 148 usable; (2) grades 7-8–91% replied, 493 usable; and (3) grades 7-8-9–85% replied, 399 usable. Replies were tabulated separately for those principals who had previous experience as principal of a four-year high school. There were 91 principals with such experience. The opinions of principals concerning the best place for the ninth grade were summarized as follows:

1. The best experience in leadership and citizenship for ninth grade pupils can be provided in the junior high school, in the opinion of most principals of all three types of schools, as well as those with experience as principal of a four-year high school. The percentage of principals of each group who indicated that the junior high school is the best place for such experiences was: (1) principals with grades 7-8-9–91%; (2) principals with grades 7-8–65%; (3) principals with grades 6-7-8–55%; (4) principals with experience as principal of a four-year high school–76%.

2. The best opportunity to develop wholesome boy-girl relationships among ninth grade pupils is in the junior high school, according to most principals in these groups: (1) principals with grades 7-8-9–81% (2) principals with experience as principal of a four-year high school–72%. Principals of schools with grades 6-7-8 were quite divided in their opinions concerning the best place for ninth grade pupils to develop wholesome boy-girl relationships as follows: (1) four-year high school–50%; (2) junior high school–43%; (3) others or no reply–7%.

3. Both ninth grade boys and girls are least likely to develop undesirable attitudes of social sophistication if the ninth grade is in the junior high school, in the opinion of a substantial majority of the principals of schools with grades 7-8-9, those with grades 7-8, and those who have also been principal of a four-year high school. Principals of schools with grades 6-7-8, however, were more divided in their opinions on this question. For ninth grade girls, principals with grades 6-7-8 indicated the least likely place to develop undesirable social sophistication was as follows: (1) junior high school–44%; (2) four-year high school–38%; (3) others or no reply–18%. For ninth grade boys, principals with grades 6-7-8 indicated the place they were least likely to develop such undesirable attitudes was: (1) junior high school–40%; (2) four-year high school–41%; (3) others–19%.

4. Steady dating is least likely to begin among ninth grade pupils if the ninth grade is in the junior high school, according to a substantial majority of three groups of principals, as follows: (1) principals with grades 7-8-9–75%; (2) principals with grades 7-8–61%; (3) principals with experience as principal of a four-year high school–68%. Principals of schools with grades 6-7-8 likewise considered the junior high school the least likely place to lead to steady dating by ninth grade pupils, though they were more divided, as follows: (1) junior high school–49%; (2) four-year high school–24%; (3) no difference–18%; (4) others or no reply–9%.

5. The junior high school is least likely to lead to dating by ninth grade girls and older boys (grades 11-12), in the opinion of a substantial majority of all groups of principals, as follows: (1) principals with grades 7-8-9–85%; (2) principals with grades 7-8–72%; (3) principals with grades 6-7-8–68%; (4) those with experience as principal of a four-year high school–85%. In fact, on no other question did such a high percentage of principals of all groups indicate that the junior high school is the best place for the ninth grade.

6. The junior high school was considered to be the best place for ninth grade academic studies by most principals (60%) of schools with grades 7-8-9 and by most principals (51%) who had previous experience as principal of a four-year high school. Principals of schools with grades 7-8 were divided, however, on this question as follows: (1) four-year high school–43%; (2) junior high school–41%; (3) others or no reply–16%. Most principals (62%) of schools with grades 6-7-8 considered the four-year high school to be the best place for ninth grade academic studies.

7. The junior high school is the best place for the "total educational experience" of the ninth grade, in the opinion of a majority of three groups of principals, with the percentage of each group expressing this opinion as follows: (1) principals of schools with grades 7-8-9–79%; (2) principals with grades 7-8–53%; (3) principals with experience as principal of a four-year high school–71%. Principals of schools with grades 6-7-8 were the only group which indicated that the ninth grade would have the best "total educational experience" in the four-year high school, with a small majority expressing this opinion–51%.

5. General Conclusion

The junior high school with grades 7-8-9 therefore had more support from the principals and state department representatives included in this study than either of the other two types of schools. Grades 7-8-9 were considered to be the best grades for the junior high school on the questions raised in the study, as compared with grades 7-8 and grades 6-7-8, and the junior high school was considered to be the best place for the ninth grade. Support for a junior high school with grades 7-8-9 was especially strong among principals of schools with grades 7-8-9, principals with experience as principal of more than one type of school, and state department representatives. Even principals of schools with grades 6-7-8 and grades 7-8, however, showed more support for a junior high school with grades 7-8-9 than for either of the other plans. Finally, there was little support from any group of principals on any of the questions raised in the study for schools with either grades 6-7-8 or grades 7-8, except from the principals of those schools. Even these principals, however, showed only limited support for these types of schools.

The 9-10 School: A Novelty or a Better Answer? *

ALLAN A. GLATTHORN

Principal, Abington High School, North Campus
Abington, Pennsylvania

CARL J. MANONE

Assistant Superintendent of Schools
Abington, Pennsylvania

How do you like your twelve years of school divided? Your choices are several: 4-4-4, 5-3-4, 8-4, 6-2-4, 7-3-2, 6-2-2-2. And each pattern of school organization has its own die-hard defenders, anxious to sell new orthodoxies to replace old ones.

In reality, if we are completely honest with ourselves and our professional colleagues, we will admit that any logical way of dividing the school years can be made to work—that each has its own advantages and disadvantages—and that the "best" answer is really an individual district matter, determined by such variables as size of school, enrollment trends, curricular offerings, student scheduling priorities, community sentiment, and personal philosophies of what constitutes quality education.

Our purpose in the present article, then, is not "to sell" the freshman-sophomore intermediate high school as one more educational panacea. Rather, with the perspective of three years of intensive research and one year of

*Reprinted from *Educational Leadership*, 23 (January 1966), 285-289, with permission of the Association for Supervision and Curriculum Development and Allan Glatthorn, principal, Abington High School, Abington, Penn., and Carl J. Manone, Assistant Superintendent, Abington, Penn.

operational experience, we would like to take a dispassionate look at how the 9-10 school meets some special needs of the teen-ager, make an honest and critical appraisal of its advantages and disadvantages, and share some practical approaches we have evolved for special problems that ensue from the 2-2-2 pattern of secondary school organization.

Abington's decision to move from a 6-3-3 organization to a 6-2-2-2 was, of course, strongly influenced by the local factors alluded to above. Our school district boasted three excellent 7-9 junior high facilities and one very fine three-year high school. The high school, built in 1956 to accommodate 1800, was bulging with 2400 students in the fall of 1963. Our enrollment projections indicated that we would shortly be facing enrollments of 1000 per grade. Adding classrooms and a variety of other educational spaces to the existing high school building was considered architecturally unsound, to say nothing of the horizontal pagoda effect on aesthetics such additions would be sure to have. Furthermore, the prospect of enrollments spiraling to 3000 in a single building suggested a bigness that we found unappealing.

Building a second three-year high school posed other kinds of problems: one school might emerge as the "status" institution; rivalries could become intense and community loyalties divided; and the likelihood of being able to offer specialized electives such as Advanced Placement courses to a senior class of 500, for example, would be much more difficult than for a class of 1000—both from the standpoint of student scheduling as well as qualified teacher availability. The more we studied organizational alternatives, the more the 6-2-2-2 pattern looked like a good answer to Abington's growing student enrollment and expanding educational program.

As our study and research continued, we discovered further advantages for the 2-2-2 or single high school concept plan. With two high schools, libraries in each school would basically be duplicates of each other. With separate 9-10 and 11-12 buildings, libraries could be more specialized; presently, in fact, the 11-12 library is partially taking on the complexion of a college freshmen facility. More effective grouping, the development of individually-tailored student schedules, the fullest use of specialized teacher talent, and the widest adaptation of individualized instruction were all relatively enhanced as a result of increasing, not the size of the school, but the number of students enrolled in one particular grade level.

Adolescent Needs

The 9-10 middle school was planned and designed around people and how they learn. In particular, we believe this arrangement gives us unique opportunities to meet certain special needs of young adolescents:

1. They need to develop a sense of independence. Many junior high schools thwart this need by placing pupils in a school situation that is too highly structured. Our 9-10 North Campus School has been able to develop a program of independent study that gives all the students many opportunities to plan for wise use of their own time, to develop interests in new fields, to get remedial help in academic areas where they are experiencing troubles, and to pursue individual projects in depth. And at the same time they are experiencing that important feeling of being on their own.

2. They need to develop leadership abilities and to gain a sense of status. Typically in the three-year high school, such a goal is attainable only for the upper classmen—usually the graduating senior. The sophomore must bide his time; his role is one of being seen without being heard. The 2-2-2 organization, on the other hand, sets up natural leadership possibilities for the student in grades 8, 10, and 12, all of whom are upper classmen.

In our new intermediate school, for example, numerous opportunities for leadership are made available through the house plan. Each grade is divided into three "houses," administrative units of ten homerooms each. Each house has its own guidance counselor, its own faculty director, its own student officers; each house produces its own assembly programs, conducts its own charity drives, has its own "varsity" teams, sponsors dances open to the entire school. In addition, students and faculty have organized over forty after-school clubs, each of which contributes in its own way to fostering opportunities for leadership development.

3. The 14- and 15-year-olds need the security of being with agemates at a similar stage of physical development. They also need the guidance of teachers and counselors who understand and know them. Although there are significant individual differences, 9th and 10th graders are much alike and seem to do better when together. In the junior high, the 9th grader often lords it over his younger and smaller school mates; at the same time, he is often not sufficiently mature to give 7th and 8th graders the kind of direction they need. The 10th grader in the senior high school is often the forgotten person.

Putting freshmen and sophomores together in the same school seems to make good educational sense to us. We find also that we are able to recruit teachers who combine a depth in subject knowledge with a concern and feeling for young adolescents in a way that makes them especially suited for the intermediate high school.

4. They need a sense of involvement, participation and activity. The young adolescent is characterized by an exuberance and energy that need to be channeled into constructive outlets. In planning the new 9-10 school and its schedule, we tried to create such channels. We schedule small seminar groups for each major subject, placing the student in a learning situation where meaningful participation is difficult to escape.

We built three smaller dining areas ("commons," also used for bus waiting, general study, and evening social affairs) instead of one large one. We built a little theater, seating only 350 (just big enough to hold one house), that provides an ideal setting for dramatic and musical productions. It is also an excellent room for largegroup instruction—and yet perhaps paradoxically, small enough to make the worry of student control largely unnecessary.

Our point is simply that the 9-10 school is especially able to meet certain major needs of the young adolescent. In many ways its special advantages over the traditional three-year junior high school grow out of the fact that it is something more—significantly more—than a building or enrollment expediency.

Advantages

First, it provides a more homogeneous group of students with respect to age, physical and mental growth pattern; and such homogeneity makes it easier for faculty and administration to tailor a program to meet pupil needs.

In our social activities, for example, we knew that we had to develop a program that would especially meet the needs of young adolescents. Many of these young people want to be socially active with the opposite sex yet usually lack the necessary maturity and finesse; consequently they usually feel ill-at-ease at a high school dance—too young for dancing and yet too old for junior high games. So, with the monthly "no-dates" dances we alternated the "North Campus Canteen" a night of informal dancing, ping-pong, table games, and hootenannies—and found the awkward ninth graders enjoying themselves in the game room yet feeling that they were attending a "grown-up" dance.

Second, the 9-10 school strengthens the academic program, especially for the ninth grade. To many, the junior high atmosphere connotes merely exploration and academic transition; as part of a 2-2 high school, the ninth grader benefits from the high school's aura of academic seriousness. Seventy percent of our ninth graders are taking five majors which include one of five available foreign languages.

In addition, ninth and tenth graders have available a broad range of more than fifteen elective subjects, ranging from a course in Humanities to Introduction to Power Mechanics and Metal. Large enrollments make possible the scheduling of dramatics, speech, personal typing, and journalism—to mention a few—for two periods a week with specialized facilities and faculty.

Third, the middle school provides many more opportunities for leadership. More than half of our students participate in junior varsity and varsity sports, and almost two-thirds are active in some type of club or extracurricular activity.

Throughout the entire year our students are involved in varied and enriching activities: students gave thirteen instrumental and vocal concerts, presented five plays, published fifteen issues of a school paper, and produced their own literary magazine.

A final major advantage of the 9-10 school is the beneficial effect it has on the 7-8 junior high and the 11-12 senior high. Junior high principals report that discipline problems have diminished sharply; senior high administrators feel that the 11-12 school has taken on many of the desirable characteristics of a junior college.

Disadvantages

In looking candidly at the liabilities of the 9-10 school, we feel that there are two areas of disadvantage: The first stems from the same homogeneity which is also a virtue: the 9-10 school places together in the same building students who are living the most volatile of the teen-age years. The 9th and 10th graders tend to be impulsive—impulsively good and impulsively bad—and they require the kinds of teachers who know when to be flexible and when not to yield, when to direct and when to keep hands off.

The second disadvantage is self-evident. The student makes three, instead of two, changes in six years. (Interestingly enough, some students and parents now feel that this is an advantage.) Close coordination from grades 7 through 12 is an absolute necessity in all phases of school life—record keeping, curriculum, disciplinary policies, and guidance.

Yet, weighing all factors, we at Abington are thoroughly convinced now, a year after opening our new 9-10 school, that we made a very wise decision. And perhaps we can be of service to other school districts contemplating such a change (we have received over a hundred inquiries during the past two years) by concluding with some practical answers we have developed to the problems that are likely to arise:

Most of the problems focus around the relationships of the two high school buildings: are they to be considered a single high school, or two completely separate schools? Each extreme poses certain dangers. If they are considered as only a single high school, the 9-10 unit is bound to suffer from being dominated by its senior counterpart; if they go their own separate ways completely, then unnecessary rivalries, frictions, and curricular gaps and overlaps are bound to develop.

We at Abington have tried to achieve a happy medium of unit autonomy with close interschool coordination. There have, of course, been difficulties; but our answers to the questions that follow will probably show that we have been able to work out most of them to our satisfaction.

QUESTIONS

1. *How is the varsity sports program organized?* Our 10th graders, with

few exceptions, compete as a high school junior varsity team, and ninth graders as a junior high varsity. As was indicated earlier, our ninth grade houses, three in number, have their own varsity teams which compete against each other and against junior high varsity teams from nearby schools.

2. *How are activities coordinated between the 9-10 building and the 11-12 building?* Rather than adopt a rigid policy, we try to find the best answer for each individual activity. Each school, for example, publishes its own four-page newspaper with its own staff and sponsor. But the combined eight-page issue is distributed to both schools. For some activities (such as our Affiliation-Exchange club) there is a single organization, with members and faculty sponsors from both buildings and with meetings held alternately in both schools. For some activities, (such as the Debate Club) there are dual clubs, which from time to time meet together. And, in a few cases, a club will exist at only one of the schools but will draw members from the other.

3. *How is curriculum coordination assured?* District-wide curriculum committees, under the direction of the assistant superintendent, coordinate closely the entire 7-12 program for each department. Because of these very active committees, we probably have better curriculum coordination now than we had with the 6-3-3 organization.

4. *Do guidance counselors move with the students or stay with the building?* There are heated and valid arguments on both sides of this question. We see the counselor as a vitally important member of the faculty team, who stays in his school, builds up strong faculty relationships, and plays an important part in the total instructional program. He has the same counselees for two years and works very closely with his counterparts in the 7-8 and 11-12 buildings.

5. *How are the two buildings administered?* Each building is administratively autonomous, with its own principal and assistants. Both administrations, of course, are responsible to the superintendent and his staff, who resolve any differences that cannot be settled in open discussion.

6. *What happens to tenth graders who fail key subjects?* Summer school takes care of most failures. The 11-12 building offers one math and one science course for 10th graders; a few students—no more than five or six—take courses at both buildings.

7. *Are there three commencements?* There is only one commencement and one yearbook—at grade twelve. Eighth graders and tenth graders have final promotion assemblies, but the usual fuss attendant upon junior high graduation has been eliminated.

What we are saying, in effect, is that the 9-10 intermediate high school is neither just a passing novelty, nor an educational panacea that will make the junior high obsolete. It can, however, be a highly effective way of meeting the special needs of the young teenager in terms of curriculum offerings, leadership opportunities, social program, and extracurricular activities.

8. *How do you build school spirit for two high schools in one?* The name

is perhaps the best indication of what we have tried to achieve: the 11-12 unit is called "Abington High School South Campus"; the 9-10 unit, "Abington High School North Campus." There is still *one* Abington High School in terms of college admissions, varsity football, school colors and cheers, and academic reputation. But there is also one very important "North Campus." This unit, through its school paper, its house organization, its ninth grade teams, its course offerings, it social activities—its own total uniqueness—has developed intense loyalties among its students.

Don't Copy the Senior High's Mistakes*

RIVERTON, WYO.—For many years we operated on a kind of 6-6 or 6-2-4 plan—the upper six grades were in the same building, although the seventh and eighth graders had their own teachers. Our schools grew to the point where we really needed a new high school. After much study it was finally decided that a new school would be built but it was to be a junior high school—in our part of the country a building that becomes antiquated or inadequate becomes the home for a junior high school far too often!

In setting up our new school we decided on a broad exploratory program for students *before* the construction began. Listed below are the differences that I believe exist between our junior high and the senior high school.

At the time we divided the two schools we selected for the junior high the personnel who had demonstrated ability to work with children on the lower age level. When new faculty members were added we made a conscientious effort to obtain people who had student teaching experience at the junior high level. None of our junior high teachers say they'd like to move.

We have consciously exerted a good deal of effort to see that the junior high did not become a "little senior high." Class rings, formal parties, and "graduation" are not found in the junior high. The student council and guidance services, however, can be found at both levels.—JAMES H. MOORE, *Superintendent, School District No. 25, Freemont County, Wyoming.*

Junior High

Grades 7-8-9 are each sectioned into nine groups per grade.

Homemaking is required for girls in Grade 8. General shop is required for boys in Grade 8 (wood, leather, metal). Woodshop is elective for 9th grade boys. Homemaking is elective for 9th grade girls.

*Reprinted with permission from *Nation's Schools*, 75 (April 1965), 33

The two lowest sections in Grades 7-8 are ability sectioned and kept to 20 to 22 students. Ability grouping is used in Grade 9 in English, math, science.

The top seven sections for Grade 8 take Spanish as a required subject (we have a language lab).

Physical education required of all 7-8 grade students. Elective in Grade 9.

Limited homeroom period everyday for all sections.

Senior High

Students are sectioned on a track plan; no set number of classes per grade.

No shop available for boys, except vocational agriculture. Homemaking for girls was discontinued for 1964-65.

Students tend to section themselves, *i.e.* poor students do not elect physics or math IV.

Purely elective–do not have a language lab in senior high.

P.E. required in Grade 10 only.

No study halls. There are "study privilege" rooms for those who wish to use them.

The Junior High School Is Dead*

EUGENE E. REGAN

The philosophy of the junior high school has been evolving since the first one was organized in 1909 in Columbus, Ohio. This concept in grade organization has been a noble experiment for over 50 years, but the grade alignment of 7-8-9, better known as a junior high school, is now dead. It died for want of identity.

In reviewing the history of the junior high school, it is noted that the first was organized to keep boys and girls in school and to expose them to the advantages of a high school education. The junior high school was organized to be truly a *junior* high school. The curriculum offerings for the freshmen year in high school were purposely programmed into the new grade alignment of 7-8-9 to encourage students to get exposure to what they would be missing by not attending high school. All the extra-curricular activities of the high school were introduced into this new intermediate school to again encourage boys and girls to continue their high school education. During this time of educational development, stress was being applied to establish a type of school where dropouts would be reduced as well as to provide terminal education for those not interested in continuing their studies. To provide experience for terminal students, vocational and prevocational courses were introduced into the new junior high school curriculum.

With the demands of the society changing in the mid-1930's and dropouts becoming less of a problem during the middle years of adolescence, the junior high school philosophy was again studied. The concept of it as an exploratory school was developed. The extracurricular activities, the 9th grade high school requirements, and the general practice of copying the high school all remained.

By 1920 there were 400 junior high schools in the United States, by 1940 approximately 2000, and by 1960 over 5000. These figures would indicate a

*Reprinted from *The Clearing House*, 41 (November 1967), 150-151, by permission of the publisher and Eugene E. Regan, Principal, Fairhaven Middle School, Bellingham, Washington.

steady and probably continued growth in the junior high school movement; however, this is not the complete picture, for over 500 school districts in the country are currently studying and many are developing middle schools with grade alignments in various groupings: 5-6-7-8, 6-7-8, and 7-8, but all having one grouping in common. The 9th grade has been removed from the alignment and returned to the high school where it belongs.

The high school has never relinquished control over the junior high school. Graduation requirements have always included the Carnegie unit credits earned as a 9th grader. The curriculum offerings of the 9th grade have had to be programmed first in setting up a total school class schedule. The class periods had to be of sufficient length of time and frequency per week to meet the demands of the Carnegie unit. The junior high school, in effect, revolved around the high school and therefore had no identity or opportunity to develop freely on its own because the high school dictated policy to one-third of the junior high school student body.

The middle school, being unencumbered by the requirements of the high school, has the opportunity to develop an identity which is uniquely characteristic of the boys and girls it serves. No outside rules can be inflicted upon it, for the only requirement placed against it is the demands of meeting the needs of boys and girls in early adolescence. Flexible scheduling, large and small groupings for learning, module scheduling, programming for basic skill development can now take place for there is no need to be concerned with the Carnegie unit in grade 9.

Aping the high school is a thing of the past. Intramurals and mass participation for all is the objective of the middle school extracurricular programs. Participation is the key concept to be developed. The excitement and rewards of interschool competition remain the sole prerogative of the high school. Social activities, drill teams, marching bands, and all the other activities associated with high school can now be enjoyed by the 9th grader in an environment conducive to the sophistication of the grade level.

Studies in recent years of adolescent development have stressed that the teen-ager of today is nearly one year advanced in maturity over his brother or sister of a generation ago. No need to worry about how the 9th grader fits into the high school because his maturational development has indicated that he has belonged there for some time.

For those who feel that moving the 9th grade to its rightful grade alignment is tantamount to heresy and that the philosophy of meeting the educational needs of boys and girls can only be developed in a junior high school environment, it should be pointed out that only through a grade structure which returns the 9th grade to the high school can the needs of boys and girls in early adolescence be truly accomplished without outside interference.

Traditions die hard. But since the junior high school has never had an identity of its own, the dying should not take long. To those who feel that the junior high school personnel of today might feel awkward in embracing the new middle school concept, it is well to remember that the objectives of public education have always been focused upon meeting the needs of boys and girls. Certainly the elimination of the 9th grade from the junior high school structure, and adding 5th or 6th to the 7th and 8th grades and calling it a middle school, should not deter one from this basic concept.

The adjustment from a junior high school concept to a middle school philosophy will be a painless one.

Why We Abandoned Our Traditional Junior High*

ROBERT N. ROWE

Two years ago in Berkeley, Calif., a determined group of educators, school board members, and lay citizens decided to change the grade level of the traditional junior high school. Many people, including some educators, vigorously resisted. They attacked the school board and suggested that the change would seriously jeopardize education in Berkeley.

A recall election to remove a majority of school board members made a major issue of the threatened demise of the junior high school. Retired educators and representatives of the junior high school associations testified to the sanctity of the seventh, eighth and ninth grade schools. Underlying the recall, in the minds of many people, was integration. The recall was defeated decisively. One reason for its defeat was the instability of the campaign to preserve the traditional junior high school at any cost. Advocates of the new plan brought forth as much evidence to support a division of the junior high grade structure as traditionalists were able to find in support of the seventh, eighth and ninth grade school. The traditionalists insisted that children who were 11 to 15 years of age should be isolated. They failed to realize, however, that the rate of social maturation, even physiological maturation, might change through successive generations. Physicians, psychologists and physiologists report that children mature at a rate of four to twelve months faster than they did 40 years ago. And it appears obvious that children are becoming more socially sophisticated at an earlier age than they did in the past.

The extensive exposure of the children through television and other modern communication media to all aspects of life makes it difficult to isolate

*Reprinted with permission from *Nation's Schools*, 79 (January 1967), 74, 82, and Robert N. Rowe, Garfield Junior High School, Berkeley, California.

or shelter them from society. If an acceleration in the rate of maturation does exist, then educators who 40 years ago said that seventh, eighth and ninth graders were physically and socially unique, must revise their age delineation and begin to include sixth graders and to eliminate ninth graders. If one of the reasons to group 11 to 15 year olds on one campus was to isolate them socially, the reason has been weakened considerably by greater student mobility and greater student access to communication media. Exposure of children to all age groups, to all races, to a wide range of economic, mental and physical variation is now an asset and may well produce better informed, better adjusted youth.

Two years have passed since school integration in Berkeley was sanctioned. All ninth graders attend school on one campus. Seventh and eighth graders are assigned to two other campuses. Education in Berkeley has not been jeopardized as prophesied by the advocates of the status quo. In fact there is an accumulation of evidence which indicates that all pupils are profiting academically as well as socially from the new school plan.

The ninth grade school has been successful. The seventh and eighth grade structure is developing a flexibility which encourages experimentation and a greater variety of course offerings.

We believe Berkeley has shown that grade structure is not sacred; there are values more important than the maintenance of traditional programs.

Berkeley did need a change. A de facto segregated junior high school situation was alienating Berkeley citizens. Three-fourths of the junior high school children were being denied the opportunity to associate with their fellow man.

Whether the existing junior high school concept is functional or obsolete is not the real issue. The real issue is whether we will allow a traditional program to stand in the way of more important goals. New ideas, including nongraded schools, the educational park in which many grades are brought together on one large campus, the Princeton Plan, the Berkeley "Ramsey Plan," are emerging. Each attempts to improve educational opportunities for all youth. Some are specifically aimed at expediting racial integration. Others do not involve this but all attempt to solve vital problems.

Every community should reanalyze its educational program, including the grade structure of its schools. If integration is important to the community, traditional grade structure should not be allowed to interfere. Although grouping of children into various age levels or in traditional elementary, junior high school, and high school campuses may be administratively convenient, and may in some communities be educationally sound, we must not be wedded to such convenience. If the nongraded concept relieves the anxiety of young people and improves their learning opportunities, we should abandon grades. If the educational park solves an integration problem and improves educational opportunities for all, let our children go to school in parks. And as progress is made, if the traditional junior high school falls by the wayside, let it fall.

What's Wrong with Junior Highs? Nearly Everything*

ARTHUR H. RICE

Has the "junior" high school been so heavily saddled with the traditions of the "senior" high school that it may never achieve a freedom and identity of its own? Can it eventually have a program that is realistic for *all* young adolescents? And can these transitional grades have a more appropriate name than "junior" high school?

The pattern of the junior high school closely parallels the senior high, but with so little evidence to justify it. It apes the senior high in athletics, social events, class scheduling, and departmentalization. Its curriculum is pushed down from the grades above it, so that in all too many instances it really is a prep school for the senior high.

Try Nongraded Approach

These intermediate grades—from the sixth or seventh through the ninth—require a curriculum, a learning environment, and methods of instruction expecially planned for young teen-agers. Students in this age bracket are learning at different rates and have a great variety of interests. The traditional pattern of grade levels is the least appropriate in the junior high. In fact, here is a place where the nongraded idea truly can find effective and logical use. The curriculum for these transitional grades should be in terms of broad objectives, expressed in an educational program that transcends or even ignores the sequence of grade levels. Slow learners could be given a greater length of time in

*Reprinted with permission from *Nation's Schools*, 74 (November 1964), 30, 32 and Arthur H. Rice, Indiana University.

which to complete a course or learning assignment that conventionally is measured in terms of a semester or a school year. It is possible that the junior high school might permit a student to stay within its time boundaries longer than the usual three years. The youth would then go on to senior high when he is really ready for its more mature program.

Here in the junior high is a need and opportunity to plan the services of the school on a year-round basis, with the summer activities appropriate to the special interests of the young adolescent—camping, for example. Here, too, in junior high is where the social standards and moral values of youth are shaped and tested—receiving proper direction or sometimes misdirection. Here, too, is where guidance from every teacher he knows may prevent the child from becoming the senior high school dropout or the juvenile delinquent looking for kicks.

Improve Health Programs

This group of grades (my favorite term for them is the "middle school") should have a realistic health program that directly benefits *every* child. Here again the "junior" high repeats the sins of the "senior" high with a disproportionate amount of teaching time and money being spent upon the physically elite who need it the least, the youngsters chosen for the varsity squads in competitive sports.

Indiana Takes A First Step

We are told that Indiana was the first (and probably the only) state to adopt a code that includes special certification for junior high school teachers. We learned more about this in a visit with John E. Reisert, who currently divides his professional services between the Indiana State Department of Public Instruction and Indiana University. He is director of teacher education and certification for the state and a lecturer at I.U.

Reisert explains that, basically, the junior high school is designed for block-of-time situations. The Indiana program was set up with this in mind. The program includes two teaching areas. Methodology courses prepare the individual to teach more than one subject, as might be desired in a team teaching approach. The teacher is trained in depth in reading procedures, because this is believed to be a weak area in all the secondary grades. The laboratory experiences, including student teaching and related activities, are geared entirely to the junior high school age group. Also required is a course in educational media.

"Is it a popular certification proposal?" I asked.

The program has had relatively few takers, Reisert reported. Although the code went into effect in March 1962, no more than 50 students throughout the state are taking this sequence. Yet the state has approximately 2,500 junior high school teachers. The fly-in-the-ointment is that the Indiana code also permits individuals to qualify for a secondary certificate which allows them to teach in *any* of the six grades in the secondary field. Consequently, commented Reisert, most students reason: Why specialize in the junior high school only, when I can get a certificate which will let me teach in the senior high school too?

"Doesn't this illustrate the crux of the problem?"

"Yes," replied Reisert. "For too long now the junior high school has employed teachers that were elementary prepared and had ambitions to teach at the secondary level, or were secondary prepared and did not fit into the secondary school. Thus the junior high has taken the cast-offs of both the elementary and secondary fields. I think that probably the only way we will have professional teachers at this junior high level is to prepare them especially for this level.

"Ultimately we will need to close the other two routes to certification for the junior high school."

Invitation to Innovators

"Will the situation improve?"

"We are beginning to see a group of people who are thoroughly committed to the junior high school years," believes Reisert. "The junior high school has been an innovating institution, with the challenge of freedom to explore and try new things.

"The teacher who wants to be an innovator and experimenter has an opportunity here that he doesn't have in the senior high school with its more traditional program."

Asked to suggest what the administrator can and should do, Reisert advised: (1) He can advocate and encourage more research in this area; (2) he should provide leadership and encouragement for an innovating and growing program for these middle grades; (3) he should provide instructional materials and technics to help junior high school teachers develop the kind of program that is needed: (4) he can arrange for a flexibility in time that will allow a program of this kind to grow; (5) he should give more recognition to the junior high school staff on committees, in faculty activities, and on award and ceremony days. If the junior high school could be recognized more, I think it would be more attractive to more teachers and prospective teachers."

Your junior high school(s) may be one of the exceptions that proves the rule. If so, why not write me about it so that I can share the fact with readers of this department.

The Junior High School—A Psychologist's View*

WILLIAM W. WATTENBERG

The junior high school, as a psychologist might look at it, has two paradoxical distinctions: First, its clientele is composed of so bewildering an assortment of young people at crucial turning points in their lives as to defy orderly description. Second, at colleges of education there is a tendency to make believe that there is no such institution: schools are considered either elementary or secondary; young people, either are children or adolescents.

Three major strands of fact give texture to the junior high school: First, due to the fact that young people do not develop in accordance with time tables, junior high school populations are heterogeneous not only as to ability and all the usual variables, but also as to developmental stage. Second, during the years over which this institution presides, youngsters may make sharp changes in the course of intellectual growth, emotional adjustment, and social goals. Third, our knowledge of what forces cause the changes is fragmentary at best.

Perhaps it would be best to pick up these strands one at a time. In doing so, we can bring an illusion of order to what probably will always be a scene of confusingly shifting patterns.

Let us begin by picturing more concretely what was implied by the observation that the junior high school student body is composed of young people in assorted phases.

Writers and research workers have found it convenient to divide human existence into a series of stages. Although everyone knows that some poetic and prosaic license is involved, that no living human being is ever entirely childish or

*Reprinted from *The Bulletin of the National Association of Secondary School Principals,* 49 (April 1965), 34-44, by permission of the National Association of Secondary School Principals and William W. Wattenburg, Wayne State University.

adolescent or adult, yet it helps us to organize our thinking if we highlight commonalties.

Recognizing that with actual individuals there will always be variations and shadings and contradictions, there are three stages that concern us at the junior high school level. Of these, the least demanding is what we might call later childhood. At this point in the development of young people, especially those from middle class homes, the individual remains fundamentally dependent upon adults. The general orientation is one of pleasing or getting along with the grown-ups. And, in the last years of this phase, most children are skillful enough as young psychologists and strong enough in their self-control so that they are usually quite delightful.

By gradual steps, young people drift into a contrasting stage which earlier writers called early adolescent but for which Redl's designation "pre-adolescence" has come to be the standard term. Here, three major shifts take place. The young people react very strongly to their agemates: Some become utterly dependent upon their peers; an equally normal but puzzling minority court relative solitude. There is considerable vaccilation in attitudes toward adults; strong revolt against childishness and sporadic displays of enmity toward parents and teachers may punctuate displays of childishness or its opposite, adult-like responsibility. While all this is happening, the young people are quite conscious of sex—their own sex roles. The boys may show the importance to them of masculinity by shunning or teasing girls; the girls, by unending, giggling conversations, or by needling the boys demonstrate their concern about femininity. Physically, rapid growth and puberty are on the agenda.

The surest sign that pre-adolescence is coming to an end is that boy-girl interests become open. Yet, there are other shifts, also. Where the pre-adolescent was concerned negatively about childishness, the true adolescent is reaching for adulthood. Now, comes the series of steps marking progress toward grown-up status: the driving of cars, the concern with grooming, the cultivating of social skills, the interest in earning money and in vocations, and the organization of values.

What has all this to do with the junior high school? In which stage are its students? The answer is that they are in all three, but at different times! To provide a clue, let us oversimplify the facts by stating that among thirteen-year-olds, half the girls but only ten per cent of the boys will have reached pubescence. At fifteen, the comparable figures are ninety per cent of the girls and fifty per cent of the boys. Only when they are seventeen and safely ensconced in senior high school classrooms will ninety-nine per cent of both sexes be fully adolescent.

If, for the sake of having numbers easy to remember, we were to assume a "typical" class of forty, then, in the sixth grade it would be composed of two fully adolescent girls, eight pre-adolescent girls, ten childish girls, four pre-adolescent boys and sixteen childish boys. A ninth grade class of the same size would consist of sixteen young ladies (adolescents) and four pre-adolescent girls, plus two childish boys, eight pre-adolescent boys, and ten fully adolescent boys.

This, then, is the first and most important fact about the junior high school. Its classes are unstable and constantly changing admixtures. There is no uniformity in needs, motivational patterns, favorite modes of relating to adults, or even social predilections.

Among experienced teachers one finds two exactly opposite but equally "successful" techniques for dealing with what can truly be termed a juvenile hodgepodge. One, often found in many math classes, is to have the work divided into short units whose duration and content permits no leeway for significant spread in time or interest. The other, used frequently in social studies or core programs, is to have the class work in small committees chosen to give some useful organizational form to the diversity.

Usually, junior high school teachers are left to find their own techniques for coping with the extreme heterogeneity of their classes. True, there is quite a bit of useful folk wisdom on such matters transmitted from teacher to teacher. Yet, from the viewpoint of a psychologist one can ask why there has been so little direct study of this aspect of the junior high school, why there has been almost a complete neglect of grouping problems as a subject for scientific study.

This, then, gives us an initial reason for introducing a theme to which we may want to return later: The existence of the junior high school provides an opportunity to cope with a set of problems for which we otherwise would not have suitable administrative structures. But, and this is a most important "but," much too little has been done to make use of the opportunity.

The second major aspect of the junior high school's student body derives from the evidence that, during and immediately after the stage here termed "pre-adolescence," rather abrupt changes may take place in the course of an individual's development. The older writers tended to speak of the changes produced by puberty. The more objective research workers who have engaged in longitudinal studies are likely to write of changes which are associated with the year of maximum growth. For, just as the curves of individual physical growth tend to reach a plateau in late childhood, then abruptly swing into the so-called "growth spurt," and then level off, so too do the curves for various psychological functions change their slope or shape.

Let us recall a few obvious indices. There is comparatively little delinquency charged against eleven and twelve-year-olds; juveniles offenses reach their peak among the fourteens and fifteens. The number who have to be hospitalized for mental illness rises tenfold after the fifteenth birthday. For quite a while psychiatrists have been bemused by the fact that pre-adolescents may display conduct amazingly similar to that shown in the most serious mental illnesses, and spontaneously recover.

At the present point in American educational history we are also struck by the fact that the phenomenon of dropouts is concentrated in the junior high school age range.

The question to which we must address ourselves is whether the personality qualities which are symptomized by delinquency, mental illness, and social maladjustment result from changes taking place at the time of their appearance or are merely the final result of events which occurred earlier in life.

From two apparently contrasting sources of ideas there has come a tendency to regard adolescent changes as the inevitable result of what had happened to the young person during his babyhood or early childhood. Behaviorists, from the boastful Watson to the Walden-thinking Skinner, have emphasized the primacy of early conditioning. Although positing more subtle but even more potent processes, the Freudians agree.

From the latter viewpoint especially, the appearance of any form of pathology later in life is likely to be considered as the precipitating out of the effects of early trauma or early relationships. The search for causes traditionally implicates malformation of personality at the oral, anal, or phallic stages.

One notes, for instance, that use of the Glueck Social Prediction scales apparently permits a fairly accurate selection in the elementary schools of the boys who will be delinquent in junior high school. Good second grade teachers are almost as accurate. Moreover, we find that the bulk of school dropouts were children who had trouble in reading and arithmetic from the start; indeed, many appear to have betrayed their future pattern of failure even as they entered kindergarten.

The facts which support the viewpoints placing prepotency on early childhood would make us hope for relatively little from the junior high school period. True, the results of childhood events finally show themselves, but can they be changed? If the cause is indeed deep-seated, the traditional recourse is to the deep therapies, which take extended periods of time. Moreover, the turbulence of emotions accompanying puberty have been long regarded by psychoanalysts as tremendously complicating the work of the therapist.

Not only is this true, but it is equally true that the kinds of trouble with which we would be concerned blossom rapidly. The causes may have been operating for years and have acquired great momentum: The results appear suddenly. Delinquency becomes full-blown in a matter of months, the decision to drop out of school becomes firm in weeks, and who would want to decide how long it takes a disturbed girl to get herself pregnant? As one thoughtful psychiatrist summed up the dilemma, "It's too late too soon."

Since hopelessness is not a congenial frame of mind for educators, we have equipped junior high schools with counselors, installed various programs of group counseling, and opened the door to courses ranging in title from home and family living to life adjustment. Is there any evidence to justify all this?

The answer is a somewhat puzzled, "Yes." A rather striking set of facts have been brought to light by the group of research workers who have made longitudinal studies of young people and applied one or another technique of curve-fitting to those sequences of data which can be placed in numerical series. Cecil Millard noted, for instance, that there was enough of an orderly character to the growth patterns of most children so that one could predict with some confidence from the early years to the later years up to the year of puberty or the year of maximum growth. Then, so to speak, the bets were off. A new growth curve with a new set of parameters appeared on the charts.

Using difference techniques and working with the data which had earlier been gathered in the Harvard Growth Study, Cornell and Armstrong, while with the Research Division of the New York State Education Department, found four rather distinct patterns of shift in course of intellectual growth which occurred at the year of maximum growth. The first is the one which we have regarded as traditional and universal. That is, the relationship between chronological age and tested mental age is a straight line. Then, there were found a large group of curves where after the year of maximum growth, there was a slowing up of apparent intelligence. In a third group, the year of maximum growth marked an upslanting change—these are the so-called "late bloomers." The fourth group followed a pattern of growth by "fits and starts;" throughout life their curves showed a step-like pattern. For us, the thing to hold our attention is that there were many cases where changes were sharply defined and where the turning point occurred during the junior high school years.

There is a smattering of evidence that similar turning points may occur in the emotional, characterological, and social spheres. At the University of California, another center for longitudinal study of juvenile development, it was noted that boys tended to have a firm masculine identification and all the goods that went with that if they had had a non-stressful relationship with their fathers either when they were four or five on the one hand or during pre-adolescence on the other. Apparently, damage done by a poor relationship early could be significantly corrected later.

In a similar vein, a pair of studies of Warbois and Cantoni on counseling processes with the same population in Flint, Michigan, found that it was almost as though good counseling on his or her personal problems could put a youngster on another track from the one he had been following.

If these data come as a surprise, if they are not among the most important intellectual equipment of junior high school teachers and administrators, isn't that fact revealing in its own right? Here, then, to return to our theme we have the interesting facts that the junior high school is the scene of events significant enough to justify its existence but that much too little has been done to seize and exploit the opportunities it offers.

Now, let us look for a moment at the fact that so little is known about the reasons behind the changes which we have been emphasizing. The extent of our ignorance is symbolized by the fact that during the past four decades, years during which 50,000 books a year on the most detailed and even inconsequential subjects of all kinds have appeared in these United States, there have been exactly three books devoted to pre-adolescence, the pivotal psychological stage of the junior high school population. Back in the late 1920's Father Furfey published a book called *The Gang Age*. More than twenty years went by before Blair and Burton published their book on pre-adolescent development. After another decade passed a book on the same subject was authored by Loomis.

The junior high school is an established institution; it is an element in most school systems. Why has its student body apparently been comparatively ignored as a field of study? Why the paucity of publication? Part of the answer lies in the fact that relatively little is known, and that with marginal reliability. The group has puzzling qualities; the changes which take place are difficult to relate to factors over which we have control.

Let me give a sampling of the information we do have. We have data gathered at the Fels Research Institute, for instance, which seem to show that the achievement motivation of elementary school children reflects the value placed on achievement by the parent of the opposite sex. Studies of high school students indicate that they are more likely to identify with the values of the parent of their own sex. Somewhere in between, presumably during the junior high school years, the shift takes place. We lack details as to how this occurs and what can be done by school people. The phenomenon of the "academic tailspin," as evidenced by adolescent boys who were pushed scholastically by their mothers, is the main topic in the chapter on adolescent pathology in English and Pearson's classic work on "Emotional Problems of Living." They are able to give some fascinating explanations using orthodox Freudian concepts. Yet, today, twenty years after this material has appeared, there is nothing approaching a reliable application of the ideas whether by counseling techniques or deep-probing psychotherapy.

Let us take another illustration, brought to light by the careful comparison of data gathered by the Adolescent Growth Study in Berkeley, California. They noted that at about the time boys and girls first displayed interest in each other and became preoccupied apparently with their lack of boy-girl social skill or rather with the success or failures of their attempts to gain such skill, at that very time the youngsters were attacking and making life miserable for even the best trained group workers at a clubhouse established for observational purposes, and at that very time their teachers were reporting a falling off in scholastic interest and quality. A short while later, when the boy-girl activities had reached the point of taken-for-granted skills, the clubhouse leaders reported that the very same young people were now behaving helpfully, as apprentice adults, and teachers reported that their scholastic work had picked up again.

Quite interesting, we'll all agree. But, now let's ask some questions. Do we know which of these three relationships stands in the causal position? Have we any tried-and-true rationale for dealing with this matter, or even for deciding whether we should do anything at all? Yes, and when Bestor and Rickover were enjoying a field day with their sneers at "life adjustment education," why weren't these relationships mentioned? If there is reason to brood over such questions, let's compound the puzzlement with an intriguing fact: the study to which I have been referring was published more than 25 years ago; it was one of the first studies making good use of the existence of a junior high school, in this case the Claremont Junior High School.

It would be interesting to regale ourselves with the many other illustrations which could be given, but the two cited above are adequate to help define the dimensions of the situation. What we appear to have is not a total absence of information, but rather a broad and relatively shallow stream of largely descriptive information whose application is not firmly determined. This exhibits a marked contrast with the tremendous volume of material on early childhood and the not-quite so voluminous but still massive accumulation of data on adolescence.

The situation as to studies on development is paralleled to some degree by the accumulation of material on pedagogical issues. We have for no junior high school subject anything coming even close to the study of psychological factors and teaching methods involved in beginning reading or arithmetic. However, research relevant to teaching fields in the junior high school does not suffer by comparison with that for the senior high school or even the colleges. In the upper reaches of all our educational institutions there has been some fascinating experimentation by a goodly company of hardy souls, but the research problems are quite intricate and the prevailing atmosphere often permeated with suspicion of educationists.

Let us return once again to our theme. Both what we know and we don't know about the young people themselves support the wisdom of establishing an institution, the junior high school, which can minister helpfully to their special needs. In this institution the very demands of the situation require faculty, administrators, and other professional personnel with the knowledge, patience, durability, and other attributes to cope wisely with rather unique opportunities for serving young people. The institutions exist. The personnel is on the job. Yet, there has been a notable lag in the appearance of professional training for this situation; there is an equally serious lag in painstaking research on the part of either junior high school people or child development experts.

Let us attempt to come to grips with the twin questions of why this should be so, and what can be done about it. Now, with cold malice aforethought, I am going to use what is a typical psychologist's trick—I am going to call attention to the very name, its implications, link to it associations, which some will regard as farfetched, which will make others righteously indignant. So be it! The name with which we have endowed this unique educational institution, this challenging opportunity for education, is junior high school. *Junior* high school.

Let us free-associate for a moment to both halves of the title. What are our usual feelings and our usual associations, our hunches, about juniors? Sons, overshadowed by fathers, even having to bear a name not quite rightfully theirs, having to be chips off the old blocks, always having to live up to a model not of their making, not quite people in their own right. Think of the junior in Junior Achievement—not quite real, playing at being grown-up, in apprenticeship to being serious.

And high school. High. The first step to college. Emphasis upon intensive effort. Where there are departments composed of experts in subject matter, with graduate degrees in the academic disciplines, just like college professors!

Viewed wryly from the proper (or perhaps, improper) angle, there is a comic note to the juxtaposition of terms. And, as is so often true of veritable comedy, there is beneath it a deep layer of pathos, bordering on the tragic. Yes, seriously I am suggesting that a portion of our problems in fulfilling the potential of the junior high school arises from the fact that the professional staff has let themselves be caught in a situation where powerful and usually unverbalized status considerations turn their eyes away from the very difficulties which should be a source of pride.

Now, this is neither a demand nor a hint that merely changing the name will in and of itself be of any value. The situation is too deeply rooted for that; the possibilities for gain are too vital.

Well, then, where do we find the answers? For the purpose of inaugurating discussion, of triggering that comparison of ideas and matching of dissents from which knowledgeable and experienced professionals may bring into the open their own solutions, let me have the temerity to suggest a few items in a strategy for basic reorientation.

First, it may be necessary to focus sharply on what makes the junior high school distinctive from the senior high school. (We do not need to worry about proclaiming a function different from the elementary school; that is easy to do emotionally, and has been done well.) The uniqueness consists in the fact that this school's population is in transition. During an older period we might have compared it to the marshalling yards of a railroad. In an era of motor travel we might find an analogy in the elaborate interchanges which link major routes with interstate freeways. This uniqueness poses problems which are included in the construction of any other road, and then call for an additional set of skills for the engineers, for the construction workers, and for the drivers.

Second, the teachers and administrators responsible for such schools may have to be painfully insistent on bringing their special needs forcefully to the attention of our teacher-educating institutions. Possibly to avoid complicating the curricular structures, partly to guard jurisdictional rights, our education faculties have assumed that the similarities between junior high schools and senior high schools so greatly outweighed the contrasts that both could be embraced as "secondary education" and, accordingly, there was positive disadvantage in looking at the differences which might require distinctive preparation and differently aimed research.

It must be admitted that to emphasize distinctivenesses which would logically lead to "fragmentation" in teacher-preparation at the present time would be to swim against the tide. But, then, there is no point in learning to swim if one is only going to go with the tide. Today one hears much talk of K through 12 programs. The implication is that there is a universality to educational principles and problems which call for so little specialized expertise as to militate against preparation or research based on meeting the peculiar needs of different age groups.

Yes, if we are to base our educational programs upon simple-minded acceptance of Skinnerian conditioning, and consider that the major mode of learning, then there is such universality. But, if that is our fundamental belief, let's turn our schools over to electronic gadgetry and clear out. However, if we are concerned with differences in cognitive styles, if we are concerned with motivation, if we are to recognize the significance of social adjustment and utilize the full power of group processes, then, we must force acknowledgement of the fact that the junior high school population is, in fact, very special. Its specialness calls for understandings in genuine depth concerning the phenomena of pre-adolescence and the ways of utilizing heterogeneities so massive as to constitute differences in kind rather than differences in degree.

The wisdom and experience of many educators gave rise to the movement which brought the junior high school into being as an institution. Now we have the grueling task of realizing the hopes and expectations with which they launched the enterprise. There can be no doubt but that the task is proving much more complicated, much more obstinate than the founders could have believed. Their expectation was that creating a new institution, engaging as it were in a neat bit of administrative legerdemain, would almost in and of itself solve the problems. It has turned out that the creation of the institution has provided a setting that has opened opportunities. Yet, progress has been slower than earlier leaders might have expected.

If we and our thousands upon thousands of colleagues could now get to work to take full advantage of the opportunities, perhaps within a generation one could boast of great achievements, could say with pride that we had learned how to help our youth negotiate the pre-adolescent transitions with confidence, had found answers to dropout problems, had brought self-destructive delinquency under control.

The jobs to be done are worth doing. Let's intensify the zest with which we tackle them.

Administrators View the Middle School*

THOMAS E. CURTIS

State University of New York

The period of school generally considered to be most appropriate for early adolescent youth has been composed of several different administrative organizations during the last half century. Ideas ranging from the 8-4 plan, which was the most common administrative arrangement of the last century, to the 6-6 plan, which is currently being more extensively utilized than any other plan, have all had their exponents through the years. The addition of still another plan might seem to be an overendowment of riches, but certainly the evolution of the 4-4-4 and the 5-3-4 arrangements, more commonly referred to as the middle school, has attracted enough attention in the last decade to warrant further observation of their favorable aspects and shortcomings.

The middle school, from its inception, has had at least a semantic advantage in that it does not have the negative connotations of the *junior* high school with all the problems inherent to the word, junior. The crucial issue at present would seem to be the identification of basic purposes for which the theoretical framework is most advantageously constructed.

The same basic purposes and functions should and can be claimed for the middle school as for the junior school. Assuming this basic framework, the chief question seems to be whether a 5-3-4 system in which children are segregated in the sixth, seventh, and eighth grades is better suited to the education of early adolescents than is the more traditional seventh, eighth, and ninth grade arrangement.

Survey of Administrators

It was with this basic thought in mind that a survey was taken of

*Reprinted from *High Points*, 48 (March 1966) 30-35, by permission of the publisher and Thomas E. Curtis, State University of New York.

administrators of middle schools in New York State. The State Education Department informed the investigator concerning those schools in the state which were using either the 4-4-4 or 5-3-4 administrative arrangement. Letters were then sent to the administrators of those schools requesting either formal statements of philosophy for their schools or an informal statement of their opinions concerning the efficacy of the middle school as an educative institution for early adolescents. Although the following statements, which are the investigator's compilation of the administrators' opinions, may have limitations, they certainly provide an interesting insight into the relative merits of the middle school as seen by a group of admittedly highly enthusiastic administrators of such schools.

There was no particular attempt on the part of the administrators to partition their comments into particular areas. For the purpose of this paper, the investigator has grouped these favorable statements into five categories: those concerning teachers, those concerning students, those concerning guidance, those concerning articulation, and those concerning curriculum.

Age Compatibility

The chief advantage, according to the administrators, of the middle school was the synthesis of elementary and secondary teacher attitudes in such a school. They perceived a movement away from the more traditional college preparatory ideas of the junior high school to the more effective domain of the elementary school. However, they did note an expression on the part of teachers: sixth grade teachers appreciating the specialized opportunity of departmentalization, and ninth grade teachers being appreciative of association with senior high school colleagues.

The administrators noted an empirical evaluation concerning student compatibility at this age level, observing on a relatively subjective level that students seemed more compatible in grades six, seven, and eight because of similar social, emotional, and physical problems. They felt that this resulted in considerably fewer discipline problems at this grade level. In a positive light, they saw great value in having sixth graders take part in activities previously considered distinctively junior high school activities. They perceived this value in the earlier acceptance of responsibilities on the part of sixth grade students and in greater self-discipline. Particular stress was given to the lessening of tension in the middle school owing to the lessening of college preparatory academic requirements. It was the feeling of some of the administrators that seventh and eighth grade students were relieved of ninth grade domination. The presence of a dramatic difference between students in grades eight and nine was particularly noted.

Particular notice was made of the earlier onset of puberty which has occurred of recent years. The implication was noted that if the middle school was intended for the early adolescent, then the onset of puberty should certainly be one of the determining factors for the grade organization. It was their empirical observation that puberty was arriving earlier than was true a few decades ago, and that this was establishing a strong theoretical foundation for the grade arrangement in their schools. In addition to the perceptions of the principals, several research notations of this earlier arrival of puberty were made.

Earlier Counseling

One of the more positive observations made by the principals concerning guidance was the possibility for earlier counseling for youngsters in the sixth grade. They felt that the individual attention possible at this age was a strong advantage for the middle school. They also noted that planning for college could be strengthened by the placing of the ninth grade in the senior high school. The Carnegie unit has long been a cross which the junior high school has had to bear. With the ninth grade removed from the middle school, this problem seemed, to them, to be placed in its proper context, that of a senior high school situation.

It was noted that senior high school principals reported fewer discipline cases in the senior high school ninth grade than had been previously reported in the ninth grade when it was a part of the junior high school. Reasons for this change were not noted and might be due to any one of a number of variables, but the difference was clearly observable.

Articulation

In the area of articulation, two advantages were listed. First, as with the teacher aspect, there seemed to be a synthesis of elementary and secondary curriculum and attitudes. The ideal junior high school should be neither complete elementary-oriented, nor secondary-oriented but should be a unique educational experience aimed toward the unique problems of early adolescence. The administrators noted that the logical transition from the elementary to the secondary curriculum seemed to come about more effectively through the middle school approach. They were particularly interested in the transition from the self-contained elementary program to the block-of-time middle school to the completely departmentalized secondary school.

In the area of curriculum variations in the two types of schools, the administrators perceived that there was more freedom to experiment with new programs in the middle school approach. The casual relationship may be slightly obscure at this point inasmuch as the question arises as to whether the flexibility is built into the middle school idea, or whether the middle school arrangement arose because of the flexibility in such a school system. Broader academic offerings were seen as being possible, particularly for grades six and nine. The administrators perceived more and better equipment as being available for these two grades because six would be in the intermediate unit and nine in the senior high school unit in the middle school organization. The possibility of some subject matter specialization in the sixth grade was also noted as a possible advantage.

Theoretical concepts concerning the structure of knowledge and the psychological aspects of its presentation to early adolescents were noted with the statement that the elementary child's factual approach would ordinarily shift toward abstract concepts around the sixth grade. This would make the middle school a more appropriate administrative organization than the present junior high school.

Disadvantages

While the administrators were enthusiastic about most phases of the middle school, some negative aspects were also noted. For example, the question of teacher certification was raised since most sixth grade teachers, would not have secondary certification. This could severely curtail the utilization of teachers across grade lines. Most syllabi and teacher handbooks are coordinated assuming the break between grades six and seven. Much attention and effort would be necessary to coordinate an articulation between grades five and six essential to this administrative organization.

The question of leadership seemed to attract the attention of some of the principals who indicated two aspects of this problem: first, the perceived apparent inability of eighth graders to assume the leadership of the sixth, seventh, and eighth grade organization and, second, the need of ninth graders for a year of leadership since there would be a tendency for them to be held down in the senior high school. It was felt that the ninth graders needed this year of leadership in order to fulfill some of the psychological needs of early adolescence. It was also noted that eighth grade girls, most of whom had passed the pubertal stage, were dissatisfied with their lot in the sixth, seventh, and eighth grade middle school since the vast majority of the boys were still physically and emotionally more immature than they.

From these statements, many theoretical and practical merits of the middle school may be inferred. Further research on grade organization, both intensive and extensive, would seem to be appropriate, considering these findings. Since the proposed adoption of the middle school approach in New York City, the nation's largest city, it would seem incumbent upon both theoreticians and administrators to seriously weigh the relative merits of various grade organizations to attempt to ascertain whether there is, in truth, a discernible difference in effectiveness in the education of early adolescents between the so-called middle school and the junior high school, and, if so, which arrangement might be more appropriate for each individual school system.

Questions Facing the Middle School*

PAUL GASTWIRTH

Bleeker Junior High School, Queens

Definition Needed

Perhaps the most important problem facing the middle school is that of *definition.* What is a middle school? Sometimes the term "middle school" is mentioned with respect and sometimes with scorn ("muddle school") but seldom with clear understanding. In a report issued by the Educational Facilities Laboratories, titled *Middle Schools,* six different types of grade organization are mentioned as middle schools: 7-8, 7-8-9, 6-7-8, 6-7-8-9, 5-6-7-8, 5-6-7-8-9. The confusion is so flagrant that the author of this brochure, Miss Judith Murphy, boldly states: "Diversity is the keynote. Least important, as suggested earlier, is the precise scheme of grades."[1]

Miss Murphy presents an *ad hoc* definition of a middle school as one "in between elementary school and high school, housed separately and—ideally—in a building freshly designed for its purpose, and covering at least three of the middle school years, beginning with grade 5 or 6." The author then pulls out the rug from under the middle school by saying, "If the middle school is kept unfrozen in program as well as in physical design, it can serve as a true expansion link in the school system, adding or subtracting grades to meet changing enrollment pressures."[2]

What should be the organizing principle of the middle school? Should it be grade organization? Should it be the chronological age of pupils? The social and psychological maturity of pupils? The logistics of building space within the

*Reprinted from *High Points*, 48 (June 1966), 40-47, by permission of the publisher and Paul Gastwirth, principal, Bleeker Junior High School, Flushing, New York.

[1]Murphy, Judith. *Middle Schools,* Educational Facilities Laboratories, 9.

[2]Murphy, *op. cit.,* 6.

system? The demands of political groups? The demands for desegregation? Administrative convenience? Economy? Unless we develop a clean-cut operational definition of a middle school, I submit that we don't know what we're talking about. Socrates annoyed people in ancient Greece by insisting on definitions of terms: What do we mean by justice, love, virtue? He was forced to drink hemlock. Although I prefer Scotch to hemlock, I shall persist in asking for a definition of terms. Fuzzy thinking is as dangerous in education as in other walks of life. Great harm was done to the junior high school movement, for example, by Conant's comment that the type of grade organization for the early adolescent is not so important as the type of program provided. In other words, any type of grade organization will do, provided the youngster has a good junior high school program. This reminds me of the mother who advises her daughter, "It doesn't matter whether the man you marry is rich or poor, as long as he has money."

Importance of Grade Organization

The nub of the issue is the question: "Is not the conventional junior high school, grades 7-8-9, the place in which the early adolescent can receive, most efficiently and economically, the kind of education most appropriate for him?" If the "precise scheme of grades" is not important, why are the proponents of the middle school so insistent upon the particular scheme of grades that they favor? It appears to me that grade organization is a vital factor in the development of both curricular and co-curricular learning experiences. Of course, in the non-graded school of the future, the concept of grade organization will be replaced by the concept of age-level organization.

Features of the Middle School

In my quest for a definition of the middle school, I have found the following items mentioned as characteristic features of a middle school:

A new building
Effective use of the school plant
Home economics and industrial arts shops
Use of television
Foreign language instruction
Language laboratories
Divisible auditorium
Large and small group activities

Air conditioning
Movable walls
Carpets
Imaginative architectural design
Set-up planned for the next superintendent; that is, for the future
Instructional swimming pool
Library carrels
Audio-visual materials
Programmed learning
Team-teaching
Specialization and departmentalization
Individualization
Flexible schedules
Non-gradedness
A program based on 20-minute 30-minute modules
A program based on 55-minute units
A program based on units of 1½ or 2 hours

As you examine the more than two dozen items you will notice that not one of them may be said to differentiate a 5-8 middle school from a conventional junior high school!

In seeking a definitive statement of what a middle school is, I have read the pertinent literature, searching for something fixed, for some invariant, for some constant among the variables. I have found nothing except the truisms that the middle school is an in-between school, a school between two other types of schools, or the middle tier in a three-tier educational system.

Problem of Identification

How can the problem of identification be solved? Certainly not on so-called "practical" grounds which vary from district to district throughout the country! The middle school, if it is to have meaning for us as educators, must have a unique philosophy and an organizing principle to implement that philosophy. It must be based on a pattern of organization that will help pre-adolescents develop into adolescents by enabling them to explore their aptitudes, to find themselves, and to achieve some measure of self-identification. Its pattern of organization should bracket those age levels at which the vast majority of pupils enter and complete the period of pubescence. Its structure should also provide a stable educational environment designed to help preadolescents achieve an inner stability. The middle school must not be permitted to become a revolving door for pupils on the way from the elementary school to the high school. Unless these conditions are met, the middle school will be in constant flux and will resemble a race track where everything is in motion, including the judges' and spectators' stands. Can you picture that?

Superficial Criticism of the Junior High School

Since the middle school concept is being proposed as an alternative to that of the junior high school, perhaps we may be able to obtain a clearer image of the middle school; first, by considering what is allegedly wrong with the junior high school and, second, by focusing our attention on one type of middle school—that which has a grade 5-8 organization.

Some of the strictures leveled at the junior high school are the following:

1. Rigid departmentalization
2. Extra-curricular fanfare
3. Marching bands
4. Elaborate graduation ceremonies
5. Excessive emphasis on interscholastic athletics
6. Sophisticated social events such as the senior prom.

With one exception, rigid departmentalization, these criticisms are superficial and peripheral. In the schools to which these criticisms apply—and the number of such schools is small—the objectionable features named can be eliminated or mitigated without undue difficulty. It must be remembered that some of these features, e.g., elaborate graduation ceremonies, are the legacy of the obsolete K-8 school!

Further, what guarantee do we have that all the co-curricular and social "hoop-la" will not be present in a 5-8 middle school? We must guard against the fallacy in logic committed by critics who believe that their valid criticism of an existing institution or policy somehow guarantees the validity of their alternative proposals. However sound their *criticism* may be, their suggestions for improvement may be just as inadequate as, or even worse than, the programs criticized. In attempting to mitigate the sophistication of the junior high school, they may succeed only in extending it to the lower grades, thus making the middle school a *junior* junior-high-school.

With respect to rigid departmentalization, many junior high school principals have for years sought to modify the departmental program of seventh graders by introducing a core of English and social studies, by having the same instructor teach two subjects to the same class, or by other methods. It is interesting to note, however, that one of the main arguments used by proponents of the 5-8 middle school is that it would provide fifth and sixth graders with a departmentalized program in which the academic subjects would be taught by specialists! Also, in some middle schools, the most sophisticated form of departmentalization—namely, individual programming—is being planned for fifth graders.

Grades 5 and 6

In view of current trends toward the vertical organization of the curriculum in a K-12 program and in view of the growing partial departmentalization of the 5th and 6th grades in the elementary school, there would seem to be less need than ever for a middle school to encompass grades 5 and 6. These trends indicate a desire to provide children with superior preparation both for the greater departmentalization that they will encounter in the junior high school and for the greater stress on the teaching of organized subject matter by specialists. On the one hand, the vertical organization of the curriculum provides built-in continuity in the subject areas, thus easing the articulation among the three school divisions; on the other hand, the use of the dual progress plan—team-teaching, partial departmentalization, and special teachers or coordinators in art, music, science, health education, and other subjects—provides children with exposure to subject specialists in the elementary school. In these ways, pupils become acquainted with several teachers and with different groups of children, while remaining attached to one teacher and to a home-base class and classroom. Thus, elementary schools in progressive school systems are already providing the type of program for fifth and sixth graders that is being blueprinted for the grades 5-8 middle school.

However we define the middle school, it would be a catastrophe to accept the concept of the middle school as an expansion link between the elementary schools and the high schools, "adding or subtracting grades to meet enrollment pressures." The middle school must be defined on the basis of educational philosophy and psychology. It must be developed as a distinctive educational institution, uniquely designed to serve the needs of early adolescents. It must be established as a school with a status and an integrity of its own, strong enough to withstand the pressures of economic and political opportunism.

Problem of Personnel

The second basic problem that will face the 5-8 middle school is that of *personnel*. The junior high schools have been criticized also for their personnel shortage and for the high percentage of provisional teachers employed. Is there any prospect, much less guarantee, that the middle school will be able to solve the problem of teacher shortage?

Teachers in the junior high school are subject specialists. They naturally tend to gravitate toward the senior high school where they will have the opportunity to teach their subjects in greater depth and at a more advanced level. The presence of the ninth grade in the junior high schools helps them retain these subject-oriented teachers. The removal of the ninth grade would simply hasten the exodus of these teachers from the middle school.

According to the literature, the middle schools that enroll fifth or sixth graders assign them usually to their own classrooms for a substantial part of the school day. The homeroom teacher carries practically the entire load of teaching in the fifth grade, with the pupils receiving greater, but not complete, departmentalization in grade 6. This practice would also accelerate the departure of subject-oriented teachers to the high schools, especially if there are no compensatory ninth-grade classes available. For these reasons, it is doubtful that the middle schools conceived as 5-8 grade organizations will do as well as the traditional junior high schools in attracting and holding personnel.

Pre-Service and In-Service Training

A third basic problem that will confront the middle school is that of *pre-service and in-service training* of teachers. It took years for the junior high school to gain the status, the stability, and the funded experience that, in the eyes of teacher colleges, warranted the establishment of separate courses in the many areas of junior high school teaching and administration. During this long period, college students continued to exercise their option of choosing between elementary and secondary school education. Preparation for junior high school teaching was included in the courses in secondary school education.

With the middle school, we face an entirely different problem. Will students who are interested in the 5-8 middle school specialize in elementary, junior high, or secondary school education? Who has the experience to give courses in middle school technique? Who, indeed, knows how to organize such a course in view of the fluidity of the concept of the middle school?

Other Considerations

There are, of course, many other problems that confront the 5-8 middle school—questions concerning the internal organization of the curriculum, the subjects to be included, methods of grouping, techniques of individualizing instruction, deployment of teacher personnel, and the like. I do not see how we can even begin to grapple with these problems unless, and until, we have a clean-cut operational definition of the middle school.

Progress in education depends on the vision, creativity, and responsiveness to new ideas of all of us who labor in the educational vineyards. Not all change, however, is progress. Dr. Sizer, dean of Harvard's Graduate School of Education, has recently cautioned educators to take stock of *where* they are going, and *why*, before they allow themselves to be pushed into innovations that are lacking in well-thought-out ideas. The pertinency and urgency of his advice is underscored by a speech made recently by the Vice-President of the Board of Education of New York City at a conference of educators. In commenting on the Board's plan to convert the established junior high schools into middle schools, he candidly declared, "We don't know exactly what the nature of the reorganization plan will be or whether the changes will improve the education and training of the individual child or whether they will reach into the classroom."[3]

In an article in our journal[4] a few years ago, Prof. Alexander, a proponent of the 5-8 middle school, advocated setting up a pilot project. He did *not* recommend the massive large-scale changeover that is being undertaken in certain urban centers without benefit of pilot programs, scientific controls, and objective evaluation. As I read the literature, I am appalled that contradictory reasons are given in different towns and cities for the establishment of grades 5-8 middle schools. It is apparent that the reasons given were "cooked up" to support decisions made on non-educational grounds. Small wonder, then, that the middle school concept lacks adequate definition!

Finally, and above all, we must remember that, although it is desirable to have an experimental frame of mind, we are experimenting with children, not guinea pigs, not white mice. To caution educators, I should like to have every child in the land wear a large placard bearing the legend: "I am a human being; please do not bend, fold, spindle, or mutilate."

[3]School Page, *World Telegram and Sun*, January 24, 1966.
[4]*Journal of the Association of Secondary School Principals.*

Middle School: A Questionable Innovation*

RICHARD L. POST

Mr. Eugene Regan's article "The Junior High School is Dead" in the November 1967 issue of *The Clearing House* contains many statements which seem to be no more than questionable opinions. Permit me to offer a few "questionable" opinions of my own based upon 18 years experience as a teacher and principal in seventh, eighth, and ninth grade junior high schools.

Possibly my greatest misgivings concerning the current interest in the middle school stem from a feeling that educational gimmickry is being substituted for genuine innovation. The innovations which intrigue me are those offering an opportunity to stimulate the individualization of instruction. Independent study, continuous progress curricula, team teaching, and flexible scheduling seem to be the issues worthy of our serious consideration. I fail to see how the transfer of the ninth grade to the senior high and the fifth and sixth grades to the middle school can help us move in this direction. In fact, if the ninth grade students are moved into a more subject-centered school, and if the fifth and sixth grade students are subjected to increased departmentalization, we may set education back 50 years. Our energies may be directed toward an innovation which does not really merit serious consideration, and the important new ideas in education may be ignored.

The grade organization adopted by a district may be 6-3-3, 5-3-4, 4-4-4 or 6-6, with little real difference in the quality of the education offered. The program and staff within each institution determine its quality, and it is improvement in these areas that should occupy our interests.

It is generally agreed that a comprehensive senior high school should have

*Reprinted from *The Clearing House*, 42 (April 1968), 484-486, by permission of the publisher and Richard L. Post, Marcus Whitman Junior High School, Port Orchard, Washington.

at least 1000 students in order to offer needed laboratories and special facilities and to utilize its staff in areas of their major strengths. If to achieve this size the district must include grade nine, then the four year school would obviously be desirable. However, if size is not a problem, prime consideration should be given to where the ninth grade student might get the most appropriate program.

Mr. Regan has evidently experienced far greater control by the senior high over the junior high curriculum than has been my lot. High school graduation requirements have been expressed as a number of credits earned in grades 10, 11, and 12. Some subjects required for graduation may be taken in junior high, but these are not limited to the ninth grade. We have offered for the past seven years a six-year sequence in each of three modern languages. This is a 7-12 sequence and is listed upon the transcript as such. Our transcript must include grades 7-12, also, since some students take algebra in grade eight and colleges are usually interested in this credit. The state requires physical education in grades 7, 8, 9, and 10 and this is also shown on the transcript. I have never felt that these requirements inhibited the development of a sound junior high program, and certainly the moving of the ninth grade to the senior high would solve no problems if they existed.

It has been my experience that teachers whose interests are more subject-centered than child-centered gravitate to the senior high. As a result I have felt that senior high schools are more inclined to set arbitrary standards and utilize more impersonal teaching methods than junior high schools. It seems unwise to place these ninth grade students in this environment until sufficient changes have been made in program and practice to insure that their needs will be met.

At age 14 decisions about continuing in school, about value systems, and about social attitudes are of prime importance to students, and a school whose primary concern is with needs of these individuals is necessary. In our junior high we utilize the block-of-time, attempt to give continuous instruction in reading, offer alternate courses for the gifted and the handicapped, and in other ways attempt to center our interest on the individual student. I'm not certain that the ninth grade student could get any better program than this if he were moved into a senior high school.

My feelings are even stronger when we discuss the social aspects of such a move. We have no night activities and our ninth grade students do not attend senior high social events. We do not permit students to drive cars to school. I do not see what useful purpose can be served by having 14-year-old girls going to the junior prom and riding home from school in cars with 18-year-old boys. Even if it were granted that ninth graders are more mature than they were 30 years ago, this maturity should be directed toward worthwhile junior high projects such as adopting a foster child, community beautification, or planning assemblies and programs. I feel that in the four year high school the few social opportunities available might encourage the wrong sort of development. The fact that students mature earlier should not lead one to the conclusion that we should encourage earlier sophistication of their social activities, since early marriage is still an economic mistake and dating activities should be deferred as long as possible.

The elimination of interscholastic athletics and its accompanying activities are often given as the major gain resulting from the transfer of the ninth grade to the senior high. I'm afraid that if the community wants a competitive athletic program for 12-, 13-, and 14-year-olds, it's going to have one regardless of the school organization. Little Leagues, Pee Wees, and Boys Clubs will fill the gap. I happen to feel that educators can do a better job administering such a program for the good of the child than the alternate leadership usually available in the communities. Moreover, junior high regulations are usually sounder than senior high regulations and superior to community sponsored substitutes.

In our state, a 9th grade boy in a 4 year school could play in 10 football games with 12 minute quarters. The same boy in a junior high can play in only 6 games with 8 minute quarters and he cannot scrimmage with any 10th, 11th, or 12th grade students. Junior highs in our league do not permit rooter buses, tournaments, or other practices available to senior high students. There are many values both to the individual and to the student body accruing from a sound athletic program, and the junior high faculty can control this program if it chooses. If practices aping the senior high are undersirable—stop them. But needs of the junior high students should determine the practices.

There are many real challenges facing educational leaders today. Because of a growing recognition of the role education plays in improving the quality of life, there is a new commitment to educational improvement. A move to shift grades from one institution to another hardly seems worthy of consideration when we are on the verge of beginning to understand the teacher-learner relationship, and when fundamental changes in the nature of teaching could result. Another realignment of grades seems ridiculous when the graded school itself may be on its way out.

We are presently completing the plans for a new junior high school in our district. Its instructional materials center will occupy one-quarter of the floor space, its classrooms will not be divided by partitions, and I hope its staff will be dedicated to the individualization of instruction. It will include grades seven, eight, *and nine,* as we have yet to see any sound educational reason for depriving the ninth grade students of the opportunity to develop in this environment. The time may come when we will need to build another senior high. The issue of what grades to include will again arise. If the proper educational plan is devised, placing the individual learner in his rightful role, even those of us who "cling loyally to the JHS banner" might recommend a four year senior high.

The Middle School: Philosophy, Program, Organization*

W. GEORGE BATEZEL

Philosophy

A carefully thought out philosophy is essential as a guide in developing the program and organization of a good middle school. The following points should be considered:

(1) A good middle school ought to provide for a gradual transition from the typical self-contained classroom to the highly departmentalized high school.

(2) Provision should be made by program and organization for each student to become well known by at least one teacher.

(3) The middle school ought to exist as a distinct, very flexible, and unique organization tailored to the special needs of pre-adolescent and early adolescent youths. It ought not to be an extension of the elementary nor seek to copy the high school.

(4) The middle school ought to provide an environment where the child, not the program, is most important and where the opportunity to succeed exists.

Program

While the child is the important factor, the program provides the vehicle to move him along intellectually in such a way that his self-image is enhanced. Transcending any program, then, is the way in which it is implemented. A

*Reprinted from *The Clearing House* 42 (April 1968), 487-490, by permission of the publisher and W. George Batezel, Temple University.

middle school program, properly conceived, is not just a series of hurdles which a child must jump, but a means to a far broader and nobler end—developing and/or increasing the self concept of each child as a valuable human being.

It is in this frame of reference that the following curriculum, program, and activities of a 6-7-8 middle school are proposed.

General Observations. In laying out specific programs for 6th, 7th, and 8th grades, a 40 period week of 40 minutes each, plus a 40 minute lunch period has been assumed. While this does not necessarily represent an ideal, it is being used to indicate the proportionate share of available time to the various subject areas.

Sixth Grade. In planning a sixth grade program it is desirable that the benefits of the close teacher-pupil relationship inherent in the self-contained classroom be maintained as far as this is possible, while still taking advantage of the enrichment which the utilization of special teachers and/or special facilities offer.

The sixth grade ought to contain a large enough block of time with one teacher so that each child is well known by that teacher.

6th Grade	*Periods Per Week*
Language arts, social studies, reading	12
Mathematics, science	12
Physical education	3
Foreign language	5*
Music	5**
Art	5**
Industrial arts—home economics	5**
Health	5**
Special interests or homeroom	3

**shortened periods*
***for one evaluation period*

(1) In the above program the student in sixth grade would have only five teachers at any one time.

(2) Teachers in the major subject areas would be paired into teams in which each team would consist of a Language Arts-Social Studies-Reading and Math-Science teacher.

Two classes of 25 each would be assigned to this team. Each member of the team would be the homeroom teacher for 25 youngsters and, as such, be responsible for the guidance, general supervision, and welfare of the homeroom student in all phases of his school career. The team would work together in developing a total coordinated program. While the two classes would be scheduled on a turn-about basis for normal operations (e.g., "A" group would be having L.A.–S.S. while "B" group was having Math-Science in the morning, and vice versa in the afternoon), nothing would preclude the team from rescheduling for days or weeks at a time into large and small groups in order to carry out a well planned unit or units within the team or in conjunction with other two-member teams.

(3) Students would have foreign language instruction in Spanish, French, or German five times per week for 25 minutes per day.

(4) Students would have a 15 minute recess or free time.

(5) There would be four evaluation periods per year. At least one—possibly two-of these would involve a parent conference with each student's homeroom teacher.

(6) The special interests program would be designed to provide:

a. Enrichment for those who have an unusual interest in a specific subject.

b. Opportunity to try out some skills not offered in the regular program (e.g., Typing).

c. Opportunity within the school day for students being transported to partake in some intramural, music, and club programs.

Some suggested special interest programs might be:

Art	Typing
Band	Mathematics
Foreign languages	Mechanical drawing
Future Homemakers of America	Newspaper
	Nursing
Choral groups	Orchestra
Clothing	Photography
Debating	Science
Dramatics	Shop
Food	Sports

(1) The seventh grader would be assigned to a homeroom teacher who *would be responsible for knowing the child well* and for providing help, guidance, and general supervision of his welfare in all aspects of school life. This teacher would remain his homeroom teacher through 8th grade. Ideally, a homeroom teacher would teach the child in at least one class while he has the child in homeroom.

7th Grade	*Periods Per Week*
Language arts, reading	7*
Mathematics	5
Science	5
Social Studies	5
Foreign language	5**
Physical education	4
Music	5***
Art	5***
Industrial arts–home economics	5***
Health	5***
Special interest and homeroom	4

**plus 5 shortened periods*
***shortened periods*
****for one evaluation period*

(2) Interdisciplinary teams would be encouraged so that teams of four teachers would have the same (approximately 100) youngsters in the major subject areas.

(3) Foreign language instruction would continue daily for 25 minutes per day. Students would be encouraged to continue the foreign language begun in 6th grade.

(4) The special interest groups would be the same as for sixth grade.

(5) There would be four marking periods with the homeroom teacher responsible for providing his students with needed assistance.

8th Grade	*Periods Per Week*
Language arts, reading	7
Mathematics	5
Social studies	5
Science	5
Foreign language or reading	5
Physical education	4
Music	5*
Art	5*
Industrial arts–Home Economics	5*
Health	5*
Special interest groups and homeroom	4

**for one evaluation period*

(1) The eighth grader would continue with the same homeroom teacher, who, with two years' experience, will be better able to guide the student throughout the year and in the initial selection of his high school program.

(2) Foreign Language instruction would be for five full periods per week. The language would be elective, the student selecting either Spanish, French, or German.

(3) Each student not selecting a foreign language will receive reading instruction (developmental and/or remedial) designed to meet his individual needs. (The student's needs, coupled with his experience in 6th and 7th grade foreign language will provide a basis for guidance in this area.)

(4) Science will have one double period per week to introduce laboratory techniques. (Assuming 9th grade program becomes a laboratory science.)

(5) Special interest groups would be for the same purpose as 6th and 7th grades.

All grades would have the benefit of a reading specialist to work with youngsters in a flexible program of small-group instruction. This specialist would also be responsible for in-service training of all our language arts teachers in reading instruction.

The physical education program would be expanded. Remedial instruction would be provided. Hopefully, swimming instruction will be possible.

The interscholastic athletic program for 7th and 8th grades will be carefully evaluated to determine its place in a middle school. An intramural program will be developed for the 6th grade and the present program expanded for the 7th and 8th grades.

Organization and Staffing

A middle school organization should not be overwhelming. Every possible device should be built into it so that each child will become a well known individual. Size is an important factor here. Large and small schools each have their distinctive advantages. Only a large enough school can provide the services and facilities a good middle school should have. On the other hand, only a small school can enhance the close personal communication and atmosphere for teacher and pupil alike. The house plan organization comes closest to making possible the advantages of a large school while maintaining the warm, human, very personal environment of a smaller school. Therefore, it is proposed that the new middle school be organized and staffed for a 900 pupil middle school as follows:

(1) The school would be divided into three distinct houses of approximately 300 students each.

(2) Each house would have a 6th, 7th, and 8th grade of about 100 students.

(3) Each house would have
- a. A full-time "Dean" or "Housemaster" in charge of and responsible for the program in his house
- b. A full-time guidance counselor
- c. A full-time secretary

(4) The "large" or overall school would have
- a. A principal
- b. An assistant principal
- c. Two secretaries
- d. One guidance director
- e. A library staff consisting of
  - 1) Two librarians
  - 2) An audio-visual specialist
  - 3) One secretary
  - 4) Lay personnel
- f. A nurse
- g. A psychologist
- h. A reading specialist

(5) Common facilities and personnel would be available to all houses equally in minor subject and special interest areas.

The above organization and staffing represents what a really good middle school ought to have in order to provide the services necessary to carry out its basic philosophy and function well.

Facilities. In order to implement the program, philosophy, and organization, the new middle school should provide for

(1) Three separate and distinct areas for each house and its own facilities as described above.

(2) A central area convenient to all "houses" for administration, guidance, and health services.

(3) Provisions in each house for at least one large group instruction area.

(4) One small theatre large enough to seat 300 to 400 students. (This theatre could double as the large group instruction area for *one* house.)

(5) The industrial arts, home economics, music, gymnasium, art, and health facilities located for convenient use by all houses.

(6) An instructional materials center (library, A-V, reading laboratory, etc.) located in the most advantageous and central position possible.

(7) Two smaller dining areas, kitchen between, which might also be used for large group instruction.

(8) A special education classroom located in one of the house units.

The facilities ought to be designed so that no one system is irrevocably locked in. They should be flexible to accommodate changes and modifications.

General Observations. The implementation of the program should be consistent with the aims expressed in the philosophy of the middle school and should strive for the following attributes:

(1) Close coordination and cooperation between teachers in developing programs tailored to the needs of the youngsters involved.

(2) Close, warm, and wholesome relationship between teacher and student.

(3) Flexibility to provide for thoughtful innovation.

(4) A new concept of evaluation designed to lessen anxiety about grades and increase self-esteem of the pupils.

(5) Individual programming for each youngster according to the level of his ability.

part **3**

Controversy and Problems

The junior high school has never lacked critics and problems, a situation which has become intensified in the past few years. It has been said that the junior high school is too academically oriented and, in constrast, that it has been too inclined toward a "play-pen" type of education. Interscholastic athletics in junior high school have furnished a rich source of strong feelings and debate, pro and con, as have the student activities which, in many junior high schools, are criticized as too sophisticated and as being carbon copies of high school activities.

The Carnegie Unit, with its rigid standards of time spent in class and credits granted, has caused difficulties in curriculum and scheduling since it became essential to schedule ninth grade classes and fit the seventh and eighth grade program around the ninth. There have been, and still are, widely separated positions concerning core, block of time, and departmentalization; grouping practices; homework; and the use of study halls. Staffing has long been an especially difficult problem for junior high schools since most teachers are prepared for elementary teaching or high school teaching, and a specific program for the preparation of junior high school teachers exists in only a few teacher training institutions.

Teacher Liability and the Law*

ALVIN W. HOWARD

Litigation of all kinds appears to be on the increase and school litigation is no exception. Teachers are not expected to know all of the many laws, regulations, and court decisions pertaining to the operation of the public schools. However, the very nature and responsibilities of the teaching profession, involving as it does care and supervision of children, make it desirable for teachers to be aware of what may or may not be areas of liability.

Guidelines of a somewhat definite nature exist for many of the more common situations met by teachers, although it is obviously impossible to anticipate all occurrences. Various court decisions have emphasized that the teacher must exercise "reasonable" caution, an "average amount of foresight," and provide "adequate supervision." Negligence is considered to exist if harm befalls as the result of an action which could have been foreseen by a prudent teacher, using ordinary care, in a reasonable effort to avoid trouble. The courts have, in various cases, stressed "prudence," "intent," "reasonableness," and caution in a situation in which danger is inherent.

Keep this clearly in mind: teachers may be sued for their negligence. School districts, because of the principle of governmental immunity, cannot be sued for damages in most states, but teachers can be and sometimes are defendants in suits for damages. Teachers are personally liable to pupils for injuries occurring because of teacher negligence. Negligence is often defined as lack of taking such care and precautions as a responsible person, one who is reasonably prudent, should take in any given situation. Children cannot be expected to behave as mature adults, the courts have held, and teachers, by reason of their training and experience, must expect that children will act in response to childish motives and must take necessary precautions accordingly.

Precautions considered necessary may vary with the age, maturity, and

*Reprinted from *The Clearing House*, 42 (March 1968), 411-413, by permission of the publisher and A. W. Howard, University of New Mexico.

intelligence of the pupils, and the question which must be decided, should the issue reach the courts, is that of determining what a reasonably prudent teacher should have done in this particular situation to forestall possible harm to any of his charges. The teacher is held to stand *in loco parentis*—that is, in the place of the parents as regards the pupil while he is under the jurisdiction of the school. This position gives the teacher the authority to control the pupils, but carries with it the responsibility to safeguard them.

In point of fact, it is indeed a curious matter that teachers who frequently have several years experience are thoughtless and careless in the presence of potentially dangerous circumstances. For example: the physical education teacher who permits students to work out on a trampoline with insufficient training or, worse yet, leaves the class to "free play" while he occupies himself in his office or the locker room; or the industrial arts teacher who allows students with little or no training to operate power tools without proper supervision; or the classroom teacher who is often late to class or who leaves before the end of the period while, in her absence, the students engage in throwing things, scuffling, and other kinds of horseplay —all of these teachers may be found guilty of negligence and liable.

The consequences of proven negligence can be disastrous for the teacher. In instances where negligence has been proven, the negligent one has been held liable for physical harm, results of fright, emotional disturbances, and shock to an injured party.

The teacher is expected to be present in all school situations although his presence alone is not enough—he must take such steps as are necessary to safeguard his charges. He must call attention to potential dangers and warn students to take those precautions as appear necessary under the circumstances.

A Wisconsin student was scraping wax off a floor in a storeroom containing chemicals. He knocked over a bottle of acid and was burned and the teacher found himself defendant in an action for damages. In deciding in favor of the teacher the state supreme court ruled:

> A teacher in the public schools is liable for injury to the pupils in his charge caused by his negligence or failure to use reasonable care . . . (but) it was found that the defendant did warn the plantiff . . . and the cork was in the bottle.[1]

An action for damages was brought against a California school district when a small boy, who was playing on a playground gate in the schoolyard, lost a finger when the gate was slammed by another child. The teacher, said the plaintiff, was negligent in not maintaining adequate supervision. The court ruled for the defendant teacher and stated:

[1]Grosso v Witteman, 226 Wis. 17, 62 N.W. (2d) 386 1954 Supreme Court of Wisconsin.

> The accident occurred while the boy was climbing the wall (although he had been told not to do so) . . . . There was no substantial evidence to show negligence on the part of the teacher and negligence could not be inferred from the mere fact that the accident occurred on school grounds while the teacher was not at the particular spot at that moment.[2]

A New York case involved an action for $45,000 damages against the Board of Education and the principal for injuries received by a child who was riding his bicycle across the school grounds. Since neither the school board nor the principal had made any rule or regulation prohibiting bicycle riding on that part of the school grounds, the court found for plaintiff and damages were awarded.[3] Obviously, specific warnings and precautions become more than desirable; they are essential.

Another example of the need for direct and specific precautions may be found in a California case where a pupil was injured in an explosion in a science class which was caused by student substitution of potassium chlorate for potassium nitrate in an experiment. The court ruled against defendant teacher saying:

> It is not unreasonable to assume that it is the duty of a teacher in chemistry, in the exercise of ordinary care, to instruct students regarding the selection, mingling, and use of dangerous ingredients . . . rather than merely hand them a textbook with general instructions to follow the text.[4]

Those warm and sunny spring days can create problems, too. A teacher who took his class out on the lawn failed to stop a student who repeatedly flipped a pocket knife into the grass. Eventually the knife ricocheted and struck another student in the eye. An action for damages was instituted against the teacher, and the court ruled that the teacher could reasonably be expected to know that the knife throwing was going on. He was negligent either in not noticing that this was happening or negligent in failing to stop it.[5]

Failure to provide adequate supervision or to permit violent play activities can lead to disaster. The court found against defendant school district in a Pennsylvania case in which a child drowned in a swimming pool operated by the district as a part of a summer recreation program. The district was held liable for

[2]Luna v Needles Elementary School District, 154 Cal. App. 803, 316 p (2d) 773 (1957) District Court of Appeal, Fourth District, Calif.

[3]Selleck v Board of Education, 94 N.Y.S. (2d) 318, 276 App Div 263, (1949).

[4]Mastrangelo v West Side Union High School District, 2 Cal. (2d) 540, 42 Pac, (2d) 634 (California 1935).

[5]Lilienthal v San Leandro Unified School District, 193 Ca. App. 2d 453, 293 P. 2d 889 (1956).

the negligence of its employees in that they failed to give adequate supervision and permitted rough and disorderly play in the water.[6]

A New York physical education teacher was found liable for negligence when he required two boys, both untrained, to box while he sat in the bleachers and watched. The court said:

> It is the duty of a teacher to exercise reasonable care to prevent injuries.... These young men should have been taught the principles of self defense, if indeed it was a reasonable thing to permit a slugging match of the kind which the testimony shows this contest was. The testimony indicates that the teacher failed in his duties and that he was negligent.[7]

Activities occurring in out-of-class circumstances are more likely to create situations conducive to pupil injury and to require increased teacher prudence. It is easier for matters to get out of hand since there is usually a feeling of excitement and also a somewhat relaxed control. Hazing is a rich source of trouble and, in spite of the incidence of injuries and even death, each year seems to see more tragedy caused by this horseplay. An initiation into a school athletic club, held on school property, sponsored by a faculty member, included as a part of the ceremony an electric shock which was given to each initiate. The power for this electric shock was provided by the regular lighting circuit with the result that one initiate died. The teacher was found liable for negligence.[8]

Field trips can provide a multiplicity of hazards for teachers and students. A common misconception of teachers is that a field trip permit slip signed by a parent or guardian relieves the teacher of responsibility. Such is not the case. The law does not permit a parent to sign away a child's rights nor discharge a teacher from providing adequate supervision. The field trip permit only indicates that the parent gives permission for his child to make the field trip.

Another practice fraught with hazard is that of teachers using their own automobiles to take students to such functions as musical programs and athletic events. The teacher can find himself liable for injuries to students who are riding in his automobile, and, even worse, the teacher who permits another teacher to use his vehicle for transporting students may be held liable for injuries suffered by passengers due to the negligence of the borrowing driver.[9] If the teacher takes payment for transporting pupils he is likely to discover that he has no protection from his own insurance in a "for hire" situation. While it is often difficult to refuse to take students to some activity, especially if no other way

[6]Morris v School District of Township of Mt. Lebanon, 393 Pa 633, 144 A. (2d) 737 (1958).

[7]Le Valley v Stanford, 272 App. Div. 183, 20 N.Y.S. (2d) 460. N.Y. (1947).

[8]De Gooyer *et al* v Harkness *et al,* 70 S.D. 26, 13 N.W., 2d (1944).

[9]Gorton v Doty, 57 Idaho 792, 69 Pac., 2d, 136 Idaho (1937).

seems to exist for them to get there, this is an instance when refusal is the best policy.

In any situation which results in pupil injury the teacher may find himself charged with negligence. The newer forms of personal liability insurance provide a degree of protection, but there is no substitute for adequate supervision, prudence, and the care which may be expected of a reasonable person.

Student Dress, School Policies, and the Law*

ALVIN W. HOWARD

What are the schools doing to regulate student appearance, particularly unorthodox hair styles and dress? Perhaps more importantly, what can school authorities legally do when confronted with the need to control student dress and grooming?

The need for adequate pupil control is so basic to the operation of free public schools that it is recognized by teachers, school officials, and legislators alike. But in various ways pupils—and often parents—have frequently tested and resisted school regulations. Current controversies center around tight short skirts for girls, Beatle haircuts for boys, and similar fads and extremes in grooming and dress. A recent "pop" song even complains that school boards "in the home of the brave, land of the free won't let kids be what they want to be."

Newspaper articles report many instances of pupil and parent unhappiness with school regulations pertaining to pupil appearance.

In Dallas, Texas, for example, when the school authorities sent three members of a professional music group home to trim their Beatle-length hair, the agent for a music company took the issue to court, saying that the long hair was written into the boys' contract and they absolutely would not trim it. The boys and two of their mothers agreed.

Lawyers for the 3 boys put 16 witnesses on the stand, ten of them teen-agers whose hair was as long as or longer than the rock and rollers and all of whom had been allowed to register in other schools without incident. Another witness, a "mod-look" clothier, testified that, "The long hair style is common among youth. . . . A full head of hair balances the look. . . . It's part of a new revolution in men's clothes."

*Reprinted from *The Clearing House* 41 (February 1967), 357-361, by permission of the publisher and A. W. Howard, University of New Mexico.

The principal who refused admittance to the three boys said the decision was made in the interest of orderly conduct in the school. The local school district has no written rule dealing with the length of boys' hair, but leaves it up to each principal to determine what length might be "disturbing to the morale of the school."

In Chadds Ford, Pennsylvania, a high school honor student, suspended from school because of his long hair, finished the 1965-1966 school year by telephone. Proceeding under a judge's orders, the local school board removed its suspension of the boy, a member of a local rock and roll group, and ruled that he could finish his classes by telephone, although he was banned from extracurricular activities and required to make up the physical education classes he missed.

In New York, the state education commissioner ruled that the school board does not have the power to compel pupils to wear a uniform or particular kind of clothing in school. This ruling was a victory for a high school girl who was sent home from school because she wore slacks to class.

Throughout the country the battle rages. In Pojoaque, New Mexico, eight boys were sent home "to crop their lengthy locks," and girls were warned that they would be sent home to change clothes if they wore short skirts to classes. The dean for discipline of a Bronx high school met returning students at the door. He was equipped with scissors and used them. The granny gown was banned from a Maryland high school, and the same action was taken by secondary principals in Roseburg, Oregon.

When confronted by such varied rulings, what position can school officials take in regard to this sticky problem? Are these extremes merely passing fads or do they truly represent a revolution in grooming and dress? Are regulations aimed at compelling conformity just for the sake of preserving what has been traditionally so, or is there good reason for rules establishing standards of dress and grooming? If there is good reason to establish such rules, what legal precedents, regulations, and actions are available to serve as guidelines for harassed educators?

Many administrators, seeking legal precedent for their regulations, have found support in rulings related to the larger problem of overall pupil conduct. Pupil behavior and the problems arising therefrom are affected by local school district regulations, court decisions and case law, state statutes, state constitutions, the Constitution of the United States, and English common law. Gauerke admonishes:

> Remember that the offense must militate against effective control by the school. This notion comes from the English common law and has a rich tradition behind it.[1]

[1]Warren E. Gauerke, *Legal and Ethical Responsibilities of School Personnel.* Englewood Cliffs, New Jersey: Prentice-Hall, Inc., 1959.

Many actions concerning pupil control which reach the courts state some violation of rights under certain amendments to the United States Constitution, usually the Fourteenth, which has had the most sweeping application to education by virtue of this sentence:

> No state shall make or enforce any law which shall abridge the privileges or immunities of citizens of the United States; nor shall any state deprive any person of life, liberty, or property, without due process of law; nor deny to any person within its jurisdiction the equal protection of laws.

In some states the legislators have passed statutes which contain express authority for the delegation of power to make rules and regulations.

In *Coggins v. Board of Education* (223 N.C. 263, 28 S.E. (2d) 527, 1944) the state Supreme Court held that

> When [such power] is so delegated it is peculiarly within the province of the administrative officers of the local unit to determine what things are detrimental to the successful management, good order, and discipline of the schools in their charge and the rules required to produce those conditions.

In the event that the local board of education has not yet established rules and regulations, superintendents, principals, and teachers may make and enforce such reasonable rules as are considered to be necessary—the key word being "reasonable." In determining whether school officials or teachers have the authority to enforce a particular rule or regulation governing the conduct of pupils, the courts apply the test of reasonableness. The reasonableness of a board rule will be determined by the facts in each particular case. The court does not substitute its own discretion for that of the board. The enforcement of a rule is not prohibited because it is unwise or inexpedient; it must clearly be unreasonable. Rules must be related to the purposes of education.

> There is a legal presumption in favor of the reasonableness of school rules. (*Bishop v. Houston Independent School District,* 119 Tex. 403, 29 S.W. (2d) 312, 1930)
>
> The rules must be reasonable and proper . . . for the government, good order, and efficiency of the schools—such as will best advance the pupils in their studies, tend to their education and mental improvement, and promote their interest and welfare. But the rules and regulations must relate to these objects. (*State* ex rel. *Bowe v. Board of Education,* 63 Wis. 234, 23 N.W. 102)
>
> The courts have consistently upheld the actions of school

> authorities in promulgating rules to insure proper conduct and decorum of the students designed for the good of the schools as a whole where such rules have not shown a clear abuse of power and discretion or a violation of law. (*McLean Independent School District v. Andrews,* 333 S.W. 886, Texas, 1960)

In the case of *McLean Independent School District v. Andrews,* a school board established a rule which prohibited the removal by students of their cars from the high school parking lot during the school day and required that all student cars be parked on the school parking lot. A girl pupil, to evade the rule, parked her car a block from school at the home of a friend and walked to school. At noon she walked back to her car and drove home to lunch. Upon her refusal to comply with the rule, she was suspended, and the suspension was upheld by the court.

Rules which are aimed at regulation of pupil dress have been supported by the courts. They must be in accord with the policies of the school, however, and as such dress, coupled with behavior, affects the satisfactory operation of the schools

> To a limited degree the regulation of school attire may be ventured by a principal without board approval. There must be apparent a proper purpose. The principal has the right to take measures against obviously grotesque affectations by pupils with respect to personal accoutrements. No statute nor board rule is needed to prevent pupils wearing rings, gay badges, or similar hoopla . . . ordinary amenities may be enforced in matters of attire.[2]

When the authority of school officials is challenged in the regulation of pupil dress, the question is: does such dress and behavior become so extreme as to affect the discipline of the school and interfere with efficient operation and management? Black leather jackets, motorcycle boots, and sideburns are recognized by police, parents, teachers, classmates, and generally the entire community as threats to the well-being of the pupils and the schools. Some cases are however more difficult to judge. The well-known action of *Puggsley v. Sellmeyer* (158 Ark. 247, 250 S.W. 538, 1923) concerned a school board ruling which prohibited the "wearing of transparent hosiery, low-necked dresses, or any style of clothing tending toward immodesty of dress, or the use of face paint or cosmetics."

This 1923 case involved an 18-year old girl who had been told to remove face makeup. She returned to school with talcum powder on her face. In upholding her suspension, the court said:

[2]Reynolds C. Seitz, *Law and the School Principal.* Cincinnati: W. H. Anderson Co., 1961.

> Courts have other and more important functions than hearing the complaints of disaffected pupils of the public schools against the rules and regulations promulgated by school boards for the government of the schools. . . The directors are in close and intimate touch with the affairs of their respective districts and know the conditions with which they have to deal. It will be remembered also that respect for constituted authority and obedience thereto is an essential lesson to quality one for the duties of citizenship, and that the schoolroom is an appropriate place to teach that lesson; so that the courts hesitate to substitute their will and judgment for that of the school boards which are delegated by law as the agencies to prescribe rules for the government of the public schools of the state. (*Puggsley v. Sellmeyer*)

The court further ruled that since local conditions might exist which would justify the adoption of a rule of this nature to aid in the discipline of the school, "We therefore decline to annul it, for we will not annul a rule of this kind unless a valid reason for doing so is made to appear; whereas, to uphold it, we are not required to find a valid reason for its promulgation."

The Supreme Court of North Dakota, in *Stromberg v. French* (60 N.D. 750, 236 N.W. 477, 1931), ruled that a board of education may forbid pupils to wear metal heel plates when they damaged the floor "more than is normal and when noise and confusion was such as to affect the conduct and discipline of the school." At the beginning of the school year (1930-31) the principal and superintendent noticed the damage to the floors and the noise and confusion caused by boys with metal heel plates on their shoes. Murray Stromberg was one of those boys who complied with the requests of the school officials to remove the heel plates. When his mother discovered that he had removed the metal plates, she told Murray to replace them. Upon his return to school, the boy was refused admission until the taps were removed. Murray's parents insisted that it was their prerogative to decide what apparel their child would wear to school. The school was, they said, arbitrary and unreasonable.

The court held that this was one of those instances where the paramount right of the parents must give way to the interests of the public generally and that "there was no hardship or indignity imposed upon the plaintiff or his son by it."

In answer to plaintiff's argument that if this rule were permitted to stand, others might be enacted which could give the school board absolute authority to prescribe wearing material for children in public schools, the court declared the "safeguard of reasonableness" would always be considered.

So far as Murray Stromberg was concerned, one may detect a certain amount of sympathy in the remarks of the court:

> Whatever Murray did was done without malice or wilful

> disregard of rules and only because of parental command... even so his conduct amounted to insubordination ... No rule or regulation could be enforced provided the parent instructed the pupil not to observe it.

A high school principal in Georgia refused to permit a girl to attend classes while she wore slacks. In the action that ensued, plaintiff's father maintained that the ban against the girl interfered with his rights guaranteed under provisions of the constitutions of the United States and Georgia. The Supreme Court of Georgia threw the case out on a technicality; the inference to be drawn was that they favored the defendant principal. (*Matheson v. Brady*, 202 Ga. 500, 43 S.E. (2d) 203, 1947.)

Many school officials, therefore, who establish rules and regulations for student dress and grooming believe that extremes in appearance go hand in hand with extremes in undesirable behavior. They feel that there is a positive correlation between appearance and conduct of students. Thus it does not matter if extremes in dress are merely passing fads or a true change in fashion if, *at this time*, such extremes disrupt school discipline.

Few cases involving pupil suspension for reasons of dress and grooming reach the courts, possibly because of parental or school district reluctance to push that far. Instead, many school authorities stress the reasonable approach—educating students, parents, and the community to the desirability of dressing and grooming in good taste. Emphasis is placed on the improved work habits, behavior, and overall conduct which result when students adopt a "dress-up" policy. Often written codes are established by student-faculty committees and student councils which set down rules for acceptable dress, grooming, and behavior. This educational and counseling approach would appear to be the most desirable in terms of maintaining good school and community relations.

Still, school authorities appear to be on fairly safe ground in establishing rules pertaining to student dress and behavior so long as such regulations relate to the efficient and orderly operation of the schools and if the rules meet the criterion of reasonableness. In the absence of statutes as specific guides, however, the schools may find themselves challenged as unreasonable, oppressive, arbitrary, or illegal. At the very least, written policies should be adopted by the local school board.

The courts have generally upheld rules which are reasonable and intended to implement the effective operation, conduct, and discipline of the schools. In the previously mentioned Dallas case, which was decided in September, 1966, the United States District judge ruled that high school principals have the authority to suspend boys whose hair is too long.

The courts will not substitute their discretion for that of the school board; and they support the assumption that the teacher acts in good faith. The courts have also sustained the contention that individual rights may, for the good of the enterprise, be sublimated to the whole.

> It is pertinent to state that none of our liberties are absolutes; all of them may be limited when the common good or common decency requires . . . Freedom in a democracy is a matter of character and tolerance. (*Satan Fraternity v. Board of Public Instruction for Dade County,* 156 Fla. 222,22 S. (2d) 892, 1945)
>
> Schools to be effective and fulfill the purposes for which they are intended must be operated in an orderly manner. Machinery to that end must be provided. Reasonable rules and regulations must be adopted. The right to attend school and claim the benefits afforded by the public school system is the right to attend subject to all lawful rules and regulations prescribed for the government thereof. If the opinion of the court or jury is to be substituted for the judgment and discretion of the board at the will of a disaffected pupil, the government of our schools will be seriously impaired, and the position of our school board in dealing with such cases will be most precarious. The court, therefore, will not consider whether such rules and regulations are wise and expedient. Nor will it interfere with the exercise of the sound discretion of school trustees in matters confided by law to their discretion. (*Coggin v. Board of Education of the City of Durham,* 223 N.C. 765, 28 S.E. (2d) 527, 1944)

While the problems of student dress and appearance are not easily eliminated, legal precedents can be found to support "reasonable" school regulations; and by careful education and counseling, the community can often come to accept such regulations without recourse to the courts.

Bibliography

1. Angle, Paul M., *By These Words,* Chicago: Rand McNally and Co., 1954.
2. Drury, Robert L., and Kenneth C. Ray, *Principles of School Law,* New York: Appleton Century-Crofts, 1965.
3. Edwards, Newton, *The Courts and the Public Schools,* Chicago: University of Chicago Press, 1955.
4. Fellman, David, *The Supreme Court and Education*, New York: Teachers College, Columbia University, 1960.
5. Flowers, Anne, and Edward C. Bolmeier, *Law and Pupil Control,* Cincinnati: W. H. Anderson Co., 1964.

6. Garber, L., and N. Edwards, *School Law Case Book Series,* Numbers 1, and 4, Danville, Illinois: Interstate Publishers and Printers, 1962-1965.
7. Gauerke, Warren E., *Legal and Ethical Responsibilities of School Personnel,* Englewood Cliffs, New Jersey: Prentice-Hall, Inc., 1959.
8. Hamilton, Robert R., and E. E. Reutter, Jr., *Legal Aspects of School Board Operation,* New York: Bureau of Publications, Columbia University, 1958.
9. National Education Research Division, *High Spots in State School Legislation, January 1-August 1, 1965,* Washington, D.C.: NEA, 1965.
10. *Proposed Revision of the Education Law,* Report of the Law Revision Committee to the Legislative Interim Committee on Education, Salem, Oregon, April, 1964.
11. Remmlein, Madaline K., *School Law,* New York: McGraw-Hill Book Co., Inc., 1950.
12. Seitz, Reynolds C., *Law and the School Principal,* Cincinnati: W. H. Anderson Co., 1961.

Wild Hairdos and Eccentric Clothes Cause Publicity but Few Problems*

MARILYN H. CUTLER

Student clothing and grooming fads cause publicity but few headaches for schoolmen, a national survey by *Nation's Schools* shows.

Most districts have dress codes that spell out what is forbidden, and most students stick to the rules, the survey found.

"Our dress regulations are all we need to control problem areas, especially in type of dress for girls and haircuts for boys," emphasized Porter I. Leach, vice-principal at Santa Monica, Calif. When students do get out of line in Leach's school, they run the risk of suspension.

But in Chicago, where "we go through this every year," Assistant Supt. David Heffernan indicated that the city's districts don't have a written policy. "Instead," he said, "principals, who must settle these problems, have a tacit agreement that's pretty specific, such as number of inches dresses should be from the floor or where necklines should come."

Chicago has its headaches with parents who become vexed when a principal restricts their child's grooming or clothing. Parents take their side of the story to the newspapers first. "Then it's a game where the reporters try to outwit me in getting to the principal first so they can pick up all the goofy statements and pictures," Heffernan said. "When they win," he added, "they call me and say, 'Ha, Ha,–I won!' "

Oklahoma City doesn't have a formal code either, and officials there say this is why they don't have problems. Bill Lillard, director of secondary education, explained: "Our interpretation is that if a pupil's appearance detracts from the general instructional atmosphere, or creates a disturbance, he's inappropriately dressed . . . I believe this flexibility is desirable. A pupil or group

*Reprinted with permission from *Nation's Schools*, 75 (April 1965), 86, 88.

of pupils cannot become martyrs to a specific fad. I have found," Lillard noted, "that if something is not specifically prohibited, the students or the rebels feel less identified with the fad."

Sun Valley High, Chester, Pa., operates under a code and it's considered a success because the students themselves drew it up. Although Sun Valley "very rarely" has "any real problems," it does have a prescribed procedure when rarities do show up at school.

The pupil is taken out of class, sent to the principal's office, and told either to borrow the right clothing from a fellow student or call a parent to bring it to school. Punishment consists of detention amounting to double the classtime he missed while arranging to get the proper attire.

With the Beatle craze in full swing, bushy haircuts that give boys a sheep dog look have stirred some superintendents to suspend students who follow the fad.

When a high school freshman at Westbrook, Conn., sported Beatlelike bangs in class, it took the state commissioner of education to straighten things out. After the boy was suspended, the commissioner advised the superintendent to invoke the state's compulsory education law to get him back in school (the boy was 15 and the law compels anyone under age 16 to attend school). Even the school board figured in the fuss when it passed a resolution ordering the boy back.

Other hair fads that have nettled superintendents enough to take immediate action:

—At Fredericksburg, Va., a boy bleached his hair and was barred from school under a policy drawn up earlier when boys dyed their hair green.

—At Jacksonville, Fla., a junior high principal took matters into his own hands and personally gave a boy with unruly locks a haircut.

—In Philadelphia, a school nurse took the bristle side of a hairbrush to girls who wore extreme hairdos.

"Our policy is specific where possible and general where necessary," said George F. Kane, guidance counselor at Interboro Junior High, Prospect Park, Pa. "We feel we have the situation well in hand," Kane said confidently, "although," he added, "the battle for good taste is a continuing one, and there always will be a few students who choose to express their defiance in terms of dress or make-up."

Interboro came to grips with girls' high, teased hairdos by going to the professionals for help. An all-girl assembly, conducted by a local school that trains professional hairdressers, showed the latest hair styles for school by demonstrating on several students. "We considered it a success," Kane commented, "and to get our message across to parents, we published 'before and after' photos of the girls in the local paper."

Officials at Interboro have dubbed Wednesday "Dress Up Day." This is assembly day and students are required to spruce up: Girls wear "Sunday best," boys wear coats and ties.

At nearby Clifton Heights, Pa., every day is shirt and tie day for junior and senior high boys. "In fact," observed John J. Kushma, supervising principal, "dress coats seem to be the latest style." Girls have followed the lead and improved their dress and grooming standards, according to Kushma.

"Boys and girls don't use week-day manners when they wear their Sunday clothes."

How Brookhaven Faces Fads

At Brookhaven (Pa.) Junior High, the dress code was drawn up through the joint effort of the student council, faculty, P.T.A., parents and school officials—and is typical of codes surveyed. Fads it helped discourage within the past year include: boys wearing red shoes, short trousers, dickeys, black turtle-neck T shirts under white shirts, and cleats on shoes; girls wearing extremely short skirts, bouffant hairdos, and knee-high boots.

Although Brookhaven's principal or assistant principal takes charge when a student doesn't follow the rules, teachers have their say through a faculty code of dress committee that assists the principal. Code below.

GIRLS

No hair clips or hair curlers are to be worn, coming to or during school. Hair must be neatly combed and not worn in extreme styles. Excessive teasing is not permitted.

Skirts and dresses must reach at least the middle of the knee. Extremely tight skirts are prohibited. No perk skirts or sheer blouses are permitted. All blouses must be tucked in, with the exception of over-blouses.

Except in physical education classes, sneakers are not permitted. Cleats may not be worn on shoes. Stockings or socks must always be worn.

Make-up is to be worn in strict moderation. Eye make-up is not permitted.

BOYS

No extremely tapered or tight pants. No dungarees are permitted. Belts must be worn with pants that provide belt loops. No suspenders may be worn.

Shirts may not be worn outside of trousers; all shirts must be tucked in. Sports shirts and dress shirts are the proper apparel. No T shirts, sweat shirts, or turtle necks are to be worn. Shirts are to be completely buttoned, excluding the top button.

Regulations on shoes: no cleats are permitted and sneakers are to be worn only in gym periods.

Hair is to be cut in conventional styles and must be combed back from the forehead.

Regulating Student Dress*

DOROTHY WALESKI

In recent months, groups of teen-agers in schools in all parts of the country seem to be making a dedicated effort to test just how far they can carry extremes of dressing and grooming. The attention they have attracted has revived an ancient debate on the question of what the schools ought to do about controlling student appearance.

Concern and indignation over Beatle haircuts; tight, hip-slung skirts on girls and tight, hip-slung trousers on boys; black leather jackets on students of both sexes; and similar teen-age fads have resulted in a number of schools' including codes for student dress in their written rules and regulations.

Is the way students look any concern of the schools? If so, are written codes the best means of ensuring proper school attire? Opinions differ on both questions.

The battle rages, but the contenders are not aligned into such neatly opposed teams as youth versus age or school personnel versus parents. Siding with the youths who are pressing their right to array themselves as they please are educators, parents, and fellow students; lined up against them are other educators, parents, and students.

The press has made a pun fest of the struggle, using such terms as "hairsplitting," "a dressing down," "unkindest cut," and "long and short of it." "School Slacks Issue Skirted," quipped a headline in the Washington, D.C., *Evening Star*. *Senior Scholastic* presented the various points of view on wayout hairdos under the title, "Splitting Hairs over Moptops or: How Lunatic is the Fringe?"

Boys' long hair and girls' short skirts are the extremes that have received the most publicity. North and South, East and West, cameras have clicked as long-haired boys and short-skirted girls have been turned away from a

*Reprinted from *The NEA Journal* 55 (April 1966), 12-14, by permission of the publisher.

schoolhouse door or as a principal or teacher, clippers in hand, has turned barber.

Parents here and there have been outspoken in defense of what they consider to be their children's civil liberties, and have referred to "American freedom" to express individuality in school clothes and hairdos. A father in Virginia complained to county police that his fourteen-year-old son had suffered an emotional shock when a teacher cut the boy's blond bangs.

Some writers have interpreted educators' demands for conformity in appearance as expressing insistence upon conformity in thought. Russell Baker, writing in the *New York Times,* says, "Schools should be less concerned with unorthodox hair lengths and more concerned with why they are turning out so many orthodox minds willing to submit to the corporate haircut."

In the *Saturday Evening Post,* Bruce Jay Friedman argues, "People should keep their hands out of a boy's hair, since when he is in his twenties he is going to get it cut off anyway by the Army . . . So why not give him a few years to look like a person and not a cipher?"

Speaking for themselves, the teen-agers who think their appearance is their own affair have asked. "Do you have to be bald for an education?" Some have pointed out seeming inconsistencies in their adversaries' arguments. "If they have all these complaints about dresses being too short or too tight," asks one girl, "why should they complain about granny gowns? They're loose and they come down to the ankles."

Newsweek quoted one lad who said of his long hair, "It may be just an immature phase I'm going through, but it's up to me to change that phase."

A New York student, Joyce Wadler, writing in *Seventeen,* described high school dress codes as "irrelevant, immaterial, and insulting."

A high school girl in Indiana who participated in a Scholastic Magazines poll said, "I believe a teen-ager; or anyone else, will act basically the same no matter what he has on. It is not the clothes, but the person inside those clothes, that matters."

Last fall, a listing of the top fifty records included a song whose lyrics protested that school boards in the home of the brave, land of the free should let kids be what they want to be.

It must be remembered that the current brouhaha involves only a small proportion of this country's students and that many of them are no more serious than one girl who explained away her high hemline by saying that she had low knees.

Educators agree that the appearance of the over-whelming majority is well within the limits of good taste. In fact, in many of the schools where written codes exist, students have participated in drawing them up and help to enforce them.

At North Quincy High School, Quincy, Massachusetts, for instance, the dress code was suggested and formulated by the student council. At John Muir High School in Pasadena, California, the "Conduct Code," set up by the boys' and girls' leagues at the school, incorporates state, county, and school regulations. The section dealing with school attire reiterates the substance of the Pasadena City Schools' policy on campus clothing for junior and senior high school students.

The John Muir code is detailed. In addition to demanding personal cleanliness and neatness of dress, it specifies what kinds of clothes are to be worn to school and lists items of clothing and styles of dress which are prohibited.

Educators who feel that the problem of student appearance falls within their domain employ varying methods of coping with it.

John A. Venable, principal of John Muir High, is one of many school officials who believe that how a student looks when he is at school is important, and that the best way to be sure he will look right is to have rules and regulations about dress and grooming. He says of his school's "Conduct Code":

> I sincerely believe that there is a positive correlation between the dress and conduct of our students. Our experience with "dress down days" (long since discontinued) and "dress-up days" is positive proof. Because we—administrators, faculty, and student body—believe in the effect of dress on student behavior, students appearing in assemblies dress for the occasion. Our athletic teams go to and from contests in suits, shirts, and ties.
>
> We have established at John Muir High School an enviable reputation for conduct, dress, and good sportsmanship and we are convinced that our dress regulations have played an important part.

Experience with "dress-up days" led to a dress code at Southeast Junior High School in Salt Lake City. According to Gloria Merback, a counselor there, Friday, when the students dressed up for weekly dances, was the teachers' favorite day of the week, because discipline was so much better than on the other days. Reasoning that if dress worked magic of Friday, it might well work the same charm on the other days of the week, the administration set up a "Dress Up for School Code." The code prohibits blue jeans, tennis shoes, shirttails worn outside, and hair hanging over the eyes.

Mrs. Merback says that the charm does work on a daily basis. Teachers notice an improvement in behavior and work habits. The code has been well accepted. Although a few students have rebelled, Mrs. Merback says they often are the same students who rebel against any restrictions. Most of the students enjoy dressing up for school, and the PTA has been 100 percent in favor of the code.

Appropriateness is a criterion for dress at Richard Montgomery High School in Rockville, Maryland. The principal, William W. Miles, regards school as the young people's place of business and believes that, as such, it demands appropriate dress. He considers any attire to be out of place at school if it disrupts a class or causes groups of students to congregate in the halls.

Mr. Miles banned the granny gown from his school not because he had any objections to the enveloping garment per se, but on the grounds that it is inappropriate school garb.

The secondary school principals of Tucson, Arizona, take a more flexible stand on such things as boys' haircuts. According to one of them, they feel that adults "should realize that some of the outlandish hairdos on boys and young men are attention getters. The fad will pass. If it were not this, it would be something else." Tucson principals insist upon a change of hair styling only if the way a boy's hair is cut seems to be a contributing factor to unsatisfactory citizenship.

Whitman-Hanson Regional High School in Whitman, Massachusetts, takes an active approach to solving dress problems. There, if a girl comes to school wearing a skirt shorter than the approved mid-knee length, she must go to the home economics class and lengthen it. After school, she makes up the class she missed while letting down her hem.

Paul M. Mitchum, assistant superientendent in charge of instruction in the public schools of Des Moines, sees the problem in another light. He says, "This problem, like most problems, will yield most effectively to an educational approach rather than to pitched battles between home and school."

Following this policy, the Des Moines schools make matters of dress and good taste the subject of class discussions and assemblies, and even include fashion departments in the school newspapers.

The educational approach is favored in Tucson, too, where girls are instructed in matters of dress, makeup, and hair styles at special assemblies for girls. Andy Tolson, principal of Tucson High School, reports that the assemblies, which usually feature student models demonstrating "right" and "wrong" ways, have been successful.

Long Beach, California, like nearby Pasadena, regulates student dress by a written list of specifics. Long Beach differs from most school systems, however, in that it deals with parents first instead of students in cases where the rules are not observed. Vernon A. Hinze, assistant superintendent, explains:

> We believe there is nothing to be gained and much to be lost in taking a quick hard and fast stand in cases of student defiance of our rules, defiance which could lead to widespread publicity and a knock-down public battle involving the rights of the individual. So often these very youngsters who dress in an outlandish fashion and

> whose parents do not "draw the line" are the attention seekers who are pleased with the notoriety that publicity brings.

So far, Long Beach has successfully solved its difficult cases by "counseling reasonableness" with the parents until they assist in enforcing the dress rules laid down by the schools.

Once again, opinions differ. Mr. Mitchum of Des Moines states the problem this way: A principal who sends a girl home for wearing slacks runs considerable risk of having the mother appear in slacks for a parental conference. Should the mother then be sent home for more suitable apparel?

Ceremonies of Humiliation in School*

EDGAR Z. FRIEDENBERG

One afternoon last March, I received a long-distance call from the Unitarian minister—who is also president of the local chapter of the American Civil Liberties Union—in a city I shall call Birchfield. He wanted me to help him defend the rights of one of the young members of his congregation at a school board hearing. This boy, whom I shall call Shaun Anderson, had been suspended from high school since the beginning of the school year last fall and had been forced to go to a private school.

Shaun's case is of a kind that has, unfortunately, become common-place. Shaun Anderson is oddly cast in the role of miscreant. His sole claim to it rests on a single action last summer after he graduated from intermediate school. He grew a beard. As beards go, his cannot be said to be notable—both his father and his elder brother have more luxuriant beards. But it was enough to lead the school board of Birchfield to bar him from high school.

The board based its position on the familiar premises of egalitarian bureaucracy: There had to be rules, and if they made an exception for Shaun where would they draw the line the next time? The county counsel argued that a beard created an atmosphere inimical to education, and several high-school principals declared that beards had become a symbol of adolescent resistance to schooling. One courageous teacher challenged his own principal by pointing out that the anxieties and resentments caused by Shaun's exclusion—he was an honor student with no previous disciplinary record—had created an atmosphere inimical indeed to learning, and one that would surely become much worse if Shaun capitulated. But after an afternoon of acrimony, the board rejected the Andersons' plea to reinstate Shaun.

It is easy to dismiss a controversy over a 15-year-old's beard as trivial. I

*Reprinted from *Education Digest* 81 (November 1966), 28-32, and *This Magazine Is About Schools* 1 (August 1966), 9-18, by permission of the publishers and Edgar Z. Friedenberg, State University of New York at Buffalo.

wish, therefore, to make it very clear that the controversy is not over Shaun's beard, but over his and other adolescents' right to a reasonable degree of respect, privacy, and freedom to establish their own tastes and govern their own actions in areas where they interfere with no one. It seems to me clear that the regulation of hair styles is an invasion of privacy difficult to justify on educational grounds.

Petty Regulations Damaging

The triviality of the regulation itself is also, I fear, illusory. Trivial regulation is more damaging to one's sense of one's own dignity and to the belief, essential to any democracy, that one does have inalienable rights, than gross regulation is. The real function of petty regulations like these is to convince youth that it has no rights at all that anybody is *obligated* to respect, even trivial ones. And this, after all, is what many—I think most—American adults believe. To confirm this, one need only note the widespread and intense hostility against youths who protest against the war in Vietnam in any public way. Those who condemn them seem honestly to feel that it is *impertinent* of the young to presume to criticize the institutions and policies that are costing them their freedom and, in thousands of cases, their lives.

Their critics seldom seem to respect the right of the young to act on their political opinions at all. They ask, instead, "What makes them so rebellious?" implying that the answer must be either Communism or psychopathology. It would be more sensible, under the circumstances, to ask why there are still so few, and what took them so long.

The beard and haircut cases suggest an answer to this question, too. Only those cases in which the parents have stood staunchly behind their sons, at considerable personal cost, have received any public attention at all. But for each of these, there have been countless others in which the parents either supported the school, or "finked out" as soon as the boy was suspended because they were afraid of controversy, or didn't want him to have a bad record, or fail to get into college, or something of the sort.

These are serious considerations, and it would be presumptuous of me to tell parents that they invariably ought to fight; it depends on their resources, and on what the student really wants. My impression of Shaun Anderson, to be sure, was that the whole episode had so far done him more good than harm. Both he and his parents behaved with quiet dignity and humor; and his education must surely have profited from the lessons he has been receiving in his intense and protracted course in civics. His family life has taught him that there really are civil liberties; and the school and its board have taught him how little value is actually placed on these in a mass society, despite its democratic pretensions.

Public Opinion

Or, indeed, *because* of those pretensions. The argument that the chairman of the school board introduced, and clearly regarded as decisive, was that the board's regulation of dress and hair styles evidently had public support, for no other parent had ever complained and public sentiment obviously favored keeping youth on a tight rein.

This argument has two features that are of special concern. The first of these is simply that the chairman's assessment of public opinion is certainly correct. In Birchfield, and everywhere else in America that I know of, public opinion would indeed be against the Andersons. It is against the defense of civil liberty generally. Countless studies of public opinion have demonstrated that the first 10 amendments to the Constitution—the Bill of Rights—could hardly be ratified if they had to be introduced today.

The second point I wish to make is that the chairman of the school board, precisely by his reliance on public opinion as the basis on which to validate his policy, demonstrated that he did not respect the privacy and autonomy of the children in his schools as civil liberties. For civil liberties are exactly those inalienable rights which are placed, without any qualification, *beyond the scope of public opinion.* There are areas of personal inviolability in which no American may be subjected by his fellow citizens to legal or official constraint, however strongly they may feel or however completely they may agree.

No American? Not quite, even yet. The Civil Rights Act destroyed all but one of the last surviving legal categories of discrimination. But youth remains a subject minority denied the legally defensible rights now provided to all other Americans—over 21. We remain unaware of these special disabilities of youth because we have been taught to regard them as special services to the immature for which you ought to be grateful. But I suspect there are many parents—and I know there are many youngsters—who, when they think what the school that serves them is really like, recognize that the compulsory attendance law is a very serious restriction.

The compulsory school attendance law gives school regulations the force of law. The quality and spirit of those regulations becomes, therefore, a matter of crucial concern to civil liberty; the liberties involved may seem trivial, but they are all an adolescent has left of the normal supply.

The devotion of the schools to docility has become a major source of irony. If our schools had developed a tradition of respect for the persons and the character of their students, those who became critical could have done so while remaining civil; for their dissent would not have turned the social system against them and alienated them from it. Our new protesters, accordingly, are not always quite as civil as either their disobedience or their rights—both of which, perhaps, were withheld much too long. In this respect, Birchfield has so far been more fortunate, I should say, than any community deserves to be in which just growing a beard can make you an outlaw.

Interscholastic Competition: Is Junior High Too Soon?*

VERNON FRYKLUND

Many professional educators, administrators, coaches, and others believe that there should be no program of interscholastic athletics in junior high schools, while others believe this is unrealistic since there are many forms of interscholastic competition about which there can be no objection. The expressed attitudes of junior high school principals in a study conducted by Ellsworth Tomkins and Virginia Roe in 1958 clearly indicate the controversial nature of this type of program.

According to this study of junior high school principals, 85 percent of the junior high schools studied have a program of interscholastic athletics. Seventy-eight percent of the principals were in favor of such a program, and 15 percent opposed it. Eighty percent of the junior high schools in this study have not changed their policy on interscholastic athletics since 1950. Of the 20 percent who are contemplating a change in policy, the large majority are planning to expand the program now in force.

It is evident from these figures that we do have a program of interscholastic athletics in the junior high school. The principals favor such a program and are not contemplating a change, and, therefore, we should attempt to arrive at some definite conclusions concerning the best possible objectives and outcomes a program of this kind can make to meet the educational needs of all junior high school students.

Many times judgment is passed on controversial phases of any educational program without observing both sides of an issue. With this thought in mind, the author attempted to review issues, pro and con, that have been written on the subject, and to attempt to determine what is being done in schools. This was

*Reprinted from *The Minnesota Journal of Education,* 46 (March 1966), 13-14, by permission of the publisher and Vernon Fryklund, Lincoln Junior High School, Hibbling, Minnesota.

done in a research paper presented to the faculty of the Graduate School of the U of M.

Authorities indicate that evidence can be found to support or oppose any phase of the program—physical, emotional, or social—as harmful or beneficial. Evidence in any of these aspects seems to be inconclusive and fragmentary at best.

There are certain basic ideas that leaders in this area agree on:

- Schools should increase opportunities for participation in a broad program of physical education activities, intramural athletics, and interscholastic competition for all students.
- Children can profit educationally as well as physically from this type of activity.
- Adequate supervision and control is essential for the successful operation of such activities.
- Instruction should be given to all pupils in physical education activities of all types.

Authorities recommend that junior high schools support a well-rounded program of athletic competition. Emphasis on winning should be lessened, and an attempt should be made to keep the school program—academic, social and athletic—in balance.

The primary purpose of the author's study was to gather information from selected junior high schools that would show what kinds of interscholastic athletic competition were offered. Personal interviews were used, and twelve main areas of comparison served as a basis to interpret the information gathered. These comparisons were: types of sports offered in the program, eligibility rules, finances, physical examinations, insurance, awards, varsity participation by junior high school students, transportation, injuries, intramural athletics, significant changes in the program, and personal opinions about the program in operation.

All the schools studied had some sort of interscholastic athletic program. Track, basketball, swimming, and football were the most popular activities. All the schools have eligibility requirements to be met before participation is allowed with the majority of the schools following the Minnesota State High School League (MSHL) requirements. A majority of the programs studied are financed by board of education funds.

In all schools, physical examinations are required of all boys before participation is allowed in any sport, and the majority of the schools studied require that the students be covered by some type of insurance protection. The most popular type of insurance was the plan sponsored by the MSHL. More than 90 percent of the schools reported that junior high school students were participants on varsity teams in various sports, and the majority reported that the school district provided transportation for practices and games.

Some form of intramural athletics program was offered in more than 80 percent of the schools. Eighty percent indicated that no change had been made recently.

The respondents indicated that the program of interscholastic athletics had a high degree of value in the following areas: promoting good citizenship, promoting school spirit, helping students build better character, helping students expand social adjustment, helping to promote physical fitness, increasing the holding power of the school, creating good attitudes of competition. They felt that the program helped, to an average degree, to develop pupils' leadership qualities.

The consensus was that the following areas were influenced to a low degree by this program: undesirable rivalry, unsatisfactory attitudes, excessive costs, emphasis on awards and winning, interference with the smooth operation of the school program, detracting from scholastic improvement, taking up too much time and effort, and tendencies to over-excite and over-strain youth of this age group. In general, the opinions of those reporting indicated that the values of interscholastic athletics were great enough to outweigh the disadvantages.

Each of the respondents was asked the following question, "Would you care to react personally as to your opinion of junior high school interscholastic athletics?" In all cases, the respondents did express personal feelings and the statements followed certain patterns. Seventy-eight percent of the respondents indicated that they were in favor of this program personally. Of those who indicated that they were not in favor, some of the comments were;

- *This program should be regulated by the MSHL and should be kept on an intramural basis.*
- *As long as other schools are allowed to compete interscholastically, we feel compelled to do likewise.*
- *I believe that the number participating in the interscholastic program is too low to warrant it over an intramural program.*
- *We should spend more time on kinds of sports that can be carried on into later adult life.*
- *We as adults and fans put too much emphasis on winning. This is not the right effect on the attitudes of students of this age group. The physical and mental strain is too high.*
- *I personally believe that a good intramural program will develop skills just as well as an interscholastic program.*

Those respondents who were in favor expressed opinions that followed certain patterns.

- *I feel that it will help a coach to do some excellent guidance work.*
- *Physically, there is less chance of injury under a well-supervised program of this sort than under sand-lot conditions.*

• *I feel that this program will interest many boys into remaining in school after they get into senior high school.*

• *More athletics, less delinquency.*

• *This program has helped the junior high school spirit and has made these students more aware of scholarship and citizenship.*

• *De-emphasize the idea of winning, but rather develop the abilities of as many boys as possible.*

• *It is a good thing as far as developing the fundamentals of the sport, building correct attitudes, learning how to win and lose graciously.*

• *I would like to see it expanded so that more students could participate. These students that participate in the athletic program tend to participate in other activities also. Development of leadership is one of the strong points of this program.*

• *I would like to see more participation because students do not receive enough physical activity in physical education because of limited facilities.*

• *The coach is a source of inspiration to the boys. This program has a place in the school to the point where administrators and coaches use good judgment as to how much competition there should be and by whom.*

• *There should be no plants or factories to turn out athletic stars at this level. We live in a society based on competition, therefore we should offer students at this level some controlled ideas of the proper ways to win and lose.*

From the findings of the study, and the related literature that was revised, certain conclusions can be drawn.

1. The program of interscholastic athletics should be closely controlled and supervised.
2. Shorter schedules, shorter periods of play, greater emphasis on fundamentals, and close supervision of games are some of the aspects which should be stressed in the operation of the program.
3. A program of intramural athletics should be stressed to allow more to participate.
4. More leisure time activities should be stressed.
5. Undue emphasis on winning should be removed and more boys should be allowed to participate in the interscholastic program.
6. Factors of child development and education should be reviewed very carefully before passing judgment of any phase of the program.
7. The guidance phase of the program is potentially very good.
8. There is less chance of personal injury in a program of this type where supervision and proper equipment are adequate than in other types of community- or other agency-sponsored programs.
9. This program can be of help in developing good citizenship, leadership qualities, good attitudes among students, physical fitness, and school spirit.

10. Costs of operating an adequate program of interscholastic athletics in the junior high school are not excessive.

11. The operation of the interscholastic athletics program should not interfere with the smooth operation of the schools' program in general. There should be a balance between the academic, social, and athletic phases of the curriculum.

12. More athletics activities in which the girls of the junior high can participate should be added to the athletic program of the junior high schools.

13. Care should be taken when selecting uniforms and equipment for use in this program. Ill-fitting and inadequate equipment or uniforms may lead to serious injury.

14. Eligibility rules which must be met before participation is allowed should be formulated by action of state, conference or local agencies if this program is to continue.

15. Care should be taken so as not to over-excite and over-strain youth of this age group.

16. The interscholastic athletic program for boys in the junior high school should supplement rather than serve as a substitute for an adequate physical education and intramural program for all students.

17. The welfare of the individual boy should be the basic criterion upon which it is determined whether the boy should participate in this program.

18. The interscholastic athletic program in the junior high school provides excellent opportunities for participants to release excess energy; to practice self discipline; to teach good work habits and sound health practices, self-control, loyalty, friendly rivalry, fair play, and good sportsmanship.

Competitive Athletics Yield Many Benefits to the Participant*

WALLACE L. JONES, JR.

America has long been a sports-loving nation; therefore, it is natural for the youth of this nation to develop enthusiasm for sports at a very early age. Coaches and physical education teachers probably do a better and more thorough job of detecting youngsters with ability in athletics than regular classroom teachers do for children of other exceptional abilities. This fact might be explained because of the emphasis placed on athletics at different levels in the school program. Whether this emphasis is good or not is a debatable point, particularly at the elementary level. The point I should like to make is that an athletic program can offer all children something of value, from those who have just a passing interest to those individuals who dream of the time when they will make the varsity team.

There are a number of reasons for encouraging children to improve their physical skills. Psychologists tell us that self-confidence is essential to the healthy development of personality. One of the best ways to learn to meet problems and overcome obstacles encountered in life is through competing with others on the athletic field. Coach Woody Hayes, successful mentor of Ohio State University, recently stated at the National Football Clinic, "The competition and the will to win that our kids learn on a football field are of utmost importance throughout their entire lives. On the football field the kids learn how to live up to their potential. They learn how to sacrifice some of their ego for the good of the team. They learn how to be leaders."

Having coached for a number of years, I know from firsthand experience that those children who are successful in physical activity usually develop self-confidence, leadership experience, and a strong sense of cooperation. On the

*Reprinted from *The Clearing House* 37 (March 1963) 407-410, by permission of the publisher and Wallace L. Jones, Jr., State Dept. of Education, Baton Rouge, Louisiana.

athletic field, the youngster learns many lessons that most of us fail to learn throughout our lifetimes. He is taught to respect rules and to think in terms of what is best not for himself but for the team. He is taught not only the importance of winning but also the art of losing gracefully. He is taught to respect the ability of his opponent and not to underestimate him. He must learn to accept and appreciate criticism offered constructively by his coaches, teachers, and teammates. He learns that certain decisions he has to make not only affect him personally but also affect his teammates. He learns that even though he is "down," he must never stop trying. He is encouraged through proper training to take care of his body, thus eliminating such bad habits as smoking, drinking, staying out late, and the like. Athletics offer youngsters the opportunity of making many friendships which, conceivably, might not have been otherwise possible, friendships that remain long and lasting. In fact, poor development of athletic skills or a lack of athletic skills or a lack of interest in sports may be a serious handicap to some children. Since most children are interested in sports and attempt to participate, the child who either cannot or will not may be ostracized from the group.

In the last several years there seems to have developed a negative attitude toward participation by youngsters in physical activities, particularly by adolescents and by older children in high school. This negative attitude toward participation may have been caused by a number of reasons. There seems to be a tendency for the modern day youth to be content with being a spectator and watching others play. The present younger generation possibly has fallen victim to the easy-living type of environment most Americans seem to enjoy these days. Johnny either drives or is driven to a school that is in easy walking distance from home. He sits at his desk practically the entire day. When school is over, he either joyrides or returns home and enjoys unlimited hours of television or telephoning in an air-conditioned room usually from a prone position. While this may seem to be an exaggerated example, it is not too far from the truth.

The fact that too many young Americans are not getting enough and the right kinds of physical exercise led to the development of President Kennedy's physical fitness program. A series of basic exercises were given to a sampling of American schoolchildren throughout the country to determine the physical fitness of American youth. When the results showed that only a small percentage of children could pass these tests, certain physical education experts became alarmed and brought this information to the attention of the President.

I, for one, should like to see more youngsters participating in the schools' athletic programs. With the many modern conveniences Americans enjoy today, the use of leisure time of youngsters is cause for concern. This is particularly true for boys. In the past, some of our schools had a tendency to overemphasize the value of winning in athletics and, in so doing, reduced the number of youngsters who would participate. Such overemphasis restricted those who would participate in the athletic program to those individuals who were highly skilled in a particular sport. While winning is very important, all youngsters should have an opportunity to "Make the team," or we will discover one day that there will not be enough youngsters interested in sports to make up a team. Good administrators and coaches can certainly keep the game in its proper perspective and not let it become a monster controlled by zealous parents, Dad's clubs, and alumni.

Realistically, an athletic program has become a necessary and integral part of the school program. Financially, it helps to keep the athletic as well as other programs going in the schools. It has become the chief money-provider in many schools. It remains the greatest promoter of school spirit and interest.

Youngsters who are taking part in athletics in a well-supervised program are less likely to become involved in any sort of trouble. Their afterschool time and energy are being used constructively in an enjoyable, healthy atmosphere. While this point may be debatable, I doubt if there are many athletes who are vandals, juvenile delinquents, or potential delinquents. In fact, I am convinced that if more youths were drawn into athletic programs, delinquency would not be so great a problem as it is today. Since it is natural for children to be extremely interested in sports, it is equally natural for children to want to compete against one another. When competition is controlled and not allowed to get out of hand, it is not only desirable but beneficial to youngsters. Somewhere along the line, someone sold us a bill of goods that competition was harmful to youngsters, particularly in elementary and junior high schools. Since we Americans are often quick to jump on the bandwagon of those who present new ideas as to what may be harmful to our children, we became afraid to let youngsters play against each other on a competitive basis. Many of us began to realize before too long that when the desire to win is removed by not allowing children to compete, their interest in playing is also removed. While this feeling against competition is still strong in some quarters, the pendulum seems to be swinging the other way.

I have heard a number of athletic directors and coaches complain of the lack of interest by young boys in taking part in athletics. They state that if time not now being used for physical activity were utilized academically or in gainful employment, there would be justification for the loss of interest in athletics; but instead, teen-agers seem to be spending most of their time riding around in automobiles and taking part in a number of unwholesome activities. Sour grapes? Possibly so, but important enough to be aware of and to bring to the attention of parents when necessary.

On the other hand, children today have so many more outside interests than a generation ago that they possible just can't find the time to do all the things they would like to do.

Athletic training can play an important role in interesting youngsters in other valuable pursuits. For instance, thousands of young men have been able to attend college and continue their education because of their athletic skills—advanced education which otherwise would not have been possible.

This opportunity for an education not only enriched their lives but greatly increased their future earning power. It is roughly estimated that a four-year college education increases the future earning capacity of an individual between $175,000 and $200,000.

This thought can be applied to other age groups as well. The desire on the part of youngsters to participate in the school athletic program has been a starting point for getting them to achieve according to their capabilities. Some youngsters before participating in sports lacked interest in their school work, were in some cases withdrawn and sullen, and, in other cases, were overly aggressive and in general were disciplinary problems. After participation, they became better students and developed healthier personalities. Since children must maintain satisfactory grades to be able to participate, students desiring to play usually make a supreme effort to do well academically so as not to be eliminated from the team. However, if the child discovers that taking part in athletics detracts from his studies, which in most cases will be unlikely, he should not be encouraged to continue.

Louisiana Training Institute, state correctional school for boys, attributes much of its success in working with wayward boys to athletics. An all-inclusive, well-rounded sports program has enabled the administration to develop confidence, responsibility, and healthier mental attitudes in a majority of boys who come to the institution. Iron bars that were once a trademark of the institution have been removed and in their places more athletic equipment has been added. There is a bare minimum of security at the institution, and the number of runaways is practically negligible. Youngsters who had previously been given up for lost causes when returned to their parish (county) schools have found "new life" through athletics.

We are missing a wonderful opportunity to help children of all ages by failure to encourage, develop, and guide our youth into more physical activity than they seem to be getting at present. If youngsters are trained in playing as in life, then those who have been critical in the past might try to duplicate in other areas the values gained through physical training to the end that all children may develop into richer personalities.

The Case Against Interscholastic Athletics in Junior High School*

ALVIN W. HOWARD

Most of those in education who oppose interscholastic athletics in the junior high schools are not resisting athletics as such; their position is that they would like to see more children participating, and a broader program of athletics developed, both in physical education classes and in intramural sports. There is a great deal of opposition to an interscholastic athletic program at this level, a feeling which apparently is not shared by the majority of junior high school principals, since surveys indicate that over 80% of our junior high schools have interscholastic athletic programs, and such a program is favored by about 75% of the principals involved. The controversy centers around the educational values to be derived from participation in competitive athletics, in an atmosphere charged with emotion and characterized by screaming children, cheering adults, blaring pepbands, excited yell leaders, and colorful drill teams and marching bands.

The arguments against an interscholastic athletic program in junior high school are as follows:

1. Junior high school students are in their early adolescent years and need a program of physical education that is different both from that of the elementary school and that operating in the senior high school. These children are experiencing an accelerated rate of growth and are, therefore, more susceptible to injuries of bones, joints, and cartilage. This is not the age for a highly organized competitive sports program with its required intensive training, accompanying pressures to win, the attendant excitement, and the physical and emotional stresses and strains. It is too easy in the heat of the game to push these children past the danger point.

2. Size of junior high school boys is not necessarily an index to strength, endurance, or coordination. Competition in body contact sports, even if the

contestants are matched on a height and weight basis, is not a firm index of physiological maturity, and can be dangerous.

3. The argument that interscholastic sports improve physical fitness may be true—for the gifted few who are chosen—but this different fitness can be developed in other physical education programs to the same extent and on a more equitable basis.

4. "They will be competing in life so they may as well start now." This is a ridiculous statement. Earning one's living in today's world requires education, knowledge, and the ability to reach wise decisions. It seldom involves physical contact of the sort encountered in interscholastic sports. Moreover, all too often the "competition" is one in which winning is all important. It is all very well for someone to say patronizingly that what is important is how you play, not winning. There are too many parents, administrators, and coaches who emphasize winning beyond all other factors. Incidents are countless in which the coach has bitterly and brutally castigated a junior high school team which was losing a game. Blistering locker room tirades key adolescent emotions to a high pitch, a grim and furious anger more suitable to a vendetta than a ball game.

5. It is frequently claimed that interscholastic sports instill sportsmanship in the team members. Probably this occasionally happens. When the main emphasis is upon winning and when pressures of the community make victory the most important goal, sportsmanship becomes secondary. Nor is the concept of sportsmanship enhanced by those coaches who post "quitters' lists", or "yellow sheets" in the locker room which list those boys who, for reasons of choice or circumstance, no longer turn out. If the sport cannot of itself hold their interest, then it seems reasonable that the list should cite the failures of the program rather than the names of those who became disgusted and gave it up. Those coaches and principals who, in the excitement of competition, lose their patience and tempers and explode against the officials, other team members, opposing coaches, or even their own team members, create an image that is anything but sportsmanlike.

6. The cost of varsity athletics in terms of money, personnel, equipment, and facilities is extremely disproportionate. Such a program is truly one for the athletically gifted child and requires a most unreasonable share of funds. It is sometimes claimed that the interscholastic athletic program, by virtue of paid admissions, not only supports itself but provides much of the funds for other school activities. This, regrettably, may be true for many high schools, but the big business of paid admissions does not usually even meet, in the junior high school, the necessary expenditures. The results are obvious: other activities and other students must do with less financial support. It is not uncommon for the interscholastic athletic program in junior high school to require more money than all other activities combined.

7. There is a frequent complaint that the high school coaches require junior high school coaches to instruct their team members in the same plays and

to use the same training that is used in the high schools so that prospective high school players will have learned a great deal of the high school patterns before they leave junior high school. The junior high school, already criticized for aping the high school, should never serve as the high school training ground.

8. Interscholastic athletics can easily become the dominating force in the school. Those boys who make the TEAM enjoy a temporary and false popularity, often to the detriment of other activities and to that of the academic program. The psychological impact upon those boys who turn out and are "cut" from the squad and to those who do not turn out is not easily measured. Coleman's studies indicate that athletic prowess is perhaps the most important single factor in the school life of the adolescent boy.

9. This same influence of varsity athletics may be found in its effect upon the schedule and educational program of the school. Pep rallies, practice sessions, and early dismissal for games cause too many disruptions in the school's primary function—that of educating all youth. Schedules are sometimes so constructed as to permit all athletes to have physical education the last period of the day so that turnout may continue uninterruptedly after school. Moreover, facilities such as playing fields and gymnasiums are pre-empted by the "team" to an extent which restricts and may prohibit the regular physical education program, intramural sports, and girls sports.

10. It is true that the public schools belong to the community, yet it is an interesting commentary that the principal who might vigorously resist parental efforts to establish the curriculum in history, may accede without a whimper to community pressure for an interscholastic sports program. By bowing to community pressures, school administrators permit sports-minded citizens to determine the school's athletic program. More will be resolved than this since the type of athletic program established will have a pronounced effect upon raising and expending of funds and upon the importance attached to athletics.

11. The entire problem of too early and excessive sophistication of junior high school children is brought sharply into focus at one of these interscholastic athletics contests. The activities and paraphernalia of high schools and even colleges is reproduced at many of these games and those schools that participate in night games run the whole gamut. The argument has been advanced that, "parents want to see their children play." Is this a sound educational reason to establish and operate a program of this sort?

12. What educational value of the varsity interscholastic athletic program has ever been established for junior high school? Is there any benefit provided which cannot be achieved equally well or better by a good physical education curriculum and a sound program of intramural sports?

The 1952 report of a joint committee made up of representatives from the National Education Association, the National Council of State Consultants in Elementary Education, the NEA Department of Elementary Principals, the

Society of State Directors of Health, Physical Education, and Recreation, and the American Association of Health, Physical Education, and Recreation issued a statement which said flatly that, "Interscholastic competitions of a varsity pattern. . .are definitely disapproved for children below the ninth grade." In 1954, the Educational Policies Commission of the NEA and the American Association of School Administrators noted that, "No junior high school should have a 'school team' that competes with school teams of other junior high schools in organized leagues or tournaments. Varsity type interscholastics for junior high boys and girls should not be permitted." James B. Conant, in 1960, stated that, "Interscholastic athletics and marching bands are to be condemned in junior high school. There is no sound educational reason for them and too often they serve merely as public entertainment."

Since these statements were issued, the AAHPER has recommended that the interscholastic athletics program for junior high school should contribute in a positive manner to the educational objectives of the school and that such a program should supplement, rather than be substituted for, an adequate program of required physical education, intramurals, and recreation for all students.

In the opinion of those who oppose interscholastic athletics in junior high school the recommendations of the AAHPER are not being met in most junior high schools and the interscholastic varsity athletic program should be eliminated without delay at this level.

Student Activities for Early Adolescents*

MORREL J. CLUTE

The most remarkable characteristic of the human organism is its growth and development. The miracles of growth and the evolution of the human personality are the schools greatest concern and responsibility. The time for being "grown-up" is long, indeed, when compared to the time for "growing-up." If we recognize that the experiences of the growing-up years have profound effect upon the grown-up years, then the responsibility of the school as a nurturer of growth is clear. Although growth and maturation are continuous processes that go on all through life, there are periods of time in the development of an individual where growth is more dramatic and the outward manifestations of rapid change are more obvious. The years of growth encompasssed by the public school are without question most dramatic during the junior high grades. Grades seven, eight and nine, almost without exception are the grades in which boys and girls are doing the most important growing of their lives. The period of adolescence has too often been thought of as a transition from childhood to adulthood—a period in which little of importance happens. It may be, as many authorities on adolescence believe, that the junior high school period is the most important of all the school years. Growth in all areas of development, physical, social, emotional, and mental are so rapid that unique problems arise. The values, attitudes, and beliefs that young people form during these years are likely to be life-long and will in a large measure determine the degree of success or satisfaction they give to or take from life. Therefore, the junior high school has unique functions because it must provide for boys and girls who have unique problems that arise from a unique period of growth.

If the school is to fulfill its unique functions, it must provide the kind of nurture that will satisfy the growth needs of boys and girls. Thus the curriculum must be defined in its broadest sense. It includes all the experiences that touch

*Reprinted from *Indiana State University Teachers College Journal,* 34 (November 1962), 62-63, 72, by permission of the publisher and Morrel J. Clute, Wayne State University.

upon the student in his school life. It includes all the activities in which students participate both in class and out. As the line between what is curricular and what is extra-curricular has become more and more obscure, junior high schools have come closer to satisfying the growth needs of adolescent boys and girls. The student activities program, then, can be considered as part of the regular instructional program. Some activities will grow out of regular class processes; others will be organized outside of the classroom.

The student activities in the junior high take on unique characteristics because adolescents have special needs. Although it is not easy to describe or classify traits of adolescent growth, it is possible to generalize. There is a wide range of *differences in physical development.* Growth in height, weight, and maturity varies greatly with individuals and particularly between boys and girls. Girls' development is usually from one to two years ahead of boys in maturity during the junior high years.

Rapid growth of external and internal organs and the development of secondary sex characteristics *create problems because of rapid change.*

Adolescents are striving for independance from adults. The peer group, the club, the chum, the hero-figure play an important role in the struggle for freedom from adult direction and in *understanding the sex role*—what it means to be a boy or girl.

Adolescents have special fears about growing up, not being accepted, not being liked, about inadequacy, or about being different.

Intellectual growth results in expanding but often unstable interests.

Early adolescents tend to be idealists, with an eagerness for social service.

This remarkable growth which results in physical and sexual maturity has a tremendous impact on all aspects of adolescent life. With the development of secondary sex characteristics which follows soon after the advent of puberty, the adolescent in reality becomes a new person in a new world. He has a new body with new feelings and sensations. It is like starting life anew with a vastly different world to discover and explore, new relationships to understand with new and different expectations and patterns for behavior.

In this struggle to understand his new world, the people in it, and himself as a person of dignity and worth, the adolescent finds that the student activity program plays a vital role.

The dominant characteristic of adolescence is the need to explore.

The exploratory function of the junior high school calls for adjustability on the part of the school. It may be desirable, at certain points, for individuals to engage in activities that are not easily proved at that time in their own classroom group. The function of personal social adjustment, too, calls for making new friends and facing new social situations. Students should have the advantage of a rich program of activities of a total school nature as well as flexible teacher-pupil planned classroom experiences. Separation of extra curriculum need not occur. There can and should be a steady flow of experience throughout the school day and week. The concepts and insights acquired in a club can enrich a class. The progressive growth of learning in the lively classroom can be the source of new stimuli in the activity program.

These adolescent growth needs should be the basis for organizing the activities program in the junior high school.

Personal-Social Adjustment

Although all school experiences provide opportunities for furthering social adjustment, it is important to recognize it as an important objective. Every activity that brings students together provides opportunities for developing peer relationships and learning social skills of interaction. Students participation in the planning, carrying-out and evaluation of special programs and activities means experience in decision making—an aid to becoming independent.

Widened corridors in newer buildings provide social living space. The lunch period often can be used for a rich program of activities. Quiet social experiences can be provided by use of the library and other rooms for reading, chess, checkers, cards, recording-listening, movies, arts and crafts and others. The list of games which provide opportunity for physical activity and social interaction is almost endless. Table tennis, volley ball, softball, shuffleboard, singing, and dancing are but a few of the activities that some schools build into a noon program. With adult guidance these activities can be student planned and directed thus fulfilling the need for social interaction and for learning democratic skills of leadership and cooperation. *Student government* is probably the most important single activity of the school. A student faculty Council which truly represents the students not only provides opportunity for learning the democratic skills necessary for democratic citizenship, but gives both students and faculty a responsible role in all school activity. School camping is growing rapidly as an activity in those states fortunate enough to have the physical facilities. The school camp combines in one activity many of the virtues sought in more diversified activity programs.

Development and Expansion of Intellectual Interests

In many ways the conventional class program satisfies the need to explore the physical and social world, but many classroom procedures are not flexible enough to provide for many and varied interests of adolescents. Forums, discussion groups, Pen Pal clubs and other activities of this type provide additional chances to explore the world and the people in it. The clubs which form around the academic subject areas are a reflection of desire of students to explore and develop their special talents.

Special Interests and Hobbies

A good club program can do much to enhance prevocational and avocational exploration. Again the list of clubs that may be organized in these two areas is almost limitless. Such clubs as Future Teachers, Future Nurses, Future Homemakers, Future Farmers, and 4-H are well known, nationally organized, and commonly found in most junior and senior high schools. The nature of special interests in the junior high, however, calls for more flexibility than in the senior high. Schools should be ready to form and close out clubs as changing interests indicate the need. Adolescents are more interested in the "here and now" and are less motivated by the long-range adult goals. Clubs for modeling, airplane building, photography, rock collecting, radio, for example, may represent short-range interests and may need to be replaced by others during the school year. Student activities growing out of the regular class program are usually exciting opportunities for students to discover special interests. The English program can develop special activities in creative writing, school paper or magazine as well as in speech and dramatic activities. The music and art areas of the school offer many opportunities for the exploration of interests and the development of talent.

Social Service

One of the very real needs of adolescents is the need to be of service to others. Their concern for justice and fair play is coupled with compassion for the less fortunate. Not only are they concerned with helping others, but they develop feelings of worth when performing a service that obviously contributes to the well-being of others. The safety patrol, service squad, ushers club, hall guides (as contrasted to hall guards), pep club, booster club, Junior Red Cross, all provide opportunities for service. Students welcome chances to be of service to their fellow students and as a rule participate enthusiastically in orientation activities at the beginning of a new school year. Older students can be of great help to incoming seventh graders. They are in the best position to communicate what school is like and they enjoy planning mixers, parties, picnics, or assembly programs to help students become acquainted with their new school.

In Summary

The objectives of a good student activities program for a junior high school can be summarized as follows:

1. It should further the personal social adjustment with peers and with adults.
2. It should promote learning the skills and concepts of democracy through actual practice.
3. It should offer an opportunity for students to pursue a wide variety of interests and adjust readily to changes in such interests.
4. It should provide for discovery and development of abilities.
5. It should provide an outlet for the altruism and idealism of junior high school youth.

In conclusion, it should be pointed out that the overall goal of student activities is an opportunity for successful participation for all students. There should be an appropriate activity for every boy and girl, and every boy and girl should be in an activity. Whether the school provides a regular period for student activities (a common practice in junior high schools) or whether they are undistinguishable for the regularly organized learning experiences, there must be concern for all students. Students who need the experiences most are often denied them because of excessive cost or by the use of academic achievement as a criterion for admission into club membership or activity. A few students should not dominate the program nor should students be exploited for aggrandizement of the school. Students need to feel pride in their accomplishments, but winning teams, and excellence of school productions must not be the only goal of such activities. Adult frustrations about the quality of finished products often denies the desired ends. Student activities provide rich nurture for adolescent growth.

The Carnegie Unit*

ALVIN W. HOWARD

The Carnegie Unit has been for many years the primary method of determining a student's movement through high school and his admission to college. One Carnegie Unit is granted a student for each class that meets for one class period each day, five days weekly, for 36 weeks of the year, i.e., one school year. A class which meets only half so often or for but one semester would, therefore, be granted only one-half of a Carnegie Unit.

The Carnegie Unit is applied to high school courses and, in the schools which follow this unit plan, usually 16 such units are required for graduation from high school.

The story of the development and adoption of a standardizing academic scorekeeping, which is what the Carnegie Unit essentially is, goes back many years. There were, in contrast to what is commonly believed today, several factors pointing up a need for some kind of uniform measure or standard.

From the time of the founding of Harvard College in 1636 to the period roughly defined as that from the end of the Civil War to 1900, there was a close relationship between schools and colleges. College admission requirements were highly specific. They stated subjects, often the books themselves, and even editions of books. Sometimes the required passages within the books were listed. The prescription of one college differed from that of another.

The introduction of the academy brought about an expansion of subjects, elective and required, which often ran into the hundreds. The curricula of the academies varied greatly, since apparently few academies taught the same subjects. Too, the amount of time allotted to the various subjects varied from school to school, so that geometry as taught by school A might have very little in common with geometry as taught by school B, either in amount of material covered or in time spent on the subject.

*Reprinted from *The Clearing House,* 39 (November 1965), 135-139, by permission of the publisher and A. W. Howard, University of New Mexico.

The development of curricula aimed at the non-college-bound student was accompanied by the growth, in the late 1800's and early 1900's, of the comprehensive high school, which was intended to provide education for a much greater segment of American youth. Public opinion pressed for a more varied list of offerings, preferably of a more practical nature.

During and following this same period, the American population became more and more mobile, so that youngsters might attend two or even several secondary schools before they graduated.

The ever-increasing number of schools, curricula, and subjects developed a need to find a common standard for the high school program. The report of the Committee of Ten in 1893 was the first attempt to bring curriculum organization to the secondary schools. The standardized time distribution proposed by the Committee of Ten was followed by the work of the College Entrance Examination Board, beginning at its inception in 1900. This Board recommended course outlines and suggested methods as well as time allotments.

In 1905 the Carnegie Foundation for the Advancement of Teaching was established to provide retirement benefits for college professors in the United States, Canada, and Newfoundland. It became involved in the first year of its existence with the problem of defining a college and distinguishing such an institution from a secondary school.

Considerable confusion existed in finding where a high school stopped and a college began. This was aggravated by those colleges which contained one or more grades normally considered as belonging in a high school, and also by those high schools, and there were many, which called themselves colleges. Since the retirement allowances were to be paid to the institution rather than the person, it became imperative to distinguish between these schools.

Thus, from its beginning, the Carnegie Foundation for the Advancement of Teaching, whose function was the dispensing of pensions to college professors, acquired an equally important function of determining, and in a sense, compelling acceptance of educational standards.

The system involving the use of the Carnegie Unit has been accepted because its theory of equivalent units makes it extremely convenient in academic bookkeeping. It did, very largely, overcome the lack of a common denominator for college admission requirements, college preparatory courses, and time allotments of subject matter fields in the secondary schools. It compares superficially the backgrounds of students from widely separated parts of the country, It has the further advantage of universal acceptance, which makes it a convenient yardstick. The Unit has been criticized for making its fundamental criterion the amount of time spent on a subject, not the results obtained. This was not the original intent.

Critics of the Carnegie Unit point out that it controls the pattern of time distribution in secondary schools. Should, for example, a faculty wish to have a course meet one hour daily three days a week, or if they wish to concentrate upon fewer subjects for a shorter period of time, they cannot consider any such course unless it carries a unit's worth of value. It is inadequate and inaccurate as a measure of scholastic attainment.

Essentially it is a year-long record of quantitative exposure to a given discipline and reflects nothing of value. This causes padding in some courses and paring in others and leads to regimentation of the program.

The Carnegie Foundation recognized the dangers of the restriction of subject matter, but it is doubtful that it intended such a result. The Foundation report observed that the units were never meant to establish a rigid pattern for admission to college. Their purpose was only that of comparison.

Unfortunately, however, the ease of use and of standardizing, the ease of scheduling in the high schools to accommodate classes meeting one period daily, five times weekly, coupled with the accompanying consolidation of the college credit system, gave the Unit a firm entrenchment.

In all fairness to the Unit is should be mentioned that other factors had considerable influence upon a school's program—although these, too, may have strengthened the Unit. The requirements of any public secondary school reflect the effects of statutory requirements, state and regional accrediting agencies, local Boards of Education, tradition, and experimentation. State requirements may be established by a state program of testing, such as the New York Regents Examination, which will determine areas to be emphasized, as well as subsidized programs under federal or state supervision. State and regional accrediting agencies have a direct influence on any program of electives. Tradition and experimentation affect a school's curriculum in such cases as a general requirement for all students to take a course in "Basic Living." The development of the science of psychology played its part in adding to confusion.

Critics pretty well agree that the trouble with the Carnegie Unit is that it interferes with good education. Increasingly a high school diploma is only a certificate of so much attendance in so many classes for a requisite number of hours for the required number of years. Sixteen units earned at one high school do not represent the same amount of learning, even for personnel of that high school, nor the same scholastic achievements, as those earned at another high school. The instruction varies, the course content varies, all subjects are not of the same importance although equal credit is given, and quantitative measurement in terms of time is a most unsatisfactory standard of educational value. Underlying all requirements and electives is the theory that certain basic skills and knowledge are necessary in order for all individuals to live successfully and that experiences and courses providing these should be required.

There is a growing movement to escape the restrictions of the Carnegie Unit, although approximately two-thirds of the high schools and colleges of the nation still use the Unit and prefer it because of its convenience. New developments in education, such as flexible scheduling and team teaching, virtually require abandonment of the strict definiton of the Unit. One of the main reasons for its retention in so many schools is that a satisfactory substitute has never been agreed upon. Too, there has not been a compelling stimulus such as the cash grants given by the Carnegie Foundation, to force a change. Neither has there been much in the way of unified action on the part of the schools.

Proposals to replace the Unit have been made, and many high schools have found and are finding new ways to avoid all its rigid time requirements.

The City Schools of Boston use a point system, as do Clevelend and the state of New Jersey, among others. The number and value of the points vary. A Carnegie Unit may be equivalent to 5, 10, or even 20 points.

Many school administrators feel that a point system merely ducks the issue and is a temporary expedient. With mounting knowledge and more understanding of how children learn and grow, they feel it cannot be ignored that not all children need the same amount of time to learn specific things. Nor do all children come to high school with the same background of knowledge, skills, and talents.

The new goal which is beginning to emerge refers not to amount and numbers (i.e., everyone in school for a given number of years)—a quantitative standard of the past—but rather to a quality of excellence to be achieved in the education provided for everyone in high school.

The high school program, as it is now organized, does not permit full use of innovations, and it is felt by many that better programs could be provided without adherence to the standard of the Carnegie Unit and its concomitant inflexible scheduling. Removal of the Unit would permit program variations—six, seven, eight subjects, some meeting two or three times weekly, others several hours weekly. Organizational plans could be tried in which it would be unnecessary to have the students in steady attendance all day every day.

If it is felt that we still need a measure for high school graduation and college admission, one suggestion is that we keep a tally of total hours in each subject, such as 70 hours of Typing, 100 hours of History. Advocates of the "hour" plan contend that it would permit high schools to continue with class rankings (though this is considered undesirable by a great many authorities), schools could offer a greater variety of courses and achieve better balance between general and special course offerings, and there would still be statistical security for registrars.

In an effort to supplement or supplant the Carnegie Unit a number of other proposals have been made. One of the most logical to many people was that used in elementary education—chronological age, implemented by information on other types of maturation. This approach requires a close, almost intimate relationship between pupils and teachers and a vast amount of written evaluations, conferences, and guidance. It has, however, been accomplished in most elementary schools, many junior high schools, and some high schools for a considerable length of time. Obviously it could be done.

Tests and examinations have played their part in evaluation for years.

College Entrance Examinations have been in use since around the turn of the century as a means of assessing prospective college students, and achievement and aptitude tests have been used for the same purpose since the 1940's.

Colleges in several states have for some time been accepting the high school diploma, "Certificate of Graduation," or completion of the high school course of study as sufficient evidence for admission to college. If the high schools involved have, however, based their courses of study, their programs, and hence their diplomas upon the Carnegie Unit, mere acceptance of such a certificate for admission to college does nothing but take the college off the hook and place the responsibility for reform upon the shoulders of the high schools.

The "Evaluative Criteria" weakened the position of the Carnegie Unit. In urging each high school to set up educational objectives, it placed more and more emphasis upon setting up objectives for each pupil in relation to his particular needs and his individual capacities.

In 1947 a new organization, the Educational Testing Service, was formed from a merger of the testing activities of the American Council on Education, the Carnegie Foundation for the Advancement of Teaching, and the College Entrance Examination Board. ETS has made progress toward better, more exact, and more comprehensive ways of appraising student progress in learning. Work by organizations such as these in developing comprehensive instruments which will diagnose accurately a student's high school achievements and his ability to succeed both in college and in life will contribute materially to the displacement of the Carnegie Unit.

A development which is regarded by some as unsound and even radical is the granting of credits or Carnegie Units for what has already been learned. The General Educational Development Test is an instrument designed to evaluate the learnings, experiences, and skills acquired by those who do not have the high school diploma. Two such batteries of tests have been developed, one for placement in high school or for issuance of a high school diploma, and the other for use on the college level. Intended originally for use of World War II veterans who had no high school diploma, the GED Tests have been highly successful and would not require a great deal of adaptation for use with high school pupils. A related problem is that of getting all colleges to accept such test results.

One method suggested is the Diederich Profile Index. This sets forth a procedure for evaluating several major elements, each with several subheadings, on a scale from zero (weak) to 100 (strong). A student might be rated under "Practical Competence," "shopping, buying wisely," at 25. Under the same major heading he might be rated at 50 in the category of "making things, making repairs."

The University of Chicago Laboratory School has developed a Progress Report which is similar in nature.

Proposals such as these share common weaknesses. They all require a wide variety of qualitative measures of pupil progress, considerable in the way of subjective value judgments, and a noticeable expenditure of funds and increase in clerical help. However, the criticism relative to subjective judgments may be made with equal validity regarding the arbitrary letter or percentage grades which accompany the Carnegie Unit. In addition, many significant learnings concomitant with mastery of selected subjects such as emotional control and character are often not evaluated either.

When Robert Maynard Hutchins was at the University of Chicago he expanded the concept of Early Admission to college, one which has received considerably more support in the past few years. Under this approach, students are given an elaborate series of tests and are placed in college according to their results. Hutchins' policy was to permit high school students to enter college early. More recent use of Advanced Placement permits teaching of certain college courses in high school, with college credit being given for them.

A method related to Advanced Placement is the high school-college agreement which is being tried in some states. In this approach high schools are given greater freedom from subject matter restrictions, upon certain conditions primarily involving preparation of massive individual records and reports.

With the increasing high school enrollments and the need to decrease dropouts, high schools have become concerned with graduation and diploma requirements. Clearly, in this time of vocational courses, business courses, and the comprehensive high school, a diploma means many different things to different people. Suggestions have been made to grant diplomas and graduation only to those who show high academic scholarship and that others be given a "Certificate of Attendance" or a "School Leaving Certificate."

Education appears to be going through a period of rapid transition. The high schools have a much bigger job to do now than when the Carnegie Unit was adopted. The type of education in today's world, involving as it does the whole spectrum of student interests, needs, and abilities, accompanied by changes in curricula and technical innovations, requires far more flexibility than the Unit permits. Although many subjects have been added in the past 50 to 60 years, the primary emphasis is too often upon the Unit and its compartmentalized organization.

A device which is a quantitative measure of time spent in a classroom only operates to place less emphasis upon a student's gaining educational competence, and actually becomes an impediment to improvements in instruction.

A Sound Core Program—What It Is and What It Isn't*

HAROLD ALBERTY

In recent years, many attempts have been made to clarify the concept of the core, as that term is applied to the high-school curriculum. Yet probably no other term in the field of education is surrounded by so much confusion and so many misconceptions. It is literally true that there is no commonly accepted meaning of the term which makes it possible for administrators, teachers, and laymen to communicate intelligently concerning it.

Some of the fairly common definitions are: a group of required subjects, a combination of two or more subjects, a large block of time in which learning activities are planned cooperatively, any course taught by "progressive" methods.

Added to this confusion is the fact that many terms such as the following are used synonymously with core: common learnings, general education, unified studies, self-contained classrooms, basic courses, fused courses, and English-social studies.

As a consequence, when one is told that a certain school has a core, it is unsafe to draw any conclusions whatever concerning the nature of the program.

In my opinion, the conception of core most likely to transform and improve general education in the high school is this: a group of structured problem areas, based upon the common problems, needs, and interests of adolescents, from which are developed teacher-student planned learning units or activities.

Following are some of the principal characteristics of an effective adolescent-problems core program based on this conception.

*Reprinted from *The NEA Journal,* 45 (January 1956), 20-22, by permission of the publisher and Harold B. Alberty, Ohio State University.

1. It deals with the area of general education and hence is directed primarily toward the development of the common values, understandings, and skills needed for effective democratic citizenship.

2. Since it provides for general education, it is required of all students at any given level.

3. It utilizes a block of time sufficiently large to deal with a broad, comprehensive unit of work, with homeroom and guidance activities, and with individualized instruction.

4. It is based upon the common problems, needs, and interests of youth as ascertained by the teaching staff and the core teacher in cooperation with his students. It draws freely upon all pertinent resources, including logically organized subjects or fields of knowledge.

5. It has a clearly defined but flexible scope and sequence based on preplanned problem areas derived from the major values of democratic living and the common problems, needs, and interests of students.

6. Instruction is based upon learning units derived principally from the established problem areas, which are planned, carried forward, and evaluated by the teacher and the students.

7. It is supported and reinforced by a rich offering of special-interest activities—both formal and informal—designed to meet the particular needs of students and to develop their unique capacities, interests, and talents.

The foregoing presentation is intended as a frame of reference for discussing what I believe to be certain misconceptions concerning a sound core program. Some other investigator might interpret one or more of these as not being misconceptions at all but rather as the only true interpretation of the core. Therefore, the misconceptions about to be discussed can be so regarded only against the backdrop of my own interpretation.

Misconception No. 1. The core concept is new and has had very limited application; hence, programs based upon it should be regarded as highly experimental, if not radical and dangerous.

As a matter of fact, the various elements of the adolescent-problems core as defined above have been in successful use for many years.

a. The practice of setting aside a significant portion of the school day for general education is commonplace, as attested by the practices of most high schools and colleges.

b. The problem approach and the utilization of direct, firsthand experience as starting points for learning have proved their effectiveness over a period of at least half a century—even before Dewey established his famous laboratory school in 1896. It was the very heart of the revolution in agricultural education which began about 1910. In 1923, Ellsworth Collings documented experimentally the desirability of a complete break with the subject-centered curriculum. Good elementary schools have used effectively the problem and direct-experience approach to learning for many years.

c. The value of utilizing the broad unit-of-work approach was documented by the early followers of Herbart and later by Morrison, Miller, Thayer, and others. By 1930, the technics of unit teaching were well known and practiced by many high-school teachers.

d. The use of student-teacher planning grew out of the success of the socialized recitation, which had its beginning in the early decades of the century. Its value has been well documented by studies in group dynamics in both education and industry.

e. The success of teaching the so-called fundamentals thru broad comprehensive units of experience has been documented over and over. Collings could again be cited as a pioneer in this field. His results have been verified in scores of experimental studies.

Thus it is evident that the features of a sound core program have long since passed the experimental stage.

Misconception No. 2. The core program is progressive or modern while the subject-centered special-interest program is conventional or even traditional.

This conception gets us into great difficulties because it tends to create a cleavage between teachers working in the core program and those in the special-interest areas when they need to work together more effectively.

There is no valid basis for this conception because the technics of curriculum development and instruction open to the core teacher are, for the most part, equally applicable to the special-interest teacher. For example, the science teacher may base his course on problems, needs, and interests of students. The program will, of course, have a narrower scope than the core, since he is dealing with a restricted field of knowledge.

He may organize the course in terms of comprehensive units of work, using the logic of his field only as a way of determining scope and sequence. He may emphasize teacher-student planning if he regards the logical system of knowledge of his field as a guide-post rather than as a mandate to "cover ground." He may also perform a highly important specialized guidance function.

The difference between the two types of program is to be found in the fact that the core program deals with the area of general education, and hence finds its scope and sequence in the broad areas of living, while the special-interest areas deal with a content determined by the *particular field.* Both types of learning experience are essential to a well-rounded education.

Actually a good core program cannot be developed without the help of the subject specialist: in planning resource units or guides, in core classroom teaching at points of need, and in teaching his special field with constant reference to what goes on in the core so as to reinforce and enrich the core program.

Misconception No. 3. The core has no definable content. It is largely process, or methodology. Its values lie in the way the students learn. Almost any content is satisfactory, so long as the students share in planning, and are achieving certain democratic values held by the teacher.

This view is held by many teachers and some authorities who find their orientation in the more radical theories of the "left-wing progressives" in education and who hold that any attempt to define scope and sequence in advance of classroom teacher-student planning is a violation of the creative process. It places too much emphasis upon the utilization of the immediate felt and expressed wishes, wants, and desires of the students in the group.

Programs designed around this misconception have done much to bring the adolescent-problems core into disrepute because it is difficult, if not impossible, to explain to inquiring parents just what Johnny is learning because the teacher himself won't know until *after* the year's work is finished. It is likewise difficult if not impossible for special-interest area teachers to plan their own programs or their participation in the core because of the highly tentative nature of the program. And it is difficult for administrators and supervisors to anticipate resources which will be needed.

It is my contention that the core program, based on a more realistic approach to education for effective citizenship, should have a content as capable of definition as that of a field of knowledge. The content can be derived: (1) from careful studies of problems of youth which grow out of their own basic drives and from the pressures and tensions of the environment which impinge upon them; and (2) from the democratic values to which we as a people are committed.

Such a definition of scope might well eventuate in a series of problem areas in the basic aspects of living from which cooperatively planned learning units would be developed. The sequence of learning would be determined largely by each individual core teacher and his students.

Misconception No. 4. The core is merely a better way of teaching the required subjects. Clearly this misconception has some kinship with the one explained immediately above. There is, however, an important distinction. Proponents of this point of view hold that the core is a *method of teaching* which has for its aim the mastery of the conventional subjects—usually English and the social studies. To the other group, the principal aim is the attainment of the values which inhere in the process of living democratically.

The program which eventuates from this misconception is known as unified studies, English-social studies, and multiple-period classes. It is taught by one teacher, in a block of time larger than one period.

Obviously there are certain advantages to such an arrangement. The teacher gets to know the students better and hence has the opportunity to develop a more effective homeroom guidance program. The student is likely to see interconnections among the subjects that are unified. However, it can be justified only as a transition from the conventional separate-subject program to the more vital adolescent-problems core.

Misconception No. 5. The core, once firmly established, will gradually absorb the entire curriculum and eventually result in the complete destruction of all subject fields.

This view is the result of a lack of understanding of the fundamental differences between education directed toward the development of the ideals, understandings, and skills needed by all for effective citizenship and education directed toward the development of the unique interests, abilities, or talents of the individual. The former is the distinctive province of the core; the latter can best be accomplished by teacher specialists in appropriately equipped shops, laboratories, and studios. Each of the two aspects of education has its distinctive functions; each reinforces the other.

The prevalence of this misconception is probably accounted for by the fact that the adolescent-problems core draws upon all pertinent fields of knowledge in dealing with common problems of living and calls for the assistance of the specialist in determining the potential contributions of such fields of knowledge. What it neglects to take into account is the need for courses or experiences designed specifically to meet the special needs, problems, and interests of students.

Misconception No. 6. The core is more suitable for the below-average or dull student who has difficulty in mastering the conventional subjects than for the bright student who expects to go to college.

There is no evidence known to the writer that indicates that the adolescent-problems core is peculiarly adapted to any *one* class of students. Current practices reveal its successful use in schools with selective enrolments as well as in schools with more heterogeneous populations. As a matter of fact, the core, with its emphasis upon broad units of work, affords the opportunity to provide for individual differences *within* the unit, so that students of all levels of ability may find stimulating experiences.

The so-called Eight-Year Study of the Progressive Education Association, conducted in the 1930s, provided ample evidence that graduates of high schools utilizing the adolescent-problems core succeeded as well in college as did graduates of conventionally organized high schools.

Misconception No. 7. The core is better adapted to the junior high school than to the senior high school.

It is difficult to understand the logic back of this familiar misconception, for no one would seriously argue that the problem-solving approach becomes ineffective at the senior-high level. The nature of the pertinent problems, of course, will change as the students develop, but that means only that the school should adapt instruction to the student's maturity level.

Surveys of core-program development indicate that 85% to 90% of all the cores are to be found in the seventh and eighth grades. In only a small number of schools is the core extended to the senior high school level.

Probably many educators are convinced that the core program is actually better adapted to the junior high school, but the present situation is due to additional factors.

Traditionally, the seventh and eighth grades were regarded as part of the elementary school, where most or all of the instruction was given by one teacher. Consequently, many principals who reacted against the extreme specialization of the early junior high schools saw the core as a way out which would have the sanction of tradition.

On the other hand, the traditional requirement of 16 Carnegie units for high-school graduation has tended to be a barrier to the extension of the core to the senior high school.

Finally, the teacher-certification problem has added to the difficulty of extension.

It is far easier to state the misconceptions concerning a sound core program which serve as blocks to its development than to suggest ways to remove the blocks.

All that the writer hopes for is that this analysis may stimulate thinking about a conception of curriculum development which has the potentiality for improving our present programs of general education in the high school.

The Rise and Fall of the Core Curriculum*

HARVEY OVERTON

The core curriculum has fallen, and only a handful of the faithful now gather at National Core Conferences to lament its demise. How has it happened that a new light that burned so brightly in the curricular heavens of American public education turned out to be a meteorite, a mere flash in our darkness, and not a new star at all?

It is obvious that the core curriculum has fallen, because it is no longer one of the central concerns in discussions of public education. A cursory examination of the *Education Index* shows that during 1963-64 only four articles were published on the core in secondary education, whereas during its golden era–roughly from 1950 to 1959–two dozen articles appeared each year in the professional journals. It could be argued that educators are not discussing the core curriculum today because it is a *fait accompli.* There are few statistics on the status of the core, however, that show convincingly that this is the case.[1] Moreover, some recently published reports on innovations and experimentation in public education do not even mention the core.[2] And James B. Conant, whose encyclicals on the shape and substance of American secondary education have been immensely influential, gives only a timid blessing to the practice of block-time scheduling in the junior high school and makes it plain that his limited endorsement "does not presuppose an endorsement of core teaching."[3]

*Reprinted from *The Clearing House,* 40 (May 1966), 532-537, by permission of the publisher and Harvey Overton, Western Michigan University.

[1]Galen J. Saylor and William M. Alexander, *Curriculum Planning for Modern Schools* (New York: Holt, Rinehart and Winston, Inc., 1966), pp. 289-290.

[2]See The Panel on Educational Research and Development, *Innovation and Experiment in Education* (Washington, D.C.: U. S. Government Printing Office, 1964). See also Henry M. Brickell, *Commissioner's 1961 Catalog of Educational Change* (Albany N.Y.: The Commissioner of Education, State Education Department).

[3]James B. Conant, *Education in the Junior High School Years* (Princeton, N.J.: Educational Testing Service, 1960), p. 23.

The dialogue over public education today centers on excellence, acceleration, automation, tracking, "spiraling," the gradeless school, the Godless classroom, and education as rehabilitation in the Great Society.

The Core and How It Grew

The core curriculum rose both as an experiment and as an enthusiasm in the 1930's, when the Commission on the Relation of School and College of the Progressive Education Association began its famous Eight-Year Study and the State of Virginia designed its ambitious "social functions" curriculum, which was to serve as a model for subsequent core programs across the country. The early core programs shared a concern with breaking away from the traditional pattern of separate subject offerings of the secondary school and discovering a vitally reorganized curriculum that would take into account the sweeping social and economic changes of the twentieth century. In addition, these programs explicitly recognized the needs of youth in American society as revealed by the expanding science of child study. And they deliberately attempted to apply the experimental findings of learning psychology to classroom teaching methods. Soon, however, a sharp schism developed between the designers of the "broad fields" or "unified studies" core, based on a reorganization of traditional subject matter, and the promoters of the "experience curriculum" core, based on the needs of adolescents. By the time the results of the Eight-Year Study were reported in the early 1940's, the break was irreparable, and the experimental intentions of the early designers of the core curriculum succumbed to the promotional activities of the sincere but over-zealous theorists. These theorists now considered the "true" core to be one that obliterated the traditional subject matter of the secondary school, a curriculum that was to be "experienced" rather than learned, with a content that was not to be fixed in advance but was to evolve according to the purposes of the learners.

This version of the core, a stepchild of William Herd Kilpatrick's project method, was to become the most clamorous enthusiasm of the secondary school in the two decades following the onset of World War II. The messianic intentions of the promoters of this concept are prophetically revealed in the frontispiece of Harold Spears' book *Secondary Education in American Life.*[4] Spears presents a cartoon drawing depicting the core curriculum as a modern Pied Piper piping "experience," "activity," "correlation," followed by rats labeled "compartmentalized and unrelated subjects" that are deserting the secondary school situated as a castle on a distant hill.

The core coterie, now replete with a jingoism borrowed from the excesses of the progressive education movement, eventually formed a splinter group with

[4]Harold Spears, *Secondary Education in American Life* (New York: American Book Co., 1941).

the reluctant blessing of the Association for Supervision and Curriculum Development. The U. S. Office of Education designated Grace S. Wright to keep count of core developments. And the professional journals abounded with glowing reports on the core curriculum as it was practiced in classrooms across the country.

The crest of core's wave of popularity came in the 1950's. The young teachers entering secondary school classrooms from the services and reaping the benefits of the G. I. Bill brought with them an idealism and a disdain for regimentation that made the core curriculum an appealing adventure. And a bumptious but short-lived renaissance of progressive education was launched.

Soon, however, the unsettling effects of a rapidly realigning world order gave rise to a morbid anxiety and cynicism that led citizens to seek a Communist under the covers of every social studies textbook. And public education became fair game for a rising host of critics, from cranks seeking self-aggrandizement to college professors seeking to restore learning as undefiled deliberation in the pristine subject matter of the traditional school. After Sputnik I in 1957, the era of reassessment of American public education began in earnest, and the core curriculum, along with most of the formal trappings of progressive education, slid into its niche in educational history as an event to be recorded and explained.

The Core and Why It Fell

A curriculum innovation that held the attention and devotion of so many teachers and theorists for nearly three decades deserves more than passing commentary on its rise and fall.

FAILURE TO ACHIEVE A COMMON DEFINITION

A difficulty that ran throughout the course of the core movement was confusion over the meaning of the term *core.* From the beginning, a number of curriculum theorists began to make militant and dogmatic declarations about what the core curriculum was and was not. Although accurate distinctions among the variety of programs that emerged in the 1930's were necessary, along with a reliable vocabulary for discussing them intelligibly, a number of theorists insisted with almost religious fervor on reserving the use of the term *core* for their own interpretation of what they believed the core curriculum to be. Nelson Bossing, in a petulant discussion of the "abuses" of the term, commented: "The modern use of the term *core* should be clearly and sharply differentiated from its traditional usage; it must be completely divorced from any patterns of subject matter courses. The two conceptions of core represent a contradiction in terms and a confusion in educational thinking."[5] Yet there is nothing in the logic of definition to deny referring to a cluster of subjects which are required of all students as a "core." Bossing's own definition of the core, which in the same book he refers to as the "true" core,[6] although circular and vague, indicates how complete the break with "any patterns of subject matter courses" had become. It reads:

> In modern education the term *core* has come to be applied to that part of the experience curriculum which refers to those types of experiences thought necessary for all learners in order to develop certain behavior competencies considered necessary for effective living in our democratic society.[7]

Harold Spears, nearly fifteen years earlier, had also assigned the term *core* an honorific value by defining the "true" core in similar terms. Spears wrote:

> The true core course, or core curriculum, might be considered as a course designed to train for the general group life and citizenship of America, in accordance with the principles of democratic action and an appreciation of the growth process.[8]

Similar definitions were given by Pierce,[9] Krug,[10] and Leonard,[11] all denying that courses retaining identifiable subject matter in correlated patterns under the labels of "fusion" or "broad fields" could properly be called core. Despite the lack of precision in definitions holding that the purpose of a school program is to produce skills and understandings needed "for effective living in our democratic society," the kind of core these theorists seemed to be describing came to be referred to in the pedagese nomenclature as the "personal-social-problems" core.

In the meantime more neutral efforts were made by other writers and groups to make more explicit what the experiences were that all youth were supposed to acquire. The Educational Policies Commission in *Education for All*

[5]Nelson Bossing, *Principles of Secondary Education* (Englewood Cliffs, N.J.: Prentice-Hall, Inc., 1955), p. 403.

[6]*Ibid.*, p. 411.

[7]*Ibid.*, p.403.

[8]Spears, *op cit.*, p. 115.

[9]Paul R. Pierce, *Developing a High School Curriculum* (New York: American Book Co., 1942), p. 129.

[10]Edward A. Krug, *Curriculum Planning* (New York: Harper & Brothers, 1950), pp. 85-96.

[11]J. Paul Leonard, *Developing the Secondary School Curriculum* (New York: Rinehart and Co., 1953), pp. 396-400.

American Youth[12] and Florence Stratemeyer and her colleagues in *Developing a Curriculum for Modern Living*[13] made commendable efforts to examine the kinds of understandings, knowledges, and skills that an education should provide in common for all young people.

By the 1950's some theorists began to break with the earlier exponents of the experience curriculum, who held that learning situations cannot be set in advance but must derive from the ongoing needs and interests of children. The Fifty-Second Yearbook of the National Society for the Study of Education, *Adapting the Secondary School Program to the Needs of Youth,*[14] represented writers who advocated a curriculum based on the personal and social needs and interests of students but planned in advance by the faculty. These writers argued that after a century of study in the behavioral sciences we now have enough reliable data to predict what the needs of youth will be in American society; consequently, we can build in advance a curriculum based on these predictions that will be logically and psychologically coherent. It was also in this volume that Harold Alberty performed a yeoman's service by describing six different usages of the term *core.* Alberty's model at least enabled school people to discuss core intelligibly by indicating which of his six types they were talking about.

Recent efforts to define the core have turned from declaration to description, with writers reporting what appear to have developed as common practices in core programs. Lurry and Alberty, for instance, list eleven practices that represent characteristics of core programs they have studied.[15] Although these writers do present a definition of the core that is in their terms the preferred one, they fail to make any analysis of which of the eleven practices are necessary conditions, and how many are sufficient conditions, for a core program to exist. As admirable as their objectivity may be, they lead us no further toward a common definition of the core.

With the failure among theorists to achieve a common definition of core, and the internecine bickering that was its consequence, it is little wonder that teachers, school administrators, and the public often were left confused or misguided about the core. At a national core conference several years ago an enthusiastic core teacher, when I asked her what she believed core was, closed her eyes and said ecstatically, "I can't tell you what it is, but, oh, it's wonderful!" Such innocence in an age of analysis should not go unacclaimed.

[12] Educational Policies Commission, *Education for All American Youth* (Washington: National Education Association, 1944).

[13] Florence B. Stratemeyer, Hamden L. Forkner, and Margaret G. McKim, *Developing a Curriculum for Modern Living* (New York: Teachers College, Columbia University, 1947).

[14] National Society for the Study of Education, *Adapting the Secondary School Program to the Needs of Youth* (Chicago: The University of Chicago Press, 1953).

[15] Lucille L. Lurry and Elsie J. Alberty, *Developing a High School Core Program.* (New York: The Macmillan Co., 1957), pp. 29-43.

EXHORTATION VERSUS EXPERIMENTATION

The Eight-Year-Study ran concurrently with the rise of core programs in the public schools. The 1930's were a decade of experimentation and boldness in public life, both in education and in politics (a revolt against tradition had already manifested itself in the arts during the previous decades). Where the Eight-Year Study, however, maintained the rigors of an experimental design with systematic measurement, many of the core programs that accompanied its development were based on the theorizing of college professors and state superintendents of public instruction. As exciting and imaginative as some of these theories were, few of them were tested with any empirical rigor in public school classrooms. And despite the fact that the Eight-Year Study, on its conclusion, did not demonstrate the superiority of any given curricular pattern, core theorists broadly used its findings to justify an extension of the particular variety of the core curriculum they were bent on promoting. Instead of holding whatever definition of the core they had in mind as an hypothesis to be tested, they rushed headlong into advocacy without adequate empirical support and almost no experimental intentions. A review of the 200 or so articles on the core appearing in the professional journals from 1944 to 1959 demonstrates that no more than a handful of them reports any serious research efforts. What little research was done during these years was for the most part conducted by graduate students completing thesis requirements at the universities. John Dewey's contention that a true science of education could not finally exist until teachers and school administrators themselves became conductors rather than consumers of research was given little comfort in the development of core programs in the schools.

THE RETURN TO DORMANCY

By the end of the 1950's it was clear that the school had relinquished whatever intentions it had held in the earlier decades to serve as an instrument to reform society. The giants of social reconstructionism for the most part were in semiretirement, serving as distinguished professors in the universities, and in the winter of their discontent found that audiences of teachers no longer responded to their clarion. The darling of the educators had become the behaviorist psychologist with his Pandora's box of gimmickery, and the focus of teaching and learning turned to the rapidity and efficiency with which children could be taught to respond to given stimuli. To a generation of youngsters nurtured on the McCarthy hearings, this focus of the school held forth the prospect of a safe and untroubled professional career. The bland young teacher in the grey flannel suit entering the profession in the 1960's was not about to be seduced by the social reformism his generation had been taught to fear and distrust. And the school superintendent, whose training in the universities had been reduced to developing the managerial skills of running the school as a business, was content to maintain his plant and his public relations and to order the materials his teachers needed in order to stimulate the desired responses in their pupils. The stress on the ends that education was to serve in American society was replaced by a stress on the means to accomplish the neutral goal of information management. While it was still legitimate, but frequently hazardous, for individual teachers to awaken the social sympathies and quicken the sensitivities of their students, a programmatic definition of the role of the school in social reform was nowhere to be found. With the introduction of Job Corps, Vista, Head Start, and Vocational Rehabilitation, the United States government became the legatee of the controversial social reforms the reconstructionists promoted for the schools in the 1930's.

In this climate, the core program, especially the personal-social-problems core, which was essentially reconstructionist in character, had little hope of surviving.

TO CULT-TO CRISIS-TO COLLAPSE

It has been observed that an inevitable progression to cult to crisis to collapse befalls all movements. Perhaps the core cannot properly be classified as a movement, but certainly it was a stepchild of the Progressive Education movement, which did not escape this progression. And no doubt it is in this larger context that we will finally find the basic reasons for the collapse of the core. How this progression could have been avoided is now a matter of retrospection. But however we may conjecture, we must acknowledge that the problems of American education to which the pioneers of the core addressed themselves are still with us, magnified and more unmanageable than before. Despite their differences in definition of the core, theorists and practitioners alike were agreed that they were all engaged in an effort to make learning meaningful in the context of contemporary life. They sought ways to reduce barriers between disciplines in order to bring knowledge into some kind of humane relationship to the growth of the individual personality. They tried to trip the balance of learning on the side of critical inquiry, discovery, and independence as opposed to repetition, regurgitation, and regimentation. They devised methodologies that would hopefully develop the skills of communication and participation believed to be the hallmark of the effective citizen in the free society. They introduced content relevant to the issues that must be met in our time and tried to create an awareness in the young of the unsolved problems of social justice that continue to nag the conscience of sensitive men. Finally, they saw education not merely as a transmitting of the cultural heritage but as a critical evaluation of this heritage as it relates to our lives today.

Whether public schooling in the United States will return to this "progressive" vision of education remains to be seen. We seem still to be attracted by the disciplined efficiency of the Russian system and by the managerial simplicity of the European system of testing and tracking. And the pervasive attitude of American parents seems to have turned from the sentimental permissiveness of the 1930's to a grim anxiousness over keeping their children in the mainstream of the educational system whose currents will carry them through college into the glory of pedigreed life in the suburbs. At the same time, however, we see a growing federal participation in educational reform, with programs such as the Job Corps using many of the core curriculum methodologies. In addition, the national curriculum programs, such as those in mathematics and physics, have broadly employed discovery methods of teaching, stressing the development of critical thinking skills. Also, again through federal monies, a number of research-demonstration centers have been established whose purpose is not to promote a given curricular design but to test its efficacy.

If out of all this disparate activity we can once more move toward a single vision of the purposes of public education in America, perhaps we can avoid some of the excesses, however sincere, and some of the confusions, however understandable, that characterized the curricular adventures of previous decades.

Do We Expect Too Much from Ability Grouping?*

CHARLES E. HOOD

At the present time, the practical principal typically believes that every up-to-date secondary school with high scholastic standards and a low dropout rate must include ability grouping in its class organization.

However, after reading extensively the professional opinion of educational authorities, and after studying the results of educational research in this field, one quickly finds that ability grouping should certainly not be considered as the panacea for our educational ills. Practically all of these people seem to take a dim view of ability grouping. The "experts" say that it is extremely difficult to group students by ability, that even if you can, they don't stay grouped by ability, and that even if they would stay grouped by ability, you would accomplish very little as far as more efficient learning is concerned.

There is, however, an educational group which takes sharp issue with the above statements. Typical classroom teachers feel very strongly that ability grouping is the solution to most of their problems. They say in no uncertain terms that—research or no research—a better job of teaching could be done if some of the poorer students were removed from their classes. Since the principal usually is more easily influenced by the teachers with whom he comes in contact daily than he is by researchers a great deal of ability grouping, for better or for worse, has been introduced in the secondary schools during the past few years. Someone has said that a practical principal, like a practical politician, should "appear to be rushing in the direction he is being pushed." However, principals must also recognize the limitations to ability grouping and be aware of a number of problems which may arise.

1. *Screening of Students.* It is somewhat discouraging to read a booklet

*Reprinted from *The Clearing House,* 38 (April 1964), 467-470, by permission of the publisher and Charles E. Hood, Montana State University.

published by the College Entrance Examination Board entitled *Guide to the Advanced Placement Program* and find these statements in regard to screening students on the basis of ability:

"We really understand very little about what makes a student outstanding."

"Motivation, desire, persistence, and a disposition to do hard work, are at least as important as a high I.Q."

"It may be advisable to use a checklist such as the following when screening students: Is he a volunteer who is interested, willing, and able to extend himself? Do his parents approve of his taking the courses? Is his past record good enough? Does he have the recommendations of his former teachers? Does he have health and emotional stability?"

Of the factors mentioned, none directly refers to scholastic ability or native intelligence.

Recently some of the colleges in the Ivy League have been taking second looks at the methods they are using in screening applications. They are going to take an "academic risk" on 10 per cent of their freshman classes and include men who are not strictly academic, but who are unusually "vigorous, humorous, mature, or original." This description could include many of the so-called problem boys in high school—at least the "Tom Sawyers."

Evidently, more than just mental ability and scholastic achievement must be considered in screening students for ability grouping, and the more factors included, the more subjective the final judgment.

2. *Increasing Schedule Conflicts.* Small or medium-sized high schools where the number of sections of courses diminishes in the upper grades will have a particularly difficult time in avoiding conflicts. For example, when a student is placed on the level of his ability in required academic courses, a problem may be created when he is prevented from enrolling in elective courses he needs.

3. *Confusing Subject Designations.* This problem is concerned with the confusion which arises in attempting to ascertain the scholastic requirements and content of a course which appears on a student's transcript or record when several different levels of a course are taught under the same name. Although some schools attempt to clarify this situation in different ways, in most cases the information is not provided or is insufficient to evaluate the type of work done. This can result in inaccurate evaluations of transcripts or school reports by registrars, counsellors, college admission people, employers, and parents. A plan in which every course that is identified by the same name would have the same standards and content would eliminate this confusion.

4. *Going Too Far or Too Fast in Ability Grouping.* This is the result of revolutionizing a curriculum to meet pressures for ability grouping, and then finding that the new plan is creating more problems than it is solving, or that ability grouping does not seem to be as "popular" as it was previously. The solution would be to adopt a plan which would not necessitate too great an

immediate change in the organization of the curriculum, so that it would be expanded or gracefully abandoned as the need might be.

5. *Inadequate Teaching Methods and Materials.* Both the teacher and the administration must be convinced that each level of instruction should be conducted by using appropriate methods and content for that level. In other words, the error of attempting to use the same textbooks and teaching techniques in classes on different levels must be avoided. Again, the solution seems to be to make haste slowly, so that a principal will not find himself financially unprepared to provide the necessary textbooks and other teaching materials and equipment necessary for the new levels of instruction.

6. *Inflexible Programs.* A student's program should be flexible enough so that needed change can be made without too much difficulty. A group which may be somewhat homogeneous at the beginning of the term may become heterogeneous after a short period. And it is certainly not uncommon for an error to be made in assigning students in ability grouping. Organizational flexibility which will allow changes under these conditions is necessary.

7. *Selecting Qualified Teachers.* The success or failure of any program of ability grouping will ultimately depend upon the teacher, who must realize that in spite of the grouping process a wide range of ability will still exist in the classroom. Consequently students will learn at varying rates, and individual differences in ability still will be quite apparent.

8. *Assigning Marks to Students.* Resistance to ability grouping comes from the academically talented student and his parents when the normal distribution curve is followed in assigning marks in classes grouped by ability. The college-bound student is well aware that grades and rank in class are of great importance for admission to college, for scholarships, and for other honors. If a "B" in a high-level class in English is going to be as difficult to earn as an "A" in a lower-level course, you can readily understand the reluctance of many top students to enroll in the high-level courses.

The most common approach to the solution of this problem is to skew the normal distribution curve so that more above-average marks are assigned in above-average classes. Another approach, which is more difficult to carry out, is to give added weight to marks earned in high-level courses when ranking students. It should be emphasized that students should not be expected to do *more* work to earn an "A" in high-level classes as compared with normal classes, but they should expect to do a normal amount of work of a *higher quality*. The able but lazy student, who has been coasting along in ungrouped classes, earning his "A" by doing very little work, will find that he has to do a normal amount of work to earn an "A" in ability-grouped classes. It is very difficult to convince this student that it is "in his own best interest" to be placed in a class which "challenges" him, if, in addition, he has to work harder.

The Custer Plan. Custer County High School in Miles City, Montana, has an enrollment of 800 students in grades 9 through 12. A junior college operates under the same administration, which facilitates the enrollment of senior honor students in college-level courses. The following plan for ability grouping adopted by this school appears to avoid many of the problems mentioned above.

1. *By requiring prerequisities for advanced courses.* This is a form of ability grouping which is traditional in all high schools. For example, a student must have taken Algebra I before he is allowed to register for Algebra II (unless he is accelerated): or a student must be a senior before he is allowed to enroll in auto mechanics. Outside of required courses, a student must earn a "C" or better in a beginning course before he is eligible to register for the advanced course.

2. *By offering general and college-preparatory subjects in science and mathematics.* This is done in many high schools. For example, a freshman may enroll in general mathematics (a general course) or in algebra (a college-preparatory course); or a junior may enroll in physical science (a general course), or in chemistry (a college-preparatory course).

3. *By acceleration in academic subjects.* The academically able student is allowed to "skip" certain beginning courses and enroll in the course at the next higher level, if evidence shows that he has the ability and background to master the course on the higher level. For example, as a freshman he may be allowed to skip English I and enroll in English II. As a senior he would enroll in a college level honors course in English.

4. *By retardation in academic subjects.* The student who is quite deficient academically in a certain area will be urged (or even required) to enroll in a remedial course which is somewhat below the freshman level and then enroll in the regular freshman course as a sophomore. For example, he would enroll in Remedial English as a freshman and enroll in English I as a sophomore. He could graduate after completing English III as a senior.

Broad criteria are used in the screening process including mental test scores, achievement test scores, previous marks, and teacher and counsellor recommendations, together with information gathered from a conference with the student and parent. The willingness of the student to be placed ahead of or behind his classmates in an area is given utmost consideration. As a general rule, no student is accelerated or retarded if his parents are still opposed after the situation has been explained during a conference. Usually the number of students considered for either acceleration or retardation is limited to 10 per cent of the grade involved.

Although this plan works out very well in this particular situation, the following criticisms have been voiced from time to time:

1. *This plan does not group students according to their I.Q.* Comment: This is true; although if students are placed in classes with other students either a year older or a year younger, they are grouped by mental age (M.A.).

2. *It is undesirable to skip courses, since some of the content is not included elsewhere.* Comment: Although this criticism has some validity, it is based on the erroneous assumption that if a student has taken a certain course

he has mastered it, and if he has not taken a course he knows nothing about it. Teachers are often very surprised to learn how well some top eighth grade students will score on a final test given to freshman English students in high school. And experience has shown that, in the majority of cases, "A" students who are allowed to skip a course will continue to be "A" students after they have been accelerated.

3. *This plan does not go far enough in ability grouping.* Comment: This is admittedly only a first short step into ability grouping. More tracks could be added, and more acceleration and retardation could be included. In view of the problems and limitations discussed above, however, it was thought that this was far enough to go at the present time.

Let's not expect too much from ability grouping. Let's not revolutionize our school organization by setting up a costly, inflexible plan which may create more problems than it solves. But let's do something, since there seems to be some gain in student achievement, and a great gain in faculty satisfaction, if the plan is carefully worked out. As a practical matter, it might be easier to include some ability grouping in your classroom organization than to explain to your teachers, board, and community why you don't have it.

But remember—no trick class organization on an ability-grouping basis is going to help provide more efficient learning without appropriate materials for instruction, small classes, and, most important, skilled and understanding teachers.

A Critical Analysis of Standardized Testing*

HARVEY S. LEVITON

In examining the criticisms that have been made concerning testing, it is necessary to have an understanding of the purposes of testing. The basic objective is to enable the examiner to learn something about the subject, and possibly, to make some predictions. What do we do if we want to make some specific prediction? We must learn something about the behavior of the individual or of ones like him. What behavior shall we use? What procedures shall we follow for evaluating the behavior which we intend to use for predictive purposes?

Testing Prerequisites

In answer to the latter question, the major procedure is sampling. A test is an economical way of predicting a larger array of behavior through the use of a smaller array. One of two methods may be followed. In the first, we examine a *true sample* of the behavior. For example, in checking apples we could examine some of the apples for their size, shape, taste, firmness, etc. In the second, we examine a *sign or correlate* of the behavior to be predicted. For example, we could examine the leaves of the apple tree in an attempt to learn about the suitability of the apples for human consumption.

But a test is more complicated than a sample of behavior. There are several other prerequisites, the most important of which is the standardization of the testing procedures. If the conditions are standard and we find test variability, then we can attribute this to the behavioral variability of the individuals. If there

*Reprinted from *The Clearing House*, 41 (March 1967), 391-399, by permission of the publisher and Harvey S. Leviton, Edina-Morningside Public Schools, Edina, Minnesota.

is no standardization, then there is no way to determine what causes variability in the test results. Our goal, therefore, is the complete standardization of testing procedures.

Another prerequisite concerns the content of or items included in the tests. While there is no restriction placed on the content or the way in which it is presented, we do assume, however, that the test content is understandable to the Subject (at least in the questionnaire type tests), that the items are relevant to the behavior being tapped, and that the items elicit scorable, or interpretable, responses.

Another prerequisite of a test is the availability of norms. A score has no meaning in a vacuum. This leads us to discussion of classification theory.

Classification Theory

Everything we do and say is based on a continuous use of a classification system. The course of study is functional or nonfunctional; the professor is interesting or he is not; the woman is attractive or she is ugly; the movie is enjoyable or boring, etc. Classification is the process by which we assign persons or things to a class based upon some defining attribute. Classifications are always man-made. No natural classification systems exist. It is the evaluation of the object by man which determines the categories. Whether a classification scheme is utilized depends upon how functional it is to the user. Librarians classify books by their content, rather than by the color of their cover, because the former is more functional to the people they serve. On the other hand, to printers and book binders the content of the book is immaterial. To them, classification by characteristics other than content is more useful.

There are three prerequisites for a system of classification. (1) The classes are exhaustive. Every member must fit somewhere. (2) The same defining attribute must be used for all classes. (3) The classes must be mutually exclusive, i.e., a member can be in only one class.

What does classification theory have to do with testing? The fact is that norms, which are required before we call an instrument a test, are nothing more than an objective basis for assigning people to classes. Why do we classify people? There are two reasons why this is advantageous. (1) By classifying, we help to simplify and enhance our understanding. (2) Based upon class membership, certain predictions can be made about class members. For example, you can classify people according to their original hair color. Thus we can divide people into the following groups: red, blonde, brown, or black. But for a classification system to be predictably useful, there must be another attribute closely associated with class membership exclusive of the defining characteristics. In our example, we can say that red heads are easily angered, blonds are dizzy, etc.

But this classification system breaks down because the individuals in a class tend to be heterogeneous. However, there is nothing intrinsic to the classification theory to suggest that we use single defining attributes. For example, we can divide humans into two sexes, male or female. Then we can concentrate on males and ask what males do on Saturday night. We can further divide our group of males into college males, those college males who are in a fraternity, and finally, those fraternity members who have a high score on a heterosexual scale of some nature. In doing this, we are refining the classes so that they are more homogeneous and for which the behavioral criterion increases in probability. The defining attribute will help in the classification if, and only if, it is relevant to the behavior being predicted. Potentially, classification can be refined infinitely, with the only restriction being the number of refining attributes.

In considering tests up to this point, an attempt to examine their reason for being has been presented. In addition, we should be aware of the technical requirements of a test. These include reliability and validity. It is assumed that the reader is familiar with these concepts and no explanation will be attempted here.

Methods of Test Construction

There are three methods of developing a test. The first is the empirical or criterion groups method. In this method, we develop a pool of items, not necessarily of any one kind. We accumulate a larger number of items than we plan to use. Then we must identify criterion groups which are clearly distinguishable on the dimension which we are interested in measuring. The large pool of items is presented to the criterion groups, and we establish empirically those items upon which we get differential performance. This process may be replicated by successive distillation of items as long as is desired. This method uses statistics to determine the test content. Subjectivity enters only in the choice of the original pool of items and in the selection of criterion groups. The advantages of this method are that (1) the test is validated in the nature of its construction, and (2) the items tend to be less transparent and more subtle than a rationally derived scale. The disadvantage is that our success at measuring is a function of the extent to which the criterion groups vary solely on the variable we are measuring. If there were other variables involved, the test might just as well be measuring the other variables. Thus, the usefulness of any scale derived by the empirical method is a function of the exclusiveness by which the groups are distinguished by that single criterion property. The Minnesota Multiphasic Personality Test is a test constructed empirically.

The second method of test construction is the rational or judgmental approach. This method is characterized by having expert opinion as to what item content relates to the variable being measured. We decide *a priori* what the item content is and what the keyed response is. The advantages of this method are: (1) it allows for a way of narrowing down the test content, and (2) it has content validity. The disadvantage is that it is a more obvious scale almost by definition. To the extent that a judge can relate the item content to a particular dimension, then to some extent the testee can make the same relation. The success of a rationally derived test is largely contingent upon the amount of *a priori* knowledge available with regard to the measured variable, the degree of expertise of the experts, and the exclusiveness of the behavior dimension.

The third method of test construction is the item analytic. It is a combination of the empirical and the rational. It identifies by statistical procedures scales or items which hang together correlationally and, having identified these scales or factors, sets about identifying their psychological meaning. The rationality concerns the degree of correlation necessary before scales are said to hang together, and concerns the naming of factors, Also, the results of an item analysis are dependent on what goes into it, which is a rational decision. It is a potential improvement over the other methods if our desire is to measure a complex variable (subsumes a wide array of different havior), because if all of these variables are related to a central dimension, this shows up in the intercorrelations. The obvious limitations are that an item analysis can be no better than its input and that the method does not include external validations.

Criticisms of Testing

With this background as to the purpose and construction of tests, let us examine the criticisms (of which there are many) that have been made of the testing movement. Most are due to a misunderstanding of the theory and practice of testing, as presented in the first part of this article. The criticism that the test questions are untrustworthy or ambiguous does not take into account the fact that they were equally so for the standardization sample and still they aided in prediction. Those criticisms made about the misuse of the test are not the fault of the testing industry. They are no more responsible for the misuse of the tests than is the razor blade manufacturing industry responsible for the deaths caused by people slitting their wrists with razor blades. It is to the credit of the testing industry that they have made prodigious efforts to inform testers about the correct methods for test use. In other words, they try to acquaint the users with the purpose and theory of testing in general and with that of the particular test being considered.

According to Dr. Feldt, Director of the Iowa Testing Program, the criticisms of tests come from four primary groups. First, there is the ultra-conservative group. These people feel that the tests are a threat to democracy, that they are a method of bootlegging Socialism into the schools. Second, there are those who regard publishers as exploiters of the schools. They feel that the schools are being financially swindled. Third, there are those who regard testing as unfair because it results in labeling or, as an external device, in controlling the curriculum. Fourth, there are those who doubt the value of tests because of the uses that schools make of them, or because they feel that the people using them are inefficient and/or unqualified.

Some of these points are valid. Competition between the publishers in testing may result in duplication and wasted human effort. On the other hand, such competition may tend to produce better tests. Also, the test user can switch from one test to another to better meet his individual needs.

If the testers do label pupils by the results of the tests, they are not using them correctly. The tests only present unbiased results, rather than personal and subjective teacher standards. Teachers do group their pupils according to their own judgment of ability, social adjustment, etc. The tests enable the teachers to make unbiased and, hopefully, more accurate estimates of pupil characteristics.

The criticism that tests control curriculum has little basis in fact. The testing organizations are professional businesses attempting to earn money. The typical test producer is trying to satisfy the largest audience. Thus, they cannot really control the curriculum but must adjust to the present curriculum. The administrators would not buy a test which did not test what their curriculum was attempting to teach. Consequently, the test producers would not make money. Thus the test producers must adapt the tests to the curriculum set up by the administrators rather than vice versa.

However, a valid criticism is that tests tend to stabilize the curriculum. The use of tests precludes independent thinking in a school system and any innovation in the curriculum may not be tested by the standardized testing program. By and large, test producers are not very experimental. They are more followers than leaders of the curriculum.

It is true that some tests are misused and that some people who administer the school's testing program are not qualified to do the job. But this is becoming less common as the educational institutions are requiring courses in testing for teachers, administrators, counselors and psychologists. Also, the industry provides manuals for administering and interpreting its tests.

Ambiguity is a big criticism. But the critics fail to place themselves in the student's position. The student probably does not see the ambiguity. The small amount which may exist, however, does not invalidate the total score. In any case, there are fewer ambiguities in standardized tests than in teacher-made tests.

Many of the criticisers of the standardized tests fail to realize how the tests are a natural outgrowth from the teacher's natural evaluatory procedures. What starts out as a teacher asking students questions may end up as a standardized national test. We admit that all tests are imperfect. But we never expect perfection in any other product. We must see whether the advantages outweigh the disadvantages or vice versa. If we throw out a test, we may have to rely on less adequate facilities or faculties. The question is not how good the test is, but rather is there anything better available?

Conclusion

Tests could be an unmitigated blessing to education if only teachers, counselors, educational administrators, students, and parents would divest themselves of a number of misconceptions.[1]

1. Aptitude or intelligence tests measure something called native ability, something fixed and immutable within the person that determines his level of expectation for all time. The fact is that the kinds of mental tasks that appear in any intelligence or aptitude test are clearly the kinds that a student learns to perform from his experiences in the world around him.
2. A prediction made from a test score is, or should be, perfectly accurate, and if it is not, the test must be regarded as ineffective. It is more meaningful to view a prediction as a statement of the odds.
3. Standardized test scores are infallible or perfectly reliable.
4. An achievement test measures all there is to measure in any given subject area.
5. An achievement test can measure only a pupil's memory of facts. In truth, it also measures the pupil's skill in reasoning about the facts he remembers and those newly presented to him.
6. A profile of scores summarizes clearly and efficiently a considerable amount of reliable information about the relative strengths and weaknesses of an individual.
7. Interest inventories measure some kind of basic orientation of a student, irrespective of the kinds of experiences to which he has been or will be exposed.
8. A personality test reveals deep and permanent temperamental characteristics unaware to the individual.
9. A battery of tests can tell all one needs to know in making a judgment about a student's competence, present and potential, and about his effectiveness as a human being. The fact is that no test or series of tests now available is capable of giving the total picture of any child.

It is hoped that such misconceptions about and misuses of standardized testing will diminish through increased educational efforts by the testing industry and by training institutions.

[1]Henry S. Dyer, "Is Testing a Menace to Education," *New York State Education,* Vol. 49 (Oct. 1961), pp. 16-19.

The Great Fault in School Marks*

PALMER DE PUE

With essentially two quite distinct but closely related meanings, the word *fault* expresses, in a nutshell, the troublesome situation today in educational measurement. Technically, the geologist uses it to describe a sharp displacement in the orderly strata of the earth's surface. Commonly, we all use it to indicate an error, or mistake, or blemish. The thesis that I here propound and defend is that (1) a sharp displacement occurred in the early years of the present century in our most common and effective system of notation for educational measurement; that (2) subsequently, or concurrently, an additional disturbance further compounded that displacement; and that (3) more recent attempts at a satisfactory system of notation have merely glossed over and hidden the original fault so that consequent errors in measuring academic achievement continue to plague with fallacious results those who, for various reasons, would attempt to evaluate and predict academic performance.

The system of marking by percentage—which admittedly is an arbitrary human, and not divine, system—was understandably the basis of school marking systems in the early years of the twentieth century because the percentage system, going back to the Romans, has become a part of the orderly strata of the modern civilized world. Two forces, since these early years, have displaced the orderly nature of the percentage or decimal system as applied to school marks and marking systems: (1) Objective testing with its almost complete use of multiple choice questions, gaining impetus after World War I, introduced the factor of definite but variable guessability, or random selection of answers; and (2) the idea of an arbitrary hurdle, set up usually at seventy, for "passing," introduced a disharmonious element when viewed in the presence of the observable natural phenomenon of the normal distribution curve.

When, in a "closed" system of a definite number of choices as opposed to

*Reprinted from *The Journal of Secondary Education,* 42 (May 1967), 217-222, by permission of the publisher and Palmer DePue, Frankford High School, Philadelphia, Pa.

an "open" system of an infinite number of choices, the possibility of guessing increases greatly, obviously a less knowledgeable examinee will have a greater chance to show an apparent capability in comparison with a highly knowledgeable examinee. And this capability will appear to increase as the guessability increases until with only two choices (or true-false) he can appear to know half of the test material while actually knowing nothing. Until this inequity of seeming knowledge is eliminated, final results of different type tests should not be compared directly. Different type tests must have results accurately adjusted to a common basis of probable knowledge to be compared on a single ratio scale. Only recently has a simple answer form been devised (OMNIQUIZ) making such adjustment possible automatically for all types of multiple choice tests by the answer form itself.[1]

The true character of the other disruptive element, the fixed hurdle of seventy for passing, can be seen clearly only when we turn to the natural phenomenon of normal distribution—and probably nothing in the whole field of education is so thoroughly misunderstood. And yet a little common sense reflection can readily illustrate a "normal curve of distribution." We all, surely, have met some workmen in any field of endeavor who are not nearly as skillful as they should be or claim to be. On the other hand, we also, hopefully, have been blessed by the work of a few highly skilled workmen, outstanding in their fields, to whom so many turn that they can demand—and deserve—a high reward for their services. These are the two extremes. Between them, in any walk of life, are far more persons of average performance. This is all that a "normal distribution" is. It must take a pretty jaundiced disposition to think that half of the doctors one meets are quacks; or half of the lawyers, shysters; or half of the teachers, misfits; *or half of the pupils, failures.*

In the light of this reflection, then, consider what happens when we set up the artificial hurdle of seventy for passing. If we are going to mark on a uniform scale of zero to 100, we will have to allow as much room for examinees with outstanding ability as for those with scant ability, with the great mass, or average, in the middle. That means a midscore of 50. Notice, the word is *midscore,* not "passing!" And most test experts agree that, for accurate discrimination, tests should be devised that produce a midscore at least approaching 50. But with 70 for *passing,* the midscore would have to be at least 80 or higher, and a large portion of the group then would not be challenged at all. Or else we must put ourselves in that unsavory group who thinks half—or more—of the people they meet are failures.

Percentile rating, the popular answer to these two disruptive elements in marking, eliminates one—70 for passing—but glosses over the other instead of correcting it. Instead of adjusting automatically for the differences in

[1]Palmer DePue, "On A Uniform Standard for Marking," *Journal of Experimental Education* (Spring 1965), p. 231.

guessability among different types of multiple choice tests, while retaining the basic idea of the test as a standard, percentile rating throws out the baby with the bath and substitutes an altogether different step-child. Instead of the test, carefully devised to be comprehensive and impartial in determining the extent of the individual's cognitive learning, the standard now becomes the immediate group of examinees itself. Now we have only the vaguest semblance of the original standard, appropriately designated with the -ile suffix, *percentile.* All standards, to be sure, are relative, but the serious fault of percentile rating lies not in a change in degree of relativity but in the very subject to which the standard is relative: a particular group of examinees instead of the carefully devised test itself, which everyone assumes is the basic reference point for a standard.

This subtle shift, from the stable standard of a carefully devised test by a knowledgeable test maker to the extreme flexibility of the average capability of the individuals making up any separate group, causes the instability of marks by percentile rating. From it arise all of our devious machinations in trying presently to arrive at a uniform, equitable notation in educational measurement. When we mark in terms of the 90th percentile and the 80th percentile, etc., regardless of where the midscore comes on a carefully devised test, we are abandoning the idea of any standard but that of the current herd, or group. And when we abandon the idea of a fixed standard, we abandon the basic idea of accurate measurement: careful and exact comparison with a stable, accurate standard.

A simple illustration will show how we have abandoned on one hand the idea of a fixed standard while trying at the same time to give recognition to some specious sort of standard the basis of which is obscure but the very obscurity of which gives the impression of security. The principal of Exburg High School (any large urban high school with which I am sure thousands of teachers can identify) announces in faculty meeting that no failing pupil is to be given a mark lower than 50. The citywide marking system is based on 70 for passing, and since marks are cumulative, a failing mark of, say, 20 or 30 would make it impossible on the next report for a pupil to pass even if he did work of 100 per cent right from then on. In other words, we would have stamped "failure" on him so indelibly before we had seen even a majority of his work that that label, no matter what he did, would stick to the last. So teachers are asked to take up the slack in a ridiculous marking system by "giving" the pupil a meaningless mark of 50 instead of *recording* an accurately observed, meaningful mark on a ratio scale of zero to 100. A yardstick that has to have the lower half ignored is something less than a measuring instrument.

To clear our thinking, at this point, let us return to the basic, orderly strata of percentage that any child can understand as soon as he learns to count money. (It is most significant that those systems of money not expressed in the decimal system are troublesome in today's world of exchange and are turning to the decimal system.) If, by waving a magic wand, all tests for any category of individuals (by age, ability, social or economic level, etc.) including all such individuals in the world, could be so devised that the midscore would always be 50, our problem automatically would be solved. Let all teachers and test constructors everywhere, then, aim their tests for results, with any given group, that will approach consistently a midscore of 50. This simple procedure will bring more immediate stability to marking than any other factor that can be brought to bear on the vexed problem of marks and marking in school and college.

Anyone who has worked conscientiously at trying to measure human ability must be aware of at least one thing: *its infinite variability*. But the more closely this variability is studied the more readily it will be seen, in any group, to approach a normal distribution curve of results. This means that by abandoning the concept of an arbitrary percentage for passing–such as 70 or 60–which an examinee *ought* to get right in a test and recognizing what actually happens, and can be observed to happen naturally, we can so adjust our tests, and should so train ourselves or be trained to adjust our tests, that the midscore, more or less closely, will approach 50. The more nearly our testing achieves a midscore of 50, the nearer we will all be to a uniform standard for marking. *And then teachers will know also where they, as test makers, stand every time they give a test.* By standing up to be counted the teacher will put himself in the marking picture, then, and if the test results vary too far from a midscore of 50, the test should be rejected as invalid for that group.

Again a simple illustration will help to clarify my meaning. If I devise a test and so poorly judge the capabilities of the group that the midscore comes out at 20, I reject those results, as being invalid measurements, because the midscore is too close to maximum guessability to have much significance. The test, however,will not have been wasted because it will show *me* how to devise one with results more highly significant for that group and will have been useful as review for the pupils. Perhaps a closer look at the old story of Procrustes will be useful here. Instead of cutting off a person to fit a bed or stretching him, as did the giant of Attica, we have observed how people grow, and have built beds accordingly. We do not have to build an infinite number of sizes of beds but need only cribs for infants, regular beds, and possibly extra long ones for very tall adults. Just so, we should have observed, by now, how people grow in mental (academic) stature. After ten years of fairly intensive observation of test results on all ability levels of high school pupils in a large city, I am thoroughly convinced that we, as classroom teachers, should be able to build tests much more nearly approaching a common standard.

Is it too much to ask that, on the tests we devise, by far the majority of pupils (80% or more) should score between 20 and 80 on a scale of zero to 100?

The question seems almost ridiculous. Isn't that what we would expect with a normal distribution curve placed ideally with its midscore at 50? Yet many people would be shocked if, to eliminate stragglers, we proposed a tentative passing hurdle at an honest 20, with guessing always adjusted for. We have become so inured to the artificial idea that a pupil "ought" to know 70 percent or more to pass, instead of observing what actually happens and setting our notations accordingly, that we completely overlook all of the stratagems by which we "help" a pupil to achieve 70%–of what!

With a small answer form available that automatically adjusts for guessing, it is now possible to eliminate that disruptive factor in the approach to more uniform results in testing and marking. And since pupils *are* people–let us never forget–all that remains for the achievement of much more accurate and consistent marking is to observe how people group normally in mental (academic) stature and to build tests accordingly. If all objective (multiple choice) tests for cognitive learning are aimed at a midscore of 50, after guessing has been eliminated, we can approach much more closely to a uniform notation in marking. Marked on a ratio scale of zero to 100, with the only possible five equal divisions for the usual correlated letter marks of A, B, C, D, F, set off at 80, 60, 40, and 20, the work of students everywhere will be seen to approach a normal distribution that we should have identified by accurate notation long before the passage of two-thirds of the twentieth century.

Such a procedure would be an excellent compromise between the authoritative standard of the test itself and the permissive standard (if such a contradictory expression makes sense) of the percentile rating, which allows the group to determine its own standard. I do not have to tell any experienced test maker that he will not always produce a test for which the midscore is 50. But by aiming for that and setting up limits of plus or minus 15, 20, or even 25, we can neatly control both the authoritarianism of the test itself and the permissiveness of the percentile rating which allows uncontrolled flexibility. The test itself remains the standard but becomes a humane and reasonable one. And if the teacher is human enough to put himself in the marking game, he should record the midscore for each test in his record book so he can keep score on himself as well as on his pupils.

When a teacher will put himself in the picture as a centralizing or standardizing factor, responsible for devising tests mathematically appropriate for any given group (and that is all that is meant by tests that approach a midscore of 50 on a ratio scale of zero to 100), a unified picture begins to appear in educational measurement that has been too long disrupted and distorted. And was it not Immanuel Kant who said that truth is unity? There is something painfully schizoid about asking everyone who hopes to pass to make a mark of 70 when the most accurately discriminating scale, based on careful observation of humanity at large, sets the *average* performance at 50. Is this a significant element in the production of our schizoid society? What more intimate aspect, outside of his immediate family, is there in the heartland of a child's maturing than the marks with which we teachers, his substitute parents, brand him in his school life? Should we "take it out" on the pupils because our ego as a teacher is deflated by the fact that we just cannot make every pupil learn 70 percent of what he "ought" to learn when we should have observed that it is not in human nature to do so?

Unless teachers are so constituted that they take sadistic pleasure in flunking large numbers of pupils—and there are some, undoubtedly, who do—they should be able to observe that, in any school system at any level, teachers and pupils both are the product of the society around them. Likewise, the standards found in the society which the schools represent should be clearly reflected in the schools themselves. It is quite beside the point to argue here whether, in the country at large, society should lead the schools or the schools should lead society. In either case the gap between the two in the nature and use of standards should not be large. If we find in society at large that there are only a few stragglers that life catches up with and passes by as failures, as well as only a few outstanding thinkers and leaders recognized as such, then the same should be true in our schools. If a school, or department within a school, decides that one third of its pupils are failing, then it should also decide that *it* is failing almost to the same degree.

We could get into very deep philosophical waters trying to decide the responsibility of the school in society. *That very fact makes it extremely important to know what we are doing in the schools.* Are we actually failing too many, or too few? Do we represent the community around us, or should we be turning out fewer failures than it turns out? Are all dropouts failures or just liabilities of a senseless and chaotic marking system? We should all be deeply concerned about such questions but especially about this basic one: are we measuring accurately the results of the work of the schools, or are we just kidding ourselves with a ridiculously inadequate marking system when there are such serious questions to be answered?

While I am most pessimistic about our system of so-called measurement in education, I am not pessimistic about our schools. I am fortunate enough to have had first-hand experience working in civil service, in private industry, and in the public schools, and I think that teachers as a group are more conscientious, concerned, and dedicated than almost any other workers anywhere. I do think they often lack imagination, and they are so conservative, like introverted parents with too many children, that they often shun the very innovations they most need to help them. It is my firm conviction, though,—to the correction of which I have dedicated the last eight years of intensive work over and beyond my classroom duties—that teachers everywhere are victims of a ridiculous marking system, or rather a lack of any accurate marking system, for which our universities, colleges, and research foundations are responsible. They (and by "they" I mean the experts in testing from these institutions) have so swallowed up—hook, line, and sinker—the specious system of percentile rating that they are incapable of looking beyond it to see its serious shortcomings, or of listening to anyone who would point them out. Theirs is a heavier burden of responsibility than that of any classroom teacher for leaving no stone unturned—or voice unanswered—in the vigorous search for more accurate marking.

But by a simple strategy of four practical elements, classroom teachers everywhere right now can achieve more unified marking by: (1) using an *accurate* scale of zero to 100, (2) equalizing the influence of guessing, (3) aiming *all* of their tests at a midscore of 50, and (4) counting as failures only the stragglers. These things, now, are not too much to ask any teacher. Together they give all of us in schools everywhere a common goal toward which we can work with a strong feeling of approaching justice in marking.

The Pros and Cons of the National Assessment Project*

LAWRENCE BEYMER

Last year the wise men of the Association for Supervision and Curriculum Development gathered with fire in their eyes not unlike that which Moses must have had when he came down from that mountain. Their denunciation of the National Assessment Program was bitter. I haven't heard anything so emotional since another group of educators attacked *Life* magazine a few years ago, urging schools to cancel their subscriptions.

What the Opponents Are Saying

First, many critics are quite upset at the manner in which this project was initiated; in fact, they feel the whole approach was rather "sneaky." They point to the facts of the matter: the Commissioner of Education went to a private foundation, bypassing other legal, responsible, policy-making groups and individuals in the process. Moreover, the Constitution of the "illegal" committee and its apparent secrecy of deliberations and decisions arouse both suspicion and resentment. Harold Hand points out that it is impossible to construct valid and reliable tests unless or until the objectives and goals which are to be considered are decided upon. These critics are able to go back as far as 1936 to quote the chairman of this committee to the effect that "In order to make a list of major objectives usable in building examinations, each objective must be defined in terms which clarify the kind of behavior that the course should help to determine among the students."(1)[1] Where, demand the critics, do these seven

*Reprinted from *The Clearing House,* 40 (May 1966), 540-543, by permission of the publisher and Lawrence Beymer, Indiana State University.

[1]Numbers in parentheses refer to references at the end of the article.

or eight individuals get their mantle of responsibility to choose what behaviors will be sought after, and which ones will be ignored?

So criticism number one seems to be, "This project is being conducted in secrecy by individuals who have no right to exercise so much power."

Second, regardless of the title, "National Assessment Program," this is in fact a national achievement testing program. "A rose by any other name," and you know the rest. The "rest," in this case, consists of all of the evils of national "standards" which have been chronicled in the literature for years. And this choice of terms, say the critics, is not at all accidental, but simply more deception by mislabeling.

A *third* criticism is somewhat complicated, but perhaps it can be summarized by saying that many fear that data from this project will be used as ammunition for more unfair, unjustified, and unwarranted attacks upon the schools. And to defend against such potential attacks, schools are likely, consciously or unconsciously, to "teach the tests."

David Goslin, in a book which has received far less notice than it deserves, (2) summarizes this phenomenon very concisely. Standardized achievement tests measure much more than the individual's level of attainment; they also measure the adequacy of his learning environments, home, school, and community, as well as the competence of those responsible for those environments—parents and teachers. Thus externally administered achievement tests tend to evaluate all of these groups together: students, parents, teachers, and administrators. Such joint involvement results in pressures toward high performance, since anything less may be interpreted as less-than-satisfactory child-raising, teaching, and/or school administration. To minimize the chances of this indirect criticism. Goslin says the most natural thing for parents, teachers, and administrators to do is to try to insure high levels of performance by students on the tests. And they do. Thus in New York much of the curriculum is geared to coaching pupils to do well on the Regents' examinations. And as if to validate the theory suggested above, the parents and teachers and school administrators would have it no other way; to do otherwise would be to run the risk of poorer test performance, and the predictable series of criticisms and seeking of scapegoats.

The National Assessment Program, say the critics, may very well unleash all sorts of pressures toward curriculum change just to improve test scores, and may keep schools from doing what they *want* to do and what they *ought* to do in way of curriculum.

Fourth and finally, many of those who include themselves among the critics of the National Assessment Program bear scars from other grand adventures in the past. Many educators today feel that they were prematurely pushed and pressured by well financed opinion and propaganda to institute such programs as language labs, programed learning, foreign language in elementary schools, team teaching, instructional television, and elementary school guidance counseling. Not only will a burned child avoid future hot stoves, but he will shun cold ones as well. So, rightly or wrongly, many see this program as little more than a source of future blisters.

What the Proponents Are Saying

Certainly not all educators, perhaps not even a majority, oppose this program; many actively support it. Some of their chief arguments seem to be as follows:

First, they insist that education is getting too big, too complicated, too expensive, and too important to continue without systematic estimation of outputs and progress. This year nearly 28 per cent of the entire United States population is enrolled in school, we are spending approximately 6 per cent of our gross national product for education, and we not only expect more but are promised more in the way of results. Unsupported opinion is no longer sufficient: more concrete facts are sorely called for. This project can furnish some of those facts, and for that reason alone it is worth supporting.

Second, the supporters claim the critics are tilting at windmills, wrestling straw men, and frightening themselves with spooks of their own creation. Ralph Tyler, in a reply to the critics, makes the following points: (3)

1. No individual pupil, classroom, or school will be identifiable in the data; thus nobody will be able to find out how specific children or schools performed.
2. The assessment project will be so designed as to present examples of what kinds of things are learned by four different age groups, 9, 13, 17, and adults, illustrating what all or almost all have learned, what the most advanced have learned, and what is learned by the "average."
3. The project was organized under private commission in order to keep the state and federal governments out of it, to exclude political misuses.
4. No school classroom and no individual will take the complete battery, nor will they get written reports of their performances.

Everybody wants to be a critic, yet nobody wants to be criticized. So the second rejoinder from the supporters is a charge that the critics are "yelling before they're hurt," crying "wolf" when in reality there is no wolf at all.

A *third* point made by the supporters is to the effect that if, indeed, the National Assessment Program reveals weaknesses, it is hardly the fault of the measuring process that they exist!

As Henry Chauncey pointed out in the 1961 Report of the Educational Testing Service, a standardized achievement test asks all students to run the same race, regardless of their economic, social, educational, cultural, or racial backgrounds. If these opportunities and environments have been seriously inadequate, the student is likely to do poorly on the test. But this only highlights the effects of failing to provide educational opportunity for all children according to their abilities. Moreover, suggests Chauncey, it may even serve the useful purpose of pointing out that talent and ability tend to be produced in direct proportion to excellence of educational opportunity.

Clifford and Fishman, in another context, liken this situation to that of residents of Bismark, North Dakota, charging bias of temperature measurement when their thermometers read minus 20 while those in Miami Beach read plus 85. (4) This is no less rational than blaming a testing program for revealing inequalities of achievement from area to area. If such differences exist, all a testing program does is to report them.

A *fourth* point made by the supporters is that critics are clearly confusing *norms* with *standards*. Norms deal with what *is*. Standards deal with what *ought to be*. The National Assessment Project is to be set up in such a fashion that it will collect information on the status of things. Of course, after this initial step standards and value judgments will be applied to these normative data, but it will be done by those individuals and groups who are responsible for making such judgments.

A *fifth* point made by supporters of the National Assessment Program: we have already had one form of a national assessment project, Project TALENT, and the results from it haven't corrupted or compromised anybody yet. Subtitled "A Census of U. S. Youth's Abilities," it involved the testing of 440,000 students in 1,353 secondary schools in the spring of 1960, and follow-up testing is scheduled through 1983.

Rather than to fight such efforts, say their supporters, the critics might very well ponder the implications of results like the following for curricular planning: (5)

1. The average high school student apparently doesn't solve simple reasoning problems as well as he memorizes simple rules (like the rules of capitalization) and applies them.

2. Less than half of the 12th grade students understand the subtler ideas in typical paragraphs from the writings of Sinclair Lewis, Jules Verne, or Rudyard Kipling. Much smaller percentages understand the writings of Thomas Mann or typical articles in the *Atlantic Monthly* or the *Saturday Review*. (My own guess is that the figures for a sample of the adult population would be even lower!)

3. From 20 to 30 per cent of the students in grade 9 know more about many subject-matter fields than does the average student in grade 12. Variability *within* grades was found to be greater than variability *between* grades. (This seems to be another powerful argument for individualizing instruction).

4. Most of the differences between the mean test scores of boys and girls were fairly small. Boys tended to do better than girls in mathematics,

particularly at the upper grade levels. (But in grade 9, for some reason, the differences were negligible). The girls performed better than boys on all tests of language skills, including English.

The National Assessment Project supporters say, "These are examples of the kind of data we are after, only in more detail, and over a wider range of subject-matter areas."

Finally I get the impression the supporters of this project are both surprised and flattered to be the target of so much concern. One gets the impression that the critics really believe that this project will in actuality bring about sweeping changes in curriculum. When you consider the results of previous attempts to bring about such change, such fear is somewhat flattering. College courses, workshops, course syllabi, and supervisors have had a most difficult time in changing actual classroom programs and practices, so one wonders why all the concern about a testing program. Perhaps the critics are over-reacting, and expecting more than could ever come to pass.

References

(1) Herbert E. Hawkes, E.F. Lindquist, and C.R. Mann, *The Construction and Use of Achievement Examinations.* Houghton Mifflin Co., 1936, pp. 9-10.

(2) David Goslin, *The Search for Ability: Standardized Testing in Social Perspective.* Russel Sage Foundation, 1963.

(3) Ralph Tyler, "Assessing the Progress of Education," *Phi Delta Kappan,* Vol. XLVII, No. 1 (September 1965), pp. 13-16.

(4) Paul A. Clifford and Joshua A. Fishman, "The Impact of Testing Programs on College Preparation and Attendance," NSSE Yearbook Part II, 1963, *The Impact and Improvement of School Testing Programs.*

(5) Project TALENT staff, *The American High School Student.* Project TALENT Office, University of Pittsburgh, 1964.

Homework—Is It Needed?*

JOHN F. CHECK

The topic of homework has always been a hotly debated issue with school people and parents alike. As early as 1926, Good (5)[1] in the *Elementary School Journal* writes:

> We do not favor, then, the abolishment of all home study; but the study must be of such a nature that it will interest the child and contribute to his growth; he must be able to do it without assistance (in fact, it should be of such a nature that he cannot well get help on it); and it must be work that he will want to do. Formal lessons should be, for the most part if not entirely, confined to the schoolroom. There should be no compulsory home tasks assigned in the lower grades, and there may be serious doubts as to the wisdom of requiring homework in any of the grades of the elementary school (although pupils in the upper grades can well do homework requiring from one to two hours daily), the reasonable plan being to have such work done voluntarily, following the inclination of the child in selecting his particular assignment.

Admissions standards of colleges and universities are more stringent now than ever before. Furthermore, there is every indication that the trend is for higher and higher grade point averages. This indisputable fact has moved parents and teachers to question children's study habits in school and at home. More and more parents ask: "Can my child learn enough at school? Doesn't he need homework assignments too?" If the latter is true (and it appears so), then what constitutes the most appropriate kind of homework; how much of it should teachers require; when should it be given; and how should it be assigned?

*Reprinted from *The Clearing House,* 41 (November 1966), 143-147, by permission of the publisher and John F. Check, Wisconsin State University.

[1]Numbers in parentheses refer to references at the end of the article.

Homework is given for various reasons, constructive and negative alike. In the following section some of the arguments for and against homework will be examined.

(1) Often assignments are too lengthy, hence they must be completed in the after-school hours. The foes of homework suggest that the teacher tailor the lesson plan to class time. Why present the leftovers to tired pupils and anxious parents?

(2) Modern educators like to offer research techniques to their classes, and pupils are challenged to seek material from home and community. But the skeptics remind us that few students will research the problem adequately. Those who do, would do so without being coerced by an assignment.

(3) Since extra curricular activities in school absorb some of the out-of-class time and thus prohibit ample study and practice periods, home assignments help offset this loss. The opposition would ask, "Is the school's only obligation to cram academic facts into the student, or should it not help him become an all-around better individual?"

(4) Instruction in public and parochial schools is handled on a mass basis. This gives validity to home assignments because the teacher is not able to devote enough individual time. The argument against this is that parents feel they are not familiar with current techniques and thus are afraid that their "help" may be a hindrance to the student. Furthermore, there are many parents who feel very strongly that the interaction with their children should be on activities other than school-oriented tasks. These parents resent homework assignments and thus they help the child establish a negative attitude toward school and learning experiences.

(5) Homework helps develop self-discipline. In other words, the student must learn that there are things in life that must be done regardless of how dissatisfying the task may be. The opposition would assert that most children must be coerced to do homework. Is this self-discipline?

(6) Homework permits more individualization of instruction and offers the student the opportunity to broaden his horizons. But there are those cynics who say that, rather than broadening his horizons, the student walks a straight and narrow path. Some undeviating pilgrims progress from parent, to telephone, to encyclopedia, to textbook, producing only token results.

(7) One of the major premises underlying homework assignments is that these stimulate independent study and research habits. This is conceivable with those students who dig in. But what about the student who whines and inveigles someone else to provide him with the answers; who abjures even the encyclopedia?

(8) Homework must be occasionally assigned as a disciplinary measure; how else can we convince the students that we mean business? "Find other ways!" say the opposition. The effective teacher maintains proper decorum in

his classroom by gaining the confidence of each student, earning this respect by manifesting respect for the student.

(9) There is also the "public relations" philosophy concerning homework. Homework impresses parents that much is happening at school; so much, in fact, that it is not possible to accomplish all of the learning experiences at school.

Lack of adequate research and research instruments, differentiated home environments and differences in personalities make generalizations about homework difficult and almost impossible. So many of the articles reported in journals are predominantly opinion articles, not experimental ones.

Consider the widely differing views of these reseachers: Ruth Strang (9) in the N.E.A. booklet concludes that there is no evidence to support the use of habitual or routine homework. Waterman (10) concurs with Strang, but modifies this strong position by pointing out that very few people would question the value of homework. Still, this in itself hardly supports the notion that the young student should be labored with 55 to 60 hours of schoolwork per week. Whalen (11) takes a stronger stand for homework than either Waterman or Strang, but he emphasizes a constructive homework program where assignments should be commensurate with the varying levels of ability. This suggests that the qualitative rather than the quantitative phase of homework must be stressed. Yet Baughman and Pruitt (2) found otherwise. They studied seventh and eighth grade students in which one group received routine homework while the other subjects received enrichment study. Findings rejected their own hypothesis. The enrichment type of homework assignments offered no appreciable acceleration over the traditional assignment. Then another psychologist, Baker (1), in summarizing the opinions and accepted assumptions that she gathered, concluded that homework assignments can be stimulating, can promote learning, and can provide material for experimentation.

What about required hours of homework? Otto (7) concludes that only a slight relationship exists between time spent on homework and pupil progress. He found that homework had no significant relationship to achievement as measured by teachers' marks and standardized tests. He suggests that the benefits accruing from homework are too small to counterbalance the disadvantages, especially for children from poor environments. The McGills (3), after conducting a study of 185 pairs of high school students, all closely matched in ability, report that there was no difference in achievement in American history between those who had homework and those who did not. In a subsequent test they found a slightly higher performance in the non-homework students. Selwyn's findings (8) correspond with McGill. She found that children read 80 per cent better after the abolition of compulsory homework and many I.Q. scores improved simultaneously. Could we conclude from the last two reports that in order to improve history, reading, and I.Q. scores, all we need to do is to abolish homework? Goldstein (4) reports to the contrary.

Of 280 articles which Goldstein reviewed, 17 were experimental in nature and the remainder were opinion articles. He summarizes these articles by stating that homework leads to higher academic achievement; that homework is more important at some grades than others, in some subjects than others, for some pupils than others; that homework develops independent work study skills; and finally, that there is no support in the research to indicate that homework had bad psychological effects.

An article by Mulry (6) states that there is little conclusive evidence available concerning positive and negative effects of homework. She concludes by stating that only too few experimental studies on homework are available and those reported are limited in number, scope, and quality.

As this writer reviewed the available articles and reports of research, he felt compelled to contribute to this topic in both an empirical and experimental fashion. In a recent survey he administered 1016 questionnaries to six diversely different populations. His respondents were (a) students of lower and upper elementary grades, from junior high and from senior high schools, (b) parents of the four levels above, (c) teachers of the four designated levels and professors from the University of Michigan, Flint College, and (d) education majors who were at that time electing educational psychology or educational sociology.

The selection of schools was designed so that reactions would be received from both public and parochial systems as well as from a predominantly professional area and from a more restricted cultural environment. Returns of questionnaires were almost 100 per cent. The items of information sought through the questionnaire were:

(a) the school in which the child was enrolled.

(b) whether the respondent was a parent, the teacher, or the student; and if a student, what grade.

(c) whether the respondent felt that homework should be assigned.

(d) to find out why or why not such assignments should be made.

After tabulating the data from the questionnaire and analyzing particular aspects of its contents, we find that the following statements are in order:

(1) Elementary, junior, and senior high students generally feel that homework assignments are necessary. Only 20 per cent were definitely against such assignments. However, almost one-half of them wanted to reserve the right to question the type of assignments given.

(2) Parochial school students are no different from public school children in regard to homework.

(3) The highest ratio of negative responses to homework came from children in the professional home. On the other hand, there was only one professional parent who was *positively* against such activities.

(4) Out of 205 parents responding, only seven of them rejected homework in any form. About one-half of them questioned the nature and the amount of homework assignments that should be given.

(5) Of 90 teacher respondents, only one desired no homework at all. Half of them were concerned about the kind of assignments given.

(6) Professors at Flint College are strongly in favor of take-home assignments.

(7) Nearly 55 per cent of education majors (candidates for teaching) want homework. Another 38 per cent are in favor of these assignments but with conditions prescribed.

It is not possible here to reproduce the large array of interesting and worthwhile remarks that were offered by all segments of the population studied. However, many of the comments are inherent in these suggestions:

(1) Class periods are too short to provide depth and breadth to the concepts studied, hence some homework is not only desirable but essential.

(2) Homework assignments should be constructive in nature, that is, they should be interrelated with class work, not mere busy work.

(3) Homework should be carefully planned and assigned so that the student knows what to do and how he is to transfer the results to the immediate classroom project.

(4) A closely coordinated plan for homework should be structured by the school so that particular courses will necessitate home activities on particular days.

(5) Week ends, as much as possible, should be devoid of homework assignments to allow the student to participate in family and personal activities and, in a true sense, to get away from it all.

(6) Scheduled curricular and extra-curricular school activities should preclude lengthy homework assignments. School spirit for conscientious students is highly improbable when extensive assignments loom over them as an ominous cloud.

(7) A well constructed and meaningful presentation of a skill and/or concept must precede the homework assignment.

(8) The amount and the nature of homework should be determined by the age and the grade of the student. If any, a very minimum of home assignments should be given to the lower elementary child.

(9) If homework is to build character, a sense of responsibility, and persevering qualities, the assignments must be such that they can be accomplished independently and with the least amount of parental help and prodding.

With few exceptions, most researchers have found that homework in some fashion or another is desirable. This writer found that most students want and expect outside-of-school assignments, but these should be well planned, of a positive learning nature, and should be meted out with moderation.

It is indeed most encouraging to observe and to learn that so many persons of various walks of life do take such serious interest in homework activities. Educators of all levels are in a unique position to make homework a desirable experience. They can achieve this by re-examining the character of homework tasks they assign to their students.

References

(1) Janet B. Baker, "College Students and Their Assignments," *Journal of Educational Research,* 54:49-53 (1960).
(2) M. Dale Baughman and Wesley Pruitt, "Supplemental Study for Enrichment vs. Supplemental Study for Reinforcement of Academic Achievement," *The Bulletin of the National Associdtion of Secondary School Principals,* 47:154-157 (March, 1963).
(3) James and Marjorie McGill, "Forget it," *Time*, 56:74-76 (1950).
(4) Avram S. Goldstein, "Does Homework Help?" *Elementary School Journal,* 60:212-224 (January, 1960).
(5) Warren R. Good, "Opinions on Homework for Elementary School Pupils," *Elementary School Journal,* 27:122 (October, 1926).
(6) June G. Mulry, "We Need Research on Homework," *Journal of the National Education Association,* 50:49 (1961).
(7) H. J. Otto, "Homework–Home Study," *Encyclopedia of Educational Research,* First Edition.
(8) Amy P. Selwyn, "No More Homework?" *This Week Magazine* (May, 1951).
(9) Ruth Strang, "Guided Study and Homework," *National Education Association Journal,* 44:399-400 (October, 1955).
(10) Albert D. Waterman, "Homework: Curse or Blessing?" *The Bulletin of the National Association of Secondary School Principals,* 49:42-45 (1965).
(11) Thomas J. Whalen, "Homework," *The Bulletin of the National Association of Secondary School Principals,* 45:121-122 (November, 1961).

Outmoded Study Halls Give Way to Learning Centers*

MELVIN P. HELLER

It is time for school administrators and teachers to analyze the purpose of study halls in their schools. A cursory glance at the usual study hall activities reveals little study, and much time wasted. Some students can learn under the most adverse circumstances, but there are great numbers who cannot, or will not, and certainly do not give evidence of intellectual activity in the typical environment which school people term study halls.

Study halls thwart teacher efficiency. The professional competence of a teacher cannot be utilized in the face of his role as a policeman, attendance taker, disciplinarian, and master of all subjects. The physical strength necessary to enforce silence in a study hall may be a personal attribute of some teachers, but common sense would dictate that mere muscle power cannot be equated with intellectual stimulation. The variety of academic activities which vast numbers of pupils in a study hall would undertake presents too great a challenge for most teachers. It is not uncommon for students to ask a teacher of English who is in charge of a study hall for help in mathematics, physics, bookkeeping, French, and, perhaps, English. Except for some chance factors, the asininity of the situation affords the teacher little opportunity to work effectively with pupils on academic considerations.

If the task of the teacher is thwarted, the task of the student is thwarted even more. If the fact that teacher assistance is seldom available does not daunt the student, he can find other obstacles in his learning path. Study halls are seldom equipped with study materials, other than the textbooks which students may or may not bring with them. Charts, maps, drill work, resource materials, slides, programed materials are seldom available in a study hall. The barren

*Reprinted from *The Clearing House,* 38 (December 1963), 231-233, by permission of the publisher and Melvin P. Heller, Loyola University.

atmosphere cannot be stimulating to the majority of students who find themselves herded together in one large area.

For those existing study hall situations which are deemed appropriate and effective, the students and teachers and administrators deserve sincere congratulations and praise. For those study hall situations where the preceding comments are descriptive, a change in the situation is essential. The use of learning centers (or resource centers, as they are sometimes called) may offer a solution to the problem where it exists.

Any school which is seriously interested in providing learning centers can find space for one or more of them. Learning centers can be located in many parts of the building. A learning center should be equipped with a variety of pupil materials which provide for individual differences in terms of interest, ability, and achievement. Examples of these materials are programed instruction, paintings, maps, charts, slides, scale models, books, reference works, magazines, photographs, and tape recorders. A classroom can be converted into a learning center through an intelligent arrangement of schedules, materials, and furniture. If a classroom is not available, portions of existing classrooms can be organized, arranged, and/or partitioned to provide the necessary physical and intellectual environment.

The size of the area is not as important as its purpose. The important consideration is that teachers be assigned to those learning centers which are devoted to their area of academic strength. With skill in classroom management techniques and with adequate planning of learning experiences, a teacher with competence in a specific subject area can perform his teaching role with those students who need help in his area of competence. A student can work on science projects in a science room and/or science resource center where a teacher of science is available for assistance. A student of foreign language can study the language with the aid of a qualified teacher in an atmosphere where the language is taught and emphasized. The teacher with competence in history can work with a student who is writing a term paper, with one who is studying for an examination, and/or with one who is interested in historiography. In a learning center, a teacher can provide assistance as needed to individual pupils whose learning activities require a one-to-one relationship. Moreover, the teacher can encourage students to help each other and to work cooperatively on topics and projects of mutual interest. The teacher assigned to a learning center will be able to guide, direct, and coordinate the various individual study pursuits of the students so that the talents of teachers and students can be utilized effectively.

The learning center is a boon in respect to the provision for and the expansion of individual study opportunities. These opportunities will free the student from the lockstep procedures which are prevalent in so many schools. In a learning center, the student will be in an atmosphere which is conducive to his pursuit of an idea, a problem, an experiment. This pursuit may result in the kind of learning which is most significant and most lasting. Educators know that students are able to learn much through contemplation and through individual research. Educators also know that the pace of learning which is considered appropriate for a group is often inappropriate for individuals within the group. The learning center concept will lead to a program of individual study which will allow each student to be taught and to learn individually.

The emphasis upon individualized learning opportunities under the supervision and guidance of a teacher with competence in the academic area around which the learning center is organized is a safeguard against the degeneration of the learning center into a conventional study hall. Ideally, there should be as many learning centers as there are curriculum areas in a school. When many learning centers are established, a student may have his choice in the selection of those which meet his particular academic needs. If this choice is exercised intelligently, he will not select a mathematics learning center for his pursuit of history. The fact that a particular learning center has been selected by a student is an indication that the pupil will endeavor to work seriously there. If a student prefers social contact to individual study, his selection privileges may be withdrawn. The teacher assigned to each learning center will have the responsibility to see that the learning activities under his supervision relate to his area of subject matter mastery. The fact that these assignments would eliminate study hall duty can be a sufficient reason for many teachers to inspire themselves and their students to emphasize learning in the learning centers. The intelligent utilization of teachers and students will minimize many of the disadvantages which have made the conventional study halls subject to much negative criticism.

The matter of student selection of learning centers does not obviate the prerogative of a teacher to assign a student to a specific center. Cooperation among the teachers is necessary if this procedure is to be successful. When the teachers do not assign a student to a certain place, the responsible student may be given the privilege of making choices among learning centers. Pupils who are judged by their teachers to be incapable of making such decisions would not be given this choice unless or until they demonstrate that they have developed the ability to act responsibly.

It should be clear that a learning center in itself can be a force towards learning. The establishment of many learning centers can develop within the student an awareness of the need to make intelligent choices concerning the most effective use of his time. If the pupil is free to go to that learning center where his academic needs will be met best, this criterion for decision-making can lead towards the development of self-responsibility and self-directiveness. It is folly to force a student to sit in a study hall where teacher help is not available, where books and materials are not available, and where idleness is at least implicitly encouraged. A student and a teacher can work more effectively on the intellectual task at hand in a learning center than in that anomaly called a study hall.

If teachers are to be professionals, they cannot spend their time as policemen. Policemen are policemen, and perhaps not even they would enjoy study hall duty.

Junior High School Teachers: Fish or Fowl

Editor's Note

The junior high school idea found widespread acceptance during its early years. The growth was phenomenal and surprising when one considers this was a radical innovation in school organization. Similarly, the junior high school idea has also been a favorite target for critics of American education. It is interesting to note that the junior high school teacher has not been the focal point of this criticism. If the junior high school is dead, as some critics claim, then part of this death knell has been triggered by the failure of higher education to prepare, and the public to demand, teachers for this specific age group. Too long has the junior high school teacher been an inhabitant of education's no-man's land. What the junior high school child needs, more than anything else, is a teacher specifically prepared to work with the early adolescent – one who views his position with enthusiasm and professional pride – and not as a stepping stone to the senior high school.

Preparing Junior High Teachers*

GORDON F. VARS

The shortage of well qualified junior high school teachers is too well known to require documentation. How can we attract and hold capable people at this level? How can we develop commitment to teaching the young adolescent? What special preparation, if any, should a junior high school teacher have? We have been wrestling with these problems since the first junior high opened around 1910, so it would be presumptuous of me to claim definitive answers now. However, since 1960 the Cornell Junior High School Project has been attempting to attract and to prepare junior high teachers through a fifth-year program for liberal arts graduates, supported by funds from the Ford Foundation. My "prof.'s eye view" of these problems is based primarily on this experience.

Preparation and Certification

Since pre-service preparation is governed to a marked extent by teacher certification requirements, we will examine both at the same time. First, because we want *special preparation* for junior high teaching, it does not necessarily follow that we should have *separate certification* for this level. It is particularly unwise if holders of a junior high certificate can teach only three grade levels. Who would want to limit his job opportunities so narrowly? Consider what is happening in Indiana, for example. A special junior high certificate, restricted to grades seven, eight, and nine, was announced in 1962 and went into effect in September, 1963. As of November, 1964, it was estimated that no more than 50 students in the entire state were working toward that certificate. With 2,500

*Reprinted from *The Clearing House,* 40 (October 1965), 77-81, by permission of the publisher.

junior high positions in Indiana, you can see how far this program goes toward meeting the demand for teachers.[1]

Values of Overlapping Certificates. Instead of closing all other routes to junior high teaching, as suggested by the Indiana certification director,[2] I believe we should more fully exploit the merits of overlapping certificates. Arrangements like Illinois' K through 9 (elementary) and 6 through 12 (secondary) certification continue to be the predominant pattern,[3] and for good reason. We need all types of teachers in the junior high school, both the broad generalist typically produced in elementary programs and the subject specialist prepared by most secondary programs. Illinois' four-year overlap is especially desirable in light of the number of "Middle Schools" being developed, embracing grades 6, 7, and 8, or even 5 through 8 or 9.

T. H. Briggs cited the elementary-trained teacher's contribution to the junior high as long ago as 1920:

> Their experience in the grades has given them an understanding of boys and girls in early adolescence and has made them appreciative of individual differences in abilities and sympathetic with any plans that will provide for differentiation of work. Whether or not they are by and large better teachers than others in the high school, as many maintain, it is unnecessary to consider, for they are usually eager to work in the new type of school, while the high-school teacher of however humble rank is likely to consider his transfer anything but a promotion.[4]

Beginning in 1966, all permanent elementary certificates in New York State will require five years of study and a minimum of 30 semester hours in a department or planned interdepartmental program of liberal arts studies. A special junior high endorsement on this K through 9 certificate is awarded for 36 hours of work in English or social studies, 42 in science, or 24 in mathematics. In addition, at least 80 of the 300 clock hours of supervised teaching must be in the junior high grades.

Unfortunately, no specific work in junior high school education, not even adolescent psychology, is listed as part of the required 30 semester hours in professional education.[5] A junior high endorsement on Indiana's four-year

[1]Arthur H. Rice, "What's Wrong with Junior Highs? Nearly Everything," *Nation's Schools,* Vol. 74, No. 5 (November, 1964), p. 32.

[2]*Ibid.*

[3]William R. Hoots, Jr., "Junior High-School Teacher Certification," *Bulletin of the National Association of Secondary School Principals,* Vol. 47 (October, 1963), pp. 44-48.

[4]Thomas H. Briggs, *The Junior High School* (Boston: Houghton Mifflin, 1920), p. 221.

[5]"Requirements for Teaching in the Elementary School" (Albany: New York State Education Department, N.D.). (Mimeographed.)

elementary certificate, on the other hand, calls for six semester hours distributed among adolescent psychology, junior high school curriculum and organization, and developmental reading. Indiana also requires 24 hours in a teaching field and two to three semester hours of supervised teaching in the junior high school.[6] These programs are not offered as ideals, but merely to show how elementary certification can be modified to fit at least some of the requirements of junior high teaching.

Another value of elementary-type preparation for junior high teachers was identified by Laura McGregor in 1929 when she said: "The experience of having taught all the major subjects of the elementary curriculum leads to a wiser interpretation of departmentalized contents in the light of subject interrelationships, and to a broader comprehension of the problems of other teachers."[7] This point is particularly important in view of the large number of junior high schools with blocktime and core programs—40 per cent at the time of the last national survey.[8]

What is needed is modest depth in at least two related fields, such as English and social studies, or science and mathematics. New York and Indiana teachers taking the elementary route to junior high certification will be able to qualify in two teaching fields, but this will use up many of their electives. Junior high teachers need more subject matter depth than elementary teachers, but less than senior high teachers.

New York is an example of the ridiculous level of specialization sometimes demanded for secondary certification—51 semester hours in English or social studies, 57 in science, or 33 in mathematics.[9] This is for a five-year program, of course, but when added to general education and professional requirements it leaves little room for breadth, and makes a second teaching field almost impossible. Any state contemplating changes in certification requirements would do well to avoid the mistakes made in New York. Both a teaching major and a teaching minor should be required of all secondary teachers, and especially those planning to work in junior high. The junior high period is much too early for narrow specialization by either teachers or students.

One influence toward specialization that some of us view with alarm is team teaching.[10] As a long-time advocate of block-time and core, I do not have

[6]Robert L. Pabst, "The Junior High School Teacher's Certificate: Something New in Teacher Education," *Junior High School Newsletter,* Vol. I, No. 1 (December, 1962), pp. 2-3.

[7]A. Laura McGregor, *The Junior High School Teacher* (Garden City, New York: Doubleday, Doran, 1929), pp. 271-272.

[8]U.S. Office of Education, *The Junior High School: A Survey of Grades 7-8-9 in Junior and Junior-Senior High Schools,* by Grace S. Wright and Edith S. Greer, Bulletin 1963, No. 32 (Washington: Government Printing Office, 1963), p. 20.

[9]*Amendment to Regulations of the Commissioner of Education Pursuant to Section 207 of the Education Law* (Albany: New York State Education Department, n.d.).

[10]See, for example, Judson Shaplin, "Toward a Theoretical Rationale for Team

to be sold on the value of continuous cooperative planning among teachers. But when a team is designed to make one teacher a specialist in grammar, another in composition, and another in literature, for example, we are in danger of re-splintering the curriculum we worked so hard in the 20's and 30's to glue back together through broad fields, block-time, and core curriculum plans.

There is some consolation in David W. Beggs' statement that "as team operation becomes more sophisticated, it tends to include interdisciplinary membership."[11] Lloyd Trump, too, has illustrated this approach in his writings.[12] Indeed, the interdisciplinary team is receiving increasingly widespread acceptance at both junior and senior high levels. Such a team can promote correlation of subject matter without the overemphasis on one field that sometimes occurs in a block-time program. I have my doubts, however, as to whether the interdisciplinary team can be as effective as block-time in accomplishing other purposes that are particularly important at the junior high level, notably guidance. The point is, whether he will teach a separate subject or block-time, individually or as a member of a team, the junior high teacher should know at least two teaching fields well enough to correlate them whenever appropriate.

Professional Preparation

Work in the teaching of reading and study skills should be required of all teachers, both elementary and secondary. Basic to success in almost any school subject, effective study also may have a special psychological significance for the young adolescent. As Mauritz Johnson puts it: "Neither economically nor emotionally can young adolescents become fully independent of adults; given help and increasing opportunity to study effectively on their own, most of them *can* become academically independent." [13]

Study of adolescent psychology and of the role of the teacher in guidance, as well as sound teaching methods, are commonly conceded to be essential for the junior high teacher. A separate course in junior high school education may be desirable, but not necessary, so long as adequate attention is given somewhere to the history and philosophy of this institution. For many students, a junior high course or seminar will make more sense if taken concurrently with practice

---

Teaching," in *Team Teaching,* ed. by Judson T. Shaplin and Henry F. Olds, Jr. (New York: Harper and Row, 1964). pp. 57-98.

[11]David W. Beggs, III, "Fundamental Considerations for Team Teaching," in *Team Teaching: Bold New Venture,* ed. by David W. Beggs, III. (Indianapolis, Indiana: Unified College Press, 1964), p. 35.

[12]See, for example, J. Lloyd Trump and Dorsey Baynham, *Focus on Change: Guide to Better Schools* (Chicago: Rand McNally, 1961), pp. 106, 116-117.

[13]Mauritz Johnson, Jr., "Preparation of Teachers for the Junior High School," *Teachers College Journal,* 34 (November, 1962), p. 58.

teaching, or else immediately afterward, while their junior high experiences are still fresh.

Student Teaching Is Crucial

Since the key to successful junior high teaching lies in how well the teacher works with the age group, professional laboratory experiences with young adolescents are of prime importance. Especially crucial is student teaching, which should take place under teachers who are themselves committed to teaching junior high youngsters. Whether the school in which the teaching takes place should approach the ideal or illustrate more typical practices is a troublesome dilemma. I would not classify the schools in which our Junior High School Project interns teach as ideal by any means, yet some of our graduates have experienced real shock at the situations they have encountered after leaving us. On the other hand, if we confront them with grim reality during their practice teaching, they might set their sights too low, missing the vision of what a junior high could be, or even becoming so discouraged as to leave the profession.

Perhaps all student teachers should have experiences in two schools that approach either end of the spectrum. Barring this, student teaching should be done in situations that illustrate at least some of the better educational practices. To quote Mauritz Johnson again, "A situation does not have to be downright poor in order to be realistic."[14]

Since teachers holding either elementary or secondary certificates are permitted to teach in the junior high grades, *both should be required to do at least some of their student teaching at this level.* Otherwise, how can we claim any uniqueness for teaching in junior high? Moreover, a good junior high experience may attract into our ranks a number of teachers who, through prejudice or ignorance, have not previously given serious thought to teaching at this level.

The net result of the total recruitment, selection, and preparation process, regardless of the certificate, should be a teacher who has a broad general education, considerable depth in two or more teaching fields, sound professional preparation, and above all, commitment to teaching young adolescents. Commitment is one of the few significant differences we have found in comparing Cornell Project graduates with a group of equally inexperienced junior high teachers. At least more of them *said* they planned to continue teaching in junior high, and indicated, believe it or not, that they would reject an offer of a senior high position at comparable salary! What they actually *do* may be another matter.[15]

[14] *Ibid.*

[15] Mauritz Johnson, Jr., "A Comparison Between Graduates of the Cornell Junior

Summary

In summary, this is what I have proposed:

1. Pre-service preparation of junior high teachers should differ in emphasis rather than kind from either elementary or secondary preparation.

2. The present practice of accepting either elementary or secondary certification at the junior high level should be continued, *provided* that both programs include some student teaching at this level. The student teaching should be under the direction of a teacher committed to this level and in a school that exemplifies at least some of the better contemporary practices.

3. A special junior high endorsement on either certificate should indicate completion of a program that includes:
   a. A broad general education
   b. Some depth in at least two teaching fields
   c. Some special attention to:
      (1) The nature of the young adolescent
      (2) The teaching of reading
      (3) The teacher's role in guidance and counseling
      (4) The history and philosophy of the junior high school.

Getting There from Here

If you accept these suggestions, how can we bring them about? First, we professors of education must provide a good junior high student teaching experience for *all* teachers whose certificates cover the junior high grades. This may mean a fight to win over our colleagues in the colleges of education, not to mention the state certification officials. Second, we must hold the line against efforts to stampede us into boosting subject field requirements for any certificate so high as to rule out a teaching minor or a second teaching major. At the same time, we must encourage our colleagues in elementary education to consider giving elementary majors who seek a junior high endorsement some depth in at least two teaching fields. Finally, we in the colleges of education must offer prospective junior high teachers practical yet substantive courses or seminars in adolescent psychology, the teaching of reading, teacher-counseling, and junior high school education.

Administrators have several key roles to play. First, they must aid college personnel in selecting really first-rate supervising teachers to guide practice teachers. At Cornell, we have learned from sad experience that even teachers nominated by junior high principals as "the best" in their schools, regardless of

---

High School Project and Other Equally Experienced Junior High School Teachers" (Ithaca, New York: Junior High School Project, Cornell University, 1965).

subject field, are not always effective either as teachers or as supervisors of beginners. Both college and public school staff should cooperate in selecting and training supervising teachers. Second, administrators bear the chief responsibility for making any junior high school a good place in which to teach and learn. Good teachers cannot be trained in poor schools; yet poor schools cannot be improved without good teachers. Here, again, cooperation of college, public school, and state education department staff is required. Continuous in-service development is especially important in junior high because of rapid teacher turnover.

Finally, administrators must remind themselves constantly that graduates of teacher preparation programs are not finished products. Beginners need special care during the first few years of teaching—decent teaching loads, adequate supervision, and lots of psychological support. One of our most creative and dynamic Project interns was ready to quit teaching because she felt she had been tossed to the wolves by her administrator, who refused to back her in maintaining discipline or to give her any help in supervising a huge and rowdy study hall.

Junior high teachers and other staff members must join with administrators and college personnel to shape certification requirements so that future junior high teachers will have appropriate preparation. They also share responsibility for making every junior high program the best that can be achieved with the time, talent, and funds available. Too, they must be willing to tolerate diversity within their own ranks. The middle school in the educational system must continue to welcome both child-centered and subject-centered teachers, generalists as well as specialists, as long as they have the necessary commitment to teaching junior high youngsters.

All of us—professors, teachers, and administrators—must maintain the highest level of professionalism. The bitter disillusion some of our graduates feel when they face the "real world" is reflected in this portion of a letter written by a Project intern after three months of full-time junior high teaching, announcing that she was leaving the profession:

> Whoever tries to defend the position that teaching is a profession might just as well give it up now. I've heard everything in teachers' rooms from dirty jokes to "dirty niggers." There's no professional pride—it's just a job to them. And gossip about the kids is their second most favorite topic of conversation. As a sick footnote, one of the married teachers has asked if he could see me some night when his wife goes out to her bridge game. (But of course any man could do that—it just rankles that he asked me in front of my class.)

Do you blame her for having second thoughts about teaching?

Each and every one of us must demonstrate by our own example the enthusiasm and dedication to teaching young adolescents that will lead students, other teachers, and the public at large to regard junior high teaching, not as a poor second choice for those who would rather do something else, but as the most rewarding and satisfying of careers.

Who Should Teach in Junior High?*

CONRAD F. TOEPFER, JR.

General opinion assumes that the junior high school evolved in an attempt to meet the educational needs of early adolescence. In reality, though, the junior high school has evolved, for the most part, because of almost every other conceivable need. The past decade, however, has seen a greater focus upon organizing the junior high school in terms of the needs of the early adolescent student. While such attempts have been spasmodic and "Topsy-like" in growth, American public education is coming to the realization that the early adolescent junior high school student is distinctly different, not only from the elementary school student, as recognized for decades, but from the senior high school student as well. If this is true, teacher education should provide the junior high school teacher with a preparation distinctly different from preparation to teach in elementary or senior high school. Overwhelmingly, this is not the case today. The junior high school has steadily become part and parcel of the American public school system and appears to be here to stay. "Who should teach in the junior high school?" The answer is obvious: junior high school teachers! What should the education of the junior high school teacher be? This answer, unfortunately, is not so readily available.

The junior high school teacher is fish as well as fowl. Most states provide an overlapping certification which allows the candidate to teach in the elementary grades as well as in the junior high grades. Certification to teach in the junior high school is usually granted the elementary school teacher upon his completion of some specific subject matter specialization above his basic elementary certification requirements. At the same time, most states similarly structure the certification of secondary school teachers to be inclusive of the early secondary or junior high school grades as well. In few such instances are there any specific or additional requirements for certification to teach in the

*Reprinted from *The Clearing House*, 40 (October 1965), 74-76, by permission of the publisher and Conrad F. Toepfer, Jr., State University of New York at Buffalo.

junior high school. Thus, the area of junior high school teacher education and certification is "no man's land." There is a tragically myopic lack of definition of the experiences needed by teachers working with the early adolescent student which the junior high school typically serves.

Some of the lack of success of the American secondary school may well stem from the beginnings of frustration developed in the junior high school. Certainly the lack of teachers specifically educated to work with a student as unique as the early adolescent junior high school student may be a strong contributing factor toward developing an educational climate in which student frustrations are germinated. Junior high school teachers commonly fail to understand the problems of early adolescence and the extremely personal nature of the difficulties typically faced by an individual in approaching, achieving, and adjusting to adolescence. Similarly, they often do not understand the causes for the erratic behavior of many early adolescent students and their relatively short attention and interest spans. The organization of curriculum and instruction in the junior high school might be significantly different from what it is, were it to be based upon a sufficiently broad and deep knowledge of the early adolescent student. Within this setting of frustration and lack of understanding, problems of student morale and holding power may well be conceived for development in the senior high school.

The important differences between the education of elementary and senior high school students can be readily enumerated by most educators. These differences have important ramifications for the areas of teaching methodology and technique, curriculum planning, and, above all, consideration for the psychological development of students. Teacher education for elementary and senior high school certification has been built upon the recognized important needs of both areas. If, however, as appears to be the growing trend, it can be agreed that the student in the junior high school is significantly different from both the elementary and the senior high school student, these differences should be translatable into a program of education not only for junior high school students but for junior high school teachers. The implications of this are two-pronged for undergraduate as well as graduate teacher education.

The University of Indiana at Bloomington has pioneered a program in junior high school teacher education and certification for almost three years. Dr. John E. Reisert developed the Indiana program in a sincere attempt to organize a teacher education experience based upon important needs of teachers at the junior high school level. The program, however, has had considerably less than monumental success, with few students having elected this sequence. This is attributable to the fact that teachers in Indiana may still qualify for a secondary certificate allowing them to teach in grades 7 through 12. The Indiana experience indicates that the development of a program of education for junior high school teachers without the support of certification requirements will, in all probability, prove to be a noble but relatively ineffective experiment. Not only must teacher education define and develop specific experiences and requirements for the education and certification of junior high school teachers, but the backdoor entrance for either elementary or secondary teachers to function at the junior high school level with a "catch-as-catch-can" preparation must be sealed off.

No matter what educational innovations may be developed to meet the needs of the junior high school student and regardless of the degree to which such changes may be implemented, the success of such attempts will be less than we should like until we develop and implement a succinct educational experience for junior high school teachers. If the junior high school student is unique, his teachers must be educated in programs distinctly different from those for prospective elementary and senior high school teachers. Awareness of the important differences in the natures of the preadolescent, adolescent, and later adolescent student served by the junior high school must be learned by junior high school teachers. They must then be prepared to organize instruction in terms of the educational needs of their students. They must also be educated to understand the importance of exploration in planning curricula and organizing instruction in the junior high school. Their techniques of instruction should also differ from those at the elementary or senior high school level.

Programs of undergraduate teacher education for junior high school teachers should carefully identify the age group in which the prospective candidate has the most interest and with which he may have better skills in terms of communication as it would affect his teaching. Opportunities to observe the differences between elementary and junior high school situations, on the one hand, and junior high and senior high school situations, on the other, should be provided so that the decision as to the level at which prospective teachers wish to specialize can be made upon a solid basis of understanding. The curricula of teacher education programs and their observation, participation, and student teaching experiences should then be directed specifically toward the appropriate level.

Graduate teacher education programs should also be organized for the special needs of the junior high school teacher. These graduate experiences must be supported by state certification requirements to add the kind of emphasis currently built into graduate experiences for elementary and senior high school teachers. Such experiences should include study of the psychology of early adolescence, teaching methods, and organization of junior high school instruction, as well as careful consideration of the role and objectives of the junior high school in the total scope of elementary and secondary education.

The junior high school has been and will be expected to achieve specific objectives in the education of students as they progress through the American public school system. The lack of definition of the education suitable for the junior high school teacher, as compared with the elementary and senior high teacher, would seem to indicate that the prospects for success of teachers in junior high schools must be considerably less than at the other two levels. This is not to imply that the junior high school has not achieved some distinct successes or that it has not been a positive movement in the development of the American public school system. It is of paramount importance that American education is realizing there are distinct differences between junior high school students and both elementary and senior high school students. However, this now must be followed by the identification of an experience in teacher education which will allow the junior high school teacher to develop greater perceptions and understandings of his task. Hopefully, the junior high school teacher might then finally be educated to operate with the realistic awareness and skills needed to achieve the objectives which the junior high school has fervently sought for well over half a century.

The Search for JHS Teachers*

NORMAN R. DIXON

The absence of systematic, large-scale efforts to prepare teachers specifically for instruction in junior high schools is a painful instance of neglect. In 1960, catalogs of 812 colleges and universities were examined (2:179)[1] and it was discovered that only 63 programs were designed to prepare junior high school teachers. Two years later, in his doctoral study involving 246 institutions approved by the National Council for the Accreditation of Teacher Education, Ackerman (1:69) found just 36 programs specifically designed to prepare teachers for junior high schools. Since the results obtained from these studies faithfully represent the lack of education programs for junior high school teachers nationally, junior high schools are generally staffed with teachers prepared for service in elementary or senior high schools.

In February, 1955, Harold B. Brooks, a former president of the National Association of Secondary School Principals, sought information on junior high school summer workshops so that "those specifically interested in the junior high school could cooperate most effectively in developing programs in junior high schools." (11:87) Nineteen institutions in 13 states reported they would conduct junior high school summer workshops. (11) In May, 1955, sixteen additional institutions (12) stated they would offer junior high school summer workshops.

Eight years later, in 1963, data on summer school courses in junior high school education were compiled by Trump and Hawley (17:165) (see table).

With the rapid increase of junior high schools throughout the nation, it is alarming that more colleges and universities are not offering summer courses for junior high school teachers—especially since summer schools are usually quite sensitive to the in-service needs of teachers.

*Reprinted from *The Clearing House*, 40 (October 1965), 82-84, by permission of the publisher and Norman R. Dixon, Southern University, Baton Rouge, Louisiana.

[1]Numbers in parentheses refer to references at the end of the article.

No. of Schools Responding to Inquiry	*Offerings on JHS*
121	One or more courses
5	Special provisions for teachers and administrators in the general area of secondary education
12	Secondary education courses with special relevance to junior high schools
50	No offerings

In 1963, Hoots (7:45) offered the following data on certification to teach in junior high schools:

12 states—special certificates or endorsements for junior high school
8 states—definite plans for special certification
7 of 12 states—with junior high school certification use teachers with elementary certificates
10 states—with certification use teachers with secondary certificates
6 states—have institutions preparing junior high school teachers and have or plan special certification.

It is generally conceded that state certification requirements tend to shape teacher education programs. (8:59) If states required special preparation of junior high school teachers, many more colleges and universities would develop programs to meet those requirements.

It is said that there "has been a crescendo of comment and criticism of the American junior high school." (14:63) Some of the major criticisms are: lack of certification requirements for teachers, lack of special education for teachers, lack of prestige of junior high school teachers, and use of junior high school positions as stepping stones to high school or elementary service. These biting indictments are true indeed, and they have plagued the junior high school from its birth to the present. No wonder the junior high school is said, in the fashion of a litany, to be "a school without teachers." (8:57) Perhaps more appropriately, it is an institution in search of teachers.

Social Significance of the Search for Teachers

The lack of specifically educated teachers for junior high schools is a far more serious social problem than most educators seem willing to admit. Consider the fact that more than half the pupils in secondary school are in junior high school. In addition, Erickson (6:172) calls the junior high school "the fastest growing component of American public education." Also, with reference to pupil population, Budde (3:390) in his doctoral study states, "The greatest increase in enrollment in the nation and in the state of Michigan during the next five years will be in the junior high school grades. More students will be attending these grades than any other three grades in public education."

For this bumper crop of rested, restless, curious, eager, bright, average, slow, interested, mischievous, "good" early adolescents the junior high school has the dubious distinction of being an institution in search of teachers. The teachers in the junior high school tend to be younger, have less experience, and be less permanent in their positions and grades when compared with other teachers. (3:390)

The problem of securing junior high school teachers is dramatically different from that faced by elementary and senior high schools. For a good many years, colleges and universities have made special efforts to prepare teachers for elementary and senior high schools. In their case, it is a matter of refining long-established teacher education programs. For junior high schools, the problem is getting colleges and universities to commit themselves to the preparation of junior high school teachers. How long this dire situation will be allowed to crawl through American education crying and begging for attention no one knows!

Of several facts one can be relatively sure. First, the American people will continue to express faith in public education by investing huge sums of money in it. Second, the American people will demand a better product from the schools as a result of the huge outlay of capital. Third, educational leaders and professional organizations are going to demand more effective performance from teachers. This is as it ought to be. Junior high schools, colleges, and universities—and educators as a group—must not sit smugly in their once-ivory towers until a Rickover or a Bestor or a Conant sets off bombs at their feet. As professionals, the impetus for excellence in junior high schools should come from educators themselves. The social significance of the continuing search for teachers is so critical that it can not enjoy the costly inattention for the next 50 years that it has had for the last half-century.

Toward Moving Out of the Dilemma

To move out of a 50-year-old dilemma, the search for unavailable junior high school teachers, several proposals are offered. First, to stimulate pre-service and in-service teacher education, local, state, regional, and national conferences should be convoked (1) to define teacher needs in terms of the purposes and functions of junior high schools and (2) to draft broad policies for programs to minister to the needs as identified. These conferences should be joint efforts of professional organizations, state departments of education, and colleges and universities. A national committee selected from the proposed sponsors cited above could well be formed to coordinate the national effort. Scholars in the several disciplines, and laymen as well, should be represented in the proposed national committee. Some state and regional conferences have been held, and they could well fit into the proposed framework of a national effort.

Second, there should be research and experimentation to determine the content and patterns of junior high school teacher education programs. There are a growing number of researches (1, 3, 5, 18, 19) whose findings could be used as hypotheses. Polemics (2, 4, 8, 9, 10, 13) and reports (6, 16) may offer a good deal of insight for developing hypotheses also. In addition, concepts as to what an effective junior high school teacher is, as expressed by administrators, teachers, and pupils, might supply the data for research and experimentation.

Third, as a result of the above proposals, pilot teacher education programs should be instituted in selected colleges and universities on a state and/or regional basis. Such programs as the Cornell University Junior High School Project (16) might well offer insights for program establishment. Provisions should be made for pooling and disseminating data gathered in the conduct of the pilot teacher education programs.

Fourth, there should be more serious study of certification for junior high school teachers. Even though there is some opposition to separate certification (8, 19), the matter should receive deliberate study by the best minds available.

Fifth, state and regional accrediting agencies should develop evaluative criteria which more adequately reflect the specific purposes and functions of the modern junior high school—and its teacher needs. All of the foregoing suggestions should supply guidelines for development of standards for evaluating junior high school teachers.

To some, the proposals herein set forth may seem daring, but they must be so conceived because of the sharp crisis they are designed to meet. Programs for the preparation of junior high school teachers should be superior models. They have the advantage of general knowledge of successes and failures accumulated by years of long and difficult experience, but it should not induce a half-hearted effort. If educators accept their responsibilities with courage, creativity, and prudence, the junior high school will not remain an institution in search of teachers!

References

(1) R.E. Ackerman, "The Preparation of Junior High School Teacher," *Journal of Teacher Education.* 13:69-71 (March 1962).

(2) E. Brainard. "The JHS Teacher–Has the Training Been Adequate?" *Clearing House.* 38:179-81 (November 1963).

(3) Ray Budde, "A Study of the Permance of Seventh-, Eighth-, and Ninth-Grade Teachers in Michigan," *National Association of Secondary School Principals Bulletin.* 46:389-90 (February 1962).

(4) James B. Conant, *Education for the Junior High School Years.* Princeton: Educational Testing Service, 1960.

(5) Leroy M. Devane, "The Qualities and Qualifications of Junior High School Teachers," *National Association of Secondary School Principals Bulletin.* 46:378-80 (February 1962).

(6) J. H. Erickson, "Specialized Training for Junior High School Teachers: The LaCrosse Plan (A Report)," *Teachers College Journal.* 35:172-3 (March 1964).

(7) W. R. Hoots, Jr., "Junior High School Teacher Certification," *National Association of Secondary School Principals Bulletin.* 47:44-8 (October 1963).

(8) Mauritz Johnson, "The Preparation of Teachers for the Junior High School," *Teachers College Journal.* 34:57-9 (November 1962).

(9) C. W. Jung, "The Teachers We Need," *National Association of Secondary School Principals Bulletin.* 47:21-5 (February 1963).

(10) "Junior High School Personnel," *National Association of Secondary School Principals Bulletin.* 47:65-71 (February 1955).

(11) "Junior High School Summer Workshops," *National Association of Secondary School Principals Bulletin.* 39:87-8 (February 1955).

(12) "Junior High School Summer Workshops," *National Association of Secondary School Principals Bulletin.* 39:105-6 (May 1965).

(13) R. A. MacNaughton, "Junior High School Teaching Deserves Its Own Training," *Ohio Schools.* 39:22 (January 1961).

(14) G. R. Rassmussen, "Junior High School: Weakest Rung in the Educational Ladder?" *National Association of Secondary School Principals Bulletin.* 46:63-9 (October 1962).

(15) H. B. Spencer, "Preparing Teachers for the Junior High School." *National Association of Secondary Principals Bulletin.* 44:85-7 (April 1960).

(16) F. H. Stutz, "The Cornell University High School Project," *High School Journal.* 43:188-91 (February 1960).

(17) J. Lloyd Trump, and L. E. Hawley (comp.), "1963 Summer Session Courses on Junior High School Education in Colleges and Universities," *National Association of Secondary School Principals Bulletin.* 47:165-89 (March 1963).

(18) John E. Walsh, "A Study of the Overt Behavioral Characteristics of Effective Teachers of Junior High School Youth," *National Association of Secondary School Principals Bulletin.* 46:380-1 (February 1962).

(19) W. D. Wiley, "Teaching Success of Junior High School Teachers as It Relates to Type of Credential Held," *National Association of Secondary School Principals Bulletin.* 46:382-4 (February 1962).

The Case for Teachers Who Are Specifically Prepared to Teach in Junior High Schools *

MARK C. SMITH

What type of educational background should the junior high teacher have? What factors should receive special attention by institutions of higher learning as they prepare such teachers? How many colleges and universities provide greater service to the junior high schools and their administrators? Such questions were the basis for recent investigation.

At the close of the school year in June 1964, questionnaires were mailed nationwide to 291 superintendents and principals. The return of 224, or 77 percent, indicated widespread interest in the subject.

Eighty percent of principals and 73 percent of superintendents returned the questionnaire. Geographically, the percentage of return was roughly the same. The length of the responses to the open-end questions indicated that the area is one of considerable concern.

One group of questions asked of both principals and superintendents was related to the subject matter and professional preparation of junior high school teachers. The data summarized in Table 1 indicate close agreement between principals and superintendents. Eighty-seven percent of the principals and 86 percent of the superintendents indicated they felt that the subject matter preparation was adequate to superior for those teachers added to their staffs during the past five years.

The data summarized in Table 2 indicate a somewhat wider divergence of opinion between the superintendents and principals as to the professional preparation of teachers. Sixty-three percent of the principals and 73 percent of

*Reprinted from *The Journal of Teacher Education*, 17 (Winter 1966), 438-443, by permission of the publisher and Mark C. Smith, Associate Secretary, American Association of Colleges for Teacher Education.

Table 1. Principals' and Superintendents' Evaluation of Subject Matter Preparation of Teachers Added to Staff During the Last Five Years

	Adequate	*Superior*	*Inadequate*
Prin.	78%	9%	13%
Supt.	81%	5%	14%

the superintendents indicated adequate to superior professional preparation for teachers added during the past five years. Thus, 24 percent of the principals and 13 percent of the superintendents found their most recently acquired teachers less adequately prepared in the professional area than in subject matter.

Table 2. Principals' and Superintendents' Evaluation of Professional Preparation of Teachers Added to Staff During Last Five Years

	Adequate	*Superior*	*Inadequate*
Prin.	59%	4%	37%
Supt.	71%	2%	27%

Tables 3 and 4 deal with a question closely related to the previous one. The administrators were asked whether requirements in subject matter and professional preparation should be changed or remain the same. In Table 3 we see that 97 percent of the principals and superintendents agreed that the subject

Table 3. Principals' and Superintendents' Recommendations for Subject Matter Preparation of Teachers

	Increase	*Decrease*	*Remain the Same*
Prin.	48%	1%	51%
Supt.	51%	1%	48%

matter requirement should either remain the same or be increased. Only 1 percent of each group recommended a decrease.

As far as professional preparation is concerned, Table 4 shows that, although 95 percent of the principals and 92 percent of the superintendents recommend either holding the professional requirement at the present level or

Table 4. Principals' and Superintendents' Recommendations for Professional Preparation of Teachers

	Increase	*Decrease*	*Remain the Same*
Prin.	51%	5%	44%
Supt.	39%	8%	33%

increasing it, there is a greater range of disagreement between them here than in subject matter requirements. Twelve percent more principals than superintendents saw the needs for increasing the professional requirement; less than 10 percent of each group saw a need for reducing it.

In looking at the responses to questions such as the ones discussed thus far, it is important to keep in mind the scope of the study. In tabulating answers from 46 different states, we must take into account the various differences in requirements for state certification, as well as the requirements of the teacher education institutions within that state. It is for this reason that responses have been grouped under "remain the same" and "increase the requirement" as opposed to "decrease the requirement." A valid case might be made for grouping these in another way, but for the purpose of this study, they have been grouped as indicated.

Answers to the next question, What training have your most successful junior high teachers received? are summarized in Table 5. The greatest disagreement between the two groups thus far appears in answer to this question. Fifty-nine percent of the superintendents favored a teacher specifically trained for the junior high school. Of the other 41 percent, a ratio of 2 to 1 favored a teacher trained for a secondary level over one trained for the elementary level. The principals, on the other hand, were overwhelmingly in favor of a teacher trained expressly for the junior high school (87 percent).

It was felt that additional insight might be gained by asking principals for an evaluation of why teachers have failed in their junior high schools in recent years. The answers contained in Table 6 are most revealing. The large majority, over 60 percent, said failure was due primarily to the teacher's inability to cope

Table 5. The Preparation of the Most Successful J.H.S. Teachers

	Elem. Training	*Sec. Training*	*J.H.S. Training*
Prin.	3%	10%	87%
Supt.	14%	27%	59%

with the junior high school youngster. Only 2 percent attributed the failure to the teacher's inability to handle the subject matter, while almost one-fourth of the failures were seen as resulting from poor human relations on the part of the teacher. Several principals indicated that a teacher with deficiencies in subject

Table 6. Primary Reasons for Failure by J.H.S. Teachers

Inability to Handle Subject Matter	*Inability to Cope with JHS Students*	*Poor Human Relations*	*Other*
2%	61%	24%	13%

matter preparation was much more easily salvaged than one who had little understanding of the junior-high-school-aged student.

The administrators were next asked to identify those areas which have been most difficult to fill with qualified junior high teachers. Table 7 shows that

Table 7. Most Difficult Areas To Fill With Adequately Prepared J.H.S. Teachers

Subject Area	*Principals' Opinion*	*Superintendents' Opinion*
Mathematics	20%	20%
Science	16%	20%
English	13%	14%
Foreign Languages	11%	11%
Girls' Phys. Ed.	9%	6%
Eng./Soc. St.	8%	9%
Ind. Arts	6%	5%
Reading	5%	7%

one-fifth of the principals and superintendents agree that the most difficult area is mathematics. Science, English, and foreign languages were listed by over 10 percent of the administrative group. Girls' physical education, English-social studies combination, industrial arts, and reading followed in that order. The other subject areas were listed by fewer than 5 percent of the respondents.

Answers to the next question, also open-ended, In what way could institutions of higher learning make the greatest contribution toward providing better junior high school teachers? are included in Table 8. The most frequent reply was: "By educating teachers specifically for work in the junior high

Table 8. Ways by Which Institutions of Higher Learning Could Make the Greatest Contribution Toward Providing Better Junior High School Teachers

	Principals	*Superintendents*
Educating teachers specifically for the junior high school	36%	42%
Better understanding of junior-high-school-aged youngsters	18%	
Give status to junior high school teaching		12%
Practice teaching in the junior high school	10%	
A junior high school internship		10%
Emphasis on subject matter as an instrument to learning, not as an end		9%
Profs. of JHS education with recent experience in public schs.	10%	6%
Better selection of students in junior high school education	6%	5%
Great mastery of subject matter	2%	6%
Increase the practice-teaching requirement	5%	4%
More stress on professionalism	3%	5%
Use an advisory committee of public school people	3%	1%
A good background in reading	1%	3%
More experience with newer techniques	1%	3%

school." Thirty-six percent of the principals and 42 percent of the superintendents listed this as the greatest contribution. It was offered twice as often by principals and three and one-half times as often by superintendents as the next most frequent suggestion. Another interesting point is noted in three answers most often given by principals: (1) to provide teachers trained specifically for the junior high school, (2) an understanding of youngsters of this age level, and (3) the student teaching should be done in a junior high school. These three account for almost two-thirds of the answers given by principals.

Principals were asked how institutions of higher learning could make the greatest contribution toward providing service to the junior high school administrator. As will be noted in Table 9, 21 percent indicated that the greatest service would be to provide leadership in the form of workshops, institutes, conferences, and in-service programs.

Table 9. Ways by Which Institutions of Higher Learning Could Make the Greatest Contribution Toward Providing Service to the J.H.S. Administrator

	Percent
Provide leadership for workshops, conferences, in-service programs, etc.	21
Train teachers specifically for the junior high school	18
Research and study to update curriculum	12
Cooperation between schools and universities in preparing and interpreting the curriculum	10
Help faculty get at persistent problems	6

A similar service received the third highest priority; namely, to conduct research and study to update the curriculum. The second most frequent reply to this question, as also to the previous question, was, "By providing the schools with teachers who are specifically trained for the junior high school." Ten percent felt cooperation between the school and university in preparing and interpreting the curriculum would be of greatest value.

The respondents usually answered the open-end questions with one to three paragraphs rather than with three or four words, as is sometimes done on questionnaires. It was replies such as these that gave insight to the problems in the area of teacher preparation as viewed by the practicing administrator in the field. The results of the preceding tables, coupled with these supporting comments, made several points quite clear:

1. Administrators found junior high school teachers added to their staff in recent years better prepared in subject matter than in professional education.

2. Very few administrators favor any decrease in either subject matter or professional education requirements.

3. The majority of administrators rate a teacher specifically trained for the junior high school as more successful than one trained for the elementary or secondary level.

4. Teacher failure in the junior high school is due primarily to inability to cope with youngsters of this age. Few teachers fail because of inability to handle the subject being taught.

5. Qualified mathematics, science, English, and foreign language teachers are the most difficult to acquire for the junior high school.

6. Colleges and universities can be of greatest service to junior high schools by providing teachers specifically trained for this level and by furnishing leadership in conferences, workshops, institutes, in-service training, and research.

Perhaps the oft-expressed idea was stated most concisely by a superintendent:

> We don't need more content. We need teachers who know the art of questioning, who can permit and stimulate student participation as opposed to teacher lecturing, who know their subject matter well enough that they do not stay just one jump ahead of the student, who demonstrate a real thrill in the learning and use of their content fields, who have time for children and their concerns in as well as outside class, and who have an image of self-success and can help children develop one.

The responses to the various items of this questionnaire indicate that administrators who shoulder the responsibility of educating junior high school boys and girls consider it ridiculous to argue whether the teacher should know his subject matter or adolescents. Overwhelmingly, they responded that the teacher must be well prepared in his subject field. However, they feel that, generally speaking, today's graduate seeking his first teaching position is sufficiently well prepared in subject matter so that a negligible few fail for this reason.

On the other hand, the emphasis highlighted in almost all of the responses was, first, to prepare teachers who are oriented to the junior high school and its purposes and who understand the adolescent with whom they will be working.

Secondly, colleges and universities should furnish leadership to help junior high personnel keep abreast of change and increased knowledge.

Herein lies the challenge, and it is a challenge which must have the coordinated efforts of public school teachers and administrators and college and university professors in the various subject areas and in professional education, as well as of state departments of education and professional organizations.

Since the greater number of early adolescents in public schools today is in junior high schools, the time has surely come to weld this link more firmly into its place in the chain of educational progress.

part **4**

Changing Patterns of Instruction

The quickened tempo of technological advances may be seen in the innovations and changed approaches to instruction in many public schools, both elementary and secondary. The junior high school too, is experiencing diversification in the traditional techniques and methods of teaching as experimentation and variation becomes more common throughout the country. Often proposals for change are met with resistance, suspicion, and a pronounced wariness while, at the other extreme, some teachers and administrators have plunged excitedly into innovations with what might charitably be characterized as a lack of caution and preparation. Talk of the "revolution in education" has been responsible for much of the trouble, and it has been said that a better description is that of an "accelerated evolution." Innovative practices that have found their way into the junior high schools include flexible scheduling, team teaching, ungraded schools, independent study programs, instructional materials centers, teaching by television, programed instruction, and the use of paperback books. While some of this may not appear to be markedly different from past practices, what is new is the intensified interest and enthusiasm for techniques that depart from the traditional.

The Brookhurst Plan*

ELAYNE B. HOFMANN

Brookhurst Junior High School, in Anaheim, California, has been experimenting for the past three years with a pilot program for ninth graders which appears to be unusual if not unique in the United States. The Brookhurst Plan, under the direction of Principal Gardner Swenson, is based on a schedule which changes daily according to requests for time and students submitted by teams of teachers. Teachers may request a single student or as many as 350 for lengths of time which vary from twenty minutes to a full day (in the case of field trips or special events).

Under the Brookhurst Plan, a history teacher, instead of giving the same lecture six times in a day to six different classes, may call the entire history section for a large group presentation. He may devote the rest of his day to a variety of activities: leading a small group discussion of material in the lecture, planning future presentations, or conducting a review session for students needing extra help.

In another instance, a home economics teacher may request a two-hour block of time for a lesson in pie baking. Under a rigid schedule of 45-minute periods, she would have to have the dough made one day, the pie baked the next, and the finished product sampled on the third. Under the Brookhurst Plan, her class could go through the entire procedure in one day.

Perhaps the best way to describe the Brookhurst Plan in any detail is to provide answers for the type of questions someone unfamiliar with flexible scheduling might ask. For example, the first question anyone might ask would be:

Who determines the amount of time, the facilities needed, the size of the group, and the time of day for a particular activity?

*Reprinted from *The NEA Journal*, 54 (September 1965), 50-52, by permission of the publisher and Elayne B. Hofmann, Brookhurst Junior High School, Anaheim, California.

Teachers working in teams decide on what activity will best meet the needs of their students for any particular day. They then submit a job order—a request for time, facilities, and students—to the program coordinator who is responsible for making up the master schedule for the day when the activity will take place. Job orders must be submitted four days in advance.

How are priorities assigned?

Job orders are divided into three categories: classes that meet only once during the day, classes that meet more than once, and electives or "project areas" that meet throughout the day. The day is divided into modules (time blocks) of twenty minutes each. The number of modules requested will depend on the nature of the activity.

Who determines what classes a student will attend each day?

Under the Brookhurst Plan, each student has some leeway in making up his own schedule. Classes that meet only once during the day, however, are scheduled for him by the office. On days when academic subjects like English are taught in more than one section, the sections are listed on a "must" master schedule from which the student—with the approval of his scheduling group (homeroom) teacher—picks the one which is most appropriate.

For example, the student may wish to take English in module 6, when the class is scheduled in the library for independent study. Or he may decide to take English in module 8, when the teacher is conducting a grammar review for students who are having difficulty.

It should be noted that in the Brookhurst Plan electives are taught on a project basis: that is, the student, with his parent's permission, signs a project sheet agreeing to complete a certain amount of work. The elective teacher decides how much work must be done to earn a semester's credit.

The student, to a great extent, determines how much time he will take to complete the project. For example, a student with facility in typing may complete a semester's work in six weeks and then sign up for another elective. Another student with less manipulative skill or with greater demands on his time might take up to a year to complete a semester's work in typing. Nevertheless, he will receive the same credit as the student who completed the work in six weeks.

In this way, highly gifted or highly motivated students can take a greater number of electives than would be possible in a rigid scheduling plan. Less able students are not hampered by having to "keep up with the class": nor must they be satisfied with acquiring only shallow skills in an elective subject.

What are the mechanics of the scheduling process?

Student programs are made up on key-sort cards. These cards are handed out to the students the day before the schedule goes into effect. The classes that have already been scheduled for them have been written in by the coordinator and his teams.

By using this type of card, the program coordinator can sort out an entire class in one motion. For instance, if the program coordinator needs to schedule all the world history classes into a large group lecture in the auditorium, he merely "needles out" all those students enrolled in the course, writes the room and module on each card, and returns them to the deck of student cards for that day.

When the student picks up his program card the next day from his scheduling group teacher, he notes the classes he has been scheduled to attend. He then consults the "must" master schedule in order to fill in the rest of his academic courses. After he has scheduled all of his academic courses, the student can fill in his elective subjects from the elective master sheet. The completed schedule is then turned in to the scheduling group teacher, who checks it and returns it to the office for redistribution.

How long does it take a student to fill out his schedule?

It takes only about five to ten minutes (before the regular school day begins) for students to fill out their schedules.

How does the office handle the problem of providing a class roll?

The key-sort schedule consists of an original and three carbons. The student receives the original copy on the day that he is to attend the classes marked on the schedule. The second and third copies are perforated so that they can be torn into four sections by girls enrolled in office practice. The parts, or tags, are then divided by class and module. The girls place the tags in the teachers' boxes the night before the classes are actually taught, and the tags serve as class rolls. All fourth copies go to the attendance office, where they are filed in alphabetical order so that the office is aware at all times of each student's program for the day.

If a student is absent from class, his tag is sent to the attendance office, where it is checked against the office copy of his schedule. This procedure saves the teacher the trouble of having to keep a daily class roll and frees him from a great deal of clerical work.

Has flexible scheduling affected academic achievement?

Brookhurst ninth graders made significantly higher scores on SRA achievement tests given in the fall and spring at Brookhurst and at a control school. Further testing and evaluating is being carried on.

The Brookhurst Plan has a number of advantages. The greatest advantage is that it permits each student to adjust his schedule constantly to match his progress and ability. The plan also permits a capable student to spend a maximum amount of time in independent study. In fact, teachers may excuse students from certain class activities or from the complete course when they feel that independent study or research would be of greater benefit to the student.

The use of a flexible schedule has been particularly helpful to us at Brookhurst in our work with potential dropouts. At one time, seventeen students who were having serious problems in school were placed in seventeen separate learning tracks—each one tailored to the needs of the individual student.

As these students gained success in their individualized programs, they were able to return to what could be called a more normal schedule.

The Brookhurst Plan also has advantages for the teachers. Working in teams to plan activities and make up job orders gives each teacher the benefit of the special talents of other members of the team. The fact that the teachers plan and direct the program of instruction provides them with a healthy sense of involvement which is not often achieved in a set program handed down from year to year by the administration.

From the administrator's point of view, the plan has a special value. It not only helps him in developing a closer rapport with his staff through a genuine delegation of authority, but it also helps him to identify the creative, dynamic teacher.

Flexible scheduling demands a special type of teacher—one who is excited by the learning process, who can benefit from working with others, and can adjust easily and well to new ideas, methods, and procedures. The Brookhurst Plan embodies more than a flexible schedule, however; it is a complete educational program designed for individual learners.

Big Opportunities in Small Schools Through Flexible-Modular Scheduling*

THOMAS G. LEIGH

Small schools have long been recognized as possessing certain innate advantages in the educational process. Small class size, individual attention, personal identification, and the opportunity to participate to a greater degree in extra-curricular activities are among those to be listed. However, for many years small schools have also been recognized as possessing some very distinct limitations and disadvantages. Among these are restricted curricular offerings, single section offerings, restricted vocational training opportunities, inter-disciplinary teaching assignments and difficulties in teacher recruitment.

Julian High School in San Diego County, California, a school of 130 enrollment, is one of 110 small high schools with an enrollment of less than 350 in the state of California. Of these 110, 55 have an enrollment of less than 200 students. It has long recognized, as has the community, the distinct advantages of a small school as well as the restrictions seemingly imposed. The purpose of this article is to recount the steps and processes through which Julian Union High School went in its attempt to meet and solve the restrictions upon small schools. It is felt that most of the steps and procedures followed would be those which might be easily transferable to other districts in their attempts to face the same problems and that the same resources would be available in other districts which might be utilized.

Through the use of a Vocational Education Act Project a survey of vocational opportunities within San Diego County was instituted in the fall of 1965. For this purpose a country-wide Vocational Advisory Committee was formed which included representatives from the State Employment Office, the

*Reprinted from *The Journal of Secondary Education,* 42 (April 1967), 175-187, by permission of the publisher and Thomas G. Leigh, Superintendent, Julian Union High School District, Julian, California.

Apprenticeship Training Program, Farm Labor Office, and local business representatives. The needs identified by this committee, after a series of meetings, were establishment of terminal vocational programs in three areas—business, welding, and small engine repair.

In addition, a course to be titled Model Home should be offered at a future date. This program would involve building a small vacation type cottage on the school grounds by the students in the shop class and would include carpentry, sheet metal, plumbing, electrical work, etc., as well as involving the business education program in all of the business aspects such as ordering, processing of invoices and bills, cost accounting, etc. The Home Economics students would be involved in planning and decoration: the Mechanical Drawing class in drawing up plans and specifications. This program would necessarily involve a large number of students and would then in essence become a core program involving almost all of the Vocational Education students in the school. However, it was felt that some ground work need be laid and thus this program should not be instituted until the fall of 1967.

Following the development of these recommendations, the problem then was faced of how to schedule such an ambitious program into an already restricted curriculum which was crowded with courses required to be taught for college entrance; to meet state requirements; and to meet local requirements. At that time the only vocational offerings were Small Engine repair, beginning and advanced Agricultural Science, General Shop, and Typing. Operating within the financial structure possible in our school district, the curricular structure was quite lopsided in favor of the 30% of students who would be going on to four years of higher education. The 70% who were not planning to do so were neglected in the number of course offerings available to meet their particular needs. The main curricular needs identified by the faculty, Board of Trustees, and administration were in the areas of Business, Industrial Arts, Shop, and enrichment courses such as Art, Music, Chorus, Music Appreciation, and Arts and Crafts.

The availability of ESEA money in February of 1966 permitted an expansion of the vocational education program for the second semester to include Business Machines, Bookkeeping, Business English, Mechanical Drawing, and two classes for girls—Clothing and Homemaking.

In addition, through the use of Elementary and Secondary Education Act funds, a curriculum study project was instituted during the second semester of the school year. The curriculum study project was directed toward examination of the feasibility of adoption of modular scheduling and was done through contract with Stanford School Scheduling System, Stanford University.

After a series of faculty meetings which outlined the above needs and parameters within our district, the information was supplied to the Stanford School Scheduling System which in turn developed a modular schedule including all of the elements outlined. This schedule was reviewed by the entire faculty and revised as necessary and resubmitted for a final run-off and scheduling.

The machine program thus developed resulted in no reduction in the total number of courses in the academic area available to students during the high school career, but did increase the number of non-academic courses both in vocational and enrichment areas to a total of 33 or an increase of 364%. This program, which included two or more sections in each course save one—New Photography—involved alternating schedules, such as offering World Geography to all freshmen and sophomores and U. S. History to all juniors and seniors one year; then offering World History and Civics to the same groups the next year. Over a four-year period, this would result in the availability of nearly 100 courses to students enrolled in school.

During this period of time, meetings were also held and informational materials supplied to the community outlining the problems identified and the proposed means of their solution. Community response varied from scepticism to enthusiastic endorsement. Practically no objections were raised to the programming after the principles underlying it were explained.

One of the greatest areas of concern to parents, school board members, administrators, and teachers in the consideration of modular scheduling was that of unassigned time necessary to permit individual research and study as well as to permit individual assistance from teachers in the subject area. Ideally a 60 to 70% loading of students and a 60% loading of faculty were deemed desirable. The remaining time would be available for the above-mentioned individual help, individual study, and consultation.

In May the district began efforts toward teacher recruitment. Previous experience had indicated that the more highly qualified teachers, being more in demand, would not be interested in a small school situation; and that difficulties in obtaining top quality personnel might be encountered. As in the past, a number of applications were received from well qualified people and these people were invited to come in for interviews. Repeatedly the impression given by teachers at the inception of the interviews was that of polite interest. However, upon learning of the modular scheduling program and discussion of the opportunities and the challenges so presented, applicant response was highly enthusiastic and top-quality teachers were obtained with a surplus of such applicants for each position vacancy. Teacher recruitment and placement thus was no problem in comparison to difficulties experienced in previous years.

It was generally accepted that the level of responsibility the individual is able to assume is directly linked to the level of his interest. For example, if the level of responsibility were measured by observing a person digging a ditch, one might assume this person to be highly irresponsible because of poor performance of the task. However, if the same individual were interested in welding and assigned to a welding project, one might judge the same individual to be highly responsible. Therefore, we assumed that by scheduling students into areas of interest, much of irresponsible behavior previously exhibited would be very apt to disappear.

Experience in schools where modular scheduling has been in operation has shown that approximately 95% of the students are able to assume the full amount of responsibility offered them. The remaining 5% have been scheduled individually for each module of the day in order that they may have no free time. Thus, the 95% are not being penalized academically in order to control the minority 5%.

Based on this experience, all students were left free at the inception of the program to use their unscheduled time at their discretion. Provisions were made, however, to schedule these students into additional classes and/or some type of restrictive environment if they proved themselves unable to handle the responsibility. As might be expected, the first few weeks gave rise to several problems of student behavior and conduct. However, the number of incidents was considerably less than had been predicted. Interestingly enough, some students tentatively identified as potential problems fell into the routine quite readily with no difficulties whatsoever.

Student, parent, and faculty reaction from the inception of the program has been quite good. No serious problems have arisen and morale within the school has been exceptionally high in comparison to previous years. Some basic assumptions were made at the beginning of the program. These were: 1) All teachers were experienced in the techniques of large group instruction, inasmuch as it is the primary method used in traditional systems; 2) Small group instruction is a new technique to be learned and developed by all teachers and, therefore, should receive primary attention in the in-service training program; 3) Individual research should receive early attention in order that the students may be guided in the use of free time, as well as teachers guided in development of techniques for making and following through assignments or work to be conducted during these periods; 4) Students will evidence responsibility in areas in which they are interested. Therefore, it is highly desirable at an early point in time to identify these areas of interest for each student and to pursue them as rapidly as a student is able. These assumptions were the ones around which the weekly inservice training meetings were built and to which particular emphasis was to be given.

From the beginning of the implementation phase, these meetings were held to discuss the problems of modular scheduling. Problems discussed are those brought up by the faculty concerning the implementation of the program and are discussed in a small group situation in order that not only may the problems, feelings, opinions of the various faculty members be shared, but also that they may gain experience in small group dynamics which can be carried back into the classroom.

Attention is also given during these in-service meetings to methods and means by which students may be encouraged to use their individual research times to best advantage. The type of assignments which teachers should make are also subject to a considerable amount of discussion and to exchange of ideas. Teacher reaction to these in-service training periods was highly enthusiastic and it is felt that much good is being accomplished.

Legal requirements dictated that a teacher must be in attendance at all times with students. Thus, the original plan to leave the multi-purpose room open as a student union during the entire day had to be abandoned. The multi-purpose room was closed for 9 of the 15 modules of the day and teachers were assigned supervision duties during the periods in which the room was open. This problem, when explained to the students, created no adverse reaction and seemed to be very well received.

Modular scheduling in itself was deemed to have no magical qualities, but was merely a rearrangement of the use of time. The schedule permitted many advantages for students in meeting their individual needs and interests. Since the program does focus on the individual, another consideration came to the fore. This consideration was that of evaluation of the students' accomplishments and issuance of credits.

For many years our curricular structure has been in a lock step "serving of time" connotation. As has been aptly said, "How do you know when you have covered a course in English? "; the answer being, "It is June." The mere serving of a particular period of time to meet course objectives is regarded as archaic and some other means of evaluation was sought. Serious consideration was given to the question, "What do we expect a student to learn? "; or in other words, "What are our course objectives in each area? " The answer to this question by teachers was relatively specific. We expect certain basic concepts, skills, and attitudes to be evidenced. Further exploration of this question resulted in the establishment of performance criteria based on the individual teacher's expectation in the particular course.

Logically it followed that if these performance criteria could be expressed in some form, then the measurement might be made, and as the student demonstrated that he or she has met these standards, credit could be given for the individual course regardless of the amount of time spent.

Let us, for a moment, consider a simile—that of knowledge as a measurable liquid such as water—and we measure the student's "glass of knowledge" at the end of a particular period of time. Previously we have said that if this glass of knowledge is over 60% full he receives a "D"; over 70% full, a "C"; over 85% full, a "B"; over 94% full, an "A." By continuing this simile in the area of performance criteria, we can now say that if a student can demonstrate at an earlier point in time that his glass of knowledge is 94% full, then we can assume that he will not gain appreciably more from the course and, therefore, may be given credit and permitted to go on to another course.

To be more specific, let us examine a skills course such as Typing. If performance criteria set up say that the skill developed should be that of 40 words per minute at the end of the course, then a student who can type 40 words a minute is given credit for Typing I, regardless of the amount of time taken to develop this skill. He is then permitted to go on to Typing II where the performance criteria might be 65 words a minute with certain other skills, such as laying out of letters, typing of stencils, and similar activities. At the time he can demonstrate his ability to meet these criteria, he is given credit for Typing II and is permitted to go into an additional business education course if he so desires.

Similar performance criteria can be established for all other courses in the curricular structure. Thus, the student has been freed of lock step conformity to the curricular structure and has been permitted to go forward at his own speed in each course according to his abilities and interest. It is conceivable that a student might take a year and a half to complete the requirements of Typing I, or another student might be capable of completing the requirements of Typing I and Typing II in a one-year period, the focus then being on skills and abilities developed rather than the amount of time spent in the class being exposed to the skills and concepts.

To illustrate the actual operation of flexible-modular scheduling, six different schedules are included. These examples typify the individuality possible in this type of scheduling. At the foot of most schedules is a key showing the symbols representing various teachers. During the periods the student has independent study time, the symbols of the teachers available for individual instruction are shown on the student's schedule.

There is one factor not indicated on these schedules. This is the Materials Resource Center which is open from 1/2 hour before school to 1 1/2 hours after school each day. Students may choose to do their independent study there.

As noted in Figure 1, this student—a discipline problem—has no independent study time. He is of average ability and low motivation and has indicated a desire to attend college after completing high school. His performance is below average and coupling this with his poor behavior, he is supplied with a schedule of directed study. It will be noted that of the 70 periods a week he is in class or in directed study, only 2 periods of directed study are not with teachers of his academic subjects.

The college-bound Senior Boy, Figure 2, represents the opposite extreme in independent study time. This student has approximately 59% of his time for independent study, but has ample time to seek individual instruction from his teachers. Because of interscholastic athletics, his Physical Education periods (the 13th and 14th periods daily) have been omitted and credit for P.E. is extended on the basis of athletic participation.

The Vocational Arts Senior Girl, Figure 3, has 38% of her time for independent study. In addition to the wide variety of business courses, a course in Drama will be noted. In addition to Business, other areas of interest are open to her. The Office Practice shown is not done in the school office, but in a model office in the business department. This model has a complete array of business machines and is set up and run in the fashion of a one- or two-girl office. During her independent study time, this girl elects to work in the school office assisting wherever possible.

The schedule shown in Figure 4, Vocational Arts Junior Boy, illustrates another feature of this form of scheduling. The Spanish I teacher has indicated this student needs individual instruction outside of class and has arbitrarily selected the 7th period on Monday and Wednesday and the 10th period on Wednesday as the time this individual instruction will take place. Any teacher of any subject may schedule students for additional individual instruction. This additional time becomes a part of the student's schedule until such time as the teacher indicates there is no longer a need on the part of the student.

The college-bound Sophomore Girl, Figure 5, has the lowest rate of independent study time of these samples during the first quarter. Her present rate is 26% independent study time, after completing Driver Education it increases to 40%, the figure originally sought in our curriculum planning. This student is of above average ability and is highly motivated. She is taking an additional course for enrichment—Instrumental Music.

Figure 6, Vocational Arts Freshman Boy, is typical of all freshmen, in that senior requirements permit only one elective course. This particular student is taking an additional course because his Physical Education credit is being earned through our athletic program. Also shown is the non-credit course of Orientation required of all freshman students. This student has 33% independent study time which represents the average for his class.

In all sample schedules there are some common factors. All class meetings, except Orientation, which meet for a single period, are designated as large group meetings. That is, all students taking this course meet at this time, e.g., World History, when all 83 freshmen and sophomores are together. All classes scheduled for two or more successive periods are designated as small group instruction. This not only refers to reduced class size but type of instruction (non-lecture) used. Small groups vary in size from Drama with 3 students to World History with 18 students, the vast majority of classes having between 5 and 9 students.

In summary, through the use of flexible-modular scheduling those limitations and disadvantages of a small school have been largely overcome. The curricular offerings have been increased by well over 100%. Students are able to have a choice of over 100 courses during their four years in the high school. Single section offerings have been all but eliminated. The vocational educational program offers terminal education in three fields with others to be added in the near future. Inter-disciplinary teacher assignments have been all but eliminated. All teachers, save one, are teaching in their major field. Difficulties in teacher

SCHEDULE CARD

Name Discipline Problem – Boy Grade Soph.

Average Ability – Low Motivation

	MONDAY	TUESDAY	WEDNESDAY	THURSDAY	FRIDAY
1	DRIVER ED.	DRIVER ED.	DRIVER ED.	DRIVER ED.	DRIVER ED.
2	DRIVER ED.	DRIVER ED.	DRIVER ED.	DRIVER ED.	DRIVER ED.
3	MATH TEACHER	ENGLISH TEACHER	MATH TEACHER	HISTORY TEACHER	MATH TEACHER
4	SHOP TEACHER	HISTORY TEACHER	ENGLISH TEACHER	MATH TEACHER	MATH TEACHER
5	BOYS P.E.	BOYS P.E.	BOYS P.E.	BOYS P.E.	BOYS P.E.
6	BOYS P.E.	BOYS P.E.	BOYS P.E.	BOYS P.E.	BOYS P.E.
7	ALGEBRA I	ALGEBRA I	WORLD HISTORY	ALGEBRA I	ENGLISH TEACHER
8	ALGEBRA I	ALGEBRA I	WORLD HISTORY	ALGEBRA I	HISTORY TEACHER
9	LUNCH	LUNCH	LUNCH	LUNCH	LUNCH
10	ARTS & CRAFTS	ORAL COM-MUNICATION	EARLY AMERICAN LIT.	ORAL COM-MUNICATION	SCIENCE TEACHER
11	HISTORY TEACHER	ORAL COM-MUNICATION	ARTS & CRAFTS	HISTORY TEACHER	ARTS & CRAFTS
12	ARTS & CRAFTS TEACHER	WORLD HISTORY	ARTS & CRAFTS	HISTORY TEACHER	ARTS & CRAFTS
13	HISTORY TEACHER	P.E. TEACHER	EARLY AMERICAN LIT.	ARTS & CRAFTS TEACHER	ARTS & CRAFTS TEACHER
14	ARTS & CRAFTS TEACHER	P.E. TEACHER	EARLY AMERICAN LIT.	ARTS & CRAFTS TEACHER	ARTS & CRAFTS TEACHER
15	SCIENCE TEACHER	SCIENCE TEACHER	SCIENCE TEACHER	SCIENCE TEACHER	SCIENCE TEACHER

Figure 1.

SCHEDULE CARD

Name College Bound – Boy Grade Senior

Above Average Ability – High Motivation

Excused from Physical Education because of Interscholastic Athletics

	MONDAY	TUESDAY	WEDNESDAY	THURSDAY	FRIDAY
1	⊗	√	ADV. MATH	ADV. COMP.	○ □
2		⋆ ⊗	ADV. MATH	JOURNALISM	○ □
3	CIVICS	PHYSICS	○ □ ⋆ ☒	PHYSICS	○ □
4	CIVICS	PHYSICS	○ □ ☒	PHYSICS	○ □
5	√ ○ □ ☒	○ □ ☒	× ○ □	ADV. COMP.	○ □ ☒
6	√ ⋆	√ ○ □	× ○ □	ADV. COMP.	×
7	√ ○ □ ⊗ ⋆	MECH. DRAW.	× ○ □ ⊗ ⋆	MECH. DRAW.	○ □ ⊗ × √ ⋆
8	○ □ ⊗ ☒ √ ⋆	MECH. DRAW.	○ □ ⊗ ☒ √	MECH. DRAW	√ ○ □ × ☒ ⋆
9	LUNCH	LUNCH	LUNCH	LUNCH	LUNCH
10	JOURNALISM	ADV. MATH	JOURNALISM	⊗ ☒ √	JOURNALISM
11	JOURNALISM	CIVICS	JOURNALISM	EARLY ENG. LIT.	JOURNALISM
12	√ × ⋆	EARLY ENG. LIT.	PHYSICS	EARLY ENG. LIT.	PHYSICS
13	√ ○ □ ☒		√	○ □	×
14	√ ☒		√	○ □	×
15	√ × ○ □ ⋆ ⊗ ☒	√ × ○ □ ⋆ ⊗ ☒	√ × ○ □ ⋆ ⊗ ☒	√ × ○ □ ⋆ ⊗ ☒	√ × ○ □ ⋆ ⊗ ☒

√ CIVICS
× MATH
○ JOURNALISM
□ ADV. COMP.
⋆ EARLY ENG. LIT.
⊗ MECH. DRAW.
☒ PHYSICS (Open Lab)

Figure 2.

SCHEDULE CARD

Name Vocational Arts – Girl Grade Senior

Average Ability – High Motivation

	MONDAY	TUESDAY	WEDNESDAY	THURSDAY	FRIDAY
1	DRAMA	DRAMA	DRAMA	×	DRAMA
2	DRAMA	○ ×	DRAMA	* ○ ⊗	DRAMA
3	GIRLS P.E.	GIRLS P.E.	GIRLS P.E.	GIRLS P.E.	GIRLS P.E.
4	GIRLS P.E.	GIRLS P.E.	GIRLS P.E.	GIRLS P.E.	GIRLS P.E.
5	* ⊗ ○ √	OFFICE PRACTICE	* ○ ⊗		* ○ ⊗
6	SHORTHAND	SHORTHAND	SHORTHAND	SHORTHAND	SHORTHAND
7	SHORTHAND	BUSINESS LAW	SHORTHAND	BUSINESS LAW	SHORTHAND
8	* ⊗ ○ □ √ ×	BUSINESS LAW	□ ×	BUSINESS LAW	□ × √ * ⊗ ○
9	LUNCH	LUNCH	LUNCH	LUNCH	LUNCH
10	* ⊗ ○ □ √	□ √ ○ * ⊗	* ○ ⊗ □ √	* ○ ⊗ □ √	□ √ ○ * ⊗
11	INTERMEDIATE TYPING	CIVICS	OFFICE PRACTICE	INTERMEDIATE TYPING	OFFICE PRACTICE
12	INTERMEDIATE TYPING	* ⊗ ○ □	OFFICE PRACTICE	INTERMEDIATE TYPING	OFFICE PRACTICE
13	√	CIVICS	√	CIVICS	
14	√	CIVICS	√	CIVICS	
15	√ × ○ * ⊗	√ × ○ * ⊗	√ × ○ * ⊗	√ × ○ * ⊗	√ × ○ * ⊗

√ CIVICS
× DRAMA
○ OFFICE PRACTICE (Not in school office)
* BUSINESS LAW
⊗ INTERMEDIATE TYPING
□ SHORTHAND

Figure 3.

SCHEDULE CARD

Name Vocational Arts – Boy Grade Junior

Low Ability – Low Motivation

Excused from Physical Education because of Interscholastic Athletics

	MONDAY	TUESDAY	WEDNESDAY	THURSDAY	FRIDAY
1	⊗	ADV. COMP.	⊗	ADV. COMP.	× ⊗
2		ADV. COMP.	⊗	○ *	× ⊗
3	SPAN I	□	SPAN I	SPAN I	SPAN I
4	SPAN I	√ ×	SPAN I	SPAN I	SPAN I
5	√ ×	EARLY ENGLISH LIT.	×	EARLY ENGLISH LIT.	×
6	√ ○ *	EARLY ENGLISH LIT.	× *	EARLY ENGLISH LIT.	*
7	(SPAN I) TEACHER	MECH. DRAW.	(SPAN I) TEACHER	MECH. DRAW.	√ × ○ □ ⊗
8	AG. ORIENTATION	MECH. DRAW.	AG. ORIENTATION	MECH. DRAW.	AG. ORIENTATION
9	LUNCH	LUNCH	LUNCH	LUNCH	LUNCH
10	SPAN I	MECH. DRAW.	(SPAN I) TEACHER	AG. ORIENTATION	√ ○ *
11	√ ○	CIVICS		√ *	⊗
12	√ ○	EARLY ENGLISH LIT.	×	× *	× ⊗
13	WELDING	CIVICS	WELDING	CIVICS	WELDING
14	WELDING	CIVICS	WELDING	CIVICS	WELDING
15	√ × ○ □ * ⊗	√ × ○ □ * ⊗	√ × ○ □ * ⊗	√ × ○ □ * ⊗	√ × ○ □ * ⊗

√ CIVICS
× ADV. COMP.
○ EARLY ENG. LIT
□ SPANISH I
* WELDING & AG. ORIENTATION
⊗ MECH, DRAW.
( ) DENOTES ADDITIONAL TIME SCHEDULED BY TEACHER

Figure 4.

SCHEDULE CARD

Name College-Bound – Girl Grade Soph.

Above Average Ability – High Motivation

	MONDAY	TUESDAY	WEDNESDAY	THURSDAY	FRIDAY
1	GIRLS P.E.	GIRLS P.E.	GIRLS P.E.	GIRLS P.E.	GIRLS P.E.
2	GIRLS P.E.	GIRLS P.E.	GIRLS P.E.	GIRLS P.E.	GIRLS P.E.
3	×	BEGINNING TYPING	⋆ ⊗ ☒ ☐	BEGINNING TYPING	×
4	☐ ×	BEGINNING TYPING	☐	BEGINNING TYPING	×
5	√ ☐	☐ ☒	× ☐	√	☐
6	DRIVER ED.	DRIVER ED.	DRIVER ED.	DRIVER ED.	DRIVER ED.
7	DRIVER ED.	DRIVER ED.	DRIVER ED.	DRIVER ED.	DRIVER ED.
8	○ ☐ √ ⋆ ⊗	INSTRUMENTAL MUSIC	GEOMETRY	INSTRUMENTAL MUSIC	√ ○ ☐ ⋆ ⊗
9	LUNCH	LUNCH	LUNCH	LUNCH	LUNCH
10	☐ √ ⋆ ⊗	ORAL COMMUNICATION	EARLY AMERICAN LIT.	ORAL COMMUNICATION	SPAN II
11	SPAN II	ORAL COMMUNICATION	SPAN II	SPAN II	SPAN II
12	SPAN II	WORLD HISTORY	SPAN II	SPAN II	SPAN II
13	GEOMETRY	GEOMETRY	EARLY AMERICAN LIT.	GEOMETRY	WORLD HISTORY
14	GEOMETRY	GEOMETRY	EARLY AMERICAN LIT.	GEOMETRY	WORLD HISTORY
15	√ × ○ ☐ ⋆ ⊗ ☒	√ × ○ ☐ ⋆ ⊗ ☒	√ × ○ ☐ ⋆ ⊗ ☒	√ × ○ ☐ ⋆ ⊗ ☒	√ × ○ ☐ ⋆ ⊗ ☒

√ HISTORY
× GEOMETRY
○ SPANISH
☐ TYPING
⋆ ORAL COMMUNICATIONS
⊗ EARLY AMERICAN LIT.
☒ DRIVER ED.

Figure 5.

SCHEDULE CARD

Name Vocational Arts – Boy Grade Frosh

Average Ability – Low Motivation

Instrumental Music lessons are scheduled as shown – Individual practice is during study time.

	MONDAY	TUESDAY	WEDNESDAY	THURSDAY	FRIDAY
1	COMP.	GEN. MATH	COMP.	GEN. MATH.	GEN. MATH
2	COMP.	GEN. MATH	COMP.	GEN. MATH	GEN. MATH
3	GEN. SCIENCE	BASIC SHOP	BASIC SHOP	BASIC SHOP	GEN. MATH
4	GEN. SCIENCE	BASIC SHOP	×	BASIC SHOP	GEN. MATH
5	B.P.E.	B.P.E.	B.P.E.	B.P.E.	B.P.E.
6	B.P.E.	B.P.E.	B.P.E.	B.P.E.	B.P.E.
7	○ ⋆ □ ⊗	INSTR. MUSIC	SUR. LIT.	INSTR. MUSIC	SUR. LIT.
8	× ○ ⋆ □ ⊗	INSTR. MUSIC	SUR. LIT.	INSTR. MUSIC	SUR. LIT.
9	LUNCH	LUNCH	LUNCH	LUNCH	LUNCH
10	√ □ ⊗	× ○ ⋆ ⊗	√ × ⋆ ⊗	⋆ □ ⊗	× ⋆ ⊗
11	GEN. MATH	SUR. LIT.	WORLD HISTORY	⋆ ⊗	WORLD HISTORY
12	COMP.	WORLD HISTORY	WORLD HISTORY	GEN. SCIENCE	WORLD HISTORY
13	× ○ ⋆ ⊗	⋆	ORIENTATION	○	√ × ⋆ □
14	× ⊗	⋆	× ⋆ ⊗	○	√ × ⋆
15	√ × ○ ⋆ □ ⊗	√ × ○ ⋆ □ ⊗	√ × ○ ⋆ □ ⊗	√ × ○ ⋆ □ ⊗	√ × ○ ⋆ □ ⊗

√ GEN. MATH
× GEN. SCIENCE
○ COMPOSITION
⋆ SURVEY OF LITERATURE
□ BASIC SHOP
⊗ WORLD HISTORY

Figure 6.

recruitment have not been evidenced. The establishment of performance criteria further frees the student to pursue his individual interests at his own speed and permits a further individualization of attention and instruction. Schedules are arranged to meet individual abilities and needs.

All of the advantages of the small school have been retained and in addition we are informed that our program now offers students a greater variety of courses and better vocational training opportunities than may be found in many schools of over fifteen hundred enrollment.

Administrative Problems as a Result of Flexible Scheduling and Team Teaching*

RALPH H. SLEIGHT

This discussion is strictly within the frame of reference of a principal as he views the administrative tasks involved when a major change is made in staffing and the use of time at a particular school. Pioneer High School, one of the high schools in the San Jose Unified School District in San Jose, California, was opened in 1960 and had operated on a conventional schedule and with conventional methods of teaching for two years before the staff began the thinking leading to planning for major reorganization to implement the ideas involved in team teaching, large group instruction, small group instruction, independent study, and flexible or modular scheduling. After two years of planning, reorganization went into effect for the 1964-1965 school year.

The problems cluster around certain areas. These areas are identified in Figure 1 entitled "Progression to Implementation." By referring to Figure 1, you

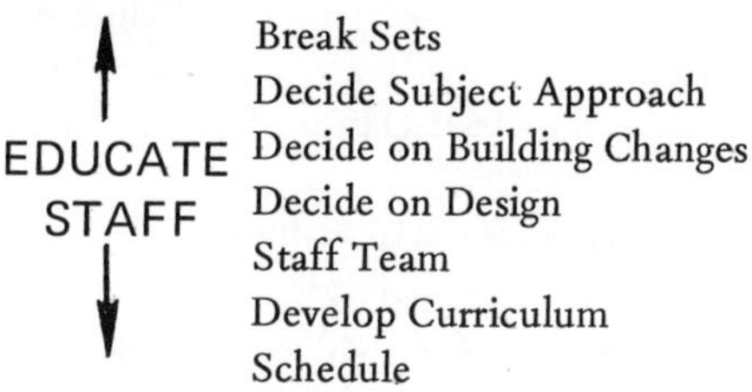

Figure 1. Progression to Implementation

will note that the education of the staff and the orientation of parents and students begin with the first ideas of major reorganization and actually never

*Reprinted from *The Journal of Secondary Education,* (December 1967), 358-362, by permission of the publisher and Ralph H. Sleight, Principal, Pioneer High School, San Jose, California.

end. These tasks, as outlined in Figure 1, obviously do not separate themselves clearly and precisely; that is, there is considerable overlapping as to when these tasks are in progress and when they are finished. To more clearly define what is meant by each task in Figure 1, each one is discussed here briefly.

Break Sets. Sets can be defined as predispositions to react to certain stimuli in certain predetermined ways. Some people refer to sets as "ruts." The strategy here is to begin working with faculty and administrators playing a kind of game wherein everyone is encouraged to challenge each other's sets; that is, whenever anyone says that something must be done in a certain pattern, he is to be challenged.

Decide Subject Approach. Involved here is the decision as to whether the school is going to follow a single subject approach or a multi-subject approach. Since so many multi-subject approaches have been unsuccessful, it seemed wise to adopt the single subject approach in the formative stages of the program.

Decide On Building Changes. Most school plants have been designed for a conventional program. A survey of facilities is required to see how the plant can be modified or expanded to accommodate large groups, small groups, library, and study centers. This decision is quite complex because it depends on determinations which will be made in the future. At this point, you can only *predict* how many large group and small group areas you are going to need because the actual number will be determined by the departmental designs and usage of time.

Decide On Design. These are the really difficult decisions for faculty. They must decide, for each course, how many large groups and small groups they will have each week and the length of time these different groups will meet. These decisions determine the pattern of the master schedule.

Staff Teams. At this time, some kind of logic must be developed to staff the teams. Many articles have been written on this subject which give direction. The logic developed at Pioneer was quite simple; place a teacher on the team for each class placed within the large group; that is, if one wants a group of 120 in the large group, it will be composed of four classes of 30 and would be staffed with four teachers.

Develop Curriculum. This procedure is actually begun when the teachers are deciding on the designs for the course. It simply means that the curriculums which have been used are re-examined and shifted so that the new activities are relevant to the time and the size of the group. Some teachers attended summer workshop sponsored by the school district to develop curriculum and the audio-visual aids which were relevant to the curriculum. Actually the year of reorganization started with the first semester being very well planned and the second semester planned during the school year.

Schedule. After the course designs have been structured and the logic developed to staff teams, the scheduling can begin. This procedure is quite similar to that followed with conventional schedules. The time that courses appear on the master schedule is determined largely by the matrix, that document that is printed out by Data Processing which tells us how many students have chosen each course. Pioneer worked with a Service Bureau who brought in experts to work out a program for the computer.

The problems discussed above and those which are to be discussed result in an increase in administrative load, particularly in the year leading to reorganization and during the first year. A few problems continue to arise just as they do with conventional organization since the reorganization leads to constant innovation because of the attitudes developed by the faculty and the community. There seems to be a conditioning process in operation here. The faculty and community expect new innovations to take place almost continually. The experienced administrator will recognize many standard problems among those presented in the following discussion, but many solutions differ as a result of the different structure. No effort is made here to present the solutions to the problems as this would make this article too lengthy, but the problems have been solved.

Setting Subject Designs. This problem has been previously discussed and it is stated here merely for emphasis, but it requires a great deal of sophistication on the part of a faculty to be able to decide on subject designs.

Schedules. Establishment of schedules for the State Testing Program, final examinations, assemblies, and student activities is made more complex. When all periods started and ended at the same time, it was relatively easy to shift periods to accommodate almost any kind of scheduling problem. However, with modular scheduling the development of these schedules becomes more difficult.

Number Of Classes A Student May Take. On the modular schedule, it became possible for some students to take as many as eight classes. The decision here is developing criteria which will determine how many classes a student will be permitted to take.

Credit. Not all classes meet for 250 minutes per week; therefore, it became necessary to determine how many minutes of class time would qualify a student for a Carnegie unit. We adopted the policy that 200 minutes per week would be the minimum time necessary to qualify for a Carnegie unit. Students can take courses and qualify for less than a full unit of credit. Procedures and symbols must be designed so that the partial unit credit can be recorded on permanent record cards.

Lunch. Do we want a lunch period for all students who eat at the same time; do we want to split the lunch hour, or do we want to have students with non-scheduled time somewhere around the noon hour and have this worked into their schedule?

Activity. We cannot follow the alternative of having a floating period for student activities. The problem then arises as to when we shall hold rallies, when we shall hold assemblies, and how we can build these activities into the schedule or how can we modify the schedule at any time to permit these activities?

Length of Day. Many alternatives are available if the day is extended, but what constitutes a reasonable day for students and a reasonable day for faculty?

Remodeling For Large Group and Small Group Areas. Each department may differ in its needs; therefore, a decision must be made on exactly how to remodel for each area. The types of materials used in remodeling must be decided upon. Is only visual separation satisfactory or must all groups be separated both audibly and visually?

Refurnishing For Large Group And Small Group Areas. Since space is usually at a premium, one must consider the use of tablet arm chairs instead of the regular standard chair desks that are found in most classrooms. Is it possible to use circular tables in small group areas?

Audio-Visual Equipment. The decision must be made as to how many areas are to have overhead projectors, and what kind of overhead projectors will be purchased. Some areas which could utilize closed circuit television must be provided for. Will this television equipment be fixed or portable?

Public Address Systems. For each large group area there is a necessity for a public address system. Do we provide this area with a type of equipment which will permit the teacher complete freedom of movement while still using the equipment, or is fixed equipment satisfactory? What kind of equipment is necessary because of maintenance problems and initial cost?

Teacher Meeting Spaces. Since teachers and students have non-scheduled time, it is essential that they have a place where they can meet with students. This was normally done in the teacher's classroom during a "free" period. However, most areas will be used and it becomes necessary to provide special places for teachers so that they can meet with students to take advantage of non-scheduled time.

Material Preparation Equipment and Supplies. When teachers begin to use overhead projectiles, a problem arises in purchasing the kind of equipment which will make the preparation of these materials rapid and of high quality. Who will prepare these projectiles—the teacher or a secretary? What happens to the school budget when you begin to purchase the supplies which are necessary for the production of projectiles? Where will this additional money come from? Where will this additional equipment be housed?

New Curriculum Materials. Will more books be needed?It was common under the conventional system to provide a set of novels in English which would be used for a week in one classroom, shifted to another classroom, so that all students would have the opportunity to use these novels. When 100 or 200 students are working on the same novel at the same time because of the large group structure, it creates a problem in that many more copies of the same books are needed.

Teacher Planning. Much of the efficiency of the program depends upon the opportunity the teachers have to meet together and to plan together. Many problems arise in this area concerning time when they can meet, place where they can meet, the personalities of the people involved in the team, and the utilization of outside personnel who are expert in certain areas of curriculum.

Team Teaching Clerks. Before reorganization there was no need for team teaching clerks, but the need immediately becomes apparent; therefore, the administrator is responsible for more personnel than he was prior to reorganization. He must decide upon where to put the clerks; will they be in a pool, or will they be with teachers, or will he have a combination of these procedures? He must decide on salary they will be paid, the time they will work, and the specific roles they will perform.

Administrative Staff Task Analysis and Assignment. A reorganization necessitates an analysis of the duties that the administrators perform and an adjustment of the duties in view of the organization. An example of this is the fact that the scheduling process becomes more complex and more experimental, requiring much more time on the part of the administrator assigned to the task.

Attendance Procedures. With classes differing in starting and stopping times all during the school day, the procedure of reporting attendance is made more complex. In order to get an accurate record of attendance during the day, it appears necessary to have at least one time during the day when all students are in class at the same time. Under the conventional schedule, if a student is out of class other than at a passing period, he becomes immediately visible to anyone observing the campus. In modular scheduling, with non-scheduled time, there are students around the school out of classes at all times during the day, so it becomes extremely difficult to identify a person as someone who is cutting a class. The procedures used in accounting for students and taking attendance in classes must be completely revised.

Teacher Education. When structuring the program and thereafter, the teachers have to be completely educated as to the alternatives available to them under this new kind of organization. This means that ways and means must be found to educate them and these procedures must be financed.

Education of Board Members, Staff Members, Supervisors. All these people who exercise control over a school must be made completely familiar with the thinking of the school personnel as this thinking progresses.

Student and Parent Orientation. We have always considered it essential to involve those most directly concerned with changes to the extent that they feel comfortable undergoing the change. The problem here is how much to involve students and parents in planning the program so that they will be completely familiar with the changes and at the same time do not inhibit the creativity of the school staff.

Staffing. Under this category we must think of teacher load; the number of students they have, the minutes per week that they teach; what's involved in adding new teachers; whether or not substitutes are always necessary; and the development of logic for staffing teams. It is possible in large group instruction to have teachers who have very high loads as far as student contacts are concerned. Therefore, we must decide what is a reasonable load. We must determine how many minutes per week the teacher can usually teach and still be efficient. Teams are structured because of the capabilities of certain people, the number of teachers needed within a certain area, and personal desires. If a new school year starts with more students than estimated and it is necessary to add teachers, it is difficult to work people into teams which have planned together and have been working together. At times when a teacher is ill, it is not always necessary to hire a substitute because a teacher may actually be unimportant to a team functioning on that particular day. There is also the problem of informing the team leader or other members of the team when a teacher is going to be absent, so that they can make modifications within the team on the day that the teacher is absent. As mentioned previously, there must be a logic established for the staffing of teams; then there must be adherence to this logic at all times because people expect this logic to be followed and become upset when it is not.

Student Location. When classes are meeting at different times on the different days of the week, the program cards listing the student's classes are inadequate. As a consequence, new locator cards must be designed. Even when new cards are designed, it is difficult to locate a student when he has non-scheduled time.

Teacher Location. The same kinds of problems exist with locating teachers that exist with students. We must design ways of locating teachers other than a simple master program. Any administrator contemplating major organizational change should be aware of the problems involved and insist that those he works with, and for, share this awareness. At this time a sufficient number of principals has been involved in team teaching and flexible scheduling to provide guidance for those moving into these areas. Those about to become involved should feel the responsibility to seek the information rather than rely on trial and error.

Can Team Teaching Save the Core Curriculum?*

GORDON F. VARS

"Both the principles and the early patterns of core are now advancing under the banner of team teaching."—Harold Spears[1]

"Team teaching and the core curriculum are as far apart as the poles in their underlying philosophical and psychological assumptions."—Nelson Bossing[2]

"Team teaching in reality can become an extension, a further refinement, and an improvement of the core."—Vernon Anderson[3]

How is it possible for eminent educators, all experts in curriculum, to come to such contradictory conclusions? Clarification of this issue is vital to anyone interested in team teaching, core, or curriculum in general.

Core Curriculum

Spears states:

> Among the common features of both core and team teaching are: 1) a large group of pupils assigned to a team of teachers, 2) a curriculum block assigned as the area to be covered, 3) a block of time longer than the usual period provided for the work, 4) the

*Reprinted from the *Phi Delta Kappa,* 47 (January 1966), 258-262, by permission of the publisher and Gordon F. Vars, Kent State University.

[1]Paraphrased from: Harold Spears, "A Second Look at *The Emerging High School Curriculu,*" *Phi Delta Kappan,* November, 1963, p 112.

[2]Paraphrased from: "S-R Bonds," *Phi Delta Kappan,* February, 1964, p. 268.

[3]Vernon Anderson, "The Evolving Core Curriculum," in *The High School Curriculum,* Harl R. Douglass (ed.), Third Edition. New York: Ronald Press, 1964, p. 266.

> provision within the program of class groups varying in size from exceedingly large to exceedingly small, 5) freedom for the teachers to plan among themselves the flexible scheduling within the program that meets the instructional objectives of the moment, and 6) the correlation of curriculum content naturally related.[4]

Here and in his earlier writing Spears applies the term "core" to any program "involving a longer period than the popular forty-to-sixty-minute period and dependence for material upon an area which under a subject curriculum would comprise two or more subject fields."[5] More appropriate for this concept is the generic term "block-time," proposed by Grace Wright in her definitive 1958 study of block-time and core programs.[6]

Both Bossing and Anderson restrict the term core to a *particular type* of block-time class that goes beyond correlation to focus directly on the needs, interests, and problems of students.[7] In such a program subject matter is brought in as needed to deal with problems, clearly distinguishing core from programs in which primary commitment is to preselected subject matter. As Anderson describes it:

> The core curriculum is a way of organizing some of the important common learnings in the high school curriculum, using a problem-solving approach as its procedure, having social and personal problems significant to youth and society as its content, and focusing upon the development of behaviors needed in a democratic society as its purpose.[8]

It is the latter, more precise definition of core that is applied in this analysis. Since both Bossing and Anderson have similar definitions of core, the clue to their disagreement must lie in their conceptions of team teaching. In listing the characteristics of core, neither Anderson nor Bossing makes explicit

[4]Spears, *op. cit.* See also Spears' introduction to: David W. Beggs, III, ed., *Team Teaching: Bold New Venture.* Indianapolis: Unified College Press, 1964, pp. 8-9.

[5]Harold Spears, *The Emerging High School Curriculum and Its Direction.* New York: American Book Company, 1940, p. 63.

[6]U.S. Office of Education, *Block-Time Classes and the Core Program in the Junior High School,* by Grace S. Wright, Bulletin 1958, No. 6. Washington: Government Printing Office, 1958, pp. ix, 9-19. See also: William Van Til, Gordon F. Vars, and John H. Lounsbury, *Modern Education for the Junior High School Years.* Indianapolis: Bobbs-Merrill, 1961, pp. 92-104.

[7]Roland C. Faunce and Nelson L. Bossing, *Developing the Core Curriculum,* Second Edition. Englewood Cliffs, New Jersey: Prentice-Hall, 1958, p. 58.

[8]Anderson, *op. cit.,* p. 248.

reference to teaching teams or to "exceedingly large groups," although both stress cooperative planning among core teachers.[9]

Team Teaching

In team teaching, two or more teachers are given joint responsibility for all or a significant part of the instruction of the same group of students. Team teaching is a key element of the plan proposed by J. Lloyd Trump and the Commission on the Experimental Study of the Utilization of the Staff in the Secondary School.[10] Besides team teaching, Trump advocates flexible scheduling, the use of nonprofessional personnel as teacher aides, and increased utilization of modern instructional media. Instruction is to be provided through independent study, small-group discussion, and presentations in groups larger than the usual class.

As indicated by its title, the commission is primarily concerned with redeployment of staff rather than curriculum reform. Implications for core must be inferred from the commission's publications, from other writings on team teaching theory, and from reports of team teaching experiments. Core is seldom mentioned in Trump's publications, but clearly consonant with the core idea are his goal of helping students learn to think and solve problems on their own, his emphasis upon the guidance role of the teacher, and such features as flexible use of large blocks of time, cooperative planning among teachers, and varying the size and composition of class groups.

Interdisciplinary Teams

Correlation of subject matter is facilitated by an interdisciplinary team, which Trump illustrates as follows:

> A teacher of United States history, a teacher of United States literature, teachers who know the music and arts of the country, and specialists who can improve students's writing and speaking could team together to teach various phases of the culture of this

[9]Faunce and Bossing, *op. cit.*, pp. 59-60, and Anderson, *op. cit.*, pp. 248-252.

[10]See for example: J. Lloyd Trump, *Images of the Future: A New Approach to the Secondary School.* Washington: National Association of Secondary School Principals, 1959; and J. Lloyd Trump, *New Directions to Quality Education: The Secondary School Tomorrow.* Washington: National Association of Secondary School Principals, 1960.

> country. . . .This approach would provide a natural synthesis of subject matter and the most competent teaching in the various subject areas.[11]

Brownell and Taylor also hypothesize "improved correlation of subject matter because of cooperative planning in team meetings,"[12] and cite as an example a three-period "core" arrangement composed of three seventh-grade teachers, specialists in English, social studies, and mathematics, respectively.

In 1940 Spears described four programs involving interdisciplinary teams, giving particular attention to the Evansville (Indiana) Plan, initiated while he was director of secondary education in that city. In this program three teachers were given responsibility for 100 ninth-graders in a three-period block of time. The "General Living Core," as it was called at the Benjamin Bosse High School, included experiences drawn from English, social studies, everyday business training, practical mathematics, art, music, and science. The "main threads of instructional experience" were school life, community life, home life, and vocational life; various ways of grouping and regrouping students were suggested for carrying out the program.[13]

Since 1958, special issues of the *Bulletin of the National Association of Secondary School Principals* have been devoted to reports of experiences with the Staff Utilization Commission's recommendations. The May, 1963, issue revealed the extent to which the interdisciplinary team idea had caught on. Fully half of the team teaching programs described in this issue included at least one team that teaches two or more subjects. Of the thirteen schools having junior high teams, nine had the "block-team" arrangement.

All these programs fall within the definition of block-time; they provide for flexible use of an extended period of time and correlation of subject matter. Many include small-group work and independent study. The interdisciplinary team may eliminate a persistent problem in block-time programs, the tendency of some teachers to stress one of the subjects absorbed into the block more than the others. Judicious use of small-group work may enable team teachers to establish rapport with a few of their students sufficient for them to exercise the guidance function typically assigned to block-time teachers. Also, the variety of teacher personalities on a team increases the likelihood that any one student will find an adult to whom he can relate easily. Little wonder, then, that team teaching may appear to be compatible with the core idea, at least in its older, more general sense of block-time, as used by Harold Spears.

[11] J. Lloyd Trump and Dorsey Baynham, *Focus on Change, Guide to Better Schools.* Chicago: Rand McNally, 1961, p. 106.

[12] John A. Brownell and Harris A. Taylor, "Theoretical Perspectives for Team Teaching," *Phi Delta Kappan,* January, 1962, p. 151.

[13] Spears, *op. cit.,* 1940, pp. 289-320.

Anderson sees further possibilities, saying:

> Team teachers have good opportunities to use teacher-pupil planning, problem solving, personal and social problems, related subject matter from different fields, and skills in relation to ongoing situations. They have the opportunity to use the experience-centered approach. Moreover, they have the propitious opportunity to use their subject specialities and talents, a lack in the core program.[14]

He makes it clear, however, that these are opportunities, not inevitable results of team teaching. It is the likelihood of this happening that is doubted by Bossing on both philosophical and psychological grounds. To examine this question we must go beyond the Trump proposals, preoccupied as they are with organizational matters, to examine team teaching theory. For this we rely on *Team Teaching,* edited by Judson Shaplin and Henry F. Olds, Jr., one of the most penetrating analyses of team teaching extant.[15]

It is important to note first that comments on the integration of learning experiences from several curriculum areas appear but rarely in this book. The word core is not listed at all in the index, is mentioned only two or three times in all 430 pages, and is used to refer to an arrangement more accurately labeled block-time. While pointing out that team teaching arrangements have forced teachers to take a new, critical look at the curriculum, Shaplin states quite frankly that "the staff utilization studies, including team teaching, have most frequently been primarily concerned with administrative reorganization and adaptation of the existing curriculum to the new organization."[16] A consistent curriculum theory of any kind is notably lacking in most of the major publications on team teaching, least of all the relationship of team teaching to the problem-centered core.[17]

Drawbacks in Team Teaching

Moreover, certain features of team teaching appear to militate against effective core teaching. Take the matter of time. Those who expect team

[14]Anderson, *op. cit.,* p. 266.

[15]Judson T. Shaplin and Harry F. Olds, Jr. (eds.), *Team Teaching,* New York: Harper and Row, 1964.

[16]*Ibid.,* p. 42.

[17]See, for example: David W. Beggs, III, *Decatur-Lakeview High School: A Practical Application of the Trump Plan.* Englewood-Cliffs, New Jersey: Prentice-Hall, 1964; David W. Beggs, III, ed., *Team Teaching, op. cit.;* Medill Bair and Richard G. Woodward, *Team Teaching in Action.* Boston: Hougton Mifflin, 1964.

teaching to give the teacher more time for planning and for counseling with students are doomed to disappointment. The many complicated administrative decisions that are delegated to the team are tremendously time-consuming. Speaking from his experience with elementary team teaching in Lexington, Joseph C. Grannis says: "It seems likely that team teaching will demand as much time as the self-contained classroom, if not more, for a long time to come."[18]

Even large-group instruction, which is supposed to give teachers some released time, may fail to deliver. "Not only do these lessons require a great deal of time to prepare," Grannis says, "but it is also generally necessary for teachers who are not directly responsible for the lesson to be present anyway, or at least to be involved in the planning, in order to insure the articulation of these lessons with others that precede and follow them."[19] Core teachers have for years complained that a major obstacle to success of their program was lack of adequate time for staff planning and for counseling with students. They may well be jumping from the frying pan into the fire if they embrace team teaching.

Teacher-student planning within a broadly defined problem area is another key feature of core that may be difficult to carry out in a team. Clearly, cooperative planning is impossible with a large group of 100 or more students. It also is difficult to see how small groups could carry out their own plans and still keep their schedules close enough together to profit from large-group instruction. In other words, classes or small groups would be so tied to the schedule of large-group instruction that their freedom to evolve their own plans would be severely restricted.

Otherwise, after the initial overview of a problem area (which might well be carried out with combined groups), each core class would inevitably go its own way. This would not rule out the possibility of combining groups whenever a film, visiting speaker, or field trip happened to be appropriate to more than one group, a practice possible in any kind of program. Joint action to carry out a unit-culminating activity, such as a school assembly or service project, also would be difficult if each group selected its own learning experiences through teacher-student planning. Loren Tompkins reports that whole-group culminating activities have been abandoned by the core team at Northern Hills Junior High School in North Topeka, Kansas, because it proved almost impossible for each teacher to finish a unit on the same day. "It is easy to fill in until the team is ready to begin a new unit," he writes, "but it is most difficult to maintain pupil interest in postponed culminating activities."[20]

Another difficulty in harmonizing team teaching and core lies in the area of guidance. Trump makes much of the opportunities for personal teacher-student conferences in a team teaching program, but we have already pointed out that teachers in a team may actually have little time for these.

[18]Shaplin and Olds, *op. cit.,* p. 163.

[19]*Ibid.,* pp. 163-64.

[20]Loren Tompkins, "Background of the Northern Hills Core Program." Unpublished manuscript, 1964, p. 7.

Assignment of a guidance specialist to a team, helpful as that may be, is hardly an adequate substitute for the teacher-counseling provided by a core teacher who has developed a close personal relationship with his students.

The small-group discussions inherent in most team teaching proposals are expected to provide excellent opportunities for developing teacher-student rapport. However, the fact that these are so often called "discussion groups" rather than counseling groups, work groups, or even study groups, leads one to wonder how far they go beyond the mere rehashing of information presented in large-group sessions.[21] Apparently little has been done thus far to exploit the guidance potential of small-group sessions. In fact, some teams deliberately rotate their small-group leadership, sacrificing sustained contact between a teacher and a few students in the hope that all team members will become somewhat acquainted with all the students.

Robert A. Anderson has this to say about the oft-reported problem of getting to know the students in a team teaching situation:

> In the beginning, elementary teachers in a team will tend to be alarmed by the fact that it takes much longer to become acquainted with the pupils than it did in the self-contained classroom. They need reassurance on this point, since the evidence from pilot teams very clearly shows that the problem is a temporary and soluble one. In fact, the data suggest that by approximately midyear the team members are in possession of much more information about each child than their counterparts in self-contained classrooms, even though the latter have only one-third to one-sixth as many pupils.[22]

A core teacher who takes his guidance responsibilities seriously would hardly be willing to wait half a year to get to know his students well. Moreover, although information about one's students is important, even more important are the emotional overtones of the teacher-pupil relationship. The continued presence of other adults in a team teaching situation may affect the quality of these relationships. Dan Lortie raises this question in discussing the high rapport possible under the "autonomy-equality" (self-contained) teaching situation:

> What we do not yet know is whether such states of high rapport can arise w ere more than one adult is teaching in a single classroom. Under autonomy-equality the teacher unselfconsciously relates directly to the class and need not concern himself with the possibly different reactions emanating from other adults. Can adults work together in a way which permits them the same free-wheeling

[21]See, for example: David W. Beggs, III, *Decatur-Lakeview High School, op. cit.*, pp. 99-113.

[22]Shaplin and Olds, *op. cit.*, p. 214.

> emotional freedom and which results in an equally intense relationship?[23]

The most serious conflict between core and teamteaching stems from the emphasis upon subject matter specialization in most team teaching proposals. Shaplin states this quite frankly:

> One of the major goals of many team teaching projects has been to increase the amount of subject specialization among teachers at all levels of the school system. At the secondary school level this means further division of a broad subject area. An English teacher, for example, may become a specialist in language, in some phase of literature, or in developmental reading.[24]

In the same book, we are told by Glen Heathers that "the self-contained classroom is being destroyed by insistent pressures toward greater teacher specialization and toward greater diversity in the instructional arrangements made available to the individual student."[25] This, despite his candid admission that "*specialization offers no guarantee whatsoever that teaching of a subject will improve with respect to such goals as critical thinking, inquiry, self-instruction, or command of theory*."[26] While no instructional arrangement can guarantee results, one cannot but wonder what motivates the drive toward specialization if there is not at least the expectation of better achievement of these vital objectives.

In addition to subject matter specialization, the hierarchical team advocated by Trump involves further specialization in terms of roles, such as team leader, general teacher, teacher aide, clerk, and the like. Even when no formal team structure is provided, some specialization of functions must take place simply to enable the team to operate. Whether specialization is planned for or "just happens," the question remains: Can a team of staff members fully exploit the interrelatedness of learnings inherent in a core problem area, or must plans be filtered through the mind of a single person, someone who knows intimately the interests, capacities, and previous experiences of a relatively small group of children?

Problems encountered whenever two teachers try merely to correlate their courses should be sufficient warning of the well-nigh insuperable difficulties facing a team who would teach core. Robert Ohm tells us that "specialization of tasks, functions, and jobs tend to pull the organization apart and to split the

[23]*Ibid.*, p. 278.
[24]*Ibid.*, p. 82.
[25]*Ibid.*, p. 372.
[26]*Ibid.*, p. 352 (Italics mine).

central unity of the teaching process."[27] Specialization, the inevitable concomitant of team teaching, is thus destructive of the very unity of teaching process which core is designed to promote.

Conclusion

Team teaching is a pattern of staff organization that seems at first glance to be eminently suited to core, when the latter is defined in the older sense of block-time. Incompatibilities begin to appear, however, when core is defined more precisely as a curriculum organization with primary focus upon the personal-social problems of the learner. The staff time absorbed in just keeping a complex team in operation, the limitations on teacher-student planning imposed by the team schedule, the difficulties of establishing close teacher-student rapport, and above all the staff specialization that seems inevitable in a team, all militate against successful core teaching. Far from being the "salvation" of core, team teaching may prove to be "the Devil in disguise."

[27] Robert E. Ohm, "Toward a Rationale for Team Teaching," *Administrator's Notebook,* March, 1961, p. 2. (Publication of the Midwest Administration Center, University of Chicago.)

Group Grope: Problems of Team Teaching*

JAMES A. MEYER

Perceptive observers in recent years have witnessed the development and expansion of team teaching from a few isolated attempts to one of the leading innovations in staff utilization. These team teaching programs have increased not only in number but also in their diversity of organizational form. Acceptance of team teaching apparently has reached epidemic proportions. In one recent Gallop Poll, it was reported that both school board members and parents approved of team teaching programs as an innovative effort by margins of 88 and 84 per cent respectively. In another study conducted in 1967 of over 7,000 accredited secondary schools, it was found that 41 per cent of the schools reportedly utilized team teaching as an instructional innovation, whereas only about 22 per cent of the nation's secondary schools utilized team teaching in 1964.

It has often been suggested that the introduction of a team teaching program would carry with it a distinct challenge for the school administrator and staff relative to administrative and instructional leadership. In this respect a number of problems have been experienced by the personnel associated with the team teaching programs in operation. It is the purpose of this article, therefore, to discuss in some detail those problems of team teaching found to be rather common in occurance; yet significant enough to result in disenchantment with team teaching, and, in some instances, an abandonment of the team teaching program altogether.

Personnel participating in team teaching programs take great pride in their innovative efforts, and this often results in attempts on the part of the team teaching staffs to encourage the formation of team teaching programs in other

*Reprinted from *The Clearing House,* 42:362-364, (February 1968), by permission of the publisher and James A. Meyer, Assistant to the Chief Administrator, New Hartford Central School District, New York.

departments and subject matter areas of the curriculum. Members of the teaching teams tend to view conventional teaching as that of teaching in "isolated" classrooms. Team teachers have a tendency to hold their combined team teaching efforts in extremely high esteem and occasionally, at the expense of rapport with the other members of the total school staff, point with pride to their team teaching program as the "finest" instructional program. There generally is an awareness and understanding among the team teachers that team teaching is perhaps not too applicable for certain subject matter areas, and that certain teachers might not work well with a team teaching program. However, morale and rapport problems have occurred as a result of à feeling of instructional superiority among the teachers participating in such a special program.

It has been found that a measure of jealousy and envy has been directed towards the team teaching programs and the concept of team teaching by those members of the instructional staffs not team teaching. Teachers not participating in the venture have reportedly been hostile toward team teaching and have rejected its theory as a result of witnessing a great number of occasions when members of teaching teams have allegedly been found relaxing in the teachers' lounge rather than being engaged in the preplanning and preparation for classroom instruction for which the flexible schedule provides.

Teachers participating in the team teaching programs at the secondary level evidently have experienced some problems with respect to the small group instruction phase of team teaching. Team teachers are inclined to utilize the same instructional methods and techniques they practiced in programs of conventional teaching. There reportedly is a tendency on their part to review and repeat the instructional content of the large group lectures rather than to further develop and enrich such content. In some cases team teachers are reluctant to meet with students in small group instruction, and they use these times for study periods or send the students to the library for nondirected "independent study." Evidently, teachers participating in team teaching programs must be orientated to the purposes of small group instruction, psychology of group dynamics, and methodology of teaching small groups of students.

Members of the teaching teams have been encouraged to offer suggestions and constructive criticism in team meetings for the purpose of an improved and creative program. The atmosphere within the structure of the teaching team is most often characterized by free and open discussion and democratic participation. This has resulted in a tendency of the team teachers to often speak out at total staff meetings and voice strong opinions. They have grown accustomed to the fact that their ideas are important and that any contribution they make will be greatly appreciated. However, this tendency has been found to result in some resentment toward them. Some staff members have interpreted the actions of the team teachers in staff meetings as attempts to be "out-spoken" and to "dominate" the meetings.

Closely linked with the inclination of team teachers to voice strong opinions at total staff meetings is the apparent practice of the personnel participating in the team teaching programs to keep together and communicate less with other members of the school staff. Clearly there is a general lack of interaction between teachers on the teaching teams and other staff members. Team teachers work closely together during the same instructional period, are scheduled together for meetings, instruct the same students, and also plan and prepare together. As a result there is the disposition to be constantly together; perhaps at the expense of total staff rapport and morale.

In some instances less experienced members of the teaching teams or team teachers with less of a dynamic personality were assigned responsibilities for large group instruction, and it was found that some of these teachers expressed feelings of inadequacy when presenting their lectures before their observing peers from the teaching team. These feelings of inadequacy were sometimes reflected in a poor state of morale and motivation, a poor self image, and a high degree of anxiety.

Members within the teaching teams have reportedly experienced conflicts regarding the number of times and manner in which responsibilities were given for the large group lectures. Some team teachers felt that their lecturing talents were being utilized to a greater extent than other members of the teaching team. This attitude seems closely related to the amount of unscheduled time allocated to members of the teaching team for the purpose of preplanning and preparation for classroom instruction. The members of the teaching team value this unscheduled time highly and are closely observant of any possible inequality of time allotments. Members of the team also seem to be quite aware of any lack on the part of fellow members in supporting their part of the team teaching program—either in terms of teaching and preparation time or adequately prepared and presented lessons.

One facet of team teaching which has affected the morale of the students participating in such programs is the considerable addition to the amount of work expected of the students. With the combined efforts of the team teachers there are more ideas and expectations as to what material and concepts the students should master. This has resulted in a steady increase in subject matter for the students to comprehend. Team teachers seem to expect more from the students; they seem to steadily increase the amount of material presented to the students in classes, and do demand more in the nature of homework and scholastic achievement.

The students considered as below average in ability and scholastic achievement appear unable or unwilling to cope with team teaching and seem to have a disinclination for participation in these programs. In some instances these students complain that their lack of scholastic success is due to participation in team teaching programs. The slower students are of the opinion that the sequences of instruction in such programs are not as understandable as the instructional programs in the self-contained classroom. Utilization of more than one teacher for the instruction of a subject seems to further confuse the slower student. The instructional flexibility inherent in team teaching is a source of contention and conflict among the poorer students and is greatly resented. Team teachers might well consider excusing the slower students from participation in team teaching programs until conditions are such that these students can be assured that they will comprehend the presentation and successfully adjust.

School administrators do spend considerable time and effort in assisting the members of the teaching teams during the initial stages of the teaching program, and certain functions such as scheduling and grouping of students are usually handled by the school administrator. As a result some staff members feel that there is greater favoritism displayed by the school administrator toward the teaching teams in contrast with teachers not participating in team teaching. There is an inclination for staff members to compare the needs of and attention to the one teaching team with that of any one teacher. Certainly this contrast is unfair and there is an apparent need for the school administrators to clarify this relationship for the purposes of team morale and total staff rapport.

Lastly, there have been feelings expressed by those teachers engaged in team teaching of being "let down" by the school administrator in the areas of instructional supervision and curriculum construction. It is quite evident that the school administrators have been occasionally inattentive toward the teaching teams and have neglected certain aspects of the team teaching program. Aside from the fact that the school administrators have assisted the team teaching programs during the early stages of operation and have expressed pride over the fact of having team teaching programs in the schools, little has been done by the school administrators on a continuing basis in supervision or curriculum help. This has resulted in a low degree of morale within certain teaching teams and feelings of discouragement.

Problems in Team Teaching*

WILLIAM GOLDSTEIN

All stories, if continued far enough, end in death, and he is no true story-teller who would keep that from you.

Ernest Hemingway

Similarly, all new approaches to teaching, if not analyzed enough, end in atrophy. Logic and research tell us that the teaming of teachers to achieve certain desirable instructional ends has become a highly accepted, fashionable mode of teaching—to date perhaps the most compelling and attractive instructional approach to inquiry, transmittal of subject matter, use of teacher talent, and flexible grouping of students known. On the other hand, it is not difficult to see how one may be blinded by the dazzle of exotica triggered by such currently romanticized notions as large group instruction, seminars, pre- and post-testing, regrouping, sophisticated team planning, instructional analysis, and the like.

No responsible schoolman would quarrel with the need to develop new teaching-learning situations to deal with new knowledge and a "new breed" of students who continue to become increasingly demanding as well as hungry for broader and more lasting mastery of that in our environment which needs to be controlled and mastered. However, vacuous acceptance of ideas which are, in the words of Riesman, "other-directed" is tantamount to the establishment of superficiality at best and, at worst, predestined to certain failure. The dream and the real experience, the symbol and its substance, appearance and reality must be viewed as distinguishable and frequently separable commodities.

*Reprinted from *The Clearing House,* 42:83-86, (October 1967), by permission of the publisher and William Goldstein, principal, Howard B. Mattlin Junior High School, Plainview, N. Y.

The Problem of Choice

In its brief but singularly successful history, team teaching, for better or for worse, has meant almost anything its constituents wanted it to mean. For instance, some secondary schools organize teams of teachers on what is commonly called a "horizontal" basis, *i.e.*, where four teachers in the academic disciplines (English, social studies, mathematics, and science) are responsible for the basic instructional program of approximately 120 students. Other secondary schools, organize teaching teams on a "vertical" basis, *i.e.*, where three teachers within a single academic discipline (let us say, mathematics) are responsible for the instructional program of all students at a grade level (*e.g.*, grade 7).

Possible variations on these two major themes are legion, and all may have considerable relevance to sound educational objectives. Whichever direction toward the teaming of teachers a school chooses to take, it must first overcome the two most conspicuous problems—those of *choice of commitment* based on theoretically determined and desired outcomes and of the *organizational schema* to fit this choice.

One is reminded of little Alice and her charming egg-acquaintance, Humpty Dumpty, in Lewis Carroll's brilliant work, *Through the Looking-Glass*:

> 'When I use a word,' Humpty Dumpty said, in a rather scornful tone, 'it means just what I choose it to mean—neither more nor less.'
>
> 'The question is,' said Alice, 'whether you can make words mean so many different things.'
>
> 'The question is,' said Humpty Dumpty, 'which is to be the master—that's all.'

Operational Problems

Humpty Dumpty, though, like all characters populating lands of fantasy, could luxuriate in dismissing problems once he tired of them; such is not the case here. Once decisions on direction have been made, they must be dealt with. Team teaching raises a number of continuous and rather deep problems which need, quite expectedly, continuous and, sometimes, rather deep analysis. Examination of some of these may prove fruitful.

THE TIME VOLCANO

C. Northcote Parkinson in his humorous "law" states that "Work expands so as to fill the time available for its completion." Team teaching formulates its own paradoxical judicial maxim: As work or the perception of needed work expands, the time available for its completion contracts. Foremost among problems central to successful programs of team teaching seems to be the problem of a lack of time to plan programs and, indeed, sometimes even to execute instructional plans. Commitment to the teaming of teachers requires new looks into the organization of the school; these "new looks" may need to include the possibility of a complete reconstruction of the teaching load to allow for better planning and, most importantly, *analysis* and *evaluation* of the teaching-learning process. Failure to come to grips with the new realities created by a new process amounts not only to playing ostrich, but perhaps also to cheating at it.

SPACE EXPLORATION

Space, like time, is a fascinating scientific contemporary phenomenon receiving much attention. New use of building space is corollary to team teaching. Nothing provides greater frustration to students and faculty alike than short-circuitry in the use of building space. Varying class sizes, frequent regroupings of students, and sophisticated uses of audio-visual devices derive much of their existence from the idea of team teaching; attendant to these notions, logic directs that new and older school buildings alike must adapt their organization of building space to the instructional demands of the team rather than allow plastic instruction to take place in an unbending container.

STAFF RELATIONSHIPS

Placing personalities into mandatory juxtaposition creates all kinds of new relationships and problems. To belabor the enigmas of human behavior is a fruitless adventure at this time; however, to ignore these enigmas altogether is similarly fruitless.

When teachers sit down to plan together (one of the essential ingredients of team teaching) and, indeed, when they stand up to teach together or separately, new roles and perceptions of roles are born. Changes in both the image a teacher has of himself as well as changes in the image he broadcasts to others must and do occur. The resulting new teacher posture gives rise to new masks which the teacher wears in his new roles.

As dialogue between teachers increases and sharpens in focus and quality, academic productivity of a new and vibrant order may result; this is no problem except insofar as harnessing the new energies is concerned. On the other hand, experience yields other results also.

Negative, sometimes destructive behavior comes about when teachers, ill-suited to cooperative efforts, are thrust into continuous professional contact with one another. Disagreements, if frequent enough, rupture the team process and children are the big losers. For if adults cannot deal with one another productively, certainly no tangible good can come of team teaching, since the name becomes hollow and the process a mockery.

When personalities clash, whether via disagreement, insecurities, perpetual defensiveness, or other aspects of human abrasion, team teaching is doomed on that particular team. Failure on the parts of responsible individuals to react and reconstruct the team immediately could calcify the breach and make irretrievable the process of team teaching for the individuals involved.

On the other hand, recognizing that human frailty is one of the most serious threats to the success of team teaching, supervisors can contain, control, or even eliminate problems to a large extent with careful screening, selection, and assignment of teaching personnel. This takes perception, insight, patience, and virtuosity with human behavior–and even then there is no guarantee, so complicated are the human factors.

PARADOX OF OVER-PRODUCTIVITY

As in the inversion of Parkinson's Law stated earlier, team teaching reaches new heights of productivity. Frequently, it finds itself so paradoxically successful, that it outruns itself both intellectually and logistically.

Intellectually, successful teams discover new relationships of, let us say, one academic discipline to another, but may not have access to the wherewithal or the mechanics to cement the relationship. New teaching techniques frequently point the way to new class sizes and new teacher-pupil ratios; yet, if the available logistical support is threadbare, the new idea predictably atrophies.

The point is that if a school commits itself to a system, in this case team teaching, it must also commit itself to supporting systems since imagination, when unbuttressed, is quickly frustrated and ultimately dissolves into mediocrity. It is hardly fair or even real to expect productivity and a new energy if a teaching team stands chained like Prometheus to a rock of convention. One cannot view new horizons and countless directions from a limited environment.

THE NEW TECHNOLOGY

Experience with team teaching proves mightily that no discussion of it is complete without pointing up relationships to the uses of educational "hardware." Several key questions need to be asked and, in the asking, the problems reify themselves:

1. To what extent do teaching teams need technicians or, at the very least, technical assistance in organizing and using educational machinery?
2. What equipment is used with what frequency in varying sized groups?
3. What is the relationship between types of educational hardware and the concept of "independent study?"
4. Is "programmed learning" obsolescent or does it have a role in the teaming process?
5. As the team plans for use of audio-visual materials, should it not also plan *against* overuse of these materials?
6. What role should teacher aides or paraprofessional personnel play in the use of machines in teaching?
7. What degree of technical competence or accomplishment may a school reasonably expect from its professional teaching personnel? Should one expect a minimal level of competence in this respect from all or should the team train individuals for this kind of specialized role?

In an exploding technological environment, in an era where students and faculty alike are bombarded by data from all kinds of mass media of communication, a whole new area of involvement opens to teachers—an area, however, which carries with it new problems requiring new answers in new surroundings.

FINANCE

Team teaching costs money; it does not save it. However stark this may sound, it is unavoidably accurate. If teaming is to succeed, it must be given more-than-adequate funding. Once the momentum of "over-production" begins, support must be available or the program withers—ironically as a result of its own success.

Cost analysis here is out of place. Suffice it to say that staffing (professional and paraprofessional) coupled with the needs of time, space, and technology make rather self-evident the need for sound and reasonably generous fiscal moorings.

NEW RESPONSIBILITIES FOR PROFESSIONAL PERSONNEL

From the ashes of traditional approaches to instruction, new responsibilities accrue to professional personnel. Teachers, for example, now must deal in new data for the regrouping of students on different bases from what once was. Guidance counselors, formerly almost the only ones concerned with initial grouping data, now work actively in new roles as members of teaching teams. The possibilities for worth, contribution, and status are almost limitless, but need focus as the idea of team teaching develops and matures. Trite as it may sound, the challenge and the problems of coping with the unknown provide teaching teams with a fuel which generates not only abundant energy, but also phenomenal candle-power for intellectual illumination.

Possible Directions for Team Teaching

Team teaching is not without its problems, but nothing else worthwhile is either. If those responsible for quality instruction in the schools attack each problem responsibly, progress is assured. Once teams of teachers are established in a school and gain experience in the new venture, there are three major options open: (1) team teaching can fail because its problems are not confronted and solved, (2) team teaching can remain at a *status quo*, superficial level, or (3) team teaching begins, through a vigorous attack on an amelioration of its problems, to provide a continuous vehicle for teacher growth, student learning, teacher involvement in key academic decisionmaking, teacher status, sound research, and modern evaluation. Team teaching is a continuous "action" device, one whose problems may even provide the sources of its major strengths. To ignore this would not be unlike Gilbert & Sullivan's Duke of Plaza-Toro, who, with such caution, "led his regiment from behind. He found it less exciting."

The Phantom Nongraded School*

WILLIAM P. MCLOUGHLIN

Research shows little superiority in either academic achievement or social adjustment for nongraded schools.

Or does it?

Mr. McLoughlin concludes that true nongradedness has seldom been tried, although up to 30 percent of U.S. districts report doing so.

Few propositions for educational change have generated and sustained as much interest as the nongraded school. It is discussed at nearly every major educational conference, and symposiums on the nongraded school are increasing in popularity. Furthermore, the body of available literature is increasing rapidly; most leading professional journals have published several articles on this topic. Through these and other means, educators have learned more of the promises of the nongraded school than they have of its accomplishments.

This is understandable, for nongrading appears to be preached more than practiced and practiced more than appraised. In fact, few dependable estimates on the present status and anticipated growth of the nongraded school are currently available and sound studies on its accomplishments are even more difficult to come by. From what is available one would be hard put to determine just how many schools have nongraded their instructional programs and how many are seriously contemplating the change. If findings in these areas are obscure, the outcomes of the evaluations of existing nongraded programs are even less definitive.

The available estimates of the number of schools with nongraded

*Reprinted from the *Phi Delta Kappan*, 49 (January 1968), 148-250, by permission of the publisher and William P. McLoughlin, St. John's University.

programs fluctuates from 5.5 percent[1] to 30 percent.[2] These, it must be pointed out, are unqualified estimates; they do not consider the quality of the programs purporting to be nongraded. When this element is added, estimates of the number of schools with *truly* nongraded programs shrink considerably. Goodlad, in 1955, estimated that less than one percent of the schools in the country were nongraded[3] and in 1961 he felt there were probably fewer than 125 schools to be found with *truly* nongraded programs.[4]

If uncertainty marks present estimates of the number of schools operating nongraded programs, certainly forecasts for future growth are dubious. In 1958 the NEA reported 26.3 percent of the respondents to its survey saying they intended to nongrade their schools.[5] Five years later, however, this estimate had dwindled to 3.2 percent.[6] On the other hand, the USOE's pollings reverse this trend. Of schools queried in 1958, only 13.4 percent expected to become nongraded,[7] but two years later this estimate doubled and 26.3 percent of the respondents reported considering nongrading their schools.[8] With these conflicting findings it is difficult to know if the nongraded school is coming into its own or passing out of existence.

One thing seems clear from these surveys, however: nongrading is related to district size. Nearly all available surveys confirm this; the larger the district, the more likely it is to have one or more nongraded units. Here we should stress that this does not mean that nongrading is the principal organizational pattern in large school districts. It simply means a nongraded unit is operating in one or more of the district's several elementary schools.[9]

Studies of the influence of nongrading on students are rare, too, and their

[1]Lillian L. Gore and Rose E. Koury, *A Survey of Early Elementary Education in Public Schools, 1960-61.* Washington, D.C.: U.S. Department of Health, Education and Welfare, 1965.

[2]National Education Association, *Nongraded Schools.* Research Memo 1965-12. Washington, D.C.: Research Division, NEA, May, 1965.

[3]John I. Goodlad, "More About the Ungraded Plan," *NEA Journal,* May, 1955, pp. 295-96.

[4]National Education Association, *Nongrading: A Modern Practice in Elementary School Organization.* Research Memorandum 1961-37. Washington, D.C.: Research Division, NEA, October, 1961.

[5]National Education Association, *Administrative Practices in Urban School Districts, 1958-1959.* Research Report 1961-R10. Washington, D.C.: Research Division, NEA, May, 1961.

[6]NEA, *Nongraded Schools, op. cit.*

[7]Stuart E. Dean, *Elementary School Administration and Organization: A National Survey of Practices and Policies*, Washington, D.C.: U.S. Department of Health, Education and Welfare, 1963.

[8]Gore and Koury, *op. cit.*

[9]William P. McLoughlin, *The Nongraded School: A Critical Assessment.* Albany, N.Y.: The University of the State of New York, The New York State Education Department, 1967.

composite findings somewhat bewildering. Thirty-three empirical studies of the influence of nongrading on student academic achievement have been identified. Not all of these, however, consider the same variables. About half of them assess the influence of nongrading on reading achievement, while 25 percent look at its influence on arithmetic performance. Only 11 percent of the studies question the impact nongrading has on the student's development in language arts. Nine percent report on the total achievement scores of children. The remaining studies are spread so thinly through the other curricular divisions that a detailed consideration of their findings is hardly profitable.[10]

Judged by these studies, the academic development of children probably does not suffer from attending a nongraded school; there is some evidence, admittedly sketchy and tentative, to indicate it may be somewhat enhanced. One thing is certain; children from graded classes seldom do better on these measures than children from nongraded classes. More commonly, children from nongraded classes excell their contemporaries from graded classes.

For example, 15 studies considered the influence of nongrading on the general reading achievement of children. Seven of these report no significant difference between children from graded and nongraded classes. In other words, nothing is lost by having children attend nongraded classes. But only two studies found children from graded classes outscoring children from nongraded classes, while six studies found the general reading attainments of children from nongraded classes superior to that of children in graded classes.

Similar though less distinct outcomes are attained when the reading subskills of comprehension and vocabulary development are examined. Again, the principal finding of 14 studies is that there are no marked differences in the accomplishments of children in these areas regardless of the type of organization in which they learn to read. Furthermore, for every study showing greater gains for children from graded classes, there is an equal number of studies counter-balancing these findings.

The mirror image of this picture emerges when the arithmetic attainments of children from graded and nongraded classes are contrasted. Eleven studies considered the influence of nongrading on children's general arithmetic achievement, and their findings are inconclusive. Three report differences favoring children from nongraded classes, five found differences favoring children from graded classes,[11] and three found no difference.

But when the arithmetic subskills of reasoning and knowledge of fundamentals are examined, different outcomes appear. Of the 12 published studies in these areas, one reports differences favoring children from graded classes but six report differences favoring children from nongraded classes. The remaining five show no real difference in the achievement of children in these areas, regardless of the type of class organization.

[10]*Ibid.*
[11]*Ibid.*

In language arts, too, there is scant evidence to demonstrate that organization influences achievement. Seven of the 10 studies in this area report no true differences in the language skills developed by children from graded and nongraded classes. One reports achievement test scores of children from graded classes as superior to those of children from nongraded classes, while two studies found the observed differences in the achievement of children from nongraded classes indeed significantly superior to that of controls in the graded classes. Apparently, nongraded classes are no more effective in developing language arts skills than are graded classes.

Total achievement test scores, too, seem remarkably immune to change because of changes in organizational pattern. Half of the eight studies using them to measure the efficacy of the nongraded school found no significant differences in the achievements of children from graded and nongraded classes. The remaining studies divide equally: Two reported differences favoring children from graded classes while two found differences favoring children from nongraded classes. So here, once again, the influence of nongrading on the academic development of children is indeterminate.

Better student achievement is not the only claim put forth for the nongraded school. Its advocates maintain, implicitly or explicitly, that superior student adjustment is attained in the nongraded school. Certainly student adjustment and personality development are crucial concerns of educators and, quite reasonably, they are interested in developing learning settings which foster this goal.

Unfortunately, studies assessing the influence of nongrading on student adjustment are even more rare than studies assessing its influence on their academic achievement. Moreover, the diversity of procedures utilized in these studies to measure adjustment lessens their cumulative value. Sociograms, adjustment inventories, anxiety scales, and even school attendance records have all been used as indices of pupil adjustment. But no matter how measured, there is scant evidence to support the contention that superior student adjustment is realized in nongraded schools. On the 32 separate indices of adjustment used in these studies, the overwhelming majority, 26, indicate that there is no significant difference in the adjustment of children from graded and nongraded classes. Only four of the measures (general adjustment, social adjustment, social maturity, and freedom from age stereotypes) showed differences favorable to children from nongraded classes, while the remaining two (social participation and freedom from defensiveness) were favorable to children from graded classes.[12]

Research, then, finds little to impel or impede practitioners interested in nongrading. Under either organization children's adjustment and achievement appear to remain remarkably constant. For those to whom the nongraded school is a magnificent obsession, these findings must come as a numbing

[12]*Ibid.*

disappointment. Taken at face value, current research on the nongraded school seems to say that its contribution to the academic, social, and emotional development of children is marginal.

But should these findings be taken at face value? It might be naive to rest the fate of the nongraded school on past research. The validity of these studies should be rigorously tested, for they depend on one tacit but critical assumption: that the experimental schools, those purporting to be nongraded, are *truly* nongraded. If this assumption is not met and the experimental schools are not nongraded, then research has told us nothing about the efficacy of the nongraded school.

Too often, on close inspection, one finds that schools credited with operating nongraded programs are not nongraded at all. Homogeneous grouping and semi-departmentalization of instruction in reading and arithmetic are frequently passed off as nongraded programs. These techniques must be recognized for what they are. They are administrative expediencies developed to make the *graded* school work. They are not nongraded instructional programs.

If these are the "nongraded" programs represented in these studies, then researching their effectiveness is an exercise in futility, for the *experimental* schools are as graded as the control schools and no experimental treatment is being tested. Research has done nothing more than contrast the performances of children from graded schools called graded schools with the performance of children from graded schools called nongraded schools. Essentially, we have simply researched the age-old question: "What's in a name?"

The nongraded school is defensible only because the graded school is indefensible. Its justification flows from its efforts to correct the instructional errors of the graded school. It is reasonably unlikely that any amount of manipulation of the physical arrangements of schools will produce discernible differences in the academic or psycho-social development of children. Every grade label can be cleansed from every classroom door in the school without influencing the school's attainments with children as long as graded instructional practices prevail behind these doors.

Nongrading begins with significant alterations in instructional, not organizational, procedures. As long as schools seek practices designed to group away differences they are *not* nongraded. The nongraded school never held this as a goal, for it is impossible. Rather, nongrading says: "Accept children as they are, with all their differences, and teach to these differences. Don't try to eradicate them!" Until educators develop instructional programs that will meet this challenge they are not nongrading. They are simply masking their old egg-crate schools with a new facade.

Ungraded High Schools: Why Those Who Like Them Love Them*

SIDNEY P. ROLLINS

The prevalent secondary school organization is based on a premise – long ago proved false – that pupils develop at an equal pace in all academic areas. If we believe that pupils deserve the opportunity to progress as rapidly as they are able, and if we accept the notion that children differ in their abilities to learn, then we need to give careful consideration to the idea of the ungraded secondary school.

Ungraded schools create an atmosphere in which individual differences among pupils can be recognized. More important, this is an atmosphere that allows schoolmen to do something about these differences.

The ungraded school provides an unbroken learning continuum through which pupils progress. School years are not divided into several parts of equal length, each with its own content and requirements. No predetermined barriers stand.

Furthermore, ungraded plans encourage continuous, individual progress. Bright children are not forced to mark time at grade barriers, waiting for their slower classmates to catch up. Slow children do not struggle in frustrated desperation to reach barriers that lie beyond their capabilities – artificial barriers are removed.

A school without formal grade designations also encourages greater flexibility in pupil grouping. Pupils are grouped not along artificial grade standards, but in terms of their own needs and abilities. They can be moved when it becomes apparent that another setting is better suited to their educational development.

This is not to imply that ungraded plans don't create problems of their

*Reprinted with permission from *Nation's Schools,* 73 (April 1964), 110, 130, and Sidney P. Rollins, Rhode Island College Copyright ©1964, McGraw-Hill, Inc., Chicago. All rights reserved.

own. They do. But these are problems that education can solve. One of them is helping teachers to understand the possibilities of the system. Just finding teachers who want – and are able – to teach groups of pupils as though they consisted of individuals is a difficult task.

Teachers who have had no experience with ungraded organization frequently find that adjusting to it is difficult. Teachers often are required to develop several lesson preparations for the same class. Record-keeping is more involved.

Teaching in an ungraded school requires a particularly flexible personality, a knowledge of curriculum development, skills at working with several groups at varying levels of achievement, and exceptional mastery of the subject which is taught.

If you're considering an ungraded plan, here are some steps to help you to get off to a good start:

1. Be sure that you understand thoroughly the concept of ungraded organization. Ungraded schools are not likely to save money for a community, but they can improve the educational program.
2. Be sure that your community also understands the concept of ungraded organization. To bring this about, it's a good idea to hold meetings involving P.T.A.s, civic groups, business groups, and fraternal groups. These organizations will help to keep members of the community apprised concerning the development of the new school program.
3. Hire as many staff members as possible as early in the planning as possible. The more teachers who must eventually do the job become involved, the more likely they will understand and appreciate what they are supposed to do.
4. Develop a clear statement of purpose and involve the staff in determining what these purposes should be. Everyone should know the directions that are being taken.
5. Reorganize the curriculum – completely. The curriculum must be developed sequentially – each step to be mastered before the pupil proceeds to the next.

In Middletown High School, Middletown, R.I., each subject in the curriculum is organized into "concepts." For example, six years of English were broken down into 111 concepts; six years of social studies into more than 300. In Nova High School, Fort Lauderdale, Fla., on the other hand, each sequential step has been organized into a unit which most pupils are expected to learn in approximately one month. Therefore, each of the subject fields in the six-year Nova school contains approximately 60 units, or steps.

Either organization can work. And as additional ungraded secondary schools are developed it is likely that additional variations in sequential development will occur.

6. Develop other aspects of the total school program. Among these are administrative policy, a revised system of reporting to parents, guidance programs, library services, extraclass activities, and scheduling devices.

7. Find someone who has had experience helping to organize an ungraded school and hire him to help you.

Who's Using Ungraded High Schools

Before the ungraded high school can be evaluated extensively, more and longer experience with the plan is needed. The reports now available from ungraded high schools show that they not only exist, they work.

In Florida, at least three schools now use the ungraded structure: Satellite High School, Satellite Beach; Nova High School, Fort Lauderdale, and Melbourne High School, Melbourne. What was probably the first completely ungraded six-year secondary school in the country was developed in Rhode Island in 1961 – Middletown High School.

Here are some of the advantages reported and, to a considerable extent, documented from ungraded schools:

Pupil progress ranges from a year or more ahead of where pupils would be had they attended a graded secondary school to a half year behind the usual achievement at a given grade level.

Dropout rate (less than one per cent at Middletown) is drastically lower than the national rate of more than 30 per cent.

Pupils recover from extended absences from ungraded schools more quickly and easily than from graded schools.

Pupils stimulate themselves to greater effort – even in April and May and June, when they normally begin to ease up on studies.

Most parents are pleased – probably because the pupils appear to be. Pupils seem to appreciate the opportunities for avoiding the boredom and frustration that the ungraded structure can offer.

Administration Problems of the Nongraded School*

SISTER MARY PAUL, R.S.M.

The subject of the nongraded school is not a new one to NCEA audiences. Various aspects of the topic have been explored in formal presentations and in debate at NCEA meetings for the past several years. We have heard the nongraded school hailed as a dramatic innovation and enthusiastically described. The historical development has been traced thoroughly, the advantages and disadvantages debated heatedly and the findings of research reported carefully. I do not intend to review all that has been said or written by experts on this subject.

Suffice it to say that Dr. John Goodlad, the patron saint to the nongraded school, has very ably delineated the philosophy underlying the organizational plan, and correspondingly we all share his belief that boys and girls differ greatly in their innate abilities and in their perception, response, approach and readiness for a given task. The facts of individual differences have prompted educators to experiment with a variety of curricular patterns to facilitate the progress of children through school. The nongraded patterns of school organization is one of the most widely discussed of the recent innovations.

Dr. Goodlad describes the nongraded school organizationally as "one in which the grade levels and grade labels representing years of vertical progress are replaced by a plan of continuous upward progress." And conceptually the nongraded school is intended to "eliminate the promotion-nonpromotion adjustment mechanism of graded schools; to raise the ceilings and lower the floors of attainment expectancies for learners, thus encompassing their individual differences; to encourage the utilization of content and materials in

*Reprinted from *The National Catholic Education Bulletin,* 64 (August 1967). 144-147, by permission of the publisher and Sister Mary Paul, R.S.M., Mount Mercy College.

accordance with pupil individuality; and to force pedagogical attention to individual differences and the individual."

No one would quarrel with a curricular pattern conceived on this philosophy and organized to provide for a continuous upward progress of individuals. This just makes good sense. However, when one comes to the implementation of the theory, some problems can and do loom large. Those who have initiated a program or have cooperated in its planning stages would readily agree that there are administration problems which must be considered. Unfortunately, some programs die on the planning board or disintegrate soon after inception because administrators become overwhelmed with anticipated or actual problems for which they do not see an immediate or painless solution. Launching a nongraded program and seeing it through is hard work and the project is not without its problems and difficulties. In the development and innovation process the five major areas described here signal potential spots.

1. Administrator

A potential "trouble spot?" Yes! Here the program begins and thrives or begins and dies. Dufay is of the opinion that "no modern elementary school program can be managed well by the ill-prepared, unimaginative administrator. The dynamic instructional leader is an essential ingredient for successful implementation of new programs." It is necessary that the administrator have strong convictions, definite ideas of what he wants to accomplish, and concrete procedures of how he plans to carry out the design of his program. He should remember that the change from graded to nongraded practice requires more than an administrative decision. Skill in human relations is indispensable for communicating effectively with those persons involved in the program. Teachers who have a role to play in the planning, parents who are accepting of change, and children who are properly oriented will be the greatest assets of the new program.

Organizational patterns reflect the commitment of the administrator, teachers, parents and children. In planning and initiating a nongraded program the administrator's problems will be minimal if he possesses the skill in human relations which provides for the harmonious interaction of these involved groups. The administrator holds the magic key to smooth interrelationships of all agencies involved in the program.

2. Teachers

The teaching staff will be responsible for breathing life into the nongraded program. If teachers are not in complete agreement with the concept or fail to understand what nongrading will permit them to do, they will undoubtedly continue to teach as they have always taught. The administrator will find that he has the same old school under a new name. Dufay is of the opinion that any program that is inflicted upon an unwilling teaching staff is beyond any hope of success. If the teachers welcome rather than resist a new program and are given a role in bringing it about the chances of success are much greater.

Dufay describes an interesting survey that he conducted among the primary teachers in his school district to determine whether or not the teachers were apt to be receptive to the notion of a nongraded program. One hundred and fifteen primary teachers participated in a short survey which asked five questions. The questions are given here with responses indicated in percentages.

(1). In your opinion, is retention a device that should be used with greater frequency in order to maintain minimum educational standards?

42% Yes 58% No

(2). Is acceleration a device that dictates to the best interests of the rapid learner?

32% Yes 68% No

(3). Individual and small group instruction requires extensive planning. On the basis of results observed and as a matter of opinion, are you prepared to say that the efforts expended will produce desirable educational results?

74% Yes 14% No 12% Qualified

(4). Is the matter of range in the physical and mental maturity of primary children a major problem?

80% Yes 16% No 4% Qualified

(5). Do you feel that the problem noted in Item 4, above, is worthy of special study?

74% Yes 26% No

With 74 percent of the teachers favorable to further study on the subject chances of cooperation on a new program were excellent. In summary, the total review of survey responses indicated that:

• Most teachers did not believe in retention or acceleration as good devices for coping with instructional problems. Comments about "flow of education" showed a high degree of teacher sophistication and of the kind necessary for initiating an ungraded program.

• Teachers felt the necessity for gearing instruction to individuals and smaller groups.

• Teachers recognized the range of physical and mental abilities in primary children as a matter of major concern and believed the problem worthy of study.

When the administrator determines that a positive attitude exists among the staff he is ready to organize planning sessions. Once the program is launched it is imperative that he conduct formal and informal meetings, provide for frequent evaluation and plan for constant supervision of the program. The teachers must never by permitted to lose sight of the fact that the primary goal of this program is to take every child from where he is to where he can go.

Another important aspect, one that could sabotage a successful program, is staff recruitment. An administrator must be able to discern the attitudes and the background of understanding and experience that a new teacher will bring to the program. A well-planned interview with a prospective teacher will help the administrator to determine whether this person will fit into the system and make a significant contribution to the quality of the educational program.

There are implications also for teacher education programs. Institutions of higher learning would be remiss if provision were not made to study and to evaluate innovations in school organization. Preservice teachers should be familiar with a variety of curricular patterns and they should have opportunities for visitations to schools where quality programs may be observed. If novice teachers are unaware of new programs or are not open to change and innovation, their presence in an experimental school can be disastrous.

3. Parents

One of the most formidable forces on the educational scene today is that of parent groups. When properly informed they can offer great support to a new venture. The nongraded concept must be thoroughly interpreted to parents, for it is a new way of thinking about progress through the school. It is not easy to escape more than a century of gradedness. They must be led to think in terms of levels of learning, to face the realities of pupil individuality and to accept the limitations as well as the talents of their children. This calls for frequent and well-planned parent meetings. With the proper orientation a parent group will tend to support and even demand the better program. If parents fail to understand the philosophy, goals and organizational structure, they will surely be resistant and perhaps antagonistic.

If the administrator and staff remember that an enlightened group of parents is their greatest asset, the problems of an uninformed or a misinformed parent group will not have to be reckoned with and one more trouble spot will have been eliminated.

4. Children

The success of a nongraded program also depends on a carefully executed pupil orientation. Some children are more grade-conscious than we believe. The pressure to complete specified amounts of work in an allotted amount of time with the good news of "pass" or the grim alternative of "fail" has always been the school child's way of life. With this new program, they should recognize, even the youngest child, that the demands upon them and the expectations for them will be geared to their abilities. The old measuring rod of school success, promotion or nonpromotion, has given way to a new plan of continuous progress. Children must then be helped to face their own limitations as well as those of their peers. Administrators, teachers and guidance personnel are all important parts of the team for establishing with these children the goal of deriving a genuine satisfaction in achieving according to one's own capabilities. Materials of instruction, school records, reporting to parents and relationships between and among pupils and teachers should reflect an emphasis on the person as a unique individual. Thus a philosophy of individualization becomes a way of life within the school.

Here it might be pointed out that the influence of the child's attitude is felt in the home. If children are accepting and appreciative of a school program this will be transmitted to the parents who will feel reassured of the program's worth.

We can see that a nongraded program depends upon a broad reeducation for the entire school community if it is to be successful. An administrator who recognizes this fact will be able to prevent problems at their inception.

5. Organizational Structure

The last area, full of variety and complexity, is that of organizational structure. The organizational plan is only the shell in which curriculum and instruction, the heart of the educational process, are contained. Careful attention to the shell, however, will help to secure a solid framework for the methods and materials of curriculum and instruction. An administrator should be familiar with the many alternative organizational patterns and practices. Organizational plans are many and varied. Goodlad has differentiated between vertical and horizontal organizations and has described the specific functions they serve.

Vertical organization provides for the classification of children as they proceed upward through the school. Vertical organization encompasses two opposing forms of structure—graded and nongraded. The graded school with its grade level designations has been the traditional form for promoting pupil progress through the elementary school. The nongraded organization, which was described earlier in this paper, is the alternative to graded structure. Choosing one of the two vertical schemes presents no problem to the administrator. He is simply choosing the alternative to the one that he is discarding. The choice is a simple one.

Horizontal designs, on the other hand, present a variety of interesting alternatives to tempt the imaginative administrator. Before he makes a selection he studies carefully all possible alternatives—homogeneous or heterogeneous grouping, self-contained or departmentalized classes, or team-teaching arrangement. Any one of these horizontal designs aligned with the nongraded vertical form challenges creative thinking and planning. Consultation with key staff members is crucial at this point. Teachers who know their own strengths and weaknesses in subject matter areas and are familiar with the needs of pupils in their care should be involved in planning. All must work together with the administrator to decide upon an organizational pattern which will accommodate teaching style of staff and learning style of children. The pattern must be feasible also in terms of enrollment, size of staff, and type of school plant.

Many combinations of vertical and horizontal patterns are possible—a real smorgasbord! The skill with which the selection is made and implemented will spell the difference between success or failure of the program. The overall school structure will be the result of a decision on vertical as well as horizontal organizations.

A successful nongraded program depends upon:

- The administrator for leadership.
- The teachers for implementation.
- The parents for cooperation.
- The children for participation.
- The organizational structure for direction.

Our rapidly moving educational scene demands creative leadership from its administrators. B. Frank Brown, whose imaginative leadership in Melbourne, Florida, has spawned one of the most successful nongraded high schools, chides administrators who might hesitate to embark on innovations:

> The big problem is that the school organization has never been properly engineered. The school administrator hesitates to try an innovation until he has seen it for the third time. The first time around it frightens him a little and arouses his suspicions. He is unable to classify it. The second time around he dismisses it because he recalls having seen it before and therefore it is old stuff. The third time it is thrust upon him he decides it must be worth considering because it is so persistent.

I hope that we will not be counted among those who wait for the third exposure. We all realize that no one has yet discovered the panacea for all the ills that affect the educational program, that all programs have advantages and disadvantages. So to all those administrators who are on the brink of a nongraded program, I echo Frank Brown's call: "Come on in, the water's fine!" I might add a word of caution . . . be sure that you know how to swim!

Independent Study—for All Students *

ALLAN A. GLATTHORN
JOSEPH E. FERDERBAR

Schools all over the nation are giving increasing attention to independent study. Thus far, most published reports indicate that schools using independent study limit it to honors students, high ability students, or some other select group. Our experience at the Abington (Pennsylvania) High School, North Campus, indicates that 97 per cent of all our students in the ninth and tenth grades can profit from our approach to independent study.[1]

First, what is "our approach"? The term "independent study" can mean so many different things that certainly a definition is in order at the outset. Here's the picture in brief:

For about one-fourth of their school time, our students are not scheduled for classes. During this unscheduled time—called "independent study" time—the student may work any place in the building either completely on his own, with a student assistant, with a teacher, or with a teacher aide. (We require teacher or aide supervision in "high-risk" areas.) No passes are used, there is no attendance check, and the student has almost complete freedom of choice as to where he studies, what he works on, and what kind of assistance he secures.

What areas may he use for independent study? The list is long and all-inclusive: library, gymnasia, art rooms, home economics suite, guidance

*Reprinted from the *Phi Delta Kappan,* 47 (March 1966), 379-382, by permission of the publisher and Allan A. Glatthorn, principal, Abington High School, and Joseph E. Ferderbar, assistant principal, Abington High School, Abington Township, Montgomery County, Pennsylvania.

[1]The student body at North Campus is like that of most suburban schools. Average I.Q. is approximately 110, although there is an extensive range in ability. About half the graduates will attend a four-year college and a total of perhaps 70 per cent will get some form of higher education. The community reflects a similar diversity. While predominantly middle-class residential, it includes families of all economic levels and varied ethnic backgrounds.

offices, industrial arts shops, music practice rooms, foreign language laboratories, photography dark room, "quiet study" commons, "talking" commons, little theater, science laboratories, mathematics seminar rooms, English independent learning center, social studies independent learning center, typing rooms, animal room, large group lectures.

Perhaps a few of these terms need clarification. The independent learning centers in social studies and in English are classroom-size study areas furnished with carrel-type desks, audio-visual aids, paperback books, magazines, reference books, programed texts, and typewriters. The "talking commons" is a large, all-purpose area furnished with cafeteria tables and chairs where students may sit and talk quietly, and with no compulsion to study—or to feign study. The "quiet study" commons are areas similarly furnished where students study in quiet. These commons, of course, are much like the traditional study halls; the chief difference is that the student decides whether he wishes to study or to talk. Enforcing quiet in the "quiet study" commons is no problem at all, since those who wish to talk are elsewhere. The large-group lectures are regularly presented to English, social studies, science, art, dramatics, public speaking, home economics, and industrial arts classes; other students are also informed which of these they may attend on their independent study time. (The art lectures seem to draw the best response here.) The seminar rooms are small rooms, about 250 square feet, between every two academic classrooms; they get heavy use during independent study time, especially in mathematics, where they are ideal for remedial tutoring, and in English, where they are used for work on the programed textbook and for lay reader-student conferences.

As the above list might suggest, many kinds of independent learning activity take place during independent study time. The following are common: 1) practicing a skill, such as typing; 2) doing advanced work on a class project, such as a shop or art project; 3) getting remedial help from a student tutor or a teacher; 4) conferring with a lay reader on an English composition; 5) doing independent research; 6) listing and responding to language lessons, tapes of lectures, recordings, and other audio materials; 7) viewing films and filmstrips (much use of 8mm single-concept film); 8) exercising and playing competitive games; 9) conferring with a teacher or fellow student; 10) working on a programed text; 11) typing a report; 12) developing a special vocational or avocational interest; 13) practicing an instrument.

Certain aspects of the program have been so highly successful that perhaps special mention should be made of them:

Intensive remedial work. Throughout the week more than 100 different remedial clinics are operated by teachers for students needing academic help. In most of these clinics the teacher is working with small groups of his own students who report at regular times mutually agreed upon. In other clinics the teacher is assigned to a clinic period and works with any students who report. A special example of the second type is the composition clinic, supervised by a lay reader available to students who need help with their writing.

Special programs. During the course of the year we have been able to use independent study time for special programs that seem needed. We started early in the year, for example, with a series of lectures on how to study. Also, during the year we have invited several speakers from the community to talk with students interested in the professions and occupations they represent. And the dramatics club presented a one-act play to enthusiastic student audiences attending during their independent study time.

Non-credit, short-term courses. Through independent study we have been able to offer a few highly specialized nine-week courses—without credit or grades—to interested students. A junior "Great Books" discussion course and a course in contemporary protest literature have been especially successful. This avenue of approach enables us to enrich the curriculum with highly specialized short-term courses that admittedly have limited appeal and yet function as a kind of cutting edge in the curriculum.

Conferences with individuals and small groups. Guidance counselors report that the number of student contacts has increased dramatically, since students are so readily available through independent study. The principal has derived much benefit from meeting every other week in informal sessions with small groups of students who want to make their views known. And it is also an effective way to reach teachers: the administrative staff meets bi-weekly with small groups of new teachers—on *their* independent study time.

Advanced research of an original nature. We have found that about 10 per cent of our students at this age level are ready to take on original research projects requiring work in depth. And they find independent study tailor-made to suit their needs. One student is concluding a major research project in genetics, involving the breeding of guinea pigs. Another is in the midst of a study of the religious attitudes of his fellow students. These students won't make the scholarly journals, but they are learning something pretty important about working on their own, carrying out a project to its conclusion, and knowing the sheer joy of discovery.

As was indicated previously, attendance (with an exception to be noted later) is not checked, and passes are not used. The emphasis is on freedom of movement and freedom of choice; the goals are self-direction and self-discipline. Such an emphasis does not mean there are no rules, however; there are a few—and they are rather strictly enforced:

1. If a student reports to a specialized independent study area and finds there is no room for him or that the help he seeks is not available, he must report at once to one of the commons areas. He may not "shop around," wasting time and disturbing classes in session.

2. Once a student arrives at an independent study area, he must remain there for the entire period. Since we are on a modular schedule and periods are only twenty-five minutes in length, this does not work a hardship on any student and also minimizes corridor traffic while classes are in session.

3. A student may not spend two or more periods in succession in the "talking" commons. This simple rule prevents the poorly motivated student from spending too much time in an area which is really intended for only occasional relaxation.

In addition to these three simple rules, the faculty retains one important control: any teacher, counselor, or administrator may require a student to work in a specialized study area—or in the "quiet study" commons—for a specified number of periods each week. The procedure is simple: The teacher tells the student, for example, "I want you to get up to the language laboratory three times this week," and puts a note in his roll book to that effect. When the student reports to the designated area, he picks up a mimeographed form which he fills out and has signed at the end of the period by the teacher or monitor on duty; he then presents this signed form to the teacher who made the study assignment.

In spite of these rules and control, there is still a heavy responsibility on the student to plan his time wisely, to get to a study center on his own, and to make good use of the time. Can all our students—and remember, these are ninth- and tenth-graders—successfully meet these challenges?

We found out rather early that about three per cent cannot. These were immature students who could not discipline themselves; they were causing trouble, breaking school rules, wasting much time. They did not need independent study; they needed close control and careful watching. And this is what they have been given. When they have independent study time, they must report to one of the classrooms ("Stalag 125," the teachers call it) where roll is checked and quiet study is required. Every two weeks, the student's record is reviewed; if the director of student discipline feels the student has made sufficient progress, he is returned to a regular independent study program. Some students have said that their confinement to this disciplinary study hall was the single most important factor in improving their behavior; others are obviously unaffected and remain "in confinement."

But how has the program worked for the rest of the students? Let's first look at some problems:

1. Some parents remain frankly skeptical. "Why doesn't my son have more homework at night?" "Why does he have so much free time?" (We don't like that term, but it persists.) We have to do a much better job orienting the parents to the program.

2. Some teachers are still skeptical. A few teachers frankly prefer a school situation where students are always accounted for and where quiet study is always enforced. As administrators, we don't expect all teachers to agree with us, but we do expect—and get—all teachers to cooperate. And as the program continues to improve, there is less faculty skepticism.

3. Some students still need help in budgeting time. The marginal achiever,

the poorly motivated student, is still spending too much time in the "talking commons." We see this as a problem for all of us—administrators, counselors, teachers, parents—to attack collectively.

So we're sharply aware of the problems. What signs of success do we see?

First, reports of independent study use submitted weekly by department chairmen show us that, in sheer numbers of students using facilities, independent study is successful. This is what figures for a typical week look like:

Center	*Independent Study Attendance for the Week*
Art workshop	75
Business rooms	135
English	1,400
Foreign language	700
Home economics	162
Industrial arts	82
Instrumental and vocal music	115
Library	6,900
Mathematics	400
Physical education	60
Reading clinic	300
Science	198
Social studies	550
Speech-drama	84
Total	11,161

We're especially proud of that library figure. Things look pretty good when you're getting about 70 per cent of the student body in the library every day. Of course two fine librarians, an excellent book collection, and an attractive library help—but we know that independent study also plays a large part in this success.

There are other statistics that we find reassuring. We surveyed students in eight English classes—about 200 altogether—representing both grade levels and all ability levels, and found overwhelming support for the program. Some interesting findings: The average student worked in four different study centers during the week; he spent more time in quiet study area than he did in the "talking" commons; he used the English learning center more than any other departmental center.

We also find reassurance in unsolicited testimonials from students and parents. Students tell us that they are getting intensive remedial help, that they like the feeling of being trusted and having responsibility, and that they have more time after school for activities and recreation. We also think there are more important dividends that can't be fully realized yet: They're learning how to learn independently—and that's one of the main points of the program.

Yet our success—and the program—did not develop overnight, and it might be helpful for other schools if we conclude this article by summarizing the way in which the program has developed.

Our school opened in September, 1964, with a new faculty, a new curriculum, and a fine new building. One of the major tasks we set for ourselves in planning for the opening of the building was to develop this program of independent study. To accomplish this, we organized an "Independent Study Task Force" under the dynamic leadership of Roland Hughes, our director of guidance. From about March to June of the term preceding the opening of the school. Mr. Hughes and his faculty task force made an exhaustive study of the literature, debated heatedly the basic philosophy, and developed some tentative rules and guidelines—all of which turned out to be fairly sound.

It was largely at their suggestion that we began the year with a rather tightly structured situation. All study areas were quiet; attendance was checked; library passes were issued; no departmental study centers were open. Departmental study centers were opened as the departments felt they were ready to operate, and teachers were released from commons supervision to work in departmental areas when needed. We stopped checking attendance when we realized it wasn't necessary; we stopped issuing library passes because we felt it was limiting attendance and complicating matters unduly. We constantly evaluate progress, identify problems, and try to refine procedures.

We know we'll probably always have that three per cent sitting in "Stalag 125." But the frightening thing is that most schools still have 97 per cent in a similar situation. So who has the problem?

Junior High Program Lets Fast and Slow Students Take Time for Independent Study*

JOE A. RICHARDSON
DONALD G. CAWELTI

We don't agree that Independent study should be reserved for high school students of superior ability. We've found it can be a success on the elementary and junior high school levels and that the majority of students–including the slow learners–can turn out a good performance under a properly planned independent study program.

As part of a learning laboratory arrangement, independent study at Winnetka (Ill.) Junior High has led to improved teaching technics and changes in the curriculum. Perhaps one reason for success stems from our basic outlook. Instead of viewing independent study as work done by a student alone–usually on a project designed specifically for independent study by someone else–we see it occurring when a student moves from the classroom to a setting where he can find and use all kinds of varied instructional materials and aids, and, at the same time, be close to library resources. The amount of time given to this segment of the student's total educational program depends upon his interest in an area that he wants to explore in depth, his willingness to work away from the group, and the amount of time his teacher feels that he can profitably use in his project or spend away from class responsibilities.

Although we can't claim that our present offerings have been proved or refined by extensive evaluative research, here are some results and observations that might help other districts that are considering independent study programs in a learning laboratory setting.

*Reprinted with permission from *Nation's Schools,* 79 (February 1967), 74, 76-77, and Donald G. Cawelti, National College of Education, Evanston, Illinois, and Joe A. Richardson, Winnetka Public Schools, Winnetka, Illinois.

Include Everybody

When our program started three years ago we reasoned that students of high intelligence and achievement would be the only ones benefiting. We were wrong. Some of the most productive study programs have been carried on by children who, by usual measures, would be classified as slow learners or low achievers.

Fit Programs to Pupils

We'd rather arrange an individual program for a child than confine ourselves to strict regulations and procedures. Our basic aims for each student: 1) provide flexibility in his program; 2) encourage self-discipline; 3) permit personal involvement with a subject area; 4) foster the ability to find material on his own initiative; 5) help him make the best use of available school time; and 6) introduce study areas that might lead to life-long avocational or vocational interests.

Establish the Right Environment

Our learning laboratory arrangement provides us with an excellent environment for independent study. It is located immediately adjacent to the library, has individual and group study areas, and has an extensive A-V inventory. Furniture is moved and different groupings can be arranged in a matter of minutes.

Include Academic Consultants

The roles of our academic consultants have developed in the three years to include giving a portion of their school day for laboratory facilities to do research. It has become a center for turning out new ideas in teaching and initiating changes in the curriculum. One of the consultant's responsibilities is to assist teachers and students in designing independent study programs.

Release Students in Three Ways

Here are the approaches we used for releasing students from regular classes for independent study:

1. A teacher can refer a pupil for a special program. The program may be related to his classes but often it grows out of his interests and may not be related to the classwork.

2. Students use the laboratory as an elective part of their program for mathematics projects, creative writing, independent foreign language study, or improved reading skills.

3. Students use the laboratory before and after school.

Pinpoint Progress

Classroom teachers receive periodic reports on student progress. From time to time, programs are changed to include adult guidance, to allow for shorter periods of independent study, shift to different instructional materials, or to do whatever will make the program more effective.

Because communication with the classroom teacher is vital, we emphasize that, while the student may be working outside the classroom, he is still the teacher's responsibility. And the learning laboratory's independent study approach is merely one more way to help teachers provide for the individual differences in students.

How a Learning Lab Director Spends His Time

Teachers aren't burdened with paper work in Winnetka's independent study program because one person takes charge of all details concerning the operation of facilities and fills out special forms that show how a student's program of independent study is progressing. The learning lab director's duties:

1. Consult with students, discussing their interests and helping them get started on their projects.
2. Assist academic consultants in designing research topics.
3. Assist consultants in initiating, coordinating and administering individual and group study.
4. Keep records for students involved in laboratory work, do bookkeeping and accounting concerning the laboratory budget.
5. Assist consultants in developing methods of evaluation.
6. Administer details of reporting pupil progress.
7. Coordinate and administer a communication system between consultants, teachers, students and administration.
8. Assist with audiovisual equipment and materials.
9. Catalog and organize instructional material that is either created in the laboratory or purchased commercially.

10. Keep the lines of communication open between the school district and commercial producers of educational programs and instructional aids.

11. Direct and coordinate experimental programs initiated by individual classroom teachers.

How Learning Lab Students Spend Their Time

The following descriptions show three different independent study programs at Winnetka's learning laboratory and how they have been developed in line with the student's ability to follow and profit from the work.

Tim S. is a sixth grade student, who spends fourth period every day in the laboratory brushing up on mathematics. He needs remedial help; and, because he needs so much direct guidance, his independent study is very limited. He works two days with a tutor and three days on independent study with material designed to meet his problems. The material is developed by his teacher and can be used for self-instructional purposes.

Tim works independently as long as the material is appropriate to his needs. An attempt at expanding his program to four days a week of independent study showed the load was too much.

Macy B. is a seventh grade student, who spends three periods of an eight-period day in the laboratory. Second period would normally be a study period for Macy; however she spends this time in the lab learning French from tapes. She listens to a master voice, tapes her response, and checks it against the master. When she thinks she has learned the material, she takes a test. The test is corrected, and, if her score is satisfactory, she continues on to the next tape. Four periods a week are devoted to this independent study. One period concentrates on discussion with a conversation leader who checks her fluency of response, accent and comprehension. Local citizens who have native fluency in the language volunteer their services as conversation leaders.

Third period is one of the three core periods programed for Macy. Because she is a very capable and intelligent student, she is released to the laboratory to study word derivation. She uses material prepared by a language arts consultant, who reviews her work periodically and reports on her progress to her core teacher.

Eighth period is Macy's mathematics class. She spends two days a week receiving formal instruction under the direction of a mathematics consultant. Three days a week she works on assigned material (semiprogramed), as well as mathematical topics of her own choosing.

George C. is an eighth grade student, who spends one period daily working on creative writing. He works with semiprogramed materials that are easy to follow. As George completes the various segments of the program, evaluations are made and recommendations for continuing study are suggested.

George's records and teacher evaluations suggest that he is considered to be an average student by the standards of our school system. He has not given any indication of being highly motivated or of being interested in doing much independent study. However, he elected to take creative writing on his own, and his progress, according to his teacher has been very good.

The Individualized School*

JOHN W. JACKSON

After six years of a developmental program at Theodore High School in Theodore, Alabama, the total instructional program is built around individualized instruction in each of the various courses. For the Theodore faculty "individualized instruction" means that the plan for a course has been developed taking into account the unique difference of students within a class or course. Each student may work independently of other members of the class and receive help as he needs it.

In this individualized school, with grades seven through twelve and an enrollment of fifteen hundred, a student may now move through more than half of the courses offered as rapidly as his ability, initiative, and perseverance will permit. When one continuous progress course is completed a student receives credit for the course and then immediately begins the following course in the same subject, begins a course in another subject, or when it will be beneficial to him, spends additional time in other courses which he is already taking. Since the student will spend a minimum of half of his time in each course in independent study, he may adjust his daily schedule to provide adequate time to carry out a laboratory experiment in science, to prepare and cook a meal in home economics, to do lengthy research in the library, or simply to devote more time to a course which is difficult for him. There are no formal study halls in the school program. Except when a student is working in the library, schedules are arranged so that in whatever subject he may be working, the teacher who teaches him that subject is always available to give him help. Courses and assignments are organized and presented in such a way that students are never without something to do. With the major exceptions of mathematics and typewriting, all courses are developed on two to five levels of difficulty, providing in each course

*Reprinted from *The Journal of Secondary Education,* 41 (May 1966), 195-200, by permission of the publisher and John W. Jackson, principal, Theodore High School, Theodore, Alabama.

instructional programs reasonably appropriate to the ability of each student. Beginning with first year algebra, courses are available in mathematics through introductory calculus. Included in the science program are the BSCS, CHEM Study and PSSC courses. English courses are organized on three levels and individualized to such a degree that in a class that is working on composition, some students may be working in a programmed grammar text, others may be using a study guide to work through a section of a grammar handbook, while others who have reasonably mastered the elementary rudiments of the language, may be devoting their time entirely to writing. In literature classes all students read selections reasonably appropriate to their own reading level and discuss the selections in small groups. Students hear few lectures, thus providing little opportunity for them to sit passively while someone talks *at* them. Social studies courses are organized on five and six levels on two planes. One plane is a survey of each course and each student moves through that plane at his own speed. The other plane is the critical thinking and skills plane, utilizing group processes and studies of particular topics in depth. Each student in grades eight through twelve attends a group guidance period every other day. Group guidance periods are attended every day by students in the seventh grade.

Unlike many innovations the individualized school, as is being developed at Theodore, is appropriate to both large and small schools. Individualized courses can provide in the small school numerous opportunities which could not otherwise be available. Individualized mathematics and science courses are good examples. One mathematics teacher can teach, at one time in one class, all courses from general mathematics through introductory calculus, or higher. It makes no difference if only one or two students are taking the higher courses. Likewise, in science, one teacher can handle all science programs without the need to alternate chemistry and physics from one year to the next. Since only a few students are at the same place at the same time the required number of basic items of science equipment is reduced.

It needs to be pointed out again that the program under way at Theodore is a developmental one. No control groups have been established and changes are made as rapidly as more promising approaches are devised. The developmental approach has provided the flexibility needed to make adjustments in the programs easily.

The courses in the various subjects are individualized in different ways. For instance, in mathematics, referred to as a continuous progress course because each student continually progresses through the course at his own speed until the course is completed, each student follows the same sequence and works through identical assignments. Other continuous progress courses are the science courses, typewriting, bookkeeping, business law, business arithmetic, mechanical drawing, and home economics. Continuous progress shop courses are being developed currently. English is an example of a course which individualizes without continuous progress throughout the course, although in some English assignments a student will proceed through the assignment at his own speed. In English courses students usually work on the same general topics for the same length of time but with individualized assignments. Further individualization is facilitated by expectancy levels which will be discussed later. The mathematics and English courses illustrate the two major approaches used in individualization.

Four principal methods are used to individualize courses. The method most frequently used is the use of study guides. Study guides are written plans which direct the student in the pursuance of his studies. In a study guide the teacher provides the student with objectives, and with activities arranged in a sequence designed to cause the student to achieve the stated objectives. Pre-determined assignments for the whole course are written for the student to follow. Instead of the teacher telling all the students or a group of students to read a chapter, view a film strip, to carry out an experiment, listen to a record, or to write a report, he writes these instructions in the study guide so that each student may progress at his own speed from one assignment to another. By this method further instructions and assignments are always available to the student and the study guide tells him what to do next. The study guide also tells the student when to report to the teacher for conferences and when to take tests. Any time a student needs help he receives it from the teacher.

All unit study guides and unit plans begin with an overview which is a brief introductory summary of the unit objectives. The overview is followed by a list of specific objectives which spell out precisely what the student will learn and/or acquire the ability to do. An attempt is made to state all objectives in terms of outcomes so that the student will know how he will be expected to demonstrate his accomplishment of the objectives. Following the specific objectives are the student assignments. Student assignments are activities (experiences) designed to cause the student to accomplish the objectives of the unit. Emphasis is placed on activities which require the student to do something to bring about the change desired in him. Needed materials and equipment are identified in the assignments. Following the assignments students are directed to report to the teacher for testing. Self appraisal tests are sometimes worked into the assignments. Teachers always approve work of assignments before students are permitted to take tests. Teachers are urged to simultaneously prepare objectives and evaluative procedures for testing accomplishment of objectives. However, the pressure of time often causes the development of tests to be delayed until last. All continuous progress courses except mathematics courses use study guides to facilitate individualization.

The use of programmed materials is a second method used to individualize instruction. All mathematics courses use programmed materials except the courses for students with extreme reading difficulties. These students are taught in a rather conventional way. In other courses a few programmed units and books are used where they serve the need of the student or students.

As with the development of other effective instructional plans, the programmer first identifies his objectives, including the knowledge, skills, and understandings to be acquired by the student. The course is then organized into the most logical sequence for achieving the objectives and is divided into small steps. Each step presents a small amount of information and asks the student a question or otherwise requires an overt response by the student. As soon as the student responds he is shown the correct response, thus reinforcing correct responses. New information, skills, clues, and suggestions are faded into the program in such an obvious way that students can hardly respond incorrectly. As the student masters the program, he finds clues gradually fading out until he finally must respond from his own knowledge and/or skills.

Regular seventh grade students are started in a programmed general mathematics course while advanced students omit that course and start with programmed modern mathematics. A student moves into algebra as soon as he completes the modern mathematics course and several units prepared locally with study guides. Students who begin with the seventh grade general mathematics course must work through it and the modern mathematics course before beginning algebra. Students who complete the modern mathematics course before the end of their ninth year and do not elect algebra are placed in a general mathematics course using study guides until work for the ninth year is completed.

A third method used to individualize learning is that of giving individual assignments which are especially appropriate for the particular student. Special assignments are used mainly in English and social studies courses. With the use of individual assignments both quantity and quality of work required are varied according to the abilities and needs of the students.

The fourth principal method used to individualize learning is the use of levels of difficulty in the development of the various instructional programs and in the use of expectancy levels in describing a student's progress and/or quality of work. Instructional plans for a course are usually developed on from two to seven levels of difficulty. Common learnings subjects always have at least three levels of development or three expectancy levels, advanced (1), regular (2), and basic (3). The social studies department aims at an ultimate seven level development. As a rule, programs for mastery subjects are developed on only regular and advanced levels.

By developing programs on levels of difficulty the need for so called "enrichment" programs is eliminated as each student is assigned to work in a level most appropriate to his ability as determined by the student's previous achievement.

Once a student is assigned to work in a particular difficulty level that level then also becomes his expectancy level. The student is then expected to achieve with the quality and quantity of work for which that level is designed and his progress is reported accordingly. Although the quality of a student's work in a regular level might be higher than the quality of the work of a student with a basic expectancy level, it is possible for the regular level student to fail while the basic level student receives an A.

In courses with a single level development such as typewriting or programmed mathematics, students determine their own level for which credit may be received by the speed at which they progress through the program; the expectancy level is determined by the teacher. Both levels are reflected in reporting the student's progress. A student whose rate of progress is fast enough for him to complete a thirty-six weeks course within twenty-eight weeks is considered working in the advanced level, and if the course is completed within that time he receives advanced level credit. A student whose rate of progress will cause him to complete a thirty-six weeks course in from twenty-nine to forty-four weeks is achieving in a regular level.

If the teacher has determined the student's expectancy level as the advanced level, but the student's rate of progress places him in the regular level, his progress might be reported as 2C. This would indicate that at the rate the student is progressing he will receive regular level credit with a grade of C. The C indicates that the student's work or diligence is considerably below what is expected of him. Any student who achieves reasonably what is expected of him will receive an A on the level in which he is working. Students who achieve less well than should reasonably be expected receive letter grades accordingly down to a failure, which of course would eliminate credit for the course.

In continuous progress courses students are usually required to score a minimum of 90 per cent on each test before being permitted to move on to the next step in the program. In basic levels the required score is adjusted by the teacher to be appropriate for each student.

Flexibility in individual and group schedules is provided for by three simple organizational procedures, with the large amount of independent study serving as the catalyst. The three procedures are a revolving period, a change-of-schedule procedure, and responsible status for responsible students.

Although the school operates on a basic six period schedule, each day also has a seventh period called the revolving period. The revolving period is placed between the first period and second period except on occasion when another position in the schedule serves best the needs for the day. Unless his schedule is changed, each student is scheduled for one of his classes each day during the revolving period. The first day all students are scheduled for their first period class during the revolving period, the second day all are scheduled for the second period, the third day the third period, and so on through the sixth day and the sixth period. On the seventh day the students are all scheduled for first period classes again, thus the six periods of the basic schedule constantly revolve in the seventh or "revolving period."

During the revolving period all students are scheduled for independent study. This makes it possible for the teachers to organize large or small groups, drawing students from any class during that period without interrupting the work of the classes. Small seminars composed of advanced students in all of one teacher's classes can be held during the revolving period. Large groups such as one composed of 300 ninth grade civics students meeting as a state legislature in a project on reapportionment, can be held.

The second organizational procedure, the change-of-schedule, provides flexibility by allowing students to rearrange their individual schedules during revolving periods or at any other time when scheduled for independent study. Since students spend a minimum of half of their time in independent study, maximum flexibility is provided. Thus a student may arrange two consecutive periods to carry out a science experiment, to cook a meal or simply to devote additional time needed in courses that are difficult for him. To make such a change the student fills out a change of schedule form and has it approved by all teachers concerned not later than the day before the date of the change, thus assuring that each teacher knows where the student belongs at that time.

The third organizational procedure, responsible status, provides the ultimate in student freedom. Any student desiring responsible status may apply for it by having each of his teachers fill out a rating form evaluating the student's citizenship and the ability of the student to accept the responsibility for his actions. After an individual conference with his counselor if the student receives tentative approval, his application is then processed through the principal's office. Once approved the student receives an identification card which can be clipped to his clothes. The student's picture is on the card. A student so approved no longer has to request a change of schedule. He may move about the school in any way that benefits his studies. It is assumed that he will conduct himself responsibly and attend all group sessions for which he is scheduled. If one should not live up to these responsibilities his responsible status will be withdrawn. The responsible status program was begun at the beginning of the second quarter of this year, and as of this writing, the beginning of the third quarter, about eight-five students have been approved.

The Theodore faculty, after working six years in the developmental program, continues to be excited about the potentialities that the program offers. They are constantly seeking more effective methods and procedures that will improve the individualized school.

An Instructional Management Strategy for Individualized Learning*

PHILIP G. KAPFER

A frequent goal of the administrator is to integrate the essential components of instruction—the teacher, the learner, and that which is to be learned. The problem of integrating these components for the purpose of individualizing instruction is the central concern of this paper.

An instructional management strategy developed at Valley High School, Las Vegas, Nevada, is potentially effective for any school whose staff is attempting to individualize instruction, regardless of the type of schedule being used. To be genuinely effective in the school for which it was designed, however, the strategy was developed within the context of the four phases of instruction which have been advocated by innovators such as Bush, Allen, and Trump. These phases include large-group instruction, small-group instruction, laboratory instruction, and independent study.

Educators should cease to be concerned primarily with the technical problems of team teaching and flexible scheduling. Rather, they should get to the heart of the matter—the opportunities to individualize instruction *provided by* these innovations. The reader may or may not feel that the technical problems of team teaching and flexible scheduling have been solved; yet progress has certainly been made toward their solution. Agreement can be reached, however, that the problems of individualizing instruction have *not* been solved.

One key to providing for individualized instruction is the preparation of individualized learning units or packages. Such learning packages are the major elements of the instructional management strategy proposed here, and will be discussed following presentation of the strategy.

*Reprinted from *The Phi Delta Kappan,* 49 (January 1968), 260-263, by permission of the publisher and Philip G, Kapfer, Valley High School, Las Vegas, Nevada.

Assumptions

If a strategy for individualizing instruction is to be effective, it should begin with the currently existing program as perceived by teachers and pupils. In devising the strategy used at Valley High School, several assumptions were made concerning the perceptions of teachers and pupils, and concerning the schedule.

The first assumption, that *the pupil's responsibility is to learn and the teacher's responsibility is to make available to the pupil that which is to be learned,* places responsibility for the teaching-learning process where it belongs. The teacher does not cover a course, but rather uncovers it; he does not need to cover—or talk about—everything that is to be learned by the pupil.

A second assumption concerns the individuality of the pupil. *The subject matter of a course must be appropriate to the learner* with reference to 1) the pace of instruction, 2) the level of difficulty of the instructional material, 3) the relevance of the instructional material to reality as perceived by the pupil, 4) the pupil's level of interest, and 5) the individual learning style of the pupil.

Both the common and the individualized experiences of the pupil result from a third assumption which is related to the schedule: *The size of a group, the composition of a group, and the time allotted to a group should be appropriate to the purposes of the group.* The common experiences which every pupil in a given course should have are primarily a function of large-group instruction. Pupil-centered discussion of large-group presentations may occur in scheduled small-group instruction. Individualized, self-paced, quantity- and quality-monitored learning (that is, the use of learning packages with built-in self-correcting mechanisms) may occur in the laboratory phase of the course. In addition, the laboratory phase should include opportunities for student interaction and should provide directly for the independent study phase of the individualized instructional program.

A fourth assumption of the instructional management strategy is that *before truly individualized instruction can become a reality, learning packages are needed which will provide for self-paced rather than group-paced instruction.*

The Strategy

The instructional management strategy is based on, but does not adhere strictly to, the principles of Program Evaluation and Review Techniques (PERT). In a PERT network diagram, an *activity* is a time-consuming element of a project which is represented on a network as a line between two *events.* An event is a specific, definable accomplishment in the project plan, which is recognizable as a particular point in time when activities start and/or finish. An activity cannot be started until the event preceding it has been accomplished. A succeeding event cannot be accomplished until all activities preceding it are complete.[1]

[1]PERT *Time Fundamentals.* Los Vegas, Nevada: Edgerton, Germeshausen & Grier, Inc., undated, p. 3.

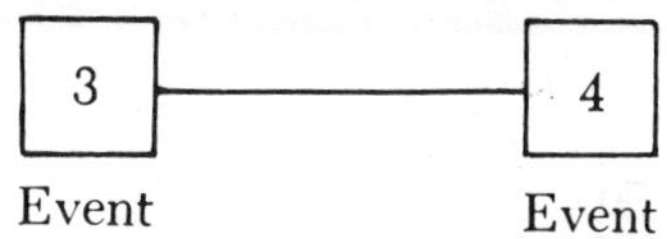

The strategy is presented as a network diagram in Figure 1, p. 372. The network is designed to show a sequence in which the pupil will attain an adequate *background* so that he is able to perceive problems and ask questions. The result of his questioning will be internal generation of a problematic *confrontation.* Through study and research the pupil will achieve *resolution* of the problem which he chose for investigation. Thus the sequence in the network is from achievement of *background* to problem *confrontation* to problem *resolution.*

Recycling, for some pupils and for some instructional objectives, may occur at various stages as indicated by arrows in the network. Thus, although the instructional management strategy may be thought of as a design for concept attainment through discovery or problem solving, it is not restricted to this interpretation. In the discovery interpretation of the strategy, the pupil might not be given a statement of the concept under study; rather, he would discover it for himself. In the presentation interpretation, a statement of the concept may be given to the pupil at the beginning of the learning package. In either case, the activities and events *following* Event 3 (see Figure 1) represent an inquiry approach. The activities surrounding Events 4 and 5, those involving minor and major quest, give the pupil the opportunity to become a researcher, and in the process of resolving problems the pupil learns information-seeking techniques. When the decision is made to proceed to a sequential learning package, options similar to those just outlined are available to the pupil.

Preparing Learning Packages

Learning packages usually include the following eight ingredients for individualizing instruction:

1. *Concepts* are abstractions which organize the world of objects, events, processes, structures, or qualities into a smaller number of categories.

2. *Instructional objectives* tell the pupil what he will have to be able to do when he is evaluated, the important conditions under which he will have to perform, and the lower limit or quality of performance expected of him.[2]

3. *Multi-dimensional learning materials* of varying difficulty are cited from commercial sources, whenever possible, and include a variety of media which require use of as many different senses as possible.

[2]Robert F. Mager, *Preparing Instructional Objectives.* Palo Alto, Calif.: Fearon Publishers, 1962, p. 52.

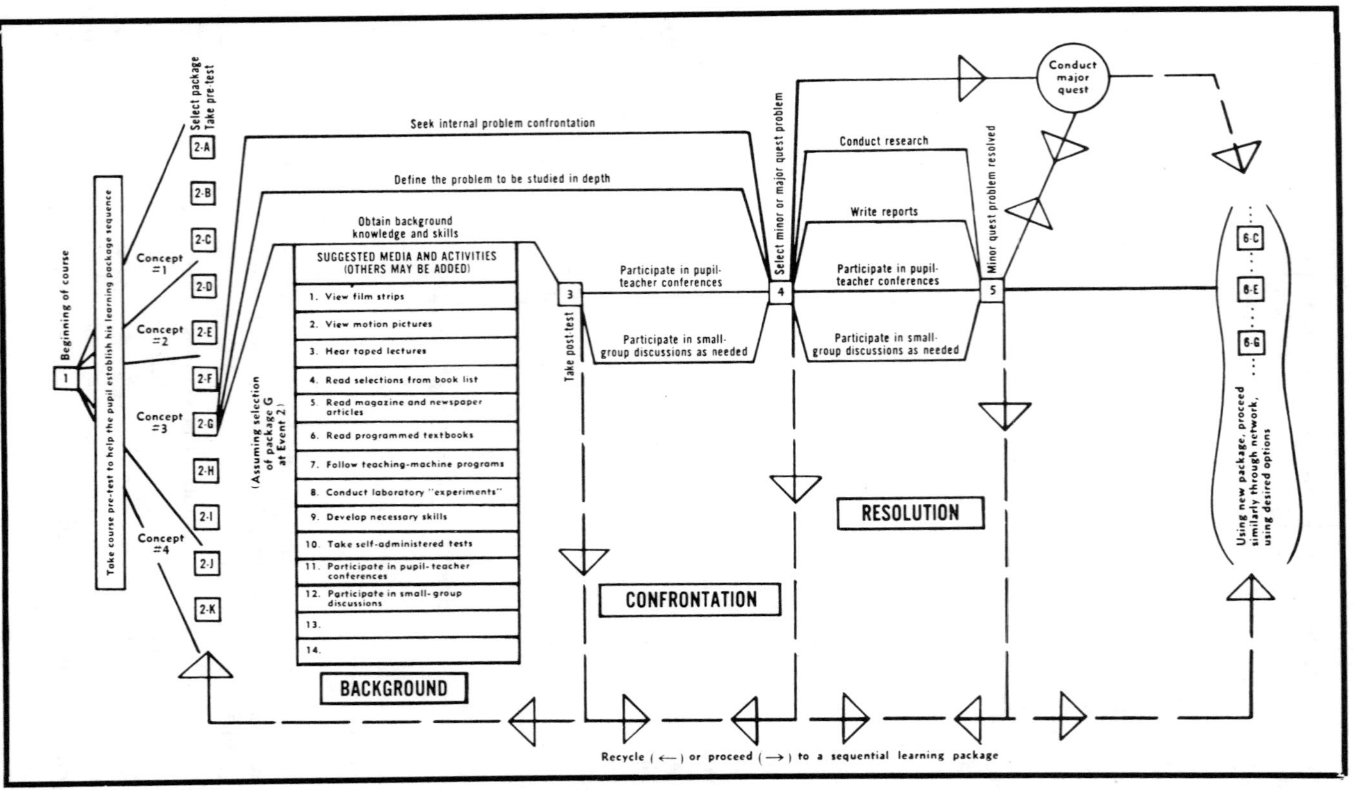

Fig. 1. The Instructional Management Strategy Network Diagram for Self-Paced Learning

4. *Diversified learning activities* provide alternative approaches for achieving the instructional objectives, and include such activities as large group and small group instruction, field trips, model building, drama productions, games, laboratory experiments, role playing, pupil-teacher conferences, reflective thinking, and the like.

5. *Pre-evaluation* is designed to assess the extent to which the pupil has already achieved the instructional objectives as a result of his earlier learning experiences. Pre-evaluation enables the pupil to invest his time wisely in areas in which he is weak.

6. *Self-evaluation* is designed to assist the pupil in determining his own progress toward achieving the instructional objectives. Self-evaluation, the results of which indicate the pupil's readiness for post-evaluation, occurs after the pupil has used the multi-dimensional learning materials and participated in diversified learning activities.

7. *Post-evaluation* is designed to assess the extent to which the pupil has achieved the instructional objectives as a result of his learning experiences.

8. *Quest* includes problem confrontation, delimitation, research, and resolution. Quest is a pupil-initiated and self-directed learning activity.

Integration of the above eight curricular elements in the form of learning packages can serve as an important advancement in providing for self-paced learning through individualized instruction. An experimental course, *Human Relations–an Interdisciplinary Study,* which is currently under way at Valley High School, is based on the instructional management strategy. One of the learning packages developed for the course is reproduced below in the form in which it is available to students. Only the pre- and post-tests have been omitted here due to space limitations.

Learning Package Topic: Stereotyping[3]

I. CONCEPT STATEMENT

Stereotyping is a learned behavior which results in loss of individuality for members of a stereotyped group or institution.

II. INSTRUCTIONAL OBJECTIVES

A. From his own experiences, the student will be able to define the term "stereotype" and give at least five examples of stereotyping. He will be

[3]Charles A. Silvestri and Kathleen Harrell, *Human Relations–An Interdisciplinary Study*. Las Vegas, Nev.: Valley High School, 1967, unpaged.

able to explain how such thinking restricts his effectiveness in human relationships.

B. Given six general headings and related terms, the student will write the response which he freely associates with each term. By looking at himself or at someone he knows, he then will be able to explain the degree of validity of his free association responses.

1. Physical appearance
   a. red hair
   b. blonde
   c. blue-eyed
   d. fat
   e. tall and dark
2. Geographical location
   a. Southerners
   b. Las Vegans
   c. New Englanders
   d. San Franciscoans
   e. Westerners
3. Occupation
   a. doctors
   b. lawyers
   c. truck drivers
   d. musicians
   e. school teachers
4. Age
   a. teen-agers
   b. over 30
   c. over 65
   d. Old Shep
   e. kindergarten
5. Socioeconomic level
   a. hicks
   b. snobs
   c. happy
   d. unhappy
6. Racial, religious, and ethnic groups
   a. Pollacks
   b. Mormons
   c. Irish

III. LEARNING MATERIALS AND ACTIVITIES[4]

A. Scan—current news media.

B. View—"Common Fallacies About Group Differences," 15-minute 16 mm. film, McGraw-Hill.

C. View—"High Wall," 32-minute 16 mm. film, McGraw-Hill.

D. View—"None So Blind," color filmstrip with sound, Anti-Defamation League of B'nai B'rith.

E. Read—Robert P. Heilbroner, "Don't Let Stereotypes Warp Your Judgment," Anti-Defamation League of B'nai B'rith (pamphlet).

F. Read—Raymond W. Mack and Troy S. Duster, "Patterns of Minority Relations," Anti-Defamation League of B'nai B'rith (pamphlet).

G. Read—Earl Raab and Seymour Lipset, "Prejudice and Society," Anti-Defamation League of B'nai B'rith (pamphlet).

H. Read—William Van Til, "Prejudiced—How Do People Get That Way?" Anti-Defamation League of B'nai B'rith (pamphlet).

[4]The student selects from the suggested learning materials and activities those which he needs in order to achieve the instructional objectives. He is neither restricted to these suggestions nor expected to use all of them.

I. Read–Howard J. Ehrlich (ed.), *Theory Into Practice,* special edition, available from Anti-Defamation League of B'nai B'rith.

J. Read–William Peters, "Why Did They Do It?" *Good Housekeeping,* June, 1962.

K. Read–G.M. Morant, *The Significance of Racial Differences.* Paris, France: UNESCO, 1958, 47 pp.

L. Read–Arnold Rose, *The Roots of Prejudice,* Paris, France: UNESCO, 1958, 35 pp.

M. Read–David Westheimer, *My Sweet Charlie.* Garden City, N.Y.: Doubleday, 1965, 255 pp.

IV. SELF-TEST

A. Define "stereotype" and give at least five examples of stereotyping. Explain how the thinking represented in each of your examples restricts one's effectiveness in human relations.

B. List your free response to each of the following terms: blond, teacher, teen-ager, parent, Mexican, truck driver, farmer, fat, red. Are your responses accurate? Explain.

V. SELF-TEST KEY

Answers on the self-test will vary. After checking your performance with the objectives and discussing your answers with other students, if you still are in doubt about acceptability you should discuss the answers with one of your instructors.

VI. QUEST SUGGESTION

Select a common stereotype and describe the process of generalization by which this stereotype might have developed. Can you find any evidence to support or refute your description?

Summary

The instructional management strategy is designed to assist teachers in establishing stepwise procedures for achieving individualized instruction. The important elements in the strategy are learning packages designed for use by individual pupils. Identification of the important concepts and instructional objectives which are to be taught by means of these packages will permit the establishment of hierarchical schemes around which the curriculum may be organized, K-12 and even higher. The packages may take many forms, but a common characteristic of each is the provision for self-pacing. As a result, the pupil is enabled to progress at his own best rate, thus avoiding the familiar difficulties of group-paced instruction.

Programed Learning: Misunderstood Tool*

ROBERT T. FILEP

You can bring a pupil to a teaching machine, but you can't make him learn from it, unless:

—It's the right program for the student.
—The teacher knows what she should be doing.
—The teacher knows what the program should be doing.

Some advocates of programed instruction maintain that a program can do a better job of teaching than a teacher can. It works equally well, they argue, with all students at a given grade level.

Contrary evidence shows that programed instruction will neither surpass all teacher achievements nor be equally effective with all students.

What it can do, however, is cover some units of work in less time than a teacher could. It can also teach as effectively as the teacher can. Programs can be used as part of a total teaching package. The package could include not only the teacher, but laboratory exercises, films, filmstrips and educational television as well.

It's a mistake to regard the confrontation of teacher and program as a competitive Indian arm wrestle. But those who do can be sure that the outcome will be determined by the quality of the program or the quality of the teacher, or both.

Use of programed materials has given teachers a new role. They serve as a guide for learning rather than as a disseminator of information. This has been a mixed blessing. Because the program covers the basic content, the teacher can

*Reprinted with permission from *Nation's Schools,* 77 (April 1966), 66-67, and Robert T. Filep, Institute for Educational Development, El Segundo, California.

concentrate on the demanding task of developing student thinking into more complex and subtle relationships. In the view of some teachers, the extra planning and effort involved may outweigh the benefits of the program. This could be a shortsighted view.

In some cases, schoolmen have balked at programed instruction because the programs available were unimaginative or inadequate. This position steadily becomes weaker, if not untenable. Now more than 450 programs are available, and new and better ones are coming right along. Most are in textbook form and do not require a teaching machine.

Programed instruction is a young field and many authorities believe the trend toward its acceptance, while bumpy, is irreversible. Whether this turns out to be the case or not, the questions and following comments can help you decide if programed instruction will work for you.

How to Make Programed Instruction Work in Your District

1. Determine if programs can help accomplish your educational objectives. The fact that programs have been used successfully for enrichment, remedial, homework, class and summer school tasks by other schools–including "leading-edge" schools–indicates they probably can. Ask yourself: what can the program do as well or better than a text, filmstrip, film or television presentation?

2. Enlist the aid of a faculty member who already may be interested in this field. He can coordinate the collection of information and programs that are potentially applicable.

3. Establish a committee to screen and evaluate programed materials. Los Angeles public schools have had much success with this approach.

4. Ask subject matter authorities to examine the subject content of all programs under consideration. Look for possible conflicts between a modern and a traditional approach. One real advantage of a good program is that the content is clearly laid out for examination and the teaching objectives are clearly stated.

5. Be ready to ask:

–Has the programer provided review sections and remedial sequences for slower students?

–Are answer sheets provided or are the programs not reusable?

–Are pretests and post tests provided?

–Are any visual prompts provided?

–Does the program have style and humor?

–Will obtaining and storing the program create problems?

–Does the majority of frames require relevant responses?

–Are field data available from developmental and evaluation testing?

6. Be prepared to start in-service training of teachers who will use the programs. A number of good potential projects have fallen flat because programs were given to teachers without prior discussion or instruction.

7. Encourage members of the committee on programed instruction to take a course in programing. They may decide to write their own programs and learn how to evolve criteria for selection and use.

If you can, have them enroll in a course where the instructor has written programs for commercial or experimental use. Be careful of programed instruction "practitioners" who have come by their knowledge secondhand.

8. Try the program out with one or two student users before adopting it. Highly verbal students generally are quick to provide feedback concerning the merits or detractions of the program.

9. Don't expect all students to finish the program at the same time. Even with a group that is basically homogenous in ability level, you will find wide variations in finishing times. But that's one big advantage of programed instruction; it permits and encourages self-pacing.

10. Remember that most programs are designed to teach either average or above-average students, or average and below-average students, but not both categories. Some programs provide enough branches to permit adaption to all student ability and motivation levels, but these are a minority.

Programmed Instruction and Unit Teaching*

DONALD G. ARNSTINE

The current quantity and variety of mechanical devices designed to aid teaching confounds the imagination. To assess all of the newer teaching aids from the standpoint of the unit approach to teaching demands either a volume or a superficial treatment. One could say that any device is useful if used properly, and possibly harmful if used inappropriately, and then elaborate the point. But since the convenience and indeed the popularity of such statements is more than overbalanced by their emptiness, we shall limit ourselves to a consideration in some detail of only one form of the newer media: programmed instruction and its implementation in the various devices known as teaching machines. Our consideration will reveal that methods of instruction are not neutral; that they do in fact determine educational goals.

We do not ask, 'How can programmed instruction aid unit teaching?' for that only begs the question. It is our purpose, rather, to ask *whether* programmed instruction can be of help in unit teaching. An answer to the question depends to some extent on what one has in mind when he says 'unit teaching', but thus far no legislation exists that would clearly define the phrase. This being the case, it might be best to put off for a while a definition of unit teaching, and instead focus on what is involved in programmed instruction. Our procedure, then, will be as follows: first we shall see what programming is designed to accomplish, and how it goes about fulfilling its ends. Next, we shall examine some of the more prevalent conceptions of unit teaching in terms of its goals and methods, and we shall then see whether programmed instruction is subsumable within, or at least compatible with the goals and methods of unit

*Reprinted from *The High School Journal,* 47 (February 1964), 194-200, by permission of the publisher and Donald Arnstine, Boston University.

teaching. We shall conclude the essay with a more general evaluative interpretation of programmed instruction with respect to any possible application of it.

A teaching program is designed "to present material to the learner and to control the student's behavior during his learning by exposing stimulus material, requiring some overt or covert response to this material,[1] and providing some form of knowledge of results[2] for each response. It is a program in the sense that it is a list of items, steps, or frames, each of which performs these functions."[3] A teaching machine, while not necessarily crucial to the process of programmed instruction,[4] is any mechanical or electronic device designed to present the program and facilitate the learner's response to it.

A teaching program, then, has as its aim the imparting of information.[5] Changes in the verbal behavior of students are brought about by getting them to make "active responses"[6]—that is, to push a button or write in an answer—to a series of questions arranged in such a manner that they cannot (presumably) answer any question correctly unless they have made correct responses to the previous questions. This arrangement of questions, designed to gradually "shape" appropriate responses, is referred to as "small steps."[7] The fact that every response *must* be either right or wrong indicates the information-giving character of the program. Indeed, one enthusiast has gone so far as to say that "if a teacher cannot ask questions requiring the student to make some discrimination that is clearly right or wrong, it is doubtful whether that teacher is teaching anything but shifting whims."[8]

What keeps the student going through the program is the immediate

[1]Recent research indicates that it may make little difference whether the response is over, covert, or indeed non-existent. See John F. Feldhusen, "Taps for Teaching Machines," *Phi Delta Kappan,* XLIV: 6 (March, 1963), 265-67.

[2]Despite the popularity of the concept, it may be the case that even feedback is not always crucial to the sort of learning that programs are intended to promote. See Feldhusen, *op. cit.*

[3]Joseph W. Rigney and Edward B. Fry, "Programming Techniques," *A V Communication Review,* 9:5 (Sept.-Oct., 1961), 7.

[4]See Lawrence M. Stolurow, "Let's be Informed on Programmed Instruction," *Phi Delta Kappan, op. cit.,* 255 f.

[5]See William R. Uttal, "On Conversational Interaction," in John E. Coulson (ed.), *Programmed Learning and Computer-Based Instruction* (New York: John Wiley and Sons, 1962), 171-190; and Stolurow, *Teaching by Machine* (Washington, D. C.: U. S. Government Printing Office, 1961), 4.

[6]See B. F. Skinner, "Why We Need Teaching Machines," *Harvard Educational Review,* 31:4 (Fall, 1961), 377-398.

[7]See B. F. Skinner, "Teaching Machines," *Science,* 128 (1958), 969-77.

[8]John W. Blyth, "Teaching Machines and Human Beings," in A. A. Lumsdaine and Robert Glaser (eds.), *Teaching Machines and Programmed Learning: A Source Book* (Washington, D. C.: Department of A V Instruction of the NEA, 1960), 415. It might be argued that some of the most important things that teachers set out to teach, e.g.

reinforcement that follows each correct response. "With humans, simply being correct is sufficient reinforcement–pigeons will not work for such meager gains."[9] Thus the pigeon may get some lunch for his efforts (or appropriate responses), while the human learner, a dupe of his own phylogenetic superiority, is expected to keep on working for the less tangible rewards of successive and minute verbal successes. Since the program and the machine are infinitely patient with the dullest of students, any length of time may be allowed for completing the program. Thus differences in learning rates are allowed for, and students are said to be "self-paced."[10] This feature of programming allows for considerable emphasis on the individual aspects of learning. One authority has recently claimed that "most of our educational goals could be achieved without interaction between individuals. We could put a child into a cubicle or leave him in the home and still accomplish most of the goals."[11]

One further aspect of programming should be noted before we go on to consider unit teaching. The *purpose* to be served by the program is the programmer's or the teacher's; it is not the learner's purpose unless it is successfully imposed on him.[12] Thus education has been defined by one sponsor of the programmed instruction as "purposefully designing and shaping human software to the needs of society."[13] Another writer, generalizing from the model of instruction appropriate to programming, goes so far as to characterize *all* instruction as "a system for controlling student behavior so as to modify it to conform to a predetermined plan."[14]

In contrast with the conception of teaching that emerges from concern with programmed instruction is the spontaneity and variability of the teaching process as often conceived by those concerned with unit teaching. As they describe "experience units" which must be "definitely related to [the students'] day-by-day life experiences," Moffatt and Howell emphasize the need for

---

information and attitudes about morality, beauty, democracy, citizenship, etc., are *not* matters that can clearly be classified as "right or wrong." And yet they are not shifting whims, either.

[9]James G. Holland, "Teaching Machines: An Application of Principles from the Laboratory," In Lumadaine and Glasser, *op. cit.*, 218 f.

[10]See B. F. Skinner, "The Science of Learning and the Art of Teaching," *Harvard Educational Review*, 24:2 (Spring, 1954), 86-97.

[11]Launor F. Carter, "The Challenge of Automation in Education," in Coulson, *op. cit.*, 7. James Finn, apparently in agreement with this conclusion, suggests that teachers and schools might even be dispensed with some day. See Finn, "Automation and Education: III Technology and the Instructional Process," *A V Communication Review*, 8:1 (Winter, 1960), 18.

[12]See B. F. Skinner, "Freedom and the Control of Men," in Skinner (ed.), *Cumulative Record* (New York: Appleton-Century-Crofts, 1961), 15.

[13]Arthur W. Melton, "The Science of Learning and the Technology of Educational Methods," *Harvard Educational Review*, 29:2 (Spring, 1959), 97.

[14]P. G. Whitmore, "A Rational Analysis of the Process of Instruction," *IRE Transactions on Education*, E-4:4 (Dec., 1961), 143.

"democratic teacher-pupil planning."[15] Lavone Hanna and her collaborators are in agreement when they claim that, in order to accept the objectives of a unit, the student "must have participated in formulating them..."[16] The predetermined purposes and design of programmed instruction would be wholly at odds with these conceptions of unit teaching.

It was noted that the aim of programmed instruction is to impart information;[17] again we find a contrast with the aim of unit teaching. Henry C. Morrison, an early but still influential advocate of unit teaching, claimed that its aim was to create a new point of view in the learner, and not merely to present a logical arrangement of material.[18] Morrison held that "it is the attitude which becomes the real and serviceable product of learning and not the experiences themselves; these may fade out of memory but the conviction abides. Conversely, there may long be retained mere memories of isolated facts, without any modifications of attitude whatsoever. In this case the individual has learned nothing..."[19] The authors mentioned earlier[20] agree with Morrison that it is the production of an attitude (and not, as in the case of programming, the acquisition of information) that is the aim of unit teaching.

A further point of contrast between unit teaching and programmed instruction lies in the wholeness aimed for in the unit, as against the fragmentary character of the teaching program. C. M. Clarke pointed out that whatever is to be learned in the unit gains its meaning from its context in the unit, which to the pupil represents a singleness of purpose, direction, and value.[21] Morrison, too, speaks of the unit as presenting a "significant and comprehensive," or whole aspect of the environment, or of a science, and contrasts this with "a mere division of descriptive or expository subject matter which cannot be understood except in relation to other chapters which themselves stand in isolation."[22] The latter would not inaccurately describe the sequence of frames in an instructional program.[23]

[15]Maurice P. Moffatt and Hazel W. Howell, *Elementary School Studies Instruction* (New York: Longmans, Green and Co., 1952), 157.

[16]Lavone A. Hanna, Gladys L. Potter and Neva Hagaman, *Unit Teaching in the Elementary School* (New York: Holt, Rinehart, and Winston, 1963), 55.

[17]That programmed instruction is able to implement aims other than those of information-acquisition has been treated as a mistaken claim in Donald G. Arnstine, "The Language and Values of Programmed Instruction," *The Educational Forum,* XXVIII:2 (January, 1964) and XXVIII:3 (March, 1964).

[18]See Henry C. Morrison, *The Practice of Teaching in the Secondary School* (Chicago: The University of Chicago Press, 1926), 177.

[19]Morrison, *op. cit.,* 26.

[20]Moffatt and Howell, op. cit., 163; and Hanna, et al. *op. cit.,* 52.

[21]C. M. Clarke, "Unit Theory in Teaching Practice." *The High School Journal* 33 (May, 1950), 106-107.

[22]Morrison, *op. cit.,* 177.

[23]Compare with Skinner and Holland, *The Analysis of Behavior* (New York: McGraw-Hill, 1961), passim., a readily available programmed textbook.

On the basis of the above comparisons of the aims and methods of both unit teaching and programmed instruction, it would appear that the two are incompatible, and that if one wanted to adopt the unit approach to teaching, he had better keep a respectable distance from programming. There are, however, two possible objections to this conclusion. The first is that the conception of unit teaching presented here has been biased; that a concern with what is sometimes called the "subject matter unit" would find unit teaching quite compatible with programmed instruction. The second objection would call attention to a possible service performed by programming *within* the sort of teaching unit that has been described in this essay. It could be claimed that, while programmed instruction might not serve as the basis or over-all plan of unit teaching, it might well be the most efficient way of presenting the information with which any teaching unit must sooner or later deal. Although they are often held by reasonable people, these two objections are mistaken. The mistake is a function of the peculiar kind of learning that results from programmed instruction. It will be the task of the concluding section of this essay to elaborate the learning products of programmed instruction, and to point out how these products unfit programmed instruction as a means for carrying out any sort of unit teaching.

Operant conditioning is the theory of learning from which programmed instruction is derived by those who claim any theory at all for such instruction. Without a doubt, the results of operant conditioning have been most thoroughly tested and most firmly established in the laboratory. The laboratory learner is usually a rat or, what has been more intriguing, a pigeon. Following the same procedures that are used in programmed instruction,[24] pigeons have been trained successfully and rather easily to play a sort of ping pong. Such a result is startling, and we do not stretch our language when we remark that these trained pigeons are now rather clever. We also remark that certain men are clever, but when we say "the pigeon is clever" and "the man is clever," we are not using the term "clever" in the same sense. That is, "clever" in these two uses commonly refers to different sorts of behaviors, and the procedures used for making a pigeon clever can only make a man clever (if they work at all with men[25]) in the *same* sense in which a pigeon can be clever. To put this in still another way, we do not expect a clever man to behave like a clever pigeon; hence we must teach the man in a manner different from the way in which we teach the pigeon. We shall now examine this argument a bit more closely.

A clever pigeon is one that performs *only those specific acts* that he has been taught. Change any significant aspect of the environmental stimuli

[24]It has been argued, however, that the human instructional program does *not* correspond to the procedures of operant conditioning used in training laboratory animals. See Arnstine, *op. cit.*

[25]See Arnstine, *op. cit.*

connected with the ping pong game, and the pigeons will no longer play. The pigeon, then, cannot use its "cleverness" to modify its acts under the press of novel circumstances. Another way of putting this is to say that *one can always specify in advance the particular acts which define cleverness in the pigeon.* Now let's look at cleverness in the man.

Unlike the pigeon, the man who is clever is one who *can* modify his acts in the face of novel circumstances. If the light over the ping pong table burns out, he replaces it. If his opponent is only a beginner, he may play with his left hand. The clever man, then, does *not* perform only those specific acts that he has been taught. Putting this in a form parallel with our conclusion about the pigeon, we may say that *one can never specify in advance the acts which define cleverness in the man.*[26]

Whatever their native capacities, then, the differences in behavior shown by clever pigeons and by clever men are differences that can be traced to the ways in which they were taught. The pigeon, having been subjected to programmed instruction, has learned to perform precisely *only* those acts that it has been taught. The man, having been subjected to instruction other than that of the programmed variety, has learned attitudes and dispositions which enable him to perform acts *other than* those that he has been taught.

Now, it has been suggested that we teach human beings by means found effective with pigeons. When it is insisted that we emphasize "the importance of the teacher's being able to specify the behavior of a learner who has reached the objectives of instruction," in order to elmininate "vague" educational goals like "appreciation" and "good citizenship,"[27] we are in effect recommending that students learn to perform *only* those acts that they have been taught. Teaching pupils, then, is reduced to the same procedures as training pigeons. The theoretical tangles involved in using the same terms (in the case we have selected, "cleverness," although the terms "response," "behavior," "intelligence," etc., have been used in other contexts) in both laboratory and classroom situations have been noted by Fred T. Tyler and Noam Chomsky.[28] The social consequences of this error, in terms of producing a generation

[26]Apparently, Harry F. Silberman (in "What Are the Limits of Programmed Instruction?" *Phi Delta Kappan, op. cit.*, 297) would disagree with this conclusion. To produce creativity in learners, he says, we must first "define operationally [i.e. specify in terms of specific, observable acts] what is meant by creative behavior." But if the behavior that we wish to produce in the learner is precisely defined *in advance* of his performing it, then that behavior is, in the light of the way in which we *define* creativity, *not creative.* Precisely the same reasoning would apply to any ill-conceived attempt operationally to define "cleverness" prior to teaching students to be clever.

[27]James D. McNeil, "The Influence of Programmed Learning Upon Curriculm Construction," *Phi Delta Kappan, op. cit.*, 262.

[28]Fred T. Tyler, "Teaching Machines, Programs, and Research on Learning," *The School Review,* 71:2 (Summer, 1963), 123-150; and Noam Chomsky, Review of B. F. Skinner's *Verbal Behavior,* in *Language,* Language, 35:1 (Jan.-March, 1959), 26-58.

of conventional, conforming human beings, have been elaborated by Donald Snygg.[29]

The conclusion should be clear. With the possible exception of such relatively isolated learnings as drill in spelling or the multiplication tables, it would seem that programmed instruction is an inadequate device for any sort of unit teaching, or any teaching at all, if our learners happen to be human beings. If we employ techniques in teaching children and youth that correspond closely to the techniques that we use in training pigeons, we should only be able to call the human products of such teaching "clever" if we mean by that term, "clever like a pigeon." Indeed, our students would in fact *be* clever (or quite intelligent), compared to other, untrained pigeons.

[29]Donald Snygg, "The Tortuous Path of Learning Theory," *Audio Visual Instruction,* 7:1 (Jan., 1962), 8-12.

The Junior High School Library Develops Investigative Skills*

FREDERICK R. CYPHERT

An article in a recent professional publication contained the thought-provoking statement that one-third of all that we know came into being prior to the year 1400; another third of the world's knowledge was discovered between 1400 and 1900; and the final third of today's understandings is the product of the twentieth century. If we, as educators, accept this geometric growth in the world of facts and ideas, we must recognize that a school program geared largely to transmitting this accumulation of culture to new generations is faced with an inextricable problem. The time has long since passed when we should alter our instructional programs to place increasing emphasis upon problem solving, research, and investigative skills. It now appears that having the skill and ability for solving problems as they are met, rather than carrying a set of answers preconceived about our rapidly changing world, is the best equipment that we can give today's youth.

The school library, filled with the treasures of the past and the promises of tomorrow, becomes the key that unlocks this modern inquiring approach to education. Unfortunately, in spite of the library's increasing importance, recent research indicates that many schools are ineptly utilizing this materials center and are thereby minimizing its curricular contributions. What can we learn from examining the strength and weaknesses of the junior high school library programs of one of our major eastern states?

Teaching the Skills of Library Usage

Virtually all junior high schools offer their students some type of

*Reprinted from *The Clearing House,* 33 (October 1958), 107-109, by permission of the publisher and Frederick R. Cyphert, University of Virginia.

preplanned library instruction. This instruction is most often given in grade seven. The responsibility for the planning and execution of it is largely the librarian's.

It is reported that library skills are most often taught in isolation from the other learning experiences of students. Pupils find themselves assigned weekly to the library to consider such topics as book classification, card catalogue, library citizenship, and general reference books. There they are confronted with methods of instruction which consist chiefly of lectures, recitations, and questions covering duplicated explanations of library routine.

Is not such a formal approach to the teaching of library-usage skills as unrealistic as attempting to teach the fundamentals of basketball through the use of a rule book? Are not skills best learned through their successful application to real situations where their need is apparent to the learner? Most librarians and administrators believe that youngsters should become familiar with the school library, but they have not accepted the concept that understanding stems from intelligent use.

Teaching Practices and Library Use

Librarians say that the techniques of classroom teachers of greatest assistance in promoting library use involve devices calling for student inquiry. The assignment of individual reports to students and teacher emphasis upon research skills are considered to be superior to required book reports and encouraged personal reading. Many librarians are sympathetic to attempts by teachers to promote investigative skills because these activities fill the library with students.

However, there is evidence to indicate that both teachers and librarians at times promote research-demanding techniques without fully comprehending the consequences or evolution of such activities. Only one librarian in four is sufficiently familiar with the classroom activities of her school to analyze the teaching methods employed. Similarly, fewer than one librarian in five visits academic classrooms for planning with students. Also, on the average, the entire faculty in these same schools consume less than one-half class period per week in curriculum planning with the librarian. Furthermore, librarians, only superficially acquainted with the details of the school's instructional program, have to select the library's supply of new instructional materials because teachers fail to make their needs known. Problem-solving skills could be developed more effectively where teachers, students, and librarians work together in the logical planning of the objectives, learning experiences, and materials of instruction that promote these abilities.

Some Schools Do the Job

There are schools, however, which are effectively teaching the skills of investigation. The following example serves to illustrate the way in which one school organizes to teach these techniques of inquiry.

In this junior high school, each year's learning experiences are organized around a series of related problems, such as, "How does man earn a living?" The professional planning for each problem unit begins in a "little school" meeting with two core teachers, a math teacher, a geography-science teacher, and the librarian participating. After this preplanning, when the students have been confronted with the problem, the librarian joins the pupils in their classroom deliberations as a resource person to help organize the search for pertinent information.

Meanwhile, the "little school" of educators continues to meet weekly to coordinate teaching method and objectives. This enables the librarian to anticipate needs and to provide flexible scheduling so that entire classes, small groups, or individual students can visit the library to satisfy the need for additional information.

Some of these visits to the library, moreover, are devoted to the consideration of research techniques for which students and teachers realize the need. As the year progresses and the solution of one problem leads to further areas of investigation, librarian, teacher, and student alike come to grips with the strengths and shortcomings of their problem-solving abilities.

Pertinent Points in Planning

Developing investigative competencies in junior high school students raises some questions of teachers and librarians:

1. Are faculty members convinced of the need for having children develop these skills and abilities?
2. Have these skills and understandings been spelled out?
3. Do teachers direct their efforts toward a growing pupil independence and responsibility rather than a dependence upon teacher domination, thinking, and ingenuity?
4. Have channels of communication among teachers and between teachers and librarians been cleared so that each knows what the other is doing?
5. Do teachers and librarians have some time and place during the day to work together?
6. Are library materials selected by librarians, after an analysis of teacher and pupil needs and objectives?

7. Is the schedule of the library flexible enough for students to visit it as needed?

8. Do both librarian and the teachers approach the teaching of investigative skills by beginning with concrete situations?

9. Do we arrange for pupils to deal with problems and develop proficiencies commensurate with their abilities?

The Challenge

In today's world of ever increasing change, we cannot, try as we will, foretell what our children will need to think. We can, at best, give them a method for approaching the challenges of life. This task demands the utilization of all we know concerning the science of learning, and the effective integration of the library and the curriculum.

Developing a Junior High School Instructional Materials Center*

RACHEL E. PLOGHOFT

When plans first were projected for a library at Brody Junior High School in Des Moines, it was with the thought that a complete instructional materials center could be developed over a period of time. An enthusiastic principal and faculty, including a librarian who was eager to promote and utilize such a concept, helped make the instructional materials center (IMC) become an actuality after only six months of school.

The IMC at Brody serves as the "center of information" for the school. Through its doors come the available material, book and non-book, which can be used for instruction and personal interests in the junior high. This does not include the basic supplies for a subject, such as thy glass tubes for science experiments. This collection would include mathematics' materials such as the abacus, the literature reading sets from *Scholastic*, models in plastic for science and social science classes, the SRA reading kits, and maps and globes.

Planned for Easy Access

This material is cataloged and filed for easy access by both teachers and students by using a color-code system in order that obtainable material on any one subject may be located in the main card catalog. For example, in the study of the Civil War there might be books (white cards), pamphlet material (salmon cards), recordings–both musical and/or speaking (blue cards), slides (color-banded orange), filmstrips (yellow cards), community resources such as a

*Reprinted from *Midland Schools,* 81 (May-June 1967), 11-12, by permission of the publisher and Rachel Ploghoft Champion, Brody Junior High School, Des Moines, Iowa.

speaker or items of interest in the community (color-banded green), and regalia such as a Civil War flag or uniform (color-banded red).

The Dewey Decimal System classification has been followed, with cross-references in the card catalog. Because of space limitations and for easier storing, the various types of media have their own storage units – vertically-divided shelving for recordings, built-to-order file drawers for slides, film loop, microfilm and tapes, and legal-sized files for informational material, transparencies, maps, and pictures.

An Audio-Visual Lab

To use all this information effectively, it is necessary to have the audio-visual equipment available in the center. What better place than the IMC! Here Brody Junior High students come to work individually or collectively with any or all the material. On the overhead projector may be a transparency of the Civil War battlefields, while on the opaque projector a picture from a reference book is being enlarged to copy for class display.

Around the tape recorder might be from one to eight students using headsets listening to a biography of Abraham Lincoln or reviewing yesterday's lecture by one of the social studies' teachers. From one to six students may have on stereophonic listening headsets to study a recording of Civil War songs. Another student may be searching the *American Heritage* microfilms via the microfilm reader for articles on that period. The filmstrip viewer and/or the slide projector may be in use along with the books, pamphlet material, pictures, and clippings also to be found in the IMC.

There is an adjoining workroom area where one may find students working on three-dimensional projects. Teachers may be utilizing the dry mount press, preparing materials for the bulletin board display, or using the primary-type typewriter for transparencies or labels.

Purpose of IMC

But why an IMC? It is believed by many of today's educators that the various kinds of media for learning should be located in one central place and easily accessible to faculty and students. By using these varied media, there is greater opportunity to develop to the fullest each child's potential learning capacity. Here at Brody it is felt that there is no better place than the library, where traditionally supplementary learning materials found in books, magazines, and other printed materials have been located.

The philosophy to which Brody subscribes is that the librarian, or director of the IMC, can provide the opportunity for teachers to look 'through' materials rather than 'for' them when planning a unit of study. Selection, classification, and organization are handled by the director who is able to help not only the faculty but also the students in their ever-broadening search for knowledge. In actual practice, then, in the Brody Junior High School IMC is found the opportunity to pursue interests and/or needs through independent study on various levels and by varied means.

Brody Junior High has been fortunate in having various sources of funds, including gifts, with which to build an IMC. All the media is not yet available, nor is there an abundance of materials, but additional services are being provided daily. Student and faculty interest is mounting with each addition, and parents are equally enthusiastic. Here is the nucleus for one of the most exciting and challenging adventures—the building of an IMC, a true "center of information."

Paperback Usage in Schools*

WILLIAM D. LITZINGER

The expanding elementary and secondary school enrollments have necessitated increased supplies of textbooks. This situation is further complicated by a burgeoning supply of new knowledge which has the effect of outdating some previous knowledge as well as adding to our overall store of information. The possibility of alleviating these difficulties by the use of paperbacks as a dissemination medium is explored in this article.

National Textbook Sales

A compilation prepared for the American Textbook Publishers Institute by Stanley B. Hunt & Associates in April, 1963, shows that the average dollar volume of sales per capita has nearly doubled in both elementary and high schools in the past decade.

Total sales at the elementary grade level increased from $155,750,000 in 1961 to $161,750,000 in 1962, an increase of about 3.8 per cent. Unit sales, however, decreased 4.6 per cent. At the high school level, a 13.3 per cent increase was made during the same period from $96,050,000 to $108,800,000. This represented a 15.7 per cent increase in unit volume.

States with the highest per capita textbook sales at the elementary and high school level were: Alaska ($10.31), Utah ($8.12), South Dakota ($7.23), and North Dakota ($7.21).

In 1962 the breakdown of textbook sales in terms of hardcover and paperback was as follows: elementary level, $101,185,000 in hardcover and $10,300,000 in paperback; the high school level, $87,855,000 in hard cover and $5,920,000 in paperback (1).[1]

*Reprinted from *The Clearing House* 38 (April 1964), 474-477, by permission of the publisher and William D. Litzinger, University of San Francisco.

[1]Numbers in parentheses refer to references at the end of the article.

Paperbacks

The introduction of the modern paperback book occurred in 1939, when Pocket Books issued its first ten titles. Red Arrow Books soon followed, and before the year was over Penguin Books had opened its first American sales office. Paperbacks had two earlier movements of substantial size, the first beginning in 1835 and the second in 1870. The paperback has now passed through two revolutions in less than a quarter-century. The first was the widespread sale of very inexpensive paperbacks through mass markets. The second was the publication and distribution of somewhat more expensive paperbacks, beginning in the early 1950's (2).

The major change of the second revolution has been qualitative. The sale of the quality paperbound is expected to increase faster than that of any other kind of book. It is predicted that 17 million copies will be sold in 1965. This contrasts with 340 million mass-market paperbacks (3).

The paperback business has grown not only in dollar volume, but also in terms of quantity of books and publishers. In 1957, there were 17 publishers of paperbacks distributed through magazine wholesale channels. Five years later there were nearly 50 publishers. There were about 970 titles recorded in *Publishers' Weekly* in 1957. This number grew to 2,200, a 130 per cent increase, by 1961. There were in 1961 nearly 16,000 active titles in print in all price ranges, of which about 3,900 were mass-market books, in contrast to about 6,000 listed five years previous (4).

There are several reasons for the boom in paperback sales: increased student reading, the lightness and small size of paperbacks, the great variety of titles available, the value of paperbacks as sources of up-to-date materials, their capacity for making difficult material look easy, and the trend to build home libraries instead of selling school books to successors.

However, one observer says paperbacks have so far made little impression on public high schools. She traces this to several factors: the ignorance of many teachers and administrators, who still link paperbacks with trash or believe that only a limited selection of titles is available; state rules on textbooks in the public schools, which do not provide for paperbacks; the confusion of publishers about whom to approach in the school system—teacher, superintendent, board of education, or principal; and school doubts about the durability of paperbacks (5).

Consider the economics of paperback publishing. Mr. Walter Oakley, senior vice-president and sales manager of the Oxford University Press, had this to say, in speaking of the related problems of production and pricing of high-priced or trade paperbacks (those that schools use primarily):

> . . . the firm's policy has been to get its money back on the first printing of a paperback. The first season's books were printed from

letterpress plates, were Smythe-sewn, and were priced relatively low. The next season, offset printing and ganged-up runs were used and the retail prices were raised. The trade paperbacks have the advantage that only the regular book trade discounts have to be allowed on them. The "get-out" (break-even) quantity on a 5,000 printing under these conditions can be as low as 1,500; on 10,000, 3,200 (6).

The economics of paperbounds is interesting and puzzling. A $4 book does not become a $1.65 book by the mere act of reducing the binding cost by 20 cents. The pricing of paperbounds reflects more than savings in cloth and boards. Apart from binding, one major saving in a paperbound is in the amount paid to the author. The author of a paperback gets about 5 per cent of the list price instead of 10 to 15 per cent. The other major saving comes from lowering printing costs through larger printings. Another saving comes from reduced promotion costs—for the most part, paperbounds are books that have become known on the strength of the promotion done in connection with the original hardbound edition (7).

Paperbacks as Textbooks

Only two comprehensive studies have been made to examine scientifically the many aspects of the practicality, feasibility, and economics of the use of paperbound textbooks in the public schools. One study was conducted by the Bureau of Educational Research of the New York City Schools, the other by the Texas Education Agency (1961) in Austin, Texas (8).

The Texas study group examined the present use of paperbacks as textbooks throughout the United States. Replies to a questionnaire were received from every state except New York and West Virginia. The responses indicated that use of paperback textbooks is spotty. Sixteen states appropriate money for paperback textbooks; fifteen of these reported general use of such texts. Ten states cited use of such books in handwriting, in band and orchestra, and as preprimers. Most states do not buy paperbacks as textbooks.

In some subjects, paperbound books have been adopted only in instances where comparable hardbound textbooks were not available: in most states, paperbound material is handled as expendable, and the life is considered as one year. One state discontinued the use of paperbound textbooks because the public did not like them. Most states report an increased use of paperbound books as supplementary books (purchased by the students), especially in conjunction with English, history, and government; and a few state officials appear to be enthusiastic about the potential of these materials for providing variety and recency to the learning of students.

Results of the New York City Study

The following tentative conclusions were drawn from the New York City Schools study:

1. It was impossible to find a solution to the problem of relative durability of hard and softcover textbooks through the inspection and a study of the relationships between the conditions of the books and the length of time in use because the editions were not actually parallel and the patterns of use of paperbound and hardbound texts were not the same.
2. If paperbound textbooks are to be approved for use in New York schools, the basis, in general, should not be that of economy.

These conclusions were justified in the New York study by the following facts:

1. In only a few subject-matter areas are paperbounds at present produced in such volume as to permit a considerable saving in purchase price.
2. The manufacture of paperbound editions of standard textbooks specifically for New York City would demand a price not far different from the price of hardcover texts, unless the editions were planned as paperbounds. In this case, some of the attractiveness (illustrations, fine paper, large type, etc.) of the hardbound editions would be lost, but educational merit might not be impaired in the case of books for young pupils.
3. The perishability of paperbound texts is such that annual replacement would probably be required. The saving in purchase price would be more than offset by the cost of frequent replacement, even excluding additional clerical labor involved.

In certain situations, a case can be made for economy in using paperbound textbooks. The low purchase price makes paperbounds valuable (a) in experimentation, (b) when a new curriculum is being initiated and it is desirable to spread costs over a period of years, or (c) when a wider variety of textbooks for meeting individual needs and interests is being tried out.

The New York study concluded that some of the possible reasons for approving the paperbound textbooks are: (1) the psychological appeal of receiving a new book annually; (2) the possibility of frequent revision; (3) lightness of weight; and (4) recency of material.

Results of the Texas Study

The Texas study, though limited in scope, of brief duration, and restricted to only 19 titles, points up significant areas related to paperback usage. The results of this study were categorized as follows:

1. *Availability of 19 titles selected in paperbound textbooks:* 93 per cent of 123 publishers responding said they did not publish paperbound texts like the 19 titles actually supplied by a dozen companies for the survey. Most indicated a willingness to produce such books, however.
2. *Testing availability and price by means of invitations for bids:* Approximately 70 per cent of those publishers responding believed that the reduction in price could not exceed 30 per cent if a book were published in a paper cover and retained the identical content and context of the hardbound textbook.
3. *Analysis of per-unit cost of hardbound textbooks already in state-wide use over many years*: The range in per-student cost of a hardbound textbook in the Texas public schools is from a high of $1 per year for a high school Texas history book to a low of 21 cents per year for a third-grade spelling book, and the "average" hardbound textbook has a per-student cost per year of 38 cents.
4. *Classroom testing of the books in the survey*: The annual per-student cost of a paperbound textbook in the Texas public schools would range from a high of $7.52 in Spanish II to a low of $2.62 in eighth-grade English. The average life expectancy for a paperbound book would be .80 years (7.92 months), as compared to an expected lifeof 5.6 years for a similar hardbound textbook.
5. *Durability tests in independent laboratory*: In the tumbling test, paper covers delaminated and split at the corners and edges; this was followed by tearing at the corners of the spine, curling of pages at the corners, and loosening of the back from the spine. After 500 tumbles the covers were in a predictably dilapidated condition.

Hardbound texts showed a consistent pattern also: first, wear on the cloth at the edges and corners; next, besides increased wear, a fallout of impregnating material at the ends of the spine; next, a loosening of joints. Still, after 500 tumbles, the hardbound books were generally in fair condition for class use. In an abrasion test, it took about 25-35 cycles to wear through the top surface of a paper cover. Cloth covers with good protective coating sustained from 50 to 800 cycles (though cloth covers with no coating resisted wear-through no better than paper covers).

Paper covers pulled off the spine because of delamination of the paper or spine tape, or failure of the adhesive line. Cloth cover failures occurred for similar reasons, but at loads many times greater.

The Texas study also made note of factors affecting durability of paperback textbooks. Climatic conditions and differences between rural and suburban types of schools did not affect durability. The following factors definitely did make a difference: method of student transportation, economic community served by the school, size of book, type of binding, type of use (whether in class, home, or school), grade level, subject area, and average number of days the book was taken home each week.

All in all, the study group felt that the findings, so far, would not justify the purchase of additional paperback texts. Publishers' bids show that the average saving on paperback texts would be less than 10 per cent, a saving that is cancelled very quickly by the average life expectancy of the paperbacks—which is one-sixth that of a hardbound text.

References

(1) "Textbook Research Planned, Major Programs Forecast," *Publishers' Weekly*, Vol. 183, May 13, 1963, pp. 17-22.

(2) Cyril O. Houle, "Two Revolutions and Their Consequences," *ALA Bulletin*, Vol. 56, July-August, 1962, p. 654.

(3) *Ibid.* p. 656.

(4) "Economic Problems and Prospects in Paperback Publishing," *Publishers' Weekly*, Vol. 181, May 14, 1962, p. 3.

(5) Nan Robertson, "Paperback Books Gain Stature with Increased Use in Schools," *The New York Times*, October 15, 1961, p. 1.

(6) "*Economic Problems and Prospects in Paperback Publishing*," op. cit., p. 30.

(7) Daniel Melcher, "Paperbounds: The Revolution in Book Distribution Patterns," *Library Journal*, Vol. 85, January 15, 1960, p. 181.

(8) "Paperbacks as Textbooks in Texas: A Tentative No," *Publishers' Weekly*, Vol. 183, February 4, 1963, pp. 84-90.

Paperback Books:
Their Role in the Schools Today*

In education, the name of the game is teaching kids how to read. Fortunes are spent annually by school districts in an attempt to find new and better ways of achieving this goal. But a recent, in-depth study indicates that a simple, *low-cost* tool–the paperback book–may be having the most pronounced effect.

In 1960-only seven years ago-this magazine ran an article encouraging the use of paperback books and suggesting that every high school should have a paperback bookstore of its own. The editors knew they were on thin ice. Relatively few educators had the courage to *use* paperbacks, then-let alone to sell them openly in the school itself. The popular image of the paperbound was a title of dubious literary worth, often pornographic, characterized by a lurid cover illustration.

To say educators and paperbacks have come a long way since 1960 is a gross understatement when you examine the findings of a recent massive study of the use of paperbacks in schools. Witness:

- Almost half of the secondary schools in the U.S. now sell paperbacks in the school.
- About 77% of the high schools use paperbacks as textbooks or supplementary texts.

*Reprinted by permission of *School Management* (September 1967), 11:103-108.

- About 63% of the high schools circulate paperbacks from the school library.
- Fewer than 3% say they refuse to use paperbacks at all.
- The average high school in the U.S. is currently spending 10% of its textbook budget on paperbacks, over 6% of its library book budget and 26% of its budget for classroom books!

Nor is the use of paperbacks confined, today, to the secondary level. Some 12% of *elementary* schools have paperback bookstores, 35% use them as texts or supplementary texts and about 30% have them in their libraries.

While the use of paperbacks for classroom reading collections and in book clubs is gaining acceptance, the two primary uses are as textbooks or supplementary texts, and as additions to the schools' library collection.

Respondents to the survey are asked *why* they use paperbacks in each of these two situations. Since it is expected that there might be many reasons in any given school, they are also asked, in a second question to identify the most important reasons for using paperbacks. Answers were then classified by elementary school and secondary school respondents (see box).

For the library: there is little doubt but that the *low cost* of paperbacks is a dominant factor when they are brought into the school library. But in both elementary and secondary schools, the fact that *students like them* is a powerful motivator—almost as strong as the cost factor. Surprisingly few respondents are concerned, in the library situation, with the fact that paperbacks might not have to be processed and cataloged. (It is interesting to note, however, that about 40% of all respondents admit that they do not classify, catalog or process library paperbacks.) In secondary schools, some 26% of the respondents say that a dominant reason for using them in the library is that "many titles are not available in hardbound books."

As texts or supplementary texts in both elementary and secondary schools, *low cost* is recited as a strong consideration in their use. But when the respondents are asked to pick the most important reasons in their decisions, *flexibility* is far-and-away the major consideration. In elementary schools, flexibility seems to be more a matter providing for the individual reading abilities of students. In secondary schools, flexibility in curriculum use is paired with flexibility for accommodating individual pupils.

Do Librarians Like Paperbacks?

It's possible to use or exploit paperbacks—and still not "like" them. In fact, there's a popular belief that most librarians abhor their existence and use them only under duress. The facts drawn from this survey put that canard to rest. It isn't even remotely true.

For example, when librarians are asked their opinion of how *other* librarians feel about paperbacks, 86% say they "favor them" or "are enthusiastic" about their use. Principals, when asked how *they* think librarians feel about paperbacks, are preponderantly certain that they "favor them" or "are enthusiastic."

The attitudes of school board members, however, is significantly different—at least when seen through the eyes of the librarian or principal. For one thing, better than half say they "don't know" how their school board feels. Among those who hold an opinion, only about 25% of the librarians feel confident that their boards favor them or are enthusiastic. Elementary school principals are equally wary. But about half of the secondary school principals feel boards favor them or are enthusiastic about using them. *It is quite possible that both librarians and principals are strongly inhibited in using paperbacks by their doubt about the board's attitude.* (Note: about 9% of all respondents state, when asked, that there are "statutes or regulations which restrict the purchase of paperbacks in their school or library." It may be conjectured whether·these impediments are real . . . or imagined.)

STUDENTS ENTHUSIASTIC

Student enthusiasm for paperbacks is one of the most striking facts confirmed by the study. As reported above, this is one of the most important factors reported by the respondents as to *why* paperbacks are used in both library and textbook programs. When the librarians and principals are asked to rate their students' attitudes, well over 80% report the pupils are "enthusiastic" or "favorable."

STAUNCH SUPPORT

But the staunchest supporter of the paperback, in both elementary and secondary schools, is the *principal.* About 90% report favorable or enthusiastic reactions. Unfortunately, many principals appear to have failed to communicate this attitude to their librarians—some 30% of the librarians "don't know" the attitude of their principal or suspect he is "indifferent."

Selling Paperbacks in School

The sale of paperback books in schools should not be confused with the mandate that students *must* buy them. In its purest and best form, the so-called paperback book store is simply a convenience for the student and an incentive to help him build a personal library. The "store" may be as simple as a wire rack in the cafeteria or hall. In some schools, it is combined with the sale of other merchandise (T-shirts, notebooks, etc.). In others, it is a remarkably complete bookstore, run by the students themselves.

Among the more than 3,000 schools represented in this study, 36% say paperbacks are sold on the school premises. Naturally, the number is higher in *secondary* schools—with 49% reporting inschool sales. Among these high schools and junior high schools, 41% have had a paperback store for five years or more.

It appears the practice is approaching saturation at the secondary level, however, for among schools that do *not* have a paperback store, only 6% say they have any plans to install one during the next year.

It is difficult to conjecture exactly *why* this should be so, since 78% of the principals in schools that do *not* sell paperbacks claim to "favor" or to be "enthusiastic" about their use by students. Nor does the economic level of the school community, or the presence or lack of a central library in the school, seem to affect the decision.

THE BEST CLUE

Perhaps the best clue can be found in the difficulty that schools claim to have in setting up a good source of supply for stocking their paperbook stores. Fifty percent of the high schools with bookstores state their chief source of supply is a *local* paperback wholesaler. By the same token, these same schools say they have "frequent" or "occasional" contact with a local wholesaler in 63% of the cases. On the other hand, over 60% of the high schools with *no* paperback store report they have no contact with local source.

It would appear that an easy and quick source of supply is certainly a key factor in whether or not the school sells paperbacks.

Paperbacks Are Used	*Schools with Stores*	*Schools without Stores*
In elementary curriculum	56%	32%
In secondary curriculum	82	71
In elementary library	44	26
In secondary library	67	60

As a corollary, it is worth noting that about half of all secondary schools with a paperback store process their orders for paperbacks used in the *classroom or library* through their own "in school" facility.

A more striking correlation, however, can be found between the extent of overall paperback usage in schools with stores, compared to schools without stores. The store clearly increases usage.

Paperbacks in the Elementary School

The use of true paperbacks (not workbooks) in elementary schools has been thwarted, until recently, by the relatively few titles available for younger children. In the last two years, however, publishers have made a deliberate effort to accomodate this group. Some of the new titles are originals, some are reprints of books that were successful as hardbounds. So it is interesting to observe that three out of four elementary school respondents say they have noticed a "substantial increase in the quality and quantity of elementary titles." This recognition has led to wider use of the available books. Some 30% of the elementary schools report that they are now using paperbacks as "textbooks or supplementary texts" and almost the same percent have introduced them into elementary school libraries. Slightly more than half are using them for classroom collections and in paperback bookclubs to encourage independent reading.

What kind of books would they like to see more of? The overwhelming plea is for titles that can be used for "reading enrichment," especially in the lower grades. About one out of five specifies the need for titles on health. And well over half state that remedial reading teachers are using paperback books in the elementary program.

In recent years, there has been a growing practice of holding one or more book fairs a year in elementary schools to encourage students to build personal libraries of their own. About 20% of all elementary school respondents say that they hold these events, to which both students and their parents may be invited. A substantially lower percentage of rural elementary schools hold book fairs—a regrettable finding, since children in these areas are normally less exposed to good book selections through normal commercial and retail channels.

More encouraging, however, is the growing incidence of paperback book clubs in these elementary schools. About half of the respondents report that book clubs are used—and, of these, the rural schools run slightly *ahead* of the suburban and urban schools!

Paperbacks in the School Library

It is not the intent of this study to measure the growth of the central library in schools. But a good estimate can be made, as a by-product of the research, by looking at the response of secondary principals to one key question. About 99% of them say they have a "central" library. In El-hi combined schools, about 83% said there is a central library. In elementary schools, about 75% claim a central facility.

If these figures are accepted as valid, they indicate an appreciable increase over accepted figures and may very well be one overlooked result of recent massive federal aid for library facilities. The extent to which these central libraries meet good standards will be known when further computer runs have been made on this study and carefully analyzed.

To what extent are paperbacks used in school libraries? About 28% of elementary libraries, 63% of secondary libraries and 53% of combined El-hi libraries use them in their collections. Only about a quarter of the librarians say they use *pre-bound* paperbacks in the library situation.

There is marked disagreement among librarians and other school officials on whether or not paperback books should be processed and cataloged in the same way as hardbounds. Those who are against it point out that such processing often costs more than the book itself and that paperbacks are better thought of as "expendables." But librarians who use paperbacks to supplement the number of titles in the collection (particularly titles not available in hardbound), insist they cannot properly provide books requested by students without a control. Actually, a good case can be made for both sides. Many have solved the problem by omitting the processing on so-called "leisure reading" books. As pointed out earlier, however, about 50% of all school libraries do not catalog more than a very few. Moreover, about 36% say they shelve their paperbacks separately from hardbounds—and it may be assumed that the bulk of the non-processing libraries are those who shelve separately.

It is also worth noting that over half of the respondents state that they expect to *increase* their use of paperbacks in the library during the coming year.

Selecting Paperback Titles

Because the school paperback bookstore is gaining increased acceptance, an effort was made in this study to determine whether there is any appreciable difference between the personnel who select the titles for the store and those who select them for curricular or library use. In fact, little or no difference can be observed-except that in over 40% of the schools with paperback stores, students are given the opportunity to participate in selections. Relatively few respondents said students are given a similar role for library or curricular uses. In both cases, better than one out of four administrators play a role in the choice of titles.

How do school people keep abreast of available titles? Two facts emerge: 1) an impressive variety of sources are used, and 2) quite different sources are used for the bookstore as opposed to the library or classroom. For example, the following three sources are most often mentioned by the respondents for classroom or library use:

Library Journal	56%
The Paperback Goes to School	40%
Paperbound Books in Print	39%

For selecting books to go into the school paperback store, these are the first three sources mentioned:

The Paperback Goes to School	46%
Paperbound Books in Print	39%
Paperbound Book Guide for High Schools	38%

Bookclubs, of course, are a form of "selection," since choices are limited to those provided by the editors of the club. About 33% of all respondents say they use a bookclub. Of these, about half say they are able to procure bookclub selections as *individual* titles.

Any Doubting Thomases?

Of the many conclusions that can be drawn from this comprehensive study about paperbacks in the schools, two stand out:

NOW THEY'RE RESPECTABLE

First, the degree to which paperbacks have been accepted by school people as a basic teaching tool is truly phenomenal–particularly when you remember that paperbacks were barely respectable, just a few short years ago.

Second, the positive effect of paperbacks on students' attitudes toward reading, on the sense of values they develop for books and on their overall reading habits cannot be denied.

NEED AMMUNITION?

In every school where paperbacks are used extensively, there is undoubtedly a small handful of people who are primarily responsible for the increased use of this new teaching tool. But there is also undoubtedly still a small handful of hold-outs *against* the paperbacks. If this survey does not provide the ammunition needed by the innovators to dispel the qualms of the Doubting Thomases . . . nothing will!

Why Paperbacks Are Used

IN ELEMENTARY SCHOOLS (BY PERCENT)

If you use paperbacks, check the most important reasons that motivate you to use them.

For your library

32%	Less expensive than hardbound books, so our budget goes farther.
24	Practical for short term use.
29	Students like them.
10	Many paperback titles are not readily available in hardbound.
1	Require less space than hardbound books.

As texts or supplementary texts

21%	Less expensive than hardbound books, so our budget goes farther.
12	Students like them.
33	Give teachers more flexibility in dealing with individual differences of students.
18	Give teachers more flexibility in curriculum (can make changes from class-to-class and year-to-year).
31	Provide useful and inexpensive supplements to regular textbooks.

IN SECONDARY SCHOOLS (BY PERCENT)

If you use paperbacks, check the most important reasons that motivate you to use them.

For your library

34%	Less expensive than hardbound books, so our budget goes farther.
23	Practical for short term use.
30	Students like them.
26	Many paperback titles are not readily available in hardbound.
4	Require less space than hardbound books.
2	Do not have to be processed and cataloged.

As texts or supplementary texts

21%	Less expensive than hardbound books, so our budget goes farther.
14	Students like them.
32	Give teachers more flexibility in dealing with individual differences of students
38	Give teachers more flexibility in curriculum (can make changes from class-to-class and year-to-year).
33	Provide useful and inexpensive supplements to regular textbooks.

Beyond The Statistics

Perhaps the most significant findings in this study can be gleaned from the "written-in" comments at the end of the questionnaires. For it is here, free from forced-choice answers, that one senses the enthusiasm of educators for the paperback as a tool to encourage reading. Librarians and principals deplore its lack of durability, but quickly rise to its defense as a stimulus for the non-reader.

"Students like the size," is repeated almost ad nauseum in comment after comment. So is: "It fits a boy's hip pocket, a girl's pocketbook."

"The children think paperbacks are shorter," says one

librarian. "They think they are abridgements. I always know when a teacher has assigned a book report because I see all the non-readers poking through our paperback shelf."

"There is something psychological about a paperback that makes a student read one when he would not read the same book hardbound."

"We have found great acceptance in our disadvantaged programs. Former non-readers are now reading with interest and perception."

"We have purchased paperbacks for our reluctant readers and placed them in the classroom. The teachers are delighted with the response—students are reading avidly."

"A God-sent blessing for the reluctant reader-gets them away from the traditional hardback."

"Students will choose a paperback over a hard cover almost 2-1."

part 5

Curricular Areas

There has been much talk concerning the "new curricula" and many academic areas are said to be experiencing a "ferment." It is unquestionably true that there has been, since the middle 1950's, a vastly increased interest in revising and improving many curricular areas. This has come to pass for several reasons: public criticism of the schools as a result of foreign scientific and engineering successes; comparisons of the American schools with European schools; massive grants of funds from private foundations and the federal government; dissatisfactions with the lack of curricular change or the lack of speed in making any changes; and the participation of scholars in the various disciplines in studying, revising, and improving content and instruction in various curricular fields. The "new" mathematics, science, English, and social studies, and the altered methods of teaching foreign languages have been reflected in texts, content, inservice training of teachers, and techniques of instruction in the junior high schools as well as at the other public school levels. While there may have been some adverse effects from these studies and proposals, one beneficial result has been a reassessment of curricular offerings and content in virtually every subject area, from physical education to algebra.

Curriculum Changes in the Junior High School*

WILLIAM T. GRUHN

Young Adolescents Today

The concern of the junior high school today, as always, is on youth—youth during early adolescence. Its concern is not only with youth as individuals, but with youth as members of a social group. The junior high school is concerned with youth as part of a young adolescent society, youth as they approach the older teenage society, and youth as they prepare for their place in the adult world. In any study of the junior high school curriculum, therefore, it is important to begin with a study of young adolescents. We need to understand young adolescents as they are today, how they may be different, and what their place is in our ever changing society.

Young adolescents are more sophisticated today than those of a generation ago. Some of this is good. They read more widely; they are better informed through television, radio, and newspapers; their speech is better—at least, when they want it to be—and they remain in school longer. They are more interested in school than young adolescents of the past, though their interests are strongest, as always, in the active studies—physical education, industrial arts, home economics, music, and art. They are also more interested in the academic studies, especially in those where new approaches are employed, such as mathematics, science, and the foreign languages.

In some respects the early sophistication of young adolescents, however, is not desirable. In a recent study among principals of junior high schools

*Reprinted from *The High School Journal,* 50 (December 1966), 122-128, by permission of the publisher and William T. Gruhn, University of Connecticut.

throughout the United States, a substantial percentage reported that among young adolescents today, as compared with a decade ago, there is more smoking, steady dating, early dating of girls with older boys (grades 11-12), drinking, and delinquency.[1] These are expressions of sophistication among young adolescents which most adults consider undesirable. Such behavior is of concern to parents and educators of junior high school youth.

The sharp differences that have developed between young adolescents and older teenage youth likewise are of concern to educators and parents. The older teenage society is a society that lives on wheels. The driver's license is the most distinguishing mark between young and older teenage youth. Practically all states issue drivers licenses at age 16 or above, although some grant junior permits below 16. Age 16 is also increasingly the age when youth may first take employment. The minimum employment age is influenced by state and federal laws, the customs of our society, and the minimum wage laws. Even though employers may employ youth under 16 years of age, they are reluctant to do so because of the need for work permits, the fact that the minimum wage law applies regardless of age, and the demands of the public for a quality of service which only older youth are likely to give. Compulsory school laws likewise distinguish rather sharply, in most states, between youth that are under 16 and older teenage youth.

The differences between young and older adolescents are complicated by the fact that they apply differently to boys as compared with girls. A girl does not need a driver's license to participate in the social activities of older youth. Spending money likewise is not as necessary for a girl as for a boy. Consequently, young adolescent girls are increasingly dating older boys and participating in social activities for which they are not sufficiently mature in their sense of values and ability to make appropriate judgments. It is problems such as these which must be considered as we study young adolescents as a basis for curriculum development in the junior high school.

Individual Differences Among Young Adolescents

The curriculum of the junior high school has always been concerned with the differences that one finds among young adolescents. There is even greater diversity among young adolescents today than at any other time in our history. There are a number of reasons for this. First, more youth remain in school through the junior high school than a generation or two ago. In the fall of 1961,

[1]Based on a study of three-year junior high schools in the United States by William T. Gruhn and Harl R. Douglass, in the spring semester of 1964, which will be summarized in a book to be published by the Ronald Press Company of New York.

according to the United States Office of Education, 94 per cent of the children who were in the fifth grade four years earlier entered the ninth grade.[2] In other words, practically all youth today remain in school into the ninth grade. This retention of pupils in school leads to a greater diversity in the backgrounds of junior high school youth, and, in turn, to problems in curriculum development.

The mobility of our population is a second reason for the greater diversity among youth in our junior high schools. The past generation has seen a rapid movement of families from farms to urban areas. The more prosperous families in our cities, in turn, have moved to the suburbs and residential rural areas. The automobile, opportunities for employment, and welfare aid policies in the various states, have also contributed to the movement of families from community to community, state to state, and one part of the United States to another. This movement of families has brought children together in school from many different parts of the country. Frequently, their speech patterns, attitudes, and customs are also greatly different. The longer children are in school, the more some of them have moved. The diversity in backgrounds of pupils, due to the mobility of our population, therefore, increases as pupils reach the junior high school.

There was a time when disadvantaged children were found primarily in rural areas. The child in the one room school, for instance, usually had educational opportunities inferior to those in the cities. It is in the cities today, however, that we find large concentrations of children with backgrounds that we consider disadvantaged. There are several reasons for this. First, the concentration in our cities of large numbers of families with low incomes alone creates a problem. Second, young adolescents in the cities are not kept busy at useful activities like they were in rural areas. Third, as families move to the cities, they often leave behind the relatives, friends, church affiliations, and community interests which provide stability to children and youth. The disadvantages youth may have had in their family backgrounds, therefore, are intensified by their concentration in the inner cities.

Disadvantaged youth present a particularly serious problem in the junior high school because, at this age, their educational, cultural, and family limitations show up more sharply. As disadvantaged youth approach the upper compulsory attendance age, they find themselves frequently unhappy in a school situation that, to them, becomes increasingly difficult. The program of the junior high school, therefore, assumes added importance for disadvantaged youth because their satisfaction and success here may determine whether or not they will continue their education into the senior high school and beyond. It is this responsibility for youth, with increasing diversity in home backgrounds, educational experiences, and motivation to remain in school, that presents the

[2]United States Office of Education, *Digest of Educational Statistics,* 1965, Washington, D. C.: Office of Education, 1965, p. 124.

greatest challenge for curriculum development in the junior high school.

Programs for the Able Pupils

The junior high school has, in recent years, introduced more new programs to meet the diversity in backgrounds and abilities of individual pupils than during any other period in its history. These programs are of many different kinds and are intended to serve the needs of many different pupils. They include programs for the more able pupils, the mentally retarded, the disadvantaged, the potential dropouts, and others. These programs should be examined by educators concerned with the junior high school curriculum.

The programs for the more able pupils, encouraged especially in the late 1950's by the emergence of space science, have received particularly wide acceptance in the junior high school. A study in 1964 revealed that 78 per cent of the junior high schools in the United States have introduced such programs, most of them since 1957.[3] Usually referred to as honors classes, they are offered most frequently in mathematics, English, and science. Most schools have honors classes to provide enrichment for the more able pupils, although in a few schools honors pupils complete the junior high school program earlier. Honors pupils in the junior high school usually take further honors work or advanced placement courses in the senior high school.

Honors classes are so new that they still present many problems. These problems include increased pressure for academic achievement, lack of a satisfactory policy for marking pupil achievement, and pressure from parents to have their children admitted to such classes even though they may not be qualified. In most schools many pupils are placed in honors classes to maintain a group of typical class size. This is indeed a mistake. The marginal pupil in the honors class is likely to suffer from the competition in such a group. Most schools place 10 to 15 per cent of the student body in honors classes. This seems high for the character of work usually demanded in such classes. Honors classes should be limited to the pupils with the motivation, ability, and health which such classes demand, even though the number of qualified pupils is insufficient to form classes of typical size.

In most schools, the approach in honors classes consists primarily of more work for the pupils, frequently as assigned homework. The pupils in honors classes are the ones, however, who are busy in other activities in school, the church, and the community. Furthermore, they have the same need for recreation and rest consistent with good health as pupils of less ability. In fact, the pressures of the honors class may demand more rest for these pupils.

[3]Based on data from the survey of junior high school education by Gruhn and Douglass.

Teachers should find more challenging approaches for the honors classes, rather than emphasizing more readings, longer assignments, and increased homework.

Programs for the Mentally Retarded

The only provision for mentally retarded pupils in small communities, until recently, was in special schools provided by the state. Today, almost every community which has junior high schools offers programs for mentally retarded pupils. Large junior high schools have their own classes, while smaller schools may have combined classes for such pupils.

The important development in present programs for the mentally retarded is that these pupils are retained in typical school situations as long as possible. It is recognized that most mentally retarded youth will live in a typical adult society, many of them supporting themselves and participating in community life. The best preparation for adult life for the mentally retarded, therefore, for many of them can be offered as part of a typical junior high school program.

The emphasis in programs for the mentally retarded today is to teach them occupational skills so that they may find employment when they leave school. Some junior high schools actually have work experience programs for these pupils, to help them make occupational adjustments under the supervision of the school. The approach to the education of the mentally retarded in the junior high school, therefore, is quite different from that of a generation ago when these children received little more than custodial care or withdrew from school.

Programs for Problem Youth

The most unique development in the junior high school curriculum in the last decade has been the programs for disadvantaged youth, socially maladjusted pupils and potential dropouts. These programs in most schools are very new. We have had, therefore, little experience with them. The success of such programs in some schools reveals, however, that much can be done to improve the educational and cultural backgrounds of disadvantaged youth. Potential dropouts, these programs show, can find sufficient success in school to be motivated to continue their education. Programs for socially maladjusted pupils likewise have been quite successful.

What is of most importance in working with problem youth is to recognize that each one is an individual case, demanding much individual help and attention. Classes for these pupils must be small, they should spend more time with one teacher, the curriculum requirements should be flexible, guidance personnel need to be continually in touch with these pupils and their teachers, and teachers must develop skill in working with each pupil as an individual. Programs for problem youth demand, therefore, imagination by teachers, flexibility in program, and adequate professional staff for unique pupil problems.

Problems of Social Sophistication

The problem of early social sophistication of youth has received much attention from educators, psychologists, sociologists and parents. That a problem exists no one seems to deny. The question is what the school should do about it.

This problem is especially important in the junior high school because it is during early adolescence when problems of social sophistication usually emerge. For many youth the junior high school is, furthermore, the last opportunity in the formal program of education where they can be helped with such problems. Because the extraclass activities are the place in the junior high school program where social sophistication seems of most concern, this problem has received little direct attention in the curriculum.

There are areas of study, however, where certain aspects of early sophistication may well receive some attention. The social studies program could emphasize better human relations, attitudes of good citizenship, and responsibility as citizens outside the school. The language arts class can emphasize good speech as a basis for better personal relations, attitudes of courtesy and consideration for others, and wholesome boy-girl relationships. Science, home economics, and health classes can give some attention to personal habits, information about sex that serves for wholesome boy-girl relationships, and personal grooming. Physical education may be an appropriate place to study personal appearance, posture, and health related to narcotics and alcohol. For the moment it is not so important precisely what should be done. It is important to recognize that there is a problem and that the school—especially the junior high school—should assume some responsibility for it.

Conclusion

These then are some aspects of curriculum development in the junior high school which are now receiving attention from curriculum workers. Progress is being made on some of these problems. Others have emerged so recently that we have done little to meet them. It is important to realize, however, that curriculum development for young adolescents is now, as always, a challenge to educators and parents.

Modernizing English Instruction*

MICHAEL C. FLANIGAN

In 1963 the Federal government granted $47,000 to Euclid Central Junior High School and Western Reserve University to demonstrate improved methods of English instruction. As a result an organization was created that was a part of Project English. The newly formed organization was called the Project English Demonstration Center, and was the only organization of its kind in the country. It was created to give teachers and administrators a chance to observe and discuss some improved and new methods and materials in English being used in a typical junior high school.

Six weekend conferences were held throughout the school year 1963-1964 and participants were given the opportunity to observe remedial, average, and academically talented classes. Noted experts in the field of English were available for group discussions of topics such as literary meaning, genre, remedial reading, composition, linguistics, honors programs, and a host of other topics of immediate importance to classroom teachers and administrators.

At each conference, participants were given copies of thematic units including ideational units, literary form units, and language study units. It was hoped that the units would be studied by the teachers and then used in their schools. It was also hoped that if the units made available were difficult to implement, the teachers would construct their own units around principles that had been formulated at the conferences.

Over 700 people—teachers, principals, and superintendents—attended the conferences, which began Thursday and ended Saturday. Many of these people took the ideas and materials developed at the Center and implemented them in their schools. Because of the enthusiastic response of most participants, the Demonstration Center was given an increased grant of $57,000 for the 1964-1965 school year.

*Reprinted from *The Clearing House,* 39 (November 1965), 167-169, by permission of the publisher.

The Center held one conference in October, 1964, entitled "Semantics and Symbolism." Three week-long conferences entitled "Research in English," "Forms and Symbol: Modern Approaches to Literature," and "Composition" were held in February, March, and April of 1965. In addition, four more three-day conferences, entitled "Language Structures," "A Concept Centered Curriculum," "Reading Skills," and "Approaches to Composition," were offered in January, February, April, and May of the same year.

The Demonstration Center uses four basic principles that it feels are essential to any vigorous and stimulating English curriculum.

The first basic principle is the idea that students must be taught approaches to meaning in order to evaluate literature and language critically. Many English curricula in junior and senior high schools simply teach students skills that they have already developed, and as a result students learn no new approaches to literature. As Wendell Johnson states in *People in Quandaries:*

> Education has been chiefly a matter of compelling the child to conform to the ways of his elders. The student has been taught answers, not questions. At least, when questions have been taught, the answers have been given in the back of the book. In the main, knowledge has been given the student, but not a method for adding to it or revising it—except the method of authority, of going to the book, of asking the Old Man. The chief aim of education has been to make of the child another Old Man, to pour the new wines of possibility into the old bottles of tradition.

The education Wendell Johnson refers to may have its place, but it would be difficult to produce students who can think critically if we relied on it solely. Therefore, we must teach new skills.

By the time they enter junior high school most average students have gained enough skill to read any newspaper or other kind of popular literature with which they are likely to come in contact. Students entering junior high also have the ability to read for main ideas and important details and can make simple inferences. The duty of the secondary school teacher is not to continue teaching these same skills, but to teach new skills that will give the student insights into the meanings of the many works of literature he will be exposed to. The student must be taught to function on his own. He must learn the more sophisticated techniques of discovering meaning in a poem, short story, or novel. The student must learn the structural areas of literature—the picture of man produced by the writer, levels of meaning, and form and genre. After the student has been systematically taught these approaches, he should be able to apply them to any literary work and should not need the teacher to point out the meaning.

Another basic principle of the Demonstration Center is the idea that language units should be used for the average students as well as for exceptional students. In order to introduce students to what their language is, what it can do for them, and how it can be abused, units have been created in the areas of semantics, dialects, morphology, syntax, and language history. In the semantics units, which build upon each other from the seventh to the ninth grades, the student learns about phenomena such as symbols, referents, reports, judgments, connotations, propaganda, euphemisms, slang, generalizations, assumptions, and deductive and inductive argumentative techniques. He is taught methods of determining an author's purpose, to question that purpose, and then to subject the purpose to close scrutiny.

The other language units are structured in such a way as to involve the students as much as possible. In the unit on language history, for example, the students learn about change in language. Then they try to create change by inventing and using a new word that they have created themselves and given meaning to. They finally evaluate whether their word was successfully introduced into the language or not. They must explain why they think the word did or did not catch on. In this kind of situation the student becomes the scientist of language. He sets up the experiment, observes it in action, and then evaluates the results.

The student is again taught a method of approach, but the final test of whether the student has learned or not is whether he can apply what he has learned. This idea that student independence should be an ultimate goal in teaching is another basic principle incorporated in the units created at the Euclid Central Demonstration Center. Units are designed so that the entire class begins to work with a concept, then the students are separated into groups to apply the concept to a new problem, and finally each student is required to apply the concept independently to an unfamiliar situation. This method seems most sensible, since students will eventually be on their own. When the students have left the school, the teacher will not be there to help them. The students must apply concepts and find meaning by themselves if the written word is to have any personal value to them.

To discuss fully all the principles that form a basis for the curriculum of the Demonstration Center would take more space than is practical here. But one last basic principle should be considered, because it has guided the creation of much of the material used and distributed by the Demonstration Center.

Most units created for the average student by the Center are thematic. Specific themes such as power, courage, coming of age, justice, the outcast, survival, protest, and man in society are used as the nucleus for teaching reading and writing skills. Although thematic units are not new to teachers of English, the thematic units of the Demonstration Center offer one unique approach to their use—they form the core of the entire curriculum. The theme is the focal point that students must refer to, time after time. They may branch out and ask new questions, but the central theme remains to indicate a direction for questioning, discussion, and composition.

The principles of the Demonstration Center have been expounded for years by many educators, but rarely have all of them been incorporated in a curriculum for average and exceptional children. It is necessary to use these principles in teaching English if we are to produce students who have the ability to approach language critically and who are able to derive the utmost meaning from what they read.

The Uses and Abuses of Junior Literature*

HARVEY R. GRANITE

Let me begin by defining what I mean by junior literature, since it is a term with many possible meanings. Generally "junior literature" refers to books written specifically for adolescents. Publishers often suggest appropriate age-levels at which the books may be used—11-14, 12-16, 13-15. Occasionally junior literature is written by authors who have distinguished themselves in other fields; Nat Hentoff, Randall Jarell, C. Day Lewis, and Bruce Catton are among the journalists, poets, and historians who have published junior fiction in recent years. Most junior literature, however, is written by specialists—skillful literary technicians who often produce two or three volumes a year, sometimes in response to a particular need indicated by publishers' surveys.

At present, many junior writers are busily grinding out thinly fictionalized tracts on such subjects as brotherhood and the evils of teen-age alcoholism. Tendentious, sentimental, stereotyped, and often wretchedly written, most junior fiction is literature only in the broadest sense of the term. Its chief raison d'être is that it offers reading to the young which their elders approve. It is with the latter kind of junior literature that this article deals.

My position on junior literature can be stated quite simply: adolescents have as much right to read bad books—hack written, stereotyped bits of slick fiction—as do adults. Adults read Irving Wallace, Leon Uris, Anya Seton, Frank Yerby, Harold Robbins; adolescents—those who are not allowed by parents or by censorship laws to read adult slicks—read Rosamund DuJardin, Betty Cavanna, Howard Pease, Henry G. Felsen, and Geoffrey Trease. These, along with the mass magazines, are the printed between-covers equivalents of other forms of popular culture: *Gidget* and *Green Acres* on television; Doris Day and

*Reprinted from *The Clearing House,* 42 (February 1968), 337-340, by permission of the publisher and Harvey R. Granite, consultant, City School District, Rochester, New York.

Beach Blanket Bingo in the movies; Perry Como and the Rolling Stones on disk-jockey radio. I would not use Perry Como in a music appreciation class, except perhaps by way of illustration, and I would not use Henry Felsen as "literature."

No one pretends that *Peyton Place* in either its printed or its televised version is great art. Its purpose is recreatory. It stimulates us or relaxes us or satisfies our desire to snoop into the kinds of lives which hack fiction-writers have led us to believe realistically portray the American people. *Peyton Place* and its antiseptic counterparts in the world of adolescents are entertainments—to use Graham Greene's description of the money-making melodramas that made possible his early serious fiction. They might better be characterized as soap opera than as literature. Literature, whether aimed at the young or the mature, focuses in some way, in a variety of ways, upon the human condition. Literature raises questions about identity, about purpose, about the meaning of existence Avoiding the great questions, *Peyton Place* and *Beach Blanket Bingo* instead plunge us into a flat two-dimensional world of unreality.

To the extent that an army of authors otherwise unknown to the general public finds a steady market among the school and public librarians who continue to be the major purchasers of junior fiction, we shall continue to have a good deal of it around. Ironically, more junior fiction is being published today than ever before, in an era when the paperback revolution has largely rendered such fiction obsolete by making it easier to buy a book than to borrow one. Librarians themselves, however, are beginning to look with suspicion upon the junior book. The Newbery Award, for example, is an award given each year to the most distinguished work written for young people. Even though awarded by librarians, the Newbery Award is often referred to by other librarians who watch circulation records as one given to "the best juvenile books for adult readers." The fact that so few award winners become popular suggests that adult judges don't always know what young people like to read.

Perhaps the same is true for English teachers. Perhaps we don't always know what our students want to read. Perhaps in an effort to convince young people that "Reading can be fun" many English teachers have been emphasizing adolescent fiction in sets with their classes, often scrutinizing such lightweight works as Dorothy Sterling's *Mary Jane* and Henry Felsen's *Hot Rod* with an intensity and a reverence that should be reserved for *The Adventures of Huckleberry Finn* or *Intruder in the Dust*.

Adolescent fiction may have its uses in the teaching of reading. Books such as *Hot Rod* or *Sorority Rebel* or *Boy Trouble* or *It can Happen to Anyone* or *A Time for Tenderness* or *The Beau Collector* may be the only book which a reluctant reader, bored stiff at fourteen by public school education, will even look at. Such books, however, are not meant to serve as an introduction to literature. They have no more place in the English program than do SRA kits or reading pacers. At best they are remedial. If the adolescent reads *Crash Club* or

A Picnic for Judy, convinces himself that the mere act of reading is not painful, perhaps even chooses another, some progress has been made. So many of the articles about reluctant readers in educational journals used to turn out that way—*"Gee," I heard one exclaim as he left my class that morning, "reading books ain't so bad after all."* During the last five years, however, some English teachers have reminded themselves that, even when working with students from impoverished homes, they are concerned with more than the mere act of reading.

Having helped the reluctant reader over that first hurdle, many teachers forget to ask themselves why they want him to be a better reader. If he never reads a better book, if he graduates from hack adolescent to hack adult literature, if he actually regresses, as so many high school terminal graduates do, from *Shane* to Zane Grey, what has he been taught? Has he learned how to read a good book? Has he gained any understanding of the richness and complexity of human existence reflected in great literature? Has he learned anything about himself, about his own values, about his direction, about those many concerns with war and injustice and conformity with which the adolescent's own major expression in mass culture today, the rock-and-roll song, is so frequently and eloquently charged? When we listen to the voice of the teen-ager through the lips of Bob Dylan, Joan Baez, The Byrds, and other folk and rock artists, we realize how much the teen-ager's concerns are still those of the major issues of our society—survival and self-identification. Most adolescent fiction avoids the major issues or covers them over with a syrup of sentiment.

I would like to suggest another definition of literature for the adolescent: A good book for an adolescent is any *worthwhile book,* juvenile, adolescent, or adult, which he is capable of reading and understanding on his own level. It is a book which responds to exploration, one in which the formal and artistic elements are significant enough to yield insight into how a literary artist works, one in which the content sincerely and honestly touches upon at least some of the important human questions with which all great literature must deal.

Paradoxically there are many such books still classed as children's literature: *Alice in Wonderland, The Little Prince, The Wind in the Willows*—but none that I have discovered which can be considered adolescent literature in terms of the definition I suggested earlier. The books to which adolescents of the last 10 or 15 years seem most often to turn were written originally for adults, or, to put it more precisely, were written as complete and mature literary statements. Novels such as *The Catcher in the Rye, A Separate Peace, Lord of the Flies,* and *Look Homeward, Angel* were never conceived of by their authors as "adolescent," even though they deal with adolescents. And it is precisely because they are mature statements, dealing with discovery and self-realization, without pat answers, without formulae, that students respond to them.

A teacher can delude herself into confusing relief from boredom with genuine love of reading. If a group of students, after spending several years making conventional responses to teacher-guide questions about *Ivanhoe* or *David Copperfield* are offered a novel such as Florence Crannel Means's *Tolliver,* which at least purports to deal with the race question in terms of today's teen-ager, of course they'll respond positively. But they are not, in dealing with *Tolliver,* engaged in the study of literature, as they could be by reading the flawed but powerful *Native Son* by Richard Wright. Not only is *Native Son* more significant as literature, but it is also more honest. John Howard Griffin's *Black Like Me* and Dick Gregory's *Nigger* are neither of them "junior" or "adolescent," but they reach the young as no junior biography can. These books are real. They are also embarrassing to many adults, including teachers.

There are many books which reach young people, which make them want to read, and which at the same time enable the English teacher to "bridge the distances between good books and the immaturity of his students," a responsibility which *Freedom and Discipline in English* calls "his primary duty as a teacher of literature." The choice of books and the method of presentation depend, of course, upon the level of reading ability, the maturity of the children, and the skill of the teacher. If tenth graders, for example, cannot read above a third or fourth grade level, the teacher may need to spend much of her time reading aloud. Mark Twain, Jack London, and John Steinbeck, whose styles adapt well to oral reading, often deal with working people as heroes without patronizing or sentimentalizing them. Inner-city youths can respond to the elemental will to live which London depicts in *The Call of the Wild* or in his stories "Love of Life" and "To Build a Fire." They too are fighting to survive in an Arctic of human indifference. Teachers who have used *Of Mice and Men* with slum children are often gratified at the insights which deprived students bring to Steinbeck's portrayal of loyalty, longing, and suffering among migratory workers. Better readers among junior high school students can read Steinbeck's *The Red Pony,* Marjorie Kinnan Rawling's *The Yearling,* and Conrad Richter's *The Light in the Forest.* Each of these is a respectable work of fiction holding special attraction for young readers. Older students, as they become more aware of social questions, find answers in books such as Upton Sinclair's *The Jungle,* James Baldwin's *Go Tell it on the Mountain,* George Orwell's *Animal Farm* and *1984,* Aldous Huxley's *Brave New World,* Frank Norris's *McTeague,* Theodore Dreiser's *Sister Carrie,* and Alan Paton's *Cry, the Beloved Country.*

There are two kinds of novels which are successful with juniors and seniors from the inner city, at least those whom I have taught. One group includes works which have received some degree of serious critical recognition, such as those discussed above, to which might be added Hemingway's *The Old Man and the Sea,* Wharton's *Ethan Frome,* and O'Flaherty's *The Informer.* The other group is of less celebrated but nonetheless mature works such as Monsarrat's *The Cruel Sea,* Pat Frank's *Alas, Babylon!,* and Knebel and Bailey's *Seven Days in May.* These novels, while "popular" in intent, deal straightforwardly with significant issues and promote discussion in the classroom. One of the peculiarities of most junior fiction is that it contains so little to discuss, Once read, most adolescent novels are forgetten.

Is there a place for adolescent literature in the English program? Yes, if by adolescent literature we mean literature appropriate for the adolescent, rather than the superficial romances written specifically for the adolescent. About most junior fiction, the Commission on English in *Freedom and Discipline in English* states: "For classes in remedial reading a resort to such books may be necessary, but to make them a considerable part of the curriculum for most students is to subvert the purposes for which literature is included in the first place. In the high school years, the aim should be not to find the students' level so much as to raise it, and such books rarely elevate."

As English teachers our job is not to entertain our students, but to teach them. Attitudes of pity or of false sympathy, particularly toward the slum child, are often disguised excuses for poor teaching. The disadvantaged student needs a strong program taught by skillful teachers, not a program of the third-rate, which insults his intelligence and denies him his potential.

Junior High School Mathematics

ALVIN W. HOWARD

Among those arguments for reorganization of schools which resulted in the establishing of the junior high school, one point frequently made was that grades seven and eight were too much oriented toward review and were, therefore, wasteful of time, dull, and repetitious. There was more than a germ of truth in this, especially as it concerned the mathematics curriculum.

One anticipated and hoped for result of the introduction of the junior high school was the movement downward into grades seven and eight of such academic courses as Latin, algebra, and geometry, since there was a strong feeling that grades seven and eight, the last two grades of elementary school, were lacking in clearcut curricula and objectives, and contained much duplication of content.

In the earlier days of the country, in colonial times and those of westward expansion, any education was a mark of achievement for the common man, and the ability to read, write, and to use arithmetic was a real accomplishment. Mathematics was taught as a mechanical technique and mathematical literacy was considered essential primarily for such purposes as navigation, surveying, engineering, and keeping books. Seventh and eighth grade courses by 1900, particularly in mathematics, were largely repetition and review and introduced but little in new material.

To an extent the hopes of the academicians were realized and in those early days in many schools the mathematics programs were revised and broadened as a part of the program of the new junior high schools. By the third and fourth decades of this century many of the same criticisms were again being voiced concerning the seventh and eighth grade curriculum in mathematics, with the added complaint that, in their efforts to make these courses practical, teachers were stressing the utilitarian features to the detriment of any real understanding of concepts of mathematics. In 1951 a group at the University of Illinois, under the direction of Max Beberman, began to develop a new curriculum, The University of Illinois Committee on Mathematics Study (the

UICMS program) which has since been followed by a variety of studies, proposals, and revisions.

The traditional mathematics programs were criticized because:

1. The program of mathematics for those students who were college bound remained relatively unchanged for over 50 years.

2. The student who did not plan to go to college found open to him only such courses in mathematics as were mostly rehashes of the arithmetic he had studied in elementary school, with occasionally some additional material on income tax, installment buying, and family budgeting.

3. There was an almost complete neglect of the cultural and esthetic aspects of mathematics. Little was taught concerning the history of mathematics or the contributions of famous mathematicians.

4. The curriculum for junior high school mathematics had evolved into a mechanically applied collection of unrelated rules and techniques which was narrow in scope, duplicatory, and boring.

The "new" mathematics, it has been said, involves nothing that is really mathematically new—all within the new mathematics has been known for years. What is "new" is the intensified interest in reorganizing the mathematics curriculum, the reduction in interest in some topics and the increased stress upon other topics which had previously been slighted. As has been the case in so many other differences, enthusiasts claim that this is not true, that mathematicians are continually creating new mathematics, and that more than half the mathematics today has been created during the twentieth century.

The several experimental projects and proposals for the new mathematics have provided some general conclusions and exhibit some common characteristics:

1. It has become apparent that junior high school students are capable of much more sophisticated reasoning than was formerly believed to be the case.

2. There is a stress upon making the language of mathematics more precise.

3. New applications are given to old ideas.

4. There is elimination of obsolete topics, and new material is added.

5. There *are* "new" mathematics included.

6. More mathematics may be taught in a shorter time.

7. There is increased stress upon the structure of mathematics.

8. The student is expected to discover mathematical relationships.

9. An added benefit is the widespread involvement of interested people, including college and public school personnel, in the revision and improvement of the mathematics curriculum.

There has been criticism of the new mathematics by those who say that this approach eliminates most of the social applications from the curriculum, that there is a concentration upon the college bound, and that there is too much thinking in terms of future mathematicians instead of the average citizen.

The trends in mathematics in junior high school include:

1. An adoption of one of the new programs for all three junior high school grades.
2. More diversity and a changed content in the mathematics curriculum.
3. Implementation of a "new" mathematics program for all ability levels of the junior high.
4. Acceleration of work to encourage better mathematics students to take algebra in grade eight and geometry in grade nine.
5. Inclusion of a course in consumer education or business mathematics, which may be elective or required.
6. A realization that the mathematics to be taught should not be the same for all students.
7. A movement toward the discovery or induction approach in developing new material.
8. More time is spent on developmental activities—experiences designed to improve student understanding.

The approach must be one of development of understandings and mathematical concepts rather than mechanical manipulations, and the junior high curriculum should include opportunities both for those who wish to puruse advanced studies in mathematics and for those who will probably not finish high school and are in real need of consumer mathematics.

Innovations in Junior High Science*

ROBERT E. YAGER

In October of 1966 seven junior high schools in Iowa began instruction with a completely new approach and new materials for their science programs. Ten teachers from the seven schools organized as the Iowa Test Center for a national curriculum study at the junior high school level in science. The program is centered at Florida State University in Tallahassee where a permanent staff is engaged during the academic year following an intensive three month writing conference during the summer of 1966. The materials used in the classrooms this year were newly written during the summer by a team of scientists, teachers, educators, and psychologists. The resulting program has many exciting features.

The seventh grade course is the only one which is in operation during the 1966-67 school year. However, during 1967-68 the new eighth year materials will be ready for use as will the ninth grade materials during 1968-69. Following each year's use the materials for each grade level will be completely rewritten reflecting the strengths and weaknesses as identified during classroom trial.

Participating Iowa Schools

The schools involved in the impressive program in Iowa include Bennett, Maquoketa, Marengo, Mount Vernon, Tipton, West Des Moines (Stillwell Junior High), and Williamsburg. The administrators and teachers in these schools were convinced that major correctives were needed in the junior high science program and that the Florida materials represented a significant step in this direction. The 10 teachers from the cities and towns previously mentioned include: Robert Hannes, Bennett; Randall Zirkelbach, Maquoketa; Charles Kline, Marengo;

*Reprinted from *Midland Schools* 81 (March-April 1967), 28-32, by permission of the publisher and Robert E. Yager, University of Iowa.

Mrs. Beverly Phillips, Mount Vernon; James DeReus, Tipton; Clare Barrett, West Des Moines; Mrs. Clarice Plager, West Des Moines; James Underfer, West Des Moines; Carroll Scott, Williamsburg; and Arthur Hutton, Williamsburg.

The Test Center

The test center headquarters is in Iowa City under the direction of the author and Jerry Underfer of the Science Education Department of the University of Iowa. Dr. William Deskin, professor of Chemistry at Cornell College, one of the writers at Tallahassee last summer, is able to provide valuable assistance with the operation of the Iowa Test Center since he has been directly involved with the preparation of the new materials.

The teachers meet bimonthly to receive equipment, to share ideas concerning their experience, and to prepare center evaluation reports that are forwarded to Florida. In addition to the classroom evaluation, an extensive testing program has been devised in order to collect specific kinds of information which will assist in the identification of specific outcomes and strengths of the new program.

Features of the Florida Project

The Florida State Junior High Curriculum Project is unique in many respects. It is the first of the so-called national curriculum programs at the secondary level to represent something more than the preparation of course materials for an existing course in the traditional curricular sequence. A continuing course for each of the three years in grades seven, eight, and nine is planned. The rationale for the sequence includes the fact that the elementary program is usually taught by a non-specialist in self-contained classrooms. In addition, the junior high sequence in most schools is followed by a general education biology course in grade 10. This emphasis in biology at grade 10 has resulted in a decrease in emphasis upon the life sciences in the sequence.

Another important feature of the project is the laboratory nature of the classroom. Each student works at his own rate in progressing through the investigative activities. The textbook includes many questions for the student to answer as he performs the various manipulations. The students progress individually with the primary role of the teacher being one of insuring that the student has an understanding of his work before he proceeds. Class discussions are infrequent; discussions with small groups of students or even with individual students are frequent. Examinations and similar types of evaluation occur only at the discretion of the teacher and are not generally a part of the program as it has evolved to date.

So-called "excursions" provide another innovation for the program. The excursions are supplementary experiences provided for the more gifted students. They provide a means for such students to carry the thought process and the experimentation to a further level. In addition to enrichment, the excursions provide a means for keeping the class together, to some degree at least.

The increased emphasis upon the laboratory approach to learning, the new role for the teacher, and the new means for providing for individual differences are exciting innovations which are being tried in the seven Iowa schools. Results of this experiment are exciting and encouraging to date. Undoubtedly there will be extensive revisions in the program materials before they appear in published form ready for general usage. However, this is the point of the classroom trials and the test center program.

Energy Is Seventh Grade Theme

The basic content theme of the seventh grade course is that of energy. All of the ideas, experiences, and techniques included are channeled into building an understanding of the concept energy, and particularly to revealing the power which this notion provides in interpreting dynamic situations of all types.

The content is organized into three distinct parts. In Phase I the general notion of work is introduced and operationally defined in a mechanical sense. Ultimately, through the vehicle of "work storage," the student is led to a simple operational definition for energy as the "cause of work." In Phase II the student is first shown that work can be accomplished through the use of heat, light, electricity, and chemical reactions, and these quantities are incorporated into his concept of energy. In addition, he is made aware of some of the more important descriptive aspects of these forms of energy, and he is finally shown that they are inter-convertible and that this conversion process proceeds in a predictable fashion with the ultimate degradation product being heat. In Phase III the student looks intensively at the question of why heat recurs so frequently as a by-product of energy conversion processes. He begins by exploring the various effects which heat has upon matter and is led to differentiate between heat and temperature. The course culminates with the student building (actually being given) a simple particule model for matter which he uses as a basis for explaining as many as possible of the heat and energy phenomena he has observed.

Eighth and Ninth Grade Courses

Although the eighth and ninth grade courses have not been prepared, the general format has been identified. The eighth grade course will deal with the structure of matter and will develop as a definite continuation of the seventh grade course. However, the direction of the investigations will be toward less structure. This will lead to the ninth grade course which will be almost non-structured. It will suggest areas for individual research study where the more complex sciences of the earth and of life will be introduced. In a sense the basic physical sciences will be applied to new situations where the student will be called upon to utilize his content and laboratory background in a new situation.

Scientist's Approach Emphasized

Certain organizing principles were identified as the new program was proposed. The fundamental assumption underlying the Florida State curriculum plan was that *science at the junior high school level serves essentially a general education function.* There are obviously other important needs to be met by such a science program and some of these argue for various types of specialized science instruction, but the Florida materials were organized around the belief that the *science curriculum in the junior high school should have as its central purpose the development in all students of a valid understanding of the nature of modern science and of the methods by which scientific knowledge is obtained.* The writers believed that the only way a student can gain a *real* understanding of science and the scientific approach to problem solving is for him to operate as a scientist does. This means that the use of reasoning and experimentation should be an important and inevitable feature of the materials developed for all grade levels.

Although the project leaders aimed to produce a course involving relatively inexpensive teaching devices, they did not plan to allow the limitations which exist in most present day junior high schools with regard to time, space, facilities, and equipment to severely limit their efforts. They assumed that changes in these matters can be made by school administrators and the taxpayers whom they represent if significant improvements in curriculum and related matters can be demonstrated and if the requested changes are realistic. Throughout the work the primary considerations were the characteristics of the learner and the nature of the science to be taught.

A key premise underlying the plan is that true scientific literacy depends upon the student's ability to successfully accomplish the intellectual transition which he must make during the junior high school years. This age level has long been recognized as a transitional one in phsyical and mental development by psychologists and perceptive teachers and parents. Without question, the child who enters the junior high school at the beginning of the seventh grade is quite different from the one who leaves at the end of the ninth grade. The writers of the new material intend to take full cognizance of the transition which the junior high school student undergoes as he moves from grade to grade. The plan assumes that seventh grade science curriculum materials must be fundamentally different from those designed for the ninth grade level.

The Florida State University program at all grade levels deals both with scientific knowledge and the process by which scientific information is unearthed, but the sophistication in approach and relative emphasis upon these two aspects of content will vary systematically from grade to grade. As the child proceeds from grade seven to grade nine the emphasis upon the formal teaching of the scientific process skills will become more casual, and the emphasis upon knowledge will proceed from relatively simple and basic situations to a series of laboratory-centered problems at a more sophisticated level from which the solution is to be achieved by the students' utilizing the tool kit of processes and knowledge which he has acquired up to that point.

Individual Effort and Attention

The pedagogical style which has been built into the materials involves providing the student with a sequence of content, or "story line," along with a fairly clear blueprint as to how he is to proceed in setting up laboratory equipment, interpreting data, etc. Hopefully this will help to free the teacher to work with individual students as they encounter specific difficulties. The concept of the teaching-learning situation is one in which much of the student's work is independent, with the teacher moving from individual to individual giving clues, answering questions, correcting misconceptions, and extending concepts to new situations.

Skill Development Process Outlined

The seventh and eighth grade materials already completed, those currently under development, and those to be completed later will have two dimensions: first, to define and give the student practice in using certain intellectual skills important in the scientific process and to help him to integrate these skills into relatively high level cognitive activity; and, second, to develop an understanding of selected basic science principles and to help the student to order these principles into major generalizations. The specific process skills which are incorporated into the three year program are as follows:

a. Recognition of significant problems in science

b. Delimiting and defining of broad problems in science to levels which allow attack by empirical means (particular attention will be given to such tools as operational definition and the systems and their relevance to this process)

c. The ability to state testable hypotheses upon which critical experiments may be designed

d. The design and conduct of experiments which yield data approximate to the testing of hypotheses

e. Interpretation of data obtained from experiments and other measurements of nature to the level of simple statistical techniques

f. Drawing conclusions from a relevant set of data and the ordering of such conclusions into generalizations

g. Testing the general applicability of conclusions drawn from limited data

h. The building of scientific "models" (with particular emphasis upon the advantages which such models provide in scientific investigation and their tentative nature)

Every effort is made to show the student how the individual skills are related to the total scientific process and, therefore, to one another. To accomplish this, more encompassing skills will be used as organizing themes for the more limited ones. In the seventh grade-materials that have been written, for example, the process organizing theme is "operational definition." All of the student's hypothesizing, experimenting, data analysis, and use of the other skills has been channeled into developing a rather simple operational definition for energy which explains the observations of forces which he has made. All materials for the course will be designed to broaden and deepen the student's concept of energy and to bring his operational definition more in line with that held by the scientist. The proposed process organizing theme for the eighth grade materials is "model building."

Four other centers are experimenting with the new material during the 1966-67 year. These other centers are located in Chicago, Indianapolis, Sarasota (Florida), and in the New Hampshire area. Dr. Ernest Burkman at Florida State University is director of the project which is funded by the U.S. Office of Education. The Iowa center is interesting because of the diverse nature of the schools in terms of size, setting, and previous offerings. Each of the schools and each of the teachers is to be commended for the part they are playing in a most promising innovation in junior high science. Progress can only be made when schools, teachers, and the supporting public are interested in assisting with such trials of an exciting idea. Schools, teachers, and students will share in the development of whatever final outcomes evolve from the attempt with the revision. The schools and teachers are sure to grow in such professional cooperation. However, the students stand the chance for the most benefit as they consider science with additional dimensions.

Music—The Uncommon Denominator in Secondary Education *

JOSEPH W. LANDON

The increasing complexity and lockstep seemingly inherent in secondary schools of the 1960's pose a variety of concerns related to the direction of curriculum. In the tight, traditional schedule patterns and rigid academic requirements imposed by higher education, many are beginning to question whether aesthetic and humanistic studies per se can long survive. This poses a strange dichotomy which is complicated by utterances from a variety of practitioners of the practical arts and sciences who claim even greater need for persons of broad perspective and liberal training.

Fortunately, the future is not especially bleak, provided that educators begin to face the facts of life and recognize that we cannot long adhere to the antiquated educational patterns to achieve a job which society and the schools say is essential. It will take, however, courage, creativity, resourcefulness and a high degree of concern for primary values rather than stereotyped educational patterns.

It seems to be generally accepted that music and the allied arts must play a significant role in the high school of today, as well as in the future. Certainly, few would disagree with the need of students for an understanding of the important role played by the creative endeavors of mankind. Obviously, these studies should be of real significance to students and must not be allowed to play the superficial role sometimes popularized in the peripheral artistic "trappings" of modern society.

The majority of students in secondary schools of today have need for courses which provide for skills, attitudes, habits and understandings in such areas as:

*Reprinted from *The Journal of Secondary Education,* 40 (February 1965), 57-61, by permission of the publisher and Joseph W. Landon, California State College at Fullerton.

Communications and rational processes of reasoning
Man's role in society
The natural and physical world
The humanities and arts
The human body and its care
One's future occupational goals and needs

Music, as one of the important areas of man's artistic development, deserves an important place in the curriculum of the secondary school. Since the importance of music is best assimilated through those unique qualities which make it an aural (or "performed") art, music must be performed to become alive. This is not to say that it should not be discussed, but rather that it has a basic medium of communication which is devoid of semantic barriers. Performance, however, cannot be confined to performance groups per se, but must be interpreted more broadly to include performances *for* as well as *by* those who participate in a musical experience. In the context of its curricular application, the various classes in music need moreover to develop aesthetic principles, skills and understandings which will provide a more diverse and broadening experience for the students of our secondary schools.

Planning of the secondary school music curriculum should be patterned from a carefully drawn blueprint which provides suitable balance between as well as within various courses. Although a common general pattern of acculturation through the study of musical aesthetics is possible, considerable latitude must be provided for a variety of learners ranging from low to high interest within a number of base groups and ranging from remedial students to both the academically gifted and subject-talented students.

Curricular planning must reflect the highest level of aspiration in the arts which is possible within the school-community milieu. The necessity for curricular flexibility and for changes in emphasis and even in design of courses must be possible at all times. It is certainly true that no secondary school can move overnight from a heavy emphasis in the performance of music, primarily aimed at the musically talented, to a comprehensive program which includes concomitant skills, knowledge and attitudes concerning the art for a *wide* segment if not all of the school population. *How* to accomplish this, still allowing for even greater finesse in the development of the musically and academically talented will be the challenge.

A look at the type of music experiences which provide breadth as well as depth indicates that secondary school students should have opportunities to:

1. Continue exploratory experiences both in listening and in performance (basic in the elementary music program) which are designed primarily to develop an increased scope of attitudes, discriminative powers and aesthetic judgments.

2. Find suitable levels of performance (either instrumental or vocal) through which the highly motivated and above-average music student may find appropriate expression for his musical interests.

3. Find courses which form the basis for a fundamental concentration in music for the student who may be interested in pursuing music as an academic major in college or as a life's vocation.

4. Supplement other secondary school studies within appropriate areas of aesthetic enrichment. This is particularly important to the academically talented student.[1]

Just how the various courses will provide vitally needed opportunities for each segment of the school population should be determined by administrators, teachers and parents who are concerned with this area of curricular determination. The Music Educators National Conference[2] has suggested that planning of the music program for the total student body should include such areas as general music, assembly participation (both as participants and as consumers) in addition to a wide spectrum of performance-oriented classes in which they may also participate. It is also urged that students having both strong interests and aptitudes in music but who do not plan on music as a career should have opportunities for group performance participation as well as some elective choices in music appreciation, theory and harmony. Finally, MENC recommends for those students who plan to make careers in music, a host of musical offerings, including solo and ensemble performance, theoretical studies, and the history and literature of music.

It is unfortunate today that in most high schools, few opportunities exist for either the general student or those whose potential for development in music could be more fully developed. Performance groups, yes–but a balanced music curriculum, no. As important as is performance to secondary school students at all levels of interest and ability, this in itself does not constitute a complete or balanced music curriculum. This becomes readily apparent when the so-called "exploratory" musical experiences of the general student and the more "serious" musical studies of the potential music major must be almost exclusively secured outside of the framework of the secondary school.

Several important steps may be recommended by which the schools may take inventory of current programs and plan for future balance in the music curriculum.

[1]William C. Hartshorn, *Music for the Academically Talented Student in the Secondary School* (Washington, D.C.: The National Education Association and the Music Educators National Conference, 1960).

[2]The Music Curriculum in Secondary Schools (Washington, D.C.: the Music Educators National Conference, 1959), pp. 8-9.

1. List present courses which are open to (a) general students, (b) students with special interests and aptitudes but whose vocational goals probably will not include music, and, (c) students either with high academic potentials or those who are particularly gifted in music (including those who will wish to pursue music as a career).

2. Check to make sure that there is balance within the music courses now offered, including a systematic imparting of knowledge regarding various periods and styles, the grammar and syntax, and aesthetic principles of the art. Make sure there are "academic" classes in music as well as performance and that the latter also include these fundamental principles.

3. Plan additional courses, as necessary, to accomplish balance in meeting the varied needs of the student population. Bring modern team-teaching and modern aids to bear in providing for larger classes for general students, while scheduling smaller classes for music majors during alternate semesters or years.

4. Provide the necessary administrative machinery to allow students to elect such courses.

It is now only too prevalent that for the vast majority of secondary school students, their last formal contact with music (or the arts) was in the elementary school. Although many junior high schools provide "general" experiences in music, these experiences tend to be superficial, cursory, and possibly overly redundant, often boring rather than stimulating students who are perhaps at the threshold of their most dramatic educational venture. High schools tend to put most of their efforts into musical productions for the very few. The result is an immense artistic vacuum. This artistic ignorance is particularly deplorable in view of the wealth of musical literature and artistic media available. If all educators took the same view of English and American literature as of the related art forms, it is quite possible that the resultant blind areas would create an almost total cultural abyss in the public secondary schools.[3]

The lack of planned, sequential and balanced music courses for the highly motivated student is particularly appalling. It means, for example, that most students entering college as music majors are deficient in those areas of study most taken for granted in other disciplines; namely, in the basic grammar and literature of their specific field of study. While it may be argued that there are insufficient numbers of such students in the secondary schools, statistics show that between 3 to 5 per cent of all students entering junior colleges or four-year collegiate institutions become music majors. With a minimum of course additions and changes but with proper planning, these students may receive the necessary secondary school exposures in music without depriving the majority of students with an excellent basic musical course fare.

Senior high schools wishing to offer either a major or an appropriate

[3]G. Scott Wright, Jr., "An Ignorant Silence," *Saturday Review,* (March 18, 1961).

emphasis in music should consider including the following four categories in their music major curriculum:

1. Major field emphasis (instrumental or vocal music)

each semester

2. Minor field supplement (if principal performing field is vocal, take instrumental; if instrumental, take vocal)

2 semesters

3. Theory and Literature of Music (minimum of 1 semester each of (a) music theory, and, (b) music history and literature)

2 semesters

4. Allied cultural fields (electives from such areas as fine art, literature, drama and social studies)

2 semesters

Any music program in the comprehensive high school which is described as a "balanced" program must provide several significant musical experiences for a variety of learners. Such a program must be available to all students in sufficient kind and degree which would help to insure that there are no artificial limitations placed on students either of low interest and ability, or, conversely, those who are highly motivated and gifted in music.

It would appear important, therefore, that some of the following objectives in music be planned for the secondary school:

1. Experiences which assist students in an awareness of the elements of musical sound, particularly through representative musical literature which can serve to illustrate the elements of music, of form, style, texture and the various performance idioms.

2. Opportunities for the performance of representative musical literature (either as a participant or a listener) of various periods, styles and composers.

3. Understandings of some of the basic principles of aesthetics as applied to man's ability to create and recreate music as an art form.

4. Perceptions of the role of music in man's civilization, both contemporary and historical.

5. Appreciations of his developmental role in relation to music, particularly with regard to the manner in which the individual may lay foundations for growing musical discrimination and taste.

6. Skills in musical understanding which are necessary for him to pursue the art of music as an independent individual.

Such programs as these just described, because they are important both to the schools and to society, should be instituted where lacking and sustained and nourished where they are on-going. With our civilization at the crossroads, it may be redundant but nonetheless important to say that man does not live by bread alone—nor do technical skills, no matter how important they may be, compensate for a lack of humanistic and artistic experiences in our lives. If they are to remain comprehensive and meet the needs of the majority of students, public secondary schools must further dedicate themselves to the concept of preserving these values in our educational system.

Forging a Junior High General Music Program*

STUART RANKIN

The justification for inclusion of music in the junior high school curriculum must be founded on its potential contribution to *general* education. At the junior high level music education for children and youth with strong interests or abilities in music should be secondary to music education for *all* pupils if music is to claim its proper place in the curriculum.

The task to be done is a thorough development of a music curriculum for general education. The parts of that task are not different from procedures of curriculum development in other disciplines. The music teachers, school administrators, and curriculum development specialists need to forge the objectives, determine the learning activities and how they shall be organized, and plan for feedback and evaluation. The quality of this curriculum development will partly determine the effectiveness of the program. The intent of this paper is to highlight a few critical factors in the development of a music curriculum which are too often neglected. Certain considerations which are usually part of a curriculum plan are omitted since this treatment is not intended to be exhaustive.

Music education will not gain a solid or central role in the junior high school program until it has undergone a critical analysis and reconstruction of its own curriculum. Every instructional program begins with objectives which need to be consistent with the school's philosophy of education and need to be teachable in terms of what we know about learning. Objectives are based in the learner, the community which supports him, and the subject or discipline under study. A thorough study of the junior-high-age pupil and of the community in

*Reprinted from *The Music Educators Journal,* 53 (December 1966), 31-32, by permission of the publisher and Stuart Rankin, Development Director, Michigan-Ohio Regional Laboratory, Detroit, Michigan.

which he must live will help identify goals for program development. But the emphasis at this time must be on the subject itself if we are to strengthen the position of music in the curriculum.

What is it that music can contribute to general education? One approach to this question requires a critical examination of the field of music to determine what is basic or central to the discipline. A depth analysis of the field of mathematics has resulted in major changes in curriculum designed to focus on continuing concepts; such as number, operation, relation, proof, and limit. Similar efforts in science have led to the PSSC physics, the CHEM study program, the BSCS biology courses in several forms, and other concept-oriented curricula. Similar movements have begun in social studies and English. Such an analysis of the essential structure of music could give direction to curriculum development.

One fact confronted in such an effort is the qualitative nature of music, which distinguishes it and the other arts from the sciences which are largely theoretical in nature. This distinction is based on the concept of representation. A theoretical symbol represents something different from itself. Words are the most common theoretical symbols. By contrast, the quality (or qualitative symbol) represents only that which it presents, namely, itself. The words "melody," "harmony," and "rhythm," are theoretical symbols which usually represent tunes, chords, and temporal spacing of sounds respectively. The actual melody, harmony, and rhythm that one hears are qualities which are symbols only in the sense that they represent what they present, namely, the contradistinctions between themselves and other qualities. This argument assumes that qualitative meanings, orderings, or mediations form a domain which is separate from the usually conceived domain of intelligence, but which is in reality a second domain of intelligence. The problem-solving process is still the heart of intelligence, but the means, methods, and ends are qualities so that control can take place in a wholly qualitative respect.

To illustrate, consider the composer who has taken on a musical problem (perhaps that of writing majestic music in a minor key without using brass instruments). He may operate solely within the realm of qualities. He is working toward a qualitative end; his means include melody, harmony, volume, rhythm, tempo, and other qualities; his method involves experimentation with qualitative means toward a qualitative end. Clearly it is possible for the composer to leave the realm of qualities and use some theoretical mediation (probably with notes on a piece of paper) and then return to the qualitative to verify his hypotheses. The point here is that music is a discipline which is predominantly qualitative but for which a great deal of theory has been developed and frequently the qualitative and theoretical parts must be models of each other. The implications for curriculum development are many. The many qualities must be heard, compared, imitated, combined. The qualitative experience should precede its symbolic representation. The skills used in creation, control and evaluation of these qualities need to be identified, ordered, organized. The relative importance of the qualitative and the theoretical must be confronted as well as the relationship between the two.

This analysis of the essence of music in one approach which may be very fruitful in the formulation of objectives for the junior high school music curriculum. It requires the separation of those elements of music which are purely musical from those elements which are common to many disciplines including music. Every teacher has responsibility for the development of symbol, form, change, contrast, meaning, problem, order, structure, and control. Only the music teacher will teach tone, rhythm, harmony, melody, pitch, tempo, and volume.

This is not to say that music is made up solely of its structural elements but surely the moods, meanings, controls, orderings, and other products of creativity in music are, in essence, combinations and structurings of these qualities. If the child's musical experience is to be extended, expanded, and appreciated, it will be done by extending and expanding his understanding of these concepts. If the junior high music planners are to forge a curriculum, then their guide question must be, "What is music that it can be of service to all people?"

A second problem which will require consideration in the determination of objectives for the teaching of music deals with the interrelation of music with other parts of the humanities. When music is song, it is linked with poetry and speech. When music is dance, it is linked with physical education. When music is opera, it is linked with drama. When music is staged, it is linked with art. It is at the intersection of disciplines where the greatest creativity is taking place at present. Any adequate plan for curriculum in music must provide for the interaction of the arts.

A third critical item in selecting objectives for a junior high music program is the decision about the importance of skills for general education. How much skill should be sought for each student? Are there listening skills which every student should acquire? What is the relative importance among performing skills, music concepts, and knowledge about particular compositions? How can we measure the achievement of skills?

Three factors which require attention in the determination of objectives for the junior high music curriculum have been identified. They are the continuing concepts of a predominantly qualitative discipline; the relation to the other humanities; and the relative importance of skills, concepts, knowledge, and appreciation. Clearly, there are other concerns in the development of objectives but the ones named have received too little attention in the past and need greater emphasis if an effective program is to be developed.

Although the curriculum builder's primary task is the determination of objectives, his job does not end there. The selection and planning of activities that will result in the achievement of these objectives is his next task.

Music teachers have done a good job of selecting songs and other compositions for both singing and music appreciation in elementary and junior high music classes where music is taught as a separate subject. However, there are a number of possible experiences which have been withheld from children and youth even though their impact on learning may be much greater than the more common activities.

Children need to experiment more with sound. The problem-solving approach should not be limited to science, mathematics, and physical education; the student can and is confronted by problems in music. However, too often these are not resolved by student-shared solutions. These might be problems involving the comparison or imitation of sounds or musical passages, or they might be problems in creating particular sounds with a variety of common, easily available materials which are not often thought of as musical instruments. Pupils should also be given an opportunity to actually play the violin, the cornet, and the clarinet in a general music class. This recommendation is made mainly to give the student experiences with the sounds and potentials of these basic instruments. Other activities should, like the ones named above, be developed as they emerge from the objectives which have been selected earlier.

The organization of these experiences horizontally and vertically in the curriculum must be done with careful consideration to the relative importance of sequence for different goals, the interrelations with other disciplines, and what we know about pre-adolescents and adolescents. An effective organization will probably require varying size of groups and different lengths of time, depending on the activity. Here is more support for modular schedules and individual programming in the junior high school.

The omission of a section on evaluation in this proposal for music curriculum development is not intended to diminish the importance of finding out whether the goals are meaningful and the experiences effective, but simply because no evaluation plan can be devised until the objectives have been forged and stated behaviorally.

Music may continue to be a prime candidate for curricular cutbacks when school financial support elections fail. Instrumental music classes may continue to be held in the boiler room, or the corridor, or even in a converted closet. Vocal music may continue to be limited largely to public relations performances by the pupils with pleasant voices some of which have been privately trained. Music education may continue to be either frill or fill-in—to be scheduled with whatever time remains after other subjects have been planned. These conditions exist now in many school systems. But it need not be so.

The thesis of this paper is that music is important for general education. The junior high school years are excellent ones for exploration. The kinds of exploration that make sense are those which highlight the essence of music and are devised intentionally to teach basic understandings of music. In other words, the argument here is that the music educators must do the same job that is being done in mathematics and science and social studies and English; they must take a long look at the structure of music itself in order to build a curriculum which will provide a richer and more meaningful life through music. Then with the artistry of a good teacher working with a sound curriculum perhaps music can take a central place in the junior high school program.

Towards a Curriculum for Understanding—Junior High School *

G. SCOTT WRIGHT, JR.

It has been suggested that there are many statements of philosophy and an infinity of descriptions of individual projects and techniques in the literature of art education, but that there is still a lack of material in the area of the art curriculum. The following is an abbreviated attempt to fill this void in respect to the junior high school.

Despite the implied injunction against generalities, it is necessary to preface the specifics with a brief summary of the philosophy on which this approach to curriculum is based. Most junior high schools (7th and 8th grades) have some provision for art as a part of the general required program. It is usually considered to be an "exploratory" course and is rarely allotted more than one period or two a week. It is even more rarely expected to teach anything of lasting value. Since art in the average high school is an elective subject and participated in by relatively few, the junior high school course can be considered terminal for most students.

While all of this should be self-evident, there seems to be little recognition of the responsibility it places on the junior high school art teacher. Thus, one finds that present courses are little more than continuations of elementary school with an increased concern with techniques.

The approach to curriculum presented here is based on the fact that man has been creating art for tens of thousands of years. Every society in history has produced its artistic expression. An understanding of man is incomplete without an understanding of his art, and an understanding of his art leads to a deeper understanding of man. It is this understanding which is the goal of this course of

*Reprinted from *Art Education* (January 1963), 4-7, by permission of the publisher and G. Scott Wright, Jr., State University College, New Paltz, New York.

study. If understanding begins in the preteenage mind, it stands a good chance of lasting for a lifetime.

The formal history of art is an academic subject concerned with dates and names and complex theories of artistic motives. As such, the history of art has little meaning to the young mind. Although there are various explanations for each work of art, it is possible to make some generalizations which are valid and illuminating. These generalized "whys" are the content of this curriculum.

It is necessary to choose the range of motivations carefully. The major motivations of man and cultures must be covered in the time given; they cannot be left to chance or the whim of current fads. Without a broad coverage there will be, at best, only partial understanding; at worst, distortion of all understanding. The following could be considered major motivations: magic, religion, political control, recording of daily events, honoring the great, expression of philosophy, expression of emotion, decoration, function, and others of a like importance.

In order to present these major motivations in some related way, they can be organized in the traditional chronological sequence of history. This organization is valuable not only as recognizable order–essential for the young mind faced with so much material–but as a way of bringing to life the dead cultures and artists of the past. And without knowing man as he has been, we cannot know him as he is now.

Thus, the historically organized curriculum offers solutions to three important problems: It provides a study of man as he has developed, thereby giving a broader understanding of what he is today; it provides sequential order to the curriculum, thereby overcoming much of the confusion inherent in such a mass of material; it provides a setting and explanation of the major motivations behind the creation of various forms of art, thereby leading directly to a deeper understanding of man and his art.

This approach to curriculum does not argue with the adage about learning from experience. It is *not* set up as a lecture course. Rather, although each motivation is introduced in its historical setting by the teacher, the student spends most of his time in active artistic experiences. However, since understanding man and his art is the goal of the whole curriculum, the artistic experiences are illustrative experiences, *not* ends in themselves.

Each illustrative experience (called "problem" in the body of the course of study) is carefully constructed to do a number of things for the student. The most obvious is to provide him with a clear illustration of the true nature of the motivation under consideration. Therefore, each problem is designed to enlighten the student about the motivation through recreating the same kind of problem faced by men in the past. However, as junior high school students are often reluctant (and justifiably so) to "pretend" they are Egyptians, or cavemen, or whatever, each problem is translated into contemporary terms. Instead of making magical pictures of bison on cave walls, they are asked to make one of their own wishes come true by creating a magical picture. The approach of placing the illustration in the modern world takes advantage of the psychology of the early adolescent and his concern with self and the world around him. (And, by the way, he is quite willing to try magic to make the world behave as he would like it to—although this is not usually mentioned in the psychology textbooks.)

A further use of the illustrative problem is to provide a series of artistic experiences which serve as an introduction to the technical aspects of art. Each student creates examples of painting, sculpture, and architecture. He learns, through experience, the fundamental similarities and differences of the major art forms. He learns a little of the techniques required by many of the different media. But, as he is not studying technique for the sake of technique, each of his creations has more meaning to him.

Another facet of the experimental problem is that it provides a vehicle for learning the abstract aspects of art. The concepts of design and their relationships to the intention of the work can be made quite clear. The psychological effects of color, shape, and form are inherent in such problems as the magic painting or designing temples for sacrifice. The concept of function as related to design is vital to the solution of the problems in architecture and decoration.

In short, the illustrative experiences serve to develop an understanding of art by helping the child face the same kinds of problems artists have faced throughout history; they introduce the child to major technical aspects of the various art forms; and they begin to develop an understanding of the abstract qualities of artistic expression such as design, psychological reaction to space, and the like.

The form of the curriculum is quite simple. The major historical and cultural periods are listed in chronological order, from Prehistoric through Egyptian: Greek, Roman, Oriental, Pre-Columbian, Gothic, Renaissance, Impressionistic, Abstract, Surrealistic, and Expressionistic. This list can easily be expanded or condensed to fit the time allotted to the course. The above is weighted at the contemporary end for two reasons: (1) It is often the most confusing to the young mind (very little help from home in most cases) and (2) it is the world in which the grown child will live, and therefore, *must* understand.

Each historical period (with the possible exception of the Prehistoric) has many major art forms from which to choose an illustrative problem. However, the factors of balance and pupil interest demand that the choices and sequence be established with the greatest possible care. It is necessary to pace the course of study so that there is variety in both the kind of art illustrated and the type of thinking needed to solve the problem. Two sculpture problems back-to-back are not as effective as a painting and sculpture sequence. Also, two religious problems in a row are not so exciting as a religious problem followed by a genre problem. Decoration goes well juxtaposed with emotion, and so forth.

In order to get this balance, it is necessary to lay out the entire range of possibilities before outlining the specific course of study. The easiest way to do this is in a chart form. Three vertical columns can contain the necessary data. The first column can list the historical periods, the second contain the major art forms of each period, and the third be made up of possible illustrative problems of each of the art forms. It should be noted that twelve historical periods with two art forms and two illustrative problems from each period will produce nearly 50 problems from which to choose. Of particular importance is the fact that these problems will not be a random, unrelated group, but will be a meaningful developmental sequence.

A few examples of this development are:

Historical Period	*Major Art Forms*	*Illustrative Problem*
Pre-Columbian	Temples	Design and build a scale model of a temple for human sacrifice
		Design a temple for sun worship
	Pottery	Make a vase to hold flowers
		Design a pitcher in the shape of an animal
Medieval & Gothic	Castles	Design and build a scale model of a castle and the surrounding town
		Design a tapestry to decorate a wall
	Cathedrals	Design a stained glass window
		Sculpt a gargoyle
	Manuscript	Design a decorative letter
	Illumination	Design own monogram

From these examples in two historical periods it is possible to see almost the full range of this subject approach. The student is introduced to a major historical period of man through his art. The relationship between the art forms and the culture is made clear. The illustrative problems have such scope that many educational ends are possible. By including examples of painting, sculpture, architecture, ceramics. lettering, stained glass, and tapestry, opportunities are provided for expressive, decorative, and functional design. Opportunities are presented for large or small projects, for long or short periods of time and for individual, small group, or combined class activities. In short, rather than being restrictive, this approach to curriculum building gives a range of possibilities as broad as the imagination of the teacher, while still being devoted to developing *lasting* understanding of man and his art.

It has been the intention of this brief statement to suggest a direction for developing a junior high school art curriculum that accepts both the limitations and responsibilities of our present educational condition. These suggestions are based on the reality of the junior high school classroom, not upon the idealistic—often unrealistic—atmosphere of the scholar's library or educator's seminar. It is intended that this approach be used to construct a curriculum that is suited to the young mind, but devoted to developing an understanding of art and man that will continue to adulthood.

What Makes a Good Junior High Art Program? *

Memo to: The Editor.

Regarding: The story on the junior high art program in Kansas City, Misouri.

As you may recall, you sent me to Kansas City to get a story on the junior high art program because we heard it is one of the best in the country. The people there impressed me, and I feel sure this is an outstanding program. Perhaps because I have no sophistication in the field of art education, I've had great difficulty putting my finger on why the K. C. program is so good. Maybe the following account of my trip will give one of us an inspiration on how the article should be written.

When I arrived in Kansas City, the long-time director of the public school art program, Rosemary Beymer, had planned a tour of art classes in junior high schools in various parts of the city, each school representing a particular socioeconomic level or racial mixture. I would have been somewhat skeptical of a guided tour if the schools had known in advance that we were coming, but they had not been told of our projected visit.

As we drove to the first school, I started asking questions on such basic facts as the number of junior high (eighteen, including a few middle schools), junior high art requirements (a semester for seventh graders, one of several electives for the required fine arts credit in eighth grade), and the role of the art consultant (who, Miss Beymer explained, is not a supervisor or a traveling teacher).

Before we reached the first school, the less tangible but ultimately more important characteristics—what one might call the underlying philosophy—of the program began to emerge. As we drove past homes in the poorer section of town, the program director spoke of how important art could be in building a favorable self-image in a disadvantaged child, of how one child had expressed the

*Reprinted from *The NEA Journal* 56 (March 1967), 14-17, by permission of the publisher.

attitude of many when he said, "Art is the only subject I like because it is the only one where *I* have the answer. In arithmetic and spelling there's only one answer, but in art, the way I feel is the answer."

When I commented on the attractiveness of a street in another part of town, Miss Beymer spoke of the importance of making children aware of the sight and feel of things around them—of the green of the trees and grass against the blue and white of the sky, of the texture of the bark of different kinds of trees, of the elaborate designs created by the veins of leaves, even of the tiny ridges of corduroy and the softness of velvet and the slippery smoothness of silk.

The first (and most impressive) classroom we visited was in a relatively new building in a middle-to high-income neighborhood. Even though I had expected to see a good art class, I was surprised at the excellence of the work displayed throughout the classroom. I wandered around enjoying watercolors, sketches, and block prints with much the same excitement one feels in good art galleries. To my uneducated-in-art eyes, some of the work looked merely pretty or striking, but some of it seemed to reflect an unusual combination of skill and emotional perception for the junior high level.

Here, I thought, was part of what had given Kansas City the reputation of having a good art program, but I still needed to discover the why—the formula for quality. External factors told me little: The number of students looked to be about average, and the classroom, which was, if anything, a little crowded, was a regular one which had been converted into an art room.

I didn't get many clues from the teacher, either, except that the school does not pressure the Art Department to produce posters, displays, and the like for other departments or for the school. Cooperation with other teachers is worked out on an individual, informal basis. Several displays in the halls indicated that art work moves outside the art class.

Before our next visit, Miss Beymer and I stopped for lunch at the William Rockhill Nelson Gallery of Art, which has a special junior gallery containing children's art and paintings representative of different periods and techniques. Special guided tours of the museum and materials to prepare the children for the tours are part of the gallery's contribution to art education in the Kansas City schools.

As we entered another school, an old one in a low-income neighborhood, we saw in the main hallway a dramatic display of glazed pottery. The designs and glazes varied, but most of the objects had a primitive-modern look, with simple but graceful lines. Revolving on a small pedestal and serving as the focal point of the display was a piece of pottery that had won a Scholastic Magazines art award.

In the art class, the walls were practically covered with students' work. Most of it was watercolor—perhaps because the materials involved are relatively inexpensive. Each picture was clearly an individual creation. I was struck by the free style, the uninhibited use of color, and a certain dramatic intensity.

This school, I was told, was known for having discipline problems—but not in the art classes. When we walked into the room, every student was intent on carrying out the assignment written on the chalkboard. The quiet concentration was all the more striking because this was the last period of the day.

That night in my hotel room, I went through the elementary and secondary curriculum guides, attractive books written by the city's art teachers and consultants and illustrated with students' work. The guides set up goals and suggested activities to help reach them but left it up to the teacher to work out his own timetable and methods.

The elementary guide indicated that students entering junior high have an unusually solid background in the use of various media, in art history, in art appreciation, and in recognizing beauty in the environment. The required seventh grade art course, which meets five hours a week, acts primarily as a transition, building on the elementary school background and beginning to stress the perfection of skills which open wider avenues of self-expression.

I had been told that many students take art as an elective in eighth grade but that the number decreases sharply in the ninth, which is really the beginning of the high school sequence. Those who have the talent and desire can take art through twelfth grade. (In one high school, one-fourth of the students enrolled in art.)

The guides also indicated that in Kansas City, the junior high program, which in many communities seems to be the weakest link in the art chain, is an integrated part of the K-12 program. Perhaps this unity is part of the answer to why the program is successful.

The next morning I talked with some of the elementary school art consultants about their work, visited an elementary school, and watched Miss Beymer give fourth graders a TV art lesson on perspective. These experiences bore out the impression I received from the curriculum guides that the elementary program provides a solid foundation for the junior high program.

That afternoon the secondary art consultant, a dynamic young woman named Dell Angerer, was my guide to one junior high and one senior high. Outside the principal's office in the junior high school was a display of student art work which the principal had collected in Yugoslavia while he was on an educators' tour, a sure sign of his interest in the art program.

Even though each classroom I had visited was different, in none of them had I seen slipshod, indifferent work, and this school was no exception. When I asked Mrs. Angerer how the system maintained such high standards, she gave much of the credit to the teachers, about half of whom, she said, are accomplished artists. An applicant for an art teaching position in Kansas City must have both a good teaching record and an impressive portfolio of his own work.

The consultant tries to give each teacher whatever help he needs. It may be no more than a casual suggestion here and there. Possibly a teacher does very well teaching watercolors but knows little about ceramics. In areas of weakness, the consultant may help the teacher with lesson plans and ordering supplies or may even give a demonstration lesson.

Another function of the consultant is to spread ideas from school to school, both by word of mouth and by means of a monthly tip sheet. In addition, five or six in-service meetings a year, each held in a different place, keep teachers up-to-date and expose them to other teachers' ideas and work.

These are the major impressions I brought back from Kansas City:

Much of the work students are doing shows what seems to me to be genuine artistic skill and surprising emotional depth for junior high students. The curriculum guides set up goals but leave room for each teacher to meet them in the context of his particular students and teaching situation. The junior high program builds on a good elementary program and toward a good senior high program.

Principals respect and support the art program, as evidenced by the prominent positions they give art displays in each school and by what teachers and principals told me. Teachers are unusually well qualified, and they receive any needed assistance from the consultant. Students respond favorably to the program, as is indicated by their work, their choice of art as an elective, and their attitude in the classroom.

As far as I can see, the program is not flashy and has no special gimmicks, what makes it outstanding is its effectiveness with students.

The Foreign Language Curriculum: Background and Problems *

ROBERT L. POLITZER

In the light of continued and recent discussion on the problems of Foreign Language Education[1] it seems appropriate to take an overall look at the "revolution" in Modern Language Education, the implications and the problems connected with it.

In order to understand the nature of the modern foreign language curriculum, we must very briefly examine the sources of this curriculum and the forces which are helping to shape it. These forces seem to be of three types: (1) public attitudes and public pressure, (2) views held by specialists in the subject matter discipline, (3) views concerning the nature of learning held by psychologists.

Perhaps the most important and dominant force without which the others could not have come into play at all counts in public attitudes. American involvement in world affairs, the possibility of contact with other peoples, the shrinking of the globe as the result of modern transportation—all of this has created an atmosphere in which foreign languages seem important. Once more they seem important as tools of communication or as tools for the understanding of foreign peoples. To what extent these goals of foreign language education are "legitimate" or "realistic" is not to be discussed here; but there can be little doubt that facility in audiolingual communication and cultural understanding are the goals that the general public has in mind when language instruction is advocated, endorsed or legislated. The PTA group clamoring for

*Reprinted from *The Journal of Secondary Education,* 40 (April 1965), 156-163, by permission of the publisher and Robert L. Politzer, Stanford University.

[1]See for instance, E. Hocking, "The Schools take over Foreign Languages," *Journal of Secondary Education,* XXXIX (1964), 243-250.

French in the elementary school wants Johnny to be able to speak French and to get along in France. The picture of Johnny reading Racine in the original is not the moving force behind the public demand. And in a similar way, the subsidies accorded to language instruction under the National Defense Education Act envisage audiolingual facility as the goal of instruction.

The impact which linguistic science has had on the Foreign Language Curriculum has been traced by myself and others at considerable length.[2] In brief, the views of the linguistic scientist, developed in the United States during the past thirty to forty years, went well hand in hand with the demands for audiolingual proficiency and cultural understanding as voiced by the public. Let me, in this context, point to three aspects of linguistic science: (1) Many American linguistic scientists were or are also cultural anthropologists. They are affiliated with departments of anthropology rather than departments of language and literature. Thus it seems natural to them that the goal of language education should be cultural understanding. (2) As anthropologist the linguistic scientist has often the function of establishing communication in a language in which written records are simply nonexistent: the learning procedures are and must be "audio-lingual." (3) For many centuries our thinking about the nature of languages has been dominated by what one might call the "common denominator approach" to grammar, in other words by the idea that certain grammatical categories could be (a) defined in semantic terms, (b) are more or less common to all languages. To give an example, we defined *noun* as a name for a place, person and thing and felt that this definition was applicable for English as well as for any other language: *boy* in English is a noun, so is *garcon* in French, *joven* in Spanish, *puer* in Latin, etc., etc. Linguistic scientists found that such universal definitions in semantic terms lacked accuracy and that at any rate these definitions were useless for the purpose of analyzing *unknown* languages. Thus linguistic scientists insist on evolving grammars based on formal criteria applicable to a specific language. Thus, a noun is *not* the name for a place, person or thing, but a noun *in English* is any word that can be substituted for *boy* in the sentence, *The boy is here*, that can be preceded by *the*, etc.

The psychological theories which helped to shape the foreign language curriculum are the various schools of behaviorism which identify learning as such as acquisition of specific responses—and language as "verbal behavior." The "old" language curricula had been very much under the influence of lingering notions of faulty psychology and "formal discipline." In other words, it was felt that language learning could somehow contribute to sharpening the student's intellect by improving his ability to think logically. The new curricula with new

[2]See, for instance, R. L. Politzer, "The Impact of Linguistics on Language Teaching: Past, Present and Future," *Modern Language Journal,* XLVIII (1944), 146-151; William G. Moulton, "Linguistics and Language Teaching in the United States 1940-1960," in *Trends in European and American Linguistics,* Utrecht, 1962, pp. 82-109.

orientation toward perfecting language skills have rejected any notion of improving the faculties and operate with the concept of behaviorist psychology. Utterances in the foreign language are treated as "responses" to specific stimuli. They are "reinforced" by "immediate confirmation" (e.g. in the language laboratory) and language learning generally speaking is viewed primarily as a process of "habit formation."

What are then, in brief, the chief characteristics of the new language curriculum which has been shaped by the above mentioned forces?[3]

1. *First of all the curriculum is definitely thought of as a long curriculum:* It comprises various "levels" and is supposed to lead the pupil to near native mastery of the language. There seems to be general agreement that the pupils should be exposed to it at an early stage-preferably in the elementary school. These two features–length of the curriculum and early beginning–are almost being taken for granted nowadays. At the same time, however, we should remember that they are really the outgrowth of the goals and assumptions discussed above. The "long" curriculum is needed to assure mastery in the skill and the "early beginning" is also tied in with the emphasis on achieving skills. (Many a language teacher of twenty or thirty years ago would have rejected the notion of the early start simply because he would have felt that elementary school children were not yet ready for the training in thinking, logic and grammar provided by foreign languages.)

2. *The curriculum is audio-lingually oriented:* This audio-lingual orientation takes various forms: (a) In the initial stages of the curriculum–the so-called "pre-reading period"–it is completely audio-lingual. (b) During the first levels of the curriculum, any new elements of language to be learned are introduced audio-lingually before they are introduced in reading and writing. During the first levels of the curriculum, audio-lingual activity generally speaking dominates over visual (e.g., reading and writing) activity. It is only in the later stages of the curriculum that the pupil is supposed to spend more time reading and writing than listening and speaking. It is only during these later and more advanced stages that new elements of language may be met in visual form *before* they are encountered audio-lingually.

3. *The presentation and teaching of grammar is deeply influenced by the assumptions and procedures of linguistic science.* Translation and the assumption of a "common denominator" grammar is avoided. Grammar is taught instead by

[3]The new curricula have been described in detail by various State Departments of Education and the following description is generally based on an analysis of these descriptions. For good examples of extensive descriptions of the new curricula the reader is referred to the New York State Education Department, *French for Secondary Schools,* Albany 1960. Connecticut, State Department of Education, *Foreign Languages* Grades 7-12, Curriculum Bulletin Series No. 5, 1958; California State Department of Education, *French, Listening, Speaking, Reading, Writing,* Sacramento, 1962.

structural manipulation within the foreign language. In other words, exercises take the form of transforming one type of sentence into another, or they consist in substituting words for each other within the same sentence. These procedures are supposed to create in the pupil an understanding of grammatical patterning based on formal criteria.

4. There is heavy reliance on the "SR" (stimulus response) kind of learning. Responses are created by repetition, and imitation. Correct responses are reinforced by being performed and rewarded in (language laboratory) exercises.

5. *Throughout the entire curriculum there is a very slow and gradual progression leading from a very strict control of the pupils responses to a more loose structuring and finally to self-expression.* Thus in the realm of speaking the emphasis shifts gradually from repetition and substitution within a structure to guided oral composition and finally uncontrolled free discussion. In writing the activities proceed from copying to controlled grammatical exercises and from guided to finally free composition. In the initial stages reading is confined to material previously studied orally. Later the pupil is allowed to read materials at least partially prepared in class, and, only in the last stage of the curriculum does the pupil face completely new reading material.

In the discussion of the problems faced by the new curriculum, I shall try to emphasize those which deal with the contents and assumptions of the curriculum rather than those that are in a sense the automatic results of its external structure. To mention just a few of the latter: In the "old" two or three year high school language curriculum, grouping of students according to ability was not a major factor. I still remember the answer given to me by a guidance counselor in a mid-western high school some ten years ago when I enquired about the policy of placing students in language classes: "It's really very simple: the smarter ones take Latin or German, or maybe French. The "in between ones" take Spanish; the dumb ones do not take a foreign language; and those who insist on taking a foreign language although they either can't or won't study, drop out after one year anyway." This policy (of questionable wisdom even ten years ago) is no longer usable in a situation in which many (in California practically *all*!) students are supposed to start and preferably finish a curriculum that spans several years. To have the capable student and the low aptitude student march in lock step is bad enough if it is done for a period of one or two years; but the harm done to both is magnified if the procedure is followed for five years. Thus, one of the major problems facing us today is to adapt the curriculum to the individual student. We must try to learn here as much as possible from the experience gained in "laning" and "sorting" in other subjects. Above all we must learn to utilize the language laboratories and various other types of audio-visual teaching aids for the one purpose that seems their *main* individual student to progress at his own rate, according to his aptitude and intelligence. Language instruction could then be programmed or partially programmed and the individual teacher could meet with students for shorter periods and in small groups in order to check on their progress, answer questions, engage in conversation, etc. Students could be easily moved from one small group to another according to their individual progress.[4]

Another important problem—again not new but magnified and intensified through the mere length of the curriculum—is that of articulation. A pupil starting a foreign language in elementary school and continuing it through college may have to pass through as many as three articulation points in the curriculum (Elementary to Junior High; Junior High to High School; High School to College). At each one of these points there lurks the danger that the pupil's foreign language experience may be, in fact, interrupted or seriously impaired by lack of coordination or agreement between the schools involved in the transition. Just to consider a few of the typical dangers that threaten at the articulation points: so far as the transition from Elementary to Junior High School is concerned, the main danger seems to be that the Elementary School experience of the pupil may simply turn out to be completely wasted. This can happen for these reasons: (1) Either because the Elementary School experience did in fact not produce any tangible, well defined results on which the Junior High School could build—or—the Junior High School may simply decide to ignore the training given in the Elementary School and to have the pupil start all over again.

At the articulation point between Junior High and High one of the typical dangers awaiting the pupil is a change in philosophy or method of instruction. In many situations the new curricula are being created by "extending backward." New teaching materials produced to implement the new curricula are typically teaching materials which start in the Junior High level. Thus we are apt to find a situation in which the Junior High School is likely to use the "new key" materials and the new, more recently trained teaching personnel. The experienced teacher with the more traditional outlook is more apt to be found on the High School level. Conflicts in teaching methodology, definition of aims, etc., are then likely to develop between Junior High School and High School language departments. Whenever there are these conflicts it is important to realize that it is neither possible or profitable to decide who is "right" and who is "wrong." In fact, I found that the experienced, traditionally minded teacher is often closer to the real spirit and intention of the modern methodology than he or she realizes, that the enthusiastic young "new key" "audio-linguist" could learn a lot from the experienced teacher who has made *successful* use of a more

[4]For a good description of a semi-programmed "ungraded" foreign language course see Albert Valdman, "How to Break the Lock Step," *Audio-Visual Instruction,* VII (1962), pp. 630-634.

traditional textbook. The really important point is, of course, that conflicts in methodology remain unresolved only at the expense of the pupil. To give example: whether or at what stage English should be used for cuing responses in the foreign language is a debatable question. What is inexcusable is use of an English to Spanish translation text for the High School placement for Junior High pupils who have been taught for three years from the point of view that it is a crime to elicit a Spanish sentence by using an English cue.

At the articulation point High School/College the problems are even more numerous. Since High Schools and Colleges belong, typically at least, to different school systems, they are even more difficult to deal with. Also, the great diversity of approaches in different language departments in different institutions makes it almost impossible to generalize. Let us just point to two fairly typical problems. The language departments in the universities are departments of Language and Literature (often with heavy stress on literature). The pupil who has gone through a long foreign language curriculum in Junior High and High School may simply find that the university or college is either incapable or not interested in providing him with a continuation of the kind of high level language experience which he expects. He may, in his Freshman year, end up in a composition course that may be only moderately challenging—or in a literature course that may be largely or completely conducted in English. Another problem: many students start the study of a foreign language in college. Such students are apt to reach the advanced literature course in their senior year. The student who has gone through the long High School curriculum may be placed in the same course as a Freshman. He may be linguistically ready but in terms of sophistication, maturity, experience he is no match for the Senior in the same course. The problems just described are not imaginary ones. I observed them in institutions (*e.g.*, Harvard) for which the Freshman coming at the end of a long foreign language curriculum (*e.g.*, in the New England Academies) has been a fact of life for a long time. The same problems of articulation are and will be developing for many other institutions of higher learning. These institutions will have to face up to the challenge of continuing rather than interrupting the foreign language experience created in the secondary school.

Yet many problems concern the philosophy of the audio-lingual curriculum as such: from my observations of operation of the curriculum in several school situations, I can comment on a few. First of all, I want to make it clear that I do not want to question the basic philosophy and assumptions: namely, the importance of audio-lingual training, especially in the initial stages of the course. We can learn to understand and speak only by engaging in those activities. I do question, however, the validity, or at least the general validity for all ages and types of students, of certain features which dominate at least the initial level of the audio-lingual curriculum. Here I am referring principally to the so-called pre-reading period and the excessive control (insistence on repetition and only minimal manipulation of structure) which is characteristic of the first level of the audio-lingual approach. If the first level of the curriculum is presented in the Elementary School, this feature presents probably not much of a problem. In the Junior High School and even more so in the Senior High School, the audio-lingual pre-reading period and the memorization of dialogue are no longer a smooth and welcome operation. Many students are bored by the *prolonged* withholding of visual (orthographic) symbols and others (often the more gifted ones) do not care for the excessive repetition and manipulation of dialogue materials. Again, it is not my purpose here to distinguish "good" methods from "bad" methods. Nor is there a simple and easy answer to the problem created by the fact that orthography on the one hand will interfere with the student's fluency and accuracy, while on the other hand the pupil may have been conditioned to ask for and to need the help of the written word in his entire learning process. There is no easy answer to the problem created by the fact that on the one hand language learning demands memorization and practice, while on the other it also requires understanding and conceptualization. The only suggestions I should like to make are that the prudent teacher will learn to compromise and will find that in *practice* there is really not much incompatibility between audio-lingual emphasis and speaking and the use of orthography, or between pattern practice and memorization and understanding of grammar and language concepts. In other words, we can very well withhold orthography in the initial stages of instruction—but only for limited amounts of material at one time and not to the point where the pupil gets worried. And I and many others have never seen any good reason why Johnny (by the time he reaches High School at least) should not fully understand the language patterns which he memorizes and manipulates.

This last observation brings us to the final point of the discussion, namely the relation of the audio-lingual curriculum with the other subjects. Here I should like to emphasize that in a very real sense the revolution in the language curriculum and those in other subjects have gone in opposite directions. The emphasis in the New Science and especially the Mathematics curricula has been away from rote learning and memorization and toward the acquisition of concepts and understanding. There is, of course, no reason why different subjects like Mathematics and Foreign Languages should necessarily go in the same direction. At the same time, however, it may be difficult for the pupil to make the switch from conceptualization to rote learning as soon as he reaches the language class. Moreover, some of the reasons which brought about the shift to a concept oriented Curriculum in Science and Mathematics apply also to the Foreign Languages. The New Mathematics was created largely in response to the fact that in today's rapidly changing world the specific mathematical skills that may be needed by the pupil in later life are quite unpredictable. Thus the curriculum insists not only in creating skills but also concepts that will in turn facilitate the learning of whatever skills may be needed. The eventual foreign language needs of our pupils are just as unpredictable. Thus in a long curriculum devoted to the learning of one single language it behooves us at least to pay more attention to creating an understanding of such concepts as are likely to facilitate the learning of language as such. Whether there is an *automatic* transfer of training from the experience of learning one language to the acquisition of another is a debatable one that has never been settled to anybody's satisfaction,[5] but there is little doubt that transfer is promoted by understanding and that it is facilitated if we teach for the purpose of bringing grammatical patterning, the nature of "meaning", etc., which appear to have a particular relation to language learning and language aptitude.[6] Our pupils should thus not only learn a language, they should also learn something about language.[7]

A final word concerning the relation of the Foreign Modern Language Curriculum to the subjects which are, or at least should be, closest to it: English and the classical languages. The relation of Foreign Modern Languages to these subject areas is difficult to assess because changes are taking place in both of these curricula. To some, but for the time being to a limited extent, the impact of linguistic science is making itself felt in those subject areas. Generally, however, the impact of linguistics in the Modern Foreign Languages has been by far more extensive, no doubt because it was accelerated through the NDEA Summer Institutes, specific teaching materials, etc. Thus, the result of the Modern languages adapting an audio-lingual approach and rejecting the "common denominator grammar" has been in many cases a rift between the Modern Languages on the one hand and English and Classics on the other. It is understandable that in this situation some classicists advocate a closer cooperation between English and Latin. Yet my own hopes are rather for a closer cooperation between the possible three language strands of the curriculum. It is perfectly true that English, Latin, Spanish, or any other languages for that matter, do not share the same *formal* grammar. It is even more true that *there are general* concepts of language and language structure (*e.g.*, transformation or substitution are processes by which one can make new sentences out of old ones in any language). Many of these concepts could profitably be taught in English and be used there to improve the pupil's language

[5]See John B. Carroll's statement in "Research on Teaching Foreign Languages," in N.L. Gage, *Handbook of Research on Teaching,* Chicago: 1963, p. 1090.

[6]See Carroll, *op. cit.* p. 1090 and John B. Carroll and Stanley M. Sapon, *Modern Language Aptitude Test Manual,* New York, 1959, p. 3.

[7]The point that language instruction should be conducted in such a way as to facilitate the learning of further languages has been especially stressed by Mortimer Graves "Languages in American Education," *DFL Bulletin* (Dept. of Foreign Languages of the NEA) II, 2(1963), p. 3-6.

skills. So far as Latin is concerned, a slight shift of emphasis in language instruction generally speaking to the creation of language concepts and grammatical principals would go far to bridge the gap which divides at present the Latin and the Modern Language Curriculum. What the Modern Foreign Language and Latin have in common is very much, what divides them is very little. Like the Modern Language, Latin gives access to a culture—a culture which will remain permanently pertinent to our own. When it comes to the creation of language concepts, Latin may very well have an edge over most of the foreign languages in the curriculum—not because its grammar is so much like English, but for the opposite reason—because the formal grammar is so radically and almost maximally different. What divides Latin from the Modern Language then is, that for an early start (in the Elementary School) and an initial audio-lingual strategy, the latter makes more sense (though some Latin teachers may even dispute that). By the time the sixth or seventh grade is reached, some pupils (*e.g.*, pupils with good language aptitude but low auditory perception) may in fact be served better by Latin rather than the audio-lingual attack on a modern language.

These are just some of the problems which confront us today. Perhaps more than anything we should emphasize that the new Curricula in Foreign Languages are still in the making. There are and will continue to be problems. The major one—which I have not discussed here because it is not part of the curriculum as such—is simply the demand made on the quality and quantity of the teaching personnel. Programmed learning, television, tapes, all of these can of course help in implementing the curriculum; but let us remember that unless the curriculum is taught well, especially in its first levels, the new "long" Foreign Language Curriculum may turn out to be short for the vast majority of our pupils.

Foreign Language Program in the Junior High School*

JOSEPH M. VOCOLO

Introduction

A discussion of foreign languages at the junior high school level invariably gets around to the problem of scheduling difficulties. This is so because (1) the school day is already pretty well filled up with mandated subjects, and (2) foreign languages are strangers to the junior high school curriculum and particularly below grade nine.

As the discussion progresses it soon is abundantly obvious that the problem involves much more than a sitting down and making decisions about the number and variety of courses to be given and deciding the hourly schedule. Of course, this is the purely mechanical aspect of the procedure, but the implications of the schedule are reflected in outlook on the curriculum, function of the junior high school, concept of the learner, and a host of considerations which go to make up an entire orientation to education. The aim of this paper will be to show that foreign languages should be part of the core program (the constants in the curriculum) open to all pupils and that there is room in the schedule for this kind of program.

The Problem

John Dewey said once of the good community and the right attitude toward education: "What the best family wants for its children, the community

*Reprinted from *The Clearing House,* 42 (February 1968), 358-362, by permission of the publisher and Joseph M. Vocolo, Director of Languages, Buffalo Board of Education, Buffalo, N.Y.

should want for all children." Authors Faunce and Clute[1] have written concerning the objectives of education:

> The fundamental purpose of education is to help the individual discover himself and the world in which he lives so that he may live a happy and useful life. In other words, education has two basic purposes; to enable each individual to realize his full potential so that he may enjoy the greatest personal happiness; and to enable him to develop to his fullest capacity for citizenship so that his fellow men profit from his service.

Now both these citations make explicit that all children should have this opportunity for self-discovery. The question, then, is what experiences are all children to have and what experiences will be had by only some of the children? And if and when we deny certain experiences to some children for whatever reason, how do we reconcile this action with the above quoted statements? On what facts, experiences, research are such decisions based? What is the reaction of the child being denied entry to an area of the curriculum?

There appears to be little justification for maintaining old ideas (which were wrong to begin with) regarding foreign languages and their place in the junior high curriculum, especially in the light of the stated purposes of the junior high school, contemporary society, learning theory, and the nature and psychology of language learning. Shane[2] has said, writing of provisions for program enrichment:

> Whether in elementary school music, junior high school sports, or secondary school dramatics, opportunities should be available for all, since some children are not more worth educating than others–although the extent of their education quite properly may vary as dictated by talent, aspiration, and intelligence. Emphasis on skill or level of performance per se, therefore, should not determine who "belongs" in an activity.

It is ironic that often the very children denied access to certain curricular areas are the very ones who would profit the most from the experience. I'm speaking here of the culturally disadvantaged who has so much to gain precisely because of the fact of disadvantagement. That Shane's proposal should apply to foreign languages is clearly indicated by the joint statement of the National

[1]Roland C. Faunce and Morrel J. Clute, *Teaching in the Junior High School* (Belmont, California: Wadsworth Publishing Company), 1961, p. 81.

[2]Harold G. Shane, "The School and Individual Differences," in *Individualizing Instruction,* 1962 yearbook–Part I, NSSE (Chicago: University of Chicago Press), 1962, p. 60.

Education Association and the Modern Language Association,[3] "Preferably not later than the third grade, all children should have the opportunity to listen to and speak a second language." All students, according to recommendations of the National Association of Secondary School Principals in 1959,[4] should have the opportunity to elect foreign language study and to continue it as long as their interest and ability permit:

> At a time when events anywhere in the world can produce immediate and profound repercussions on our everyday life, when decisions in this country involving other world areas are commonplace, and when an individual from any part of our country may find himself dealing with non-English-speaking peoples, some experience with another modern language and some understanding of another modern culture became extremely important.

Essentially the same recommendation is made by the United States Office of Education.[5] The New York State Education Department recommends foreign language programs beginning in grade seven. Thus the case for foreign languages as part of the core program and not solely for the edification of the exclusive few has gained some very powerful advocates. In matter of fact, no governmental body, no important organization would disagree with these views. The recent action of the state of California mandating the study of foreign languages for three years and for all pupils beginning no later than grade six may portend a future course of events. A little known fact is that similar bills have been introduced in the New York State legislature.

Status of Foreign Languages in the Junior High School

Yet, despite the weight of all this support, what is the state of foreign languages in the junior high school? In short, persons charged with responsibility for curriculum at this level don't appear to be listening. As one reads textbooks and other professional literature in the area of the junior high school, it is quickly and abundantly obvious that this area has been totally ignored. Even in the area of exploratory experiences curriculum writers choose not to pay much attention to this question. Foreign languages usually appear as a ninth grade elective presumably for the more able or academically inclined individual.

[3]Ilo Remer, *A Handbook for Guiding Students in Modern Foreign Languages* (Washington: U.S. Government Printing Office), 1963, p. 3.

[4]NASSP, "Modern Foreign Languages in the Comprehensive High School," *Bulletin of the NASSP* (September), 1959, p. 4.

[5]Remer, *op. cit.*, p. 1.

What is the present situation regarding enrollments in foreign languages at the junior high level? While no completely accurate count is available, it is safe to assume that less than 25 per cent of the grades seven to nine population is involved in such programs and the largest portion of these pupils would be found in the grade nine program. One notable exception is the program in three Buffalo junior high schools which enrolls approximately 70 per cent of all pupils in grades seven and eight. Incidentally, two of these schools can be labeled disadvantaged or core-area schools.

Scheduling Foreign Languages

The policy regarding foreign languages, where they are offered in junior high schools, is usually one of election. Most often it is a ninth grade elective. Generally speaking, guidance policy recommends the election of a foreign language to the college bound youngster and one can assume that the kinds of youngsters that are in these programs are the high I.Q. and college oriented groups. This applies to the grades seven and eight program as well as grade nine. Authors Faunce and Clute,[6] while they make no recommendations for foreign languages other than as electives in grade nine, frown on the idea of electives below grade nine.

> In a lively, well adapted program in which account is taken of pupils' choices and interests, the elective system contributes little in grades seven and eight. Grade nine may offer elective opportunity that makes some sense because elections are built up as continuations of the various exploratory programs of grades seven and eight. We repeat that specialization is not the function of this program, or of the junior high school (or of the foreign language program).

One might hasten to ask: On what exploratory experiences in foreign languages can an election be made in grade nine when such programs are not generally found below grade nine? Furthermore, is not the goal of exploration just as important in grade nine?

Why, then, have not foreign languages made the inroads in the junior high school that one might reasonably assume would follow on the advice of all the expert opinion? Answers usually heard are (1) there is no room in the already crowded schedule, and (2) persons charged with responsibility are not cognizant of or do not accept the new thinking concerning foreign languages. Perhaps the real answer is due to the usual time lag associated with acceptance of innovations

[6] Faunce and Clute, *op. cit.*, pp. 115-116.

which incidentally has attended all aspects of the development of the junior high school.

Recommendations

Concerning the problem of the tight schedule, while it is true there is not an overabundance of unused time, it is clear there is room for foreign languages. The many schools all over the country–Buffalo and especially now California–testify to this possibility. One wonders how much room there would be for art, music, or industrial arts and homemaking were it not for the fact that these subjects are usually mandated, which leads to the speculation that the example of California may offer the solution.

Scheduling hints are offered by Faunce and Clute[7] with their "Alternate Day" and "Short Course" schedules. Foreign language can be scheduled in the former plan three days per week opposite homemaking or art. Incidentally, minimal exposure to foreign language is recommended as three days weekly. Since both homemaking and art are constants (required of all pupils) this plan has the added recommendation that all pupils may move in groups throughout the week. This assumes, of course, that all pupils will take foreign languages. In the "Short Course" plan foreign languages could be scheduled on alternate days with physical education.

In Buffalo junior high schools foreign languages in grade seven and eight are scheduled on the alternate-day plan three days per week opposite music or art. In grade nine foreign language is an elective and is scheduled the customary five days per week. However, because of exploratory experiences in grades seven and eight, which we would hope are both pleasurable and profitable, the pupils have some basis for making elections in foreign languages. In grade nine some pupils, with the help of guidance, may decide to continue with the same foreign language, others may switch languages, and still others may terminate their foreign language education. In any event larger numbers of pupils will have experiences with a foreign language.

In summation, there seems to be little justification for the lack of involvement of large numbers of pupils in junior high school foreign language programs. The recommendations of organizations and governmental bodies such as the NEA, MLA, NASSP, and USOE require curriculum makers at this level to take stock of the situation and evolve a fresh approach to the problem unbiased by previous expectations and experiences.

It should be mentioned here that research studies[8] have indicated that

[7] Faunce and Clute, *op. cit.,* pp. 107-108.

[8] Barbara Von Wittich, "Prediction of Success in Foreign Languages Study," *Modern Language Journal* (April, 1962), p. 211; and Elton Hocking, *Language Laboratory and Language Learning* (Washington: NEA), 1964 p. 72.

I.Q., achievement, reading level in English, success in other school subjects, results of prognostic tests are all poor predictors of success in a foreign language. The only reasonable way to determine if an individual will succeed is to give him an experience in the foreign language.

Thus, in terms of the stated purposes of the junior high school, the nature of the task as revealed by research and experience, and the needs of contemporary society and the learner, there is no basis in fact for continuing the program of foreign languages prevalent in the junior high school. Indeed, the junior high school may offer the last opportunity for the large masses of pupils to have an experience in a foreign language as part of their general education.

Provide the Tools: A Basic Program for the Nonacademic Pupil *

EDWARD J. DAVEY

A core program, centered around the industrial arts area with special emphasis on automobile and electrical appliances repairs, was introduced at the Seaford Junior-Senior High School, Seaford, New York, in September of 1963. The program was designed for the nonacademic male pupil by a small work group of teachers. Included were two periods of instruction for one semester in automobile servicing and repairs, and one period of instruction in related science. The second semester was devoted to instructing boys in servicing and repairing household electrical appliances, and the third period was concerned with the teaching of related science.

It has been our experience at Seaford that the critical year for school dropouts occurred during the ninth grade for nonacademic boys. Therefore we concentrated our efforts toward identifying, screening, and selecting boys in the eighth grade who might profit educationally if placed in this experimental program.

The criteria used for the selection of pupils for the program as developed by the teacher work group and approved by the administration were as follows:

(1) Dull normal or low average (approximately 76-95 I.Q.).
(2) At least 15 years of age as of September of the entering year.
(3) Two or more years retarded for grade level.
(4) Preference to candidates expressing a sincere interest in the program.
(5) Parents' approval.

A total of 16 boys were selected, and group guidance sessions were arranged to outline the objectives and content of the program. During the several

*Reprinted from *The Clearing House,* 39 (February 1965), 351-2, by permission of the publisher and E.J. Davey, principal, Seaford Junior High School, Seaford, New York.

guidance sessions the following goals were carefully reviewed by the counselor:

1. The program will attempt to teach boys elementary work disciplines: punctuality, ability to take orders from a boss, ability to work cooperatively with others in a team, responsibility on the job.
2. The program will be adapted to the interest and ability of the group.
3. The program is designed to lead directly into stable adult jobs.
4. The courses will be organized in such a manner that a work-study program may be planned in the eleventh and twelfth grades.
5. The aim of the program is to encourage boys to remain in school and graduate.

At one guidance session the industrial arts instructor presented a general outline of the content and skills to be pursued during the first year. This course outline was distributed to the boys and contained the following work-study experiences:

1. General Service to the Automobile (first ten weeks)
   a. Change and repair tires
   b. Wheel balancing
   c. Window replacement
   d. Muffler replacement
   e. Windshield wiper service
   f. Test generator
   g. Fuel pump test and repair
   h. Rear spring replacements
   i. Grease car, change oil and; oil filter
   j. Adjust brakes
   k. Check battery, check lights for shorts
   l. Wheel bearings (repack)
   m. Car washing and polishing
   n. Minor carburetor adjustment
   o. Clutch adjustment
   p. Shock absorbers (test and replacements)
2. General Auto Mechanics (second ten weeks)
   a. Check and replace points
   b. Check and replace spark plugs
   c. Check and replace condensor
   d. Timing
   e. Radiator–removal and replacement
   f. Water pump–removal and replacement
   g. Hoses and connections–repair and/or replace
   h. Thermostat–removal, testing, replacement

3. General Service and Repair of Electrical Appliances (20 weeks)
   a. Theory of electricity
      (1) series, (2) parallel, (3) sources
   b. Mechanical operations
      (1) Splices, (2) soldering, (3) attaching and holding wires
   c. Problems in wiring
      (1) Series wiring (low voltage)
      (2) Parallel wiring (low and high voltage)
   d. Use of the multi meter
   e. Small appliances repair
      (1) How to take appliances apart
      (2) How to check components
      (3) Replacement of parts (equipment not operating)
         (a) ordering
         (b) recognizing defective parts and using parts catalog
      (4) Replacement of parts due to wear
         (a) brushes
         (b) elements
         (c) clean armature
         (d) replace and oil bearing
   f. Large appliance repair
      (1) Take apart washing machine
      (2) Recognize defective parts
      (3) Reassemble washing machine
      (4) Take apart electric dryer
      (5) Reassemble electric dryer
      (6) Observe the operation of a refrigerator and trace the various components

At the conclusion of the group guidance sessions 15 boys indicated interest in participating in the program. The counselor listed the boys' names and the principal communicated with their parents by letter. The program was explained in detail to the parents and they were requested to approve by signing an enclosed schedule card. All 15 parents gave their approval for their sons to be enrolled in the program. Several parents made favorable comments concerning this approach for meeting the needs and interest of the slow-learning child.

We have completed the first year of the program, and the results have been most gratifying. Fourteen boys successfully completed the program and have indicated a desire to continue with the experiment during the next school year. In addition, not one boy participating in the program was referred to the Dean of Students for disciplining. Attendance, attitude toward school, appearance, and social participation in school functions showed a noticeable improvement.

Our plans for the next school year are to continue this program in depth and to select a beginning group from our present eighth grade boys. Looking to the future, it is our desire to develop a work-study program in the eleventh and twelfth grades.

At Seaford we believe the nonacademic pupil has a place in this great land of ours and the school is duty bound to help him find it. This is our attempt to provide a practical program to educate the slow learner and to help him to get along in society and hold a job that will give him financial independence.

Communications Course for Junior High School *

DONALD F. HACKETT

Drafting is frequently provided in Grade 7, 8, or 9 for a variety of purposes—all of which have some justification. Unfortunately, the justifications seldom have more foundation than those used to explain why Latin, algebra, history, and the like are offered to this age-grade group. Furthermore, we have probably been guilty of perpetuating a tradition rather than looking for ways to establish new traditions.

Drafting does have academic respectability and, when sold as being the language of engineers and industry, meets with little opposition. However, in and of itself, this is slim justification for running boys and girls through the typical drafting course. The claim that this experience is "exploratory" should make us view it most critically.

About 35,000 years ago, human beings like ourselves appeared. During the next 20,000 years they developed stone tools and the first forms of art—drawing and sculpturing.

At first these drawings and carvings, scratched on cave walls with a sharp stone, only said, "This is a bison" or "This is a deer." They were "thing" pictures. When the pictures were made to show two deer fighting, they would recall to those who had seen a reindeer fight, what the artist had in mind.

Unless the observer knew something about the story, a picture story could not convey what the artist had in mind. As an improvement, a series of related pictures were drawn showing an action step by step.

In time man learned that a symbol (such as a stick figure) could be used to represent the lifelike picture. By adding characteristic features to his symbols, he

*Reprinted from *Industrial Arts and Vocational Education*, 55 (January 1966), 20-22, by permission of the Bruce Publishing Co., and Donald F. Hackett, Georgia Southern College.

could add meaning. A man symbol with a spear in his hand meant *hunter*.

Idea Symbols

"Idea symbols" were probably first made by joining two thing symbols. The symbol for mouth (a picture of two lips) when added to the symbol for water (a wavy line) gave the idea symbol *drink*.

Next, the ancients used the sounds of their spoken words to give their picture language greater meaning. A picture of a *bee* and a *leaf* were read *belief*.

Some words and ideas were impossible to draw. Until man learned to use pictures for letters rather than symbols, his capacity for written communication was limited.

About 6000 years ago, the Egyptians first used pictures to represent letters of an alphabet. Their system of writing, known as hieroglyphics, combined thing pictures, idea pictures, sound pictures, and letters, plus an explanatory symbol or two for each word. (See symbols above.)

The Phoenicians were expert traders, sailors, and manufacturers. They needed a written language for their business records. So, about 3000 years ago, they borrowed and simplified the Egyptian system and produced an alphabet.

The Greeks borrowed 19 characters from the Phoenicians and by the fifth century B.C. had established the shapes of a 24-letter alphabet.

The 23-letter Roman alphabet had its origin in the Greek alphabet of about 700 B.C. They used 13 standard Greek letters and added 10 new ones by remodeling and finishing other Greek letters. The Romans did not need J, U, and W. U and W were developed from the letter V about 1000 years ago, and J developed from the letter I about 500 years ago to give us our 26-letter alphabet.

Throughout this period of alphabet development, tools and materials determined the shapes of the letters. The Egyptians carved their letters in stone with a chisel and mallet. Later they invented papyrus and the brush and quill pen to write on it. These new writing tools permitted changes in the letter shapes.

The shapes of the Phoenician letters were influenced by the wedge and clay tablet they used in writing. The Greeks scribed their letters in wax with a stylus thus accounting for the square shape of most Greek characters. The Romans developed a twin-pointed scriber for laying out letters on stone and developed the beautifully proportioned, graceful letters we use today.

The scribes and monks who laboriously copied manuscripts during the Dark Ages developed what we call the lowercase or small letters and from these, cursive writing.

About 1450 Johan Gutenberg's movable type made the written word available to one and all and created the printing and publishing industry. To keep up with demands, a paper industry developed and other industries appeared to supply the needs of still other industries.

Electricity was discovered in the early seventeenth century, and 234 years later Morse used it to communicate by wire over a short distance. About 40 years later, Bell's telephone permitted anyone who could speak to communicate with someone at the other end of a wire. Twenty years later the wireless telegraph opened many new communications devices. The time between invention, discovery, and application was reduced to decades. It is measured in weeks today—and behind it all is better communications and the need for still better communications.

Communications, then is a larger and much more fertile area of study than is drafting for the junior high school. It is my hypothesis that a course of instruction in communications is of more concern and value to junior high school children than drafting—a relatively narrow offering.

I am suggesting a course in communications as a substitute. This course is intended to develop concepts, attitudes, skills, and knowledge that give junior high school children a more realistic picture of the world today.

(The idea for such a course in communications is several decades old. It has met with little acceptance, but maybe it was born before its time. Maybe 1966 will be a better year.)

Some of the concepts to be developed in this course are:

- Man is a tool maker and tool user.
- Man civilized himself through technology.
- Communications enable man to civilize himself more rapidly.
- Man communicates in many ways.
- Social and economic problems result from changes in communications technology.
- All industries are interdependent and therefore dependent upon communications.

The course is organized into the following areas:

COURSE ORGANIZATION

I. The Graphic Arts	*Activities*
A. The development of our alphabet	Letter nameplates, signs
1. Cave drawings	
2. Egyptian hieroglyphics	Tool copper nameplate
3. Phoenician simplification	
4. Grecian adaptation	
5. Roman influence	Design a monogram

6. Scribes	
7. Importance of tools and materials	
B. Printing and duplicating	Print from type
1. History and evolution of printing	Lithograph a print
2. History and evolution of printing presses	Linoleum block print
3. History and evolution of paper and ink	Silk-screen print
4. Materials and products	Prepare news bulletin
5. Printing technology	
6. Industrial processes and occupations	Make paper; ink
C. Photography	Take pictures
1. History and development of photography	Develop film
2. Amateur and commercial equipment	Print and enlarge Mount pictures
3. Materials and products	Design and exhibit
4. Technology of photography	
5. Industrial processes and occupations	Take and project movies
D. Drafting	Sketch familiar objects
1. Sketching	Measure object and draw mechanically
2. Language of industry	
a) Origin and development	
b) Detail drawings	
c) Assembly drawings	
3. Architecture	Draw house floor plan
4. Industrial design	Make model house
5. Manufacturing processes	
6. Materials and equipment	Make model tool, car, etc.
7. Industrial application and occupations	Design toy, tool, auto, rocket
E. Painting, drawing, and sculpturing	None
1. History and development	
2. Tools and materials	

3. Color	
4. Industrial applications and occupations	
II. Wire Communication	
A. Telegraph; telephone; teletype	Hook up key and sounder
1. History and development	
2. Equipment and its technology	Hook up telephone
3. Operation and uses	Design a remote reading wind vane
4. Manufacture and products	
5. Industrial processes and occupations	
B. Recording equipment (phonograph, tape)	Record message on tape
1. History and development	
2. Equipment and its technology	Plan and record program for radio; TV
3. Operations and uses	
4. Manufacture and products	
5. Industrial processes and occupations	Demonstrate motion picture sound recording
III. Wireless Communication	
A. Radio; radar; television; navigation devices	Assemble kits: one or two tube receivers; code oscillator; transmitter; walkie-talkie
1. History and development	
2. Equipment and technology	
3. Operation and uses	
4. Manufacture and products	
5. Industrial processes and occupations	Mass produce a printed circuit intercom
B. Semaphore; blinker; signal flags	Assemble blinker
1. History and applications	Learn semaphore

Home Economics in the Junior High School

ALVIN W. HOWARD

Home economics education in the junior high school has had a somewhat erratic acceptance, a situation which to a considerable extent still exists today. When the junior high school was first established, "Domestic Arts," or homemaking was considered a basic part of the curriculum; indeed it was hoped and planned that such a course would not only aid in reducing school dropouts but would be of considerable practical use to its students. The Smith-Hughes Act lent strength to the home economics programs and the trends of the 1920's and 1930's which stressed the utilitarian features of course offerings reinforced the position of the home economics curriculum.

The concern in recent years with academic programs and the stress upon the importance of a pre-college education, combined with rising school costs have caused many, both within the schools and in the community, to regard the program of home economics as a frill, a non-essential, and a good place to make cuts. This problem has been aggravated, at least in part, by the sometimes aggressive efforts of those involved in home economics to conform to the trends and increase the academic features of the home economics course offerings. In their sincere belief in the importance of the homemaking curriculum some rather sweeping statements and proposals have been made: for example, it has been recommended that a basic two to four-year sequence should be established on a required basis for all girls in grades 7-12. One state supervisor of home economics suggested somewhat pensively to a junior high school principal that what was really desirable was a junior high school three-year overall program in which *all* course work for all students was developed around home economics. There has also been resentment on the part of some teachers in other fields because home economics teachers frequently have smaller classes, have more planning time, and, because of the vocational aspect of ninth grade classes, home economics teachers often receive extra pay.

What is too often overlooked by critics is that only a part of the student enrollment goes on to college, that home economics has a considerably broadened field of content and interest than was formerly the case, and that a considerable number of girls receive little if any homemaking instruction out-of-school. It is common to hear a mother say, "This is a waste of time. I can teach her these things at home." This is unquestionably true and some mothers *do* teach much of the homemaking content to their daughters at home. But it is equally true that many others do not, either because they cannot, because the girls do not take the time to learn, or because the mothers find it too time consuming and conclude that it is easier to perform the homemaking tasks themselves. The traditional conception of homemaking as consisting of cooking and sewing has hampered its acceptance since it is often not generally realized that a competent, interested, and enthusiastic teacher of home economics does much more than teach cooking and sewing to her classes. A further hindrance to the junior high school program of home economics is the attitude, criticism, and complaint of many of the high school home economics teachers who accuse the junior high school teachers of going too far with their students and infringing upon the content that rightfully belongs to the high school – a complaint that is restrictive to the junior high school program and appears to indicate a need for the high school teachers to take a critical look at what they could be doing with and offering to their classes.

Home economics in the junior high school should:

1. Be required for all girls for at least one year and probably two. A good case can also be made for requiring all boys to have at least one semester of homemaking.

2. Realize that there are several levels of economic status and adjust the program accordingly. Content for girls in the upper middle class should not be the same as that for the economically deprived. A program in Montgomery County, Maryland, has been successful with a group of potential girl dropouts by taking the girls to the "Next-to-New Shop," showing them how to select worthwhile garments, buy carefully, and then remodel the clothing in the school homemaking class.

3. Accept that, in these times of rising prices and inflation, it becomes essential that boys and girls learn something of consumer education, budgeting, buying wisely, and the hazards and problems of installment buying, sales, and discounts. This may be offered in business education or homemaking, but it should be a required course.

4. Understand that homemaking courses should be just that, content which relates to the everyday lives of the students and has an immediate or imminent application. Young people need to know about the necessities of nutrition, money management, personal grooming, child care, home furnishing, and the possibilities for creative expression in home decorating and art.

5. Refuse to let the high school determine content, scope, and sequence of the junior high school curriculum in home economics. What is desirable is the best program for junior high students, not a docile acceptance of standards imposed by high school teachers.

6. Be certain that students who are potential dropouts are sure to receive a program which is of real interest to them, excites their curiosity, creates a desire to learn more, and includes content of relevance to their situation.

The usual seventh grade curriculum includes clothing selection and construction, foods, textiles, personal finances, and nutrition. In the eighth grade, course offerings commonly include more clothing and foods, purchasing food and clothing, and home management. Offerings in the ninth grade are generally comprised of consumer education, clothing and foods, home management, child care and development, health and home nursing, personal grooming, and home decorating.

There is a distinct problem in that there is no dearth of suggestions and recommendations as to what should be taught, and some excellent syllabi and course outlines are available. There is, however, a marked difference in what actually *is* taught, depending upon the administration, the community, the facilities, the funds available, pressures from the high school, and the teacher. An extreme instance of this may be found when seventh grade girls in one school are making excellent clothing while seventh grade girls in another school are restricted to hemming a dish towel or spend the bulk of their time with a text book.

There is a distinct need for an appreciation of the merit and use of the home economics curriculum for both girls and boys and an understanding of the requirements for this area in facilities and finance. Teachers of home economics should stress the application of their material to the lives of their students and select content relevant to student needs. It is also time for junior high school principals to stop regarding the home economics teachers as a source of coffee and cookies for meetings, and realize that this area is an integral part of the junior high school curriculum.

Industrial Arts in the Junior High School

ALVIN W. HOWARD

Industrial arts programs in the junior high school have often been characterized as "dumbbell classes," "Mickey Mouse" courses, a dumping ground for the academically unsuccessful, and even an educational "frill." Principals have cursed the industrial arts departments because of their expense and high pupil cost of instruction, yet have blessed them for providing a place for students who did not fit into the academic program. To an extent the teachers of industrial arts have aggravated the difficulties in those schools where the course of study is so rigid and stultified that every student is required to work on the same project, such as bookends – all being expected to begin and complete the work simultaneously. Further, in an effort to achieve academic respectability, some teachers of industrial arts have required long textbook units on "The History of the Jack Plane," and similar topics.

The industrial arts program in the junior high school has no need to scramble desperately to justify its existence. There is a definite need for this kind of education and it has a long and honorable history. When the junior high school was first established, one of the reasons often stated for its need was that of prevocational training – a course for the non-college bound. Originally titled "Manual Training," or "Manual Arts," the curriculum at that time emphasized hand skills, woodworking, and some metal work. By World War I many junior high schools, in addition to these offerings, had added courses in mechanical drawing, electricity, and graphic arts. Since then compulsory attendance laws, child labor laws, shorter work weeks, and technological advances have expanded the curricular areas to such an extent that a good case can be made for requiring industrial arts in the junior high school for both boys and girls.

The junior high is supposed to provide exploratory offerings, either for interest or of a prevocational nature; the present industrial culture makes it highly desirable for all citizens to understand as much of our technology as possible; our citizens may have been improving in academic preparation but there certainly appears to have been an increase in mechanical ignorance and lack of handiness; and industrial arts education is becoming increasingly useful and valuable to all citizens because of the expanded amount of leisure time available.

In junior high schools industrial arts is usually required of boys for one year and often for more. Industrial arts in the ninth grade is usually an elective offering. Most programs are limited to boys but a small and increasing number of junior high schools offer industrial arts for girls, sometimes elective, sometimes required, often in coeducational classes.

A good industrial arts program has come a long way from the traditional concept of one year of wood shop, one of metal shop, and one of mechanical drawing. A sound industrial arts curriculum is generally exploratory in several areas, including industrial crafts, drafting, electricity, electronics, graphic arts, metal work, wood work, and often work with plastics, cement, and rock and gems. The trend is toward a comprehensive "general" shop in junior high school which may include a variety of offerings such as work with wood, ceramics, radio, concrete, plastics, drafting, photography, welding, small motors – both electric and gasoline – forging, textiles, lapidary, and graphic arts. Larger junior high schools may have a general shop "heavy," and a general shop "light." Newer schools are even replacing the comprehensive shops with the industrial arts laboratory, which eliminates the traditional division of materials and processes previously found in the unit shop concepts.

Especially for the junior high school student, the program in industrial arts should emphasize the exploratory functions and work toward relating to curricular offerings in other fields. It is possible and desirable, for example, for the science and industrial arts teachers to coordinate their instruction to permit students to develop projects and studies which use the facilities of both laboratories. The required junior high school program should emphasize breadth, not depth of offerings and provide opportunities for some specialization in electives in such areas as graphic arts, drafting, metal, wood, plastics, and power mechanics. Students need to develop manipulative abilities and skills and to learn the proper use of hand tools.

Industrial arts should be accepted for what it can be and is: a necessary part of the junior high school comprehensive program. To help to reach this goal, it is essential that the teachers of industrial arts break away from the compartmentation and limitations of wood shop, metal shop, and drafting, with the required "projects" for every class member, and strive for the variety and interest of student selected individual projects. It is also necessary for school administrators to realize that the industrial arts program is not cheap, must have adequate financial support, and should be made available to every boy and girl regardless of their ability to pay for materials. It has been said that money spent on a junior high school interscholastic athletic program for a limited few students would, in many cases, provide the supplies for a junior high school industrial arts program for the entire student body.

All Pupils Take Agriculture in Los Angeles*

LESTER O. MATTHEWS

Agriculture Introduced Early in Schools

Agricultural education has been an integral part of the instructional program of the Los Angeles City Schools since 1908. During the early years of this program, when the schools operated on the 8-4 plan, agricultural education for the pupil of junior high-school age was divided between the seventh and eighth grades of the elementary schools and the ninth grade in the high schools. In the 1920's, when junior high schools were established, general agriculture was offered in the seventh grade as a required exploratory course and in the eighth and ninth grades as elective courses.

During this early period, Los Angeles was considered a rural area with agriculture the major industry in the county, which ranked number one in the nation in agricultural production. The major purposes of the agricultural education program during the early years were vocational in nature. During the depression years and World War II the emphasis was changed to food production for family use.

Program Changed after World War II

Following World War II, Los Angeles changed rapidly from an agricultural to an urban area, dropping to a third position in national agricultural

*Reprinted from *The Bulletin of the National Association of Secondary School Principals,* 46 (February 1962), 77-80, by permission of the National Association of Secondary School Principals and Lester O. Matthews, Supervisor of Agriculture, Los Angeles City Schools. Copyright © 1962 by the National Association of Secondary School Principals.

production. This brought changes in the agricultural education program. Although general agriculture was offered in almost every junior high school, the courses of study consisted of a basic outline, with the development of the program in each school depending largely upon the individual teacher's ingenuity and initiative. The facilities available in each school were limited to a small plot of ground, a few tools, and whatever buildings could be obtained.

With the development of building standards for junior high schools about 1948, the pattern for agricultural education in junior high schools began to change. Today, a standard agriculture unit for junior high schools consists of a classroom with toolroom, storage, lavatory facilities, a lath house, potting room, compost bins, and approximately one acre of ground. The planting area is divided into plots, approximately 25 feet by 50 feet with cement walks and adequate watering facilities. Not only are these facilities being provided in all new junior high schools, but existing schools are being brought up to the new standard as rapidly as funds permit.

The nature of facilities was based on the development of a well-defined course of study, including a statement of basic philosophy, aims, objectives, and instructional units. With the development of the new course of study has come the adoption of textbooks, audio-visual materials, and standard supply and equipment items.

These changes in teaching facilities have been accompanied by a change in the type of agriculture teacher who is employed. The typical junior high-school teacher of agriculture today is a college graduate, is 34 years of age, has taught five years, and had a college major in ornamental horticulture or landscape architecture. Half of the teachers presently employed had their practice teaching in the Los Angeles City Schools.

Objectives of the Program

The development of the junior high-school course of study in agriculture recognized the following basic interests of boys and girls: (1) natural curiosity in living and growing things; (2) desire to explore; (3) desire for self-expression and personal satisfaction; (4) eagerness to demonstrate ability; (5) ambition to achieve success; (6) desire to be practical rather than theoretical; and (7) desire for immediate application of acquired skills.

Based on these interests of students, broad objectives for the program are as follows:

1. To develop an appreciation of living things and an appreciation for beauty
2. To develop proper attitudes and responsibility
3. To develop useful skills and good work habits

4. To improve command of the three R's through the application of these fundamentals
5. To develop appreciation for outdoor living
6. To develop the spirit of cooperation and good citizenship
7. To develop avocational interests and explore vocational interests.

Content of the Program

The junior high-school program in agriculture is based upon the above objectives as follows:

J1 Gardening (Exploratory)–10 weeks–B7 Boys–Required–Includes instruction in garden tool identification, safety, preparing soil, planting and harvesting a crop, planting a seed flat, making of simple cuttings and preparation of a notebook, which includes drills in vocabulary, spelling, and arithmetic.

J2 Gardening (Elective)–20 weeks–A8, B9 Boys–Reviews B7 instruction and adds experience in producing a long-term crop of vegetables and flowers, plant identification, advanced plant propagation, simple landscaping, and garden maintenance.

J3 Floriculture (Elective)–20 weeks–A9 Girls and Boys–This course, designed primarily for girls, includes instruction in preparation of soil and planting of flowers, how to cut, preserve, and use flowers in arrangements and corsages, propagation of plants by seed and cuttings, plant identification, and planting and maintaining dish gardens and planters.

Major Activities in the Program

The outcomes of the program have been extremely rewarding. It has provided worth-while and meaningful experiences for boys and girls of all ability levels. It develops in students an appreciation for and an awareness of the importance of agriculture in everyday life. Some of the most satisfying phases of the program are school competition related to the improvement of the pupils' homes and their community environment. The "Los Angeles Beautiful" program, sponsored by the Los Angeles Chamber of Commerce and co-sponsored by the Sears-Roebuck Foundation and the Women's Architectural League of Southern California, has spearheaded community improvement. The program is divided into three categories, improvement of school gardens, home beautification, and community improvement projects. It is culminated by an awards banquet where trophies are presented to school and pupil winners. Over 250,000 pupils have participated in the "Los Angeles Beautiful" program in the past twelve years.

Another annual event is the Horticulture Contest sponsored by the California Nurserymen's Association. There is student competition in demonstrations of knowledge and skills relating to the plant and soil sciences.

The newest project is the development of turf-grass experimental plots in school gardens. The purpose of this project is to demonstrate the required knowledge and skill necessary in the selection of the best and most economical turfs grown under varying conditions. This activity is co-sponsored by the Los Angeles County Farm and Home Adviser and the Southern California Turf Grass Association.

The junior high school was originally established to provide exploratory experiences for boys and girls. The program in agricultural education in Los Angeles is designed to provide exploratory experiences in natural science. It is hoped that, through the junior high-school agriculture program, students will develop an awareness of their responsibilities toward the stewardship of the wondrous world in which they live.

Business Education in the Middle School*

WALTER NARDELLI

Business education must catch up with the changing economic world and meet the changing nature and demands of the Middle School learner. The Middle School comprises the sixth, seventh, and eighth grades. In the sixth grade business education will be related directly to the learner's experiences in his immediate community.

With the introduction of the new concept in intermediate public education organization-the Middle School- business education must be evaluated with a new educational philosophy. The old concepts of typing, shorthand, and record keeping must give way to a new philosophy and responsibility of preparing all Middle School pupils for a meaningful and practical understanding of the American economy so that they may participate more fully in a business world that has given them the highest level of living that any country in the world has ever attained.

Great curriculum changes will take place in the Middle School in the near future. All students should be oriented to the demands of the American economy through a study of their business and industrial community. All phases of economics will be the vanguard of business education because no business today has any reality unless it is related to the economic influences and demands of the local, community, state, and Federal governments. Free enterprise is American, and the sooner Americans begin to understand the term, the better for the general health of the country. The pupils of the Middle School will be introduced to the following factors:

1. *Community industries*
2. *Community service businesses*

*Reprinted from *The Balance Sheet*, 48 (March 1967), 307-309, by permission of the publisher and Walter Nardelli, South Burlington High School, South Burlington, Vermont.

3. *Community recreational businesses*
4. *Community "home" products*
5. *Community organizations that bring in new businesses and industries*
6. *Community "share" of new businesses, new families, new schools, new fire and police protection programs, new water and sewerage problems, etc.*
7. *Community economics of non-profit organizations*
8. *Community "image" building*

The sixth grader of today as opposed to the sixth grader of 10 years ago is more attuned to adult society, more conscious of the value of a dollar, more biologically susceptible to the emotional problems of girl and boy relationships, more cognizant of the inconsistencies and contradictories of the adult community, and more vulnerable to the wooings of Madison Avenue marketeers. Business education must upgrade itself to meet the challenge of the inquiring mind of the sixth grader, who wants to know "why" and "how" the American economy is the most successful in the world. He wants to know things about his community business and industrial worlds so that he may relate what he reads, sees, and hears to his immediate vicinity. He is curious about wars and the peace that follows them. He is curious about the part the Federal government plays in the economic welfare of his community. He is curious why the church is something that happens on Sundays only. He is curious why wars seem to come in the U. S. during periods of economic depressions.

These are some of the factors of business education that will put the word "business" in a respected atmosphere for the youngster. Many times the word "business" is associated with unfavorable connotations. Business in the expression business education should mean to the sixth grader the world of opportunity and challenge opened to anyone who has training, education, imagination, courage, and faith in himself. Business means the world that will supply the sixth grader with a level of living not equaled by any other nation today. This is the meaning of business in business education—not the narrow stagnant spectrum of typing, shorthand, and bookkeeping.

The seventh grader will be introduced to the concepts of the business and industrial world, economically, politically, socially, and morally. Now the seventh grader must understand that there are tools that implement, supplement, and complement his participation in the business world. Tools are needed in terms of typewriting, shorthand, and bookkeeping not for the use of the knowledge per se, but for a clearer understanding by the learner of his greater and more fruitful initiation into the economic adult world with some of these prerequisites. All students in the seventh grade will learn to type for personal use. Fingers can type faster than they can write. Writing will become a symbolic leisure-time activity in the years to come. Writing, as we understand it now, will be a personal matter for personal correspondence. Typing is fundamental to the study of the mechanized office to come in another generation. Typing will be a second-nature skill in the years to come just like driving a car. Typing will be learned as an agent educationally in the following situations:

1. *Learning spelling of English and foreign languages*
2. *Learning the grammar of English and foreign languages*
3. *Learning data processing machines with their various kinds of keyboards*
4. *Learning to prepare better reports; teaching and learning of organization and presentation of material*
5. *Learning arithmetical sets and arrangements for tabulation and interpretation*
6. *Learning keyboards of ordinary business office machines*

These are just a few of the related activities to the "why" of typewriting in the seventh grade. The typewriter (made of lighter and stronger material) will be transistorized so that it will be as basic to tomorrow's business education as the common pencil is to elementary data processing. Typing will be required of all seventh graders along with an introduction to adding machines, calculators, and some simple data processing machines. Typing will be like a catalyst that will intrigue a child to try his hand at English, arithmetic, geography, French, drawing, and others in a "different" way. Typing per se has no value educationally unless it becomes an aid in the learning process.

As part of the seventh grade business education program, the learner should be introduced to record keeping, which should be slanted to his learning level of experiences. He should be familiar with the following aspects of the business world:

1. *Bank account*
2. *Checking account*
3. *Budget*
4. *Taxes (all kinds)*
5. *Purchase invoice*
6. *Sales invoice*
7. *Discount*
8. *Trade-ins*
9. *Marginal utility*
10. *Form utility*
11. *Place utility*
12. *Financial statements*

These are just a few of the factors involved in elementary record keeping, which stress those things that the learner can see, feel, fill out, and relate to the adult business world. Record keeping is an offshoot of economics. More vocabulary can be introduced from the headings taken from newspapers and magazines.

In grade eight all pupils will take bookkeeping, an abbreviated longhand version of shorthand, business arithmetic, and an introduction to distributive educational courses. The eighth grade is still a period of orientation in business education, and the period is to reveal to the learner what other tools are needed for a fuller understanding of American economy.

Bookkeeping will unravel the five books of original entry that most businesses have in use. The material will be related to the types of businesses that are in the community. Emphasis would be placed on the "why" and "how" of such books and other papers of an original nature. Areas that would stir the curiosity of the learners would be the following:

1. *How a company can keep track of all its inventory?*
2. *How do they know any week if the company is making a profit?*
3. *Who keeps the books of original entries?*
4. *Why is a warehouse needed for most manufacturing plants?*
5. *What is the difference between a retail store and a manufacturing plant as to books of original entry?*
6. *What is the break-even point?*
7. *How does a company keep track of all the different prices of its merchandise?*
8. *How is the payroll done?*
9. *What part does the state government have in the way the books are kept? The Federal government?*

Thus, bookkeeping will be taught as an agent to understanding American economy—not just to produce bookkeepers. The study of bookkeeping will emphasize the reasons for automation in certain types of industries. The learner will be able to apply his typing skills (still being taught in the eighth grade) and his business machines skills to his bookkeeping assignments. As mentioned above, typing will be taught with emphasis on speed, control, accuracy, and "marketable" production. Business letters will be a part of the English requirements. The abbreviated longhand version of shorthand should be experimented with at the eighth grade level because the typewriter of tomorrow will probably be of a stenoscript model so that notes, letters, and reports can be done expediently. As Latin has lost its efficacy in the modern concept of written and oral communication, so will the present "liberal arts English" lose its function and purpose in the present dynamic business world. The abbreviated longhand version of shorthand is based upon the phonetic alphabet. The pupil doesn't have to learn new symbols or characters. Shorthand can be taught as a foreign language is taught today—another means of communication. All pupils will be introduced to shorthand to help make their studying easier and in the long run more effective. It is possible that a form of abbreviated longhand will be the language accepted in the public schools as a supplementary language with its own function and purpose. The "liberal arts English" will fade from use in the face of voluminous reading materials that are hitting the markets. It is possible that a type of shorthand will be available through a contrivance(not yet developed)that will convert "liberal arts English" to shorthand. Books can be read for content material if printed in this shorthand. Books can be read in the "liberal arts English" for pleasure aesthetically. Notes in shorthand form are invaluable to the learner in any course. Imagine the ease of learning a content course through concrete meaningful language. Perhaps in the future there will be greater use for this form of language that the eighth grader learns as the language of the business world. What a challenging thought!

Thus, the Middle School may well be the starting point of a complete reevaluation of business education in American public and private schools and colleges. The Middle School is a period of exploration for the youngster. What greater exploration could a child have than in the American business world that supplies him and his family with the highest level of living in the world. Business education must grow up to meet the new challenges that begin in the Middle School grades. By the time the Middle School learner reaches the high school, business education should give him a practical and workable knowledge of the American economy—such knowledge being a form of liberal arts like the studies of Cicero, Descartes, and Shakespeare.

Physical Education in the Junior High School

ALVIN W. HOWARD

The junior high school student, preadolescent and early adolescent, needs a program of physical education which is designed and presented specifically for this age group. Physical changes and growth spurts for these children are extreme—shoes bought in September do not fit in December, coordination is frequently so changed that parents are puzzled and concerned. Muscular development does not keep up with bone growth and physical size is no index to endurance; fatigue is likely to come easily. The physical education program should be, but frequently is not, one which is developmental and sequential, articulating with both that of the elementary school and that of the high school. There is a need for a wide range of activities, both within the required physical education curriculum and within the intramural program. These activities should permit every student some measure of success, encourage him to continue a variety of physical activities in out-of-school time, help in the development of bodily control, and improve his physical condition.

A real problem in junior high school physical education is that of definition since "required" physical education may mean that it is required for only grade seven or perhaps grade eight. It may mean that physical education is "required" for but one or two days a week, or perhaps for one semester and it may alternate with another subject. The difficulty is aggravated when the course is titled, "Health and Physical Education," which often means that much time intended for physical education is spent in class and book work. The junior high school program of physical education has also been criticized because of the "ball and whistle" instructors who throw a half dozen footballs or basketballs out to the students and let them work out their own games.

A sound physical education program for junior high school boys and girls will take into account several considerations:

1. There is a definite need in our mechanized age for a regular, sequential, planned, and developmental curriculum in physical education which builds bodies, promotes physical fitness, and encourages a carryover and longtime interest in sports and physical activities suitable for out-of-school use.

2. The physically educated student has developed an extreme range of basic skills in running, walking, jumping, throwing, and controlling his body.

3. The physically educated junior high school boy and girl have learned team sports, the need for team action, the necessity for learning the rules of the game and abiding by them, and the desirability of good sportsmanship. There is too little emphasis upon character and sportsmanship and too much stress upon winning and upon proselyting for varsity teams—which have but dubious value, if any, in junior high school.

4. Physical education instructors should not have coaching assignments. It is truly said that no man can serve two masters, and in this situation it is certain that one or the other of the duties will suffer. Because of the importance generally attached to varsity athletics, the required physical education program is often that which is slighted.

5. There is a place for some academic work in physical education but there is no justification for the avalanche of paper work which is sometimes proliferated in physical education classes. A girls' physical education instructor in one junior high school constructed an eleven page written objective examination for the unfortunate girls in her classes, based upon the classwork. Her final grades for the semester were weighted one-third for class work, one-third for a project, and one-third for "dressing-out and showering." Presumably one might earn a high grade without ever participating in a single activity.

6. A good physical education program teaches a wide knowledge of games and sports. The student knows the rules and backgrounds of many games which permits him to derive more pleasure as a participant and spectator.

7. A basic physical education program includes instruction and participation in:

a. Games, sports, athletics, and play activities.
b. Self-testing activities and gymnastics.
c. Rhythmical activities.
d. Physical fitness and developmental activities.

The program for girls is often better organized, better planned, and has a better range of activities than does that for boys. The program for boys is often characterized by football in the fall, basketball in the winter, and track and baseball in the spring.

8. Physical education should be a required course which meets daily for one period for all three years of junior high school. A schedule which plans P.E. classes for two or three days weekly for one semester loses much of its value. Physical education is an integral part of the overall program and should be treated as such.

9. There *must* be adequate funds, facilities, equipment, and personnel for the required program. There is absolutely no jusfication for diverting the bulk of these to an interscholastic program and treating the required curriculum in physical education as a poor relation. Neither should the physical education classes be treated as a dumping ground for problem students nor be assigned twice as many students as other classes in the junior high school. The values inherent in a sound program are many: it not only improves physical development, it contributes to social growth, mental health, and emotional growth. Adolescents can profit from opportunities to work off tensions and pressures and to secure a measure of peer status.

10. The measures taken to develop citizenship, respect for the rights of others, recognition of the worth of the individual, and the habit of courtesy and good manners must be implemented and continued in the physical education classes. The instances are countless of locker room bullying, refusals of students to permit less skillful students to participate, and the use of strong and undesirable language in physical education classes. Unfortunately, coaches are sometimes not completely innocent of this last charge.

11. Body contact sports should be avoided, it not eliminated, in junior high school. This is not the place for boxing, hockey, and probably not for tackle football.

12. There should be a diversified, well-staffed intramural program which is adequately funded, encourages wide-spread participation, and is so scheduled as to permit maximum student involvement. The intramural program for junior high school students should include such sports as badminton, ping pong, tennis, soccer, speedball, touch or flag football, basketball, track, wrestling, and softball. There should be no requirements for student participation in intramural sports except that of student desire and interest. A failing grade in English is not a valid reason for refusal to permit a student to engage in intramural basketball.

A good physical education program in junior high school does not stress team nor varsity sports at the expense of individual or dual activities. It encourages maximum interest and participation and gives training that has carryover to out-of-school and adult life.

Curriculum Trends in the Junior High School*

PHILO T. PRITZKAU

In any reasonable assessment of the Curriculum trends in the Junior High School it would seem appropriate to do much more than merely indicate those changes which have occurred and others which are now occurring. The changes which have occurred and those now taking place need to be viewed in terms of purposes of the Junior High School. Are the purposes the same as they have always been or are they changing? And what is the nature of the change which occurs? Is it an intensification of the persistent purpose, for example, of exploration? Or is the purpose being changed in terms of new conceptions about the whole purpose of education? To what degree is there a continued emphasis on the adolescent and his peculiar needs?

As one views the above questions it becomes apparent to the careful observer that perhaps more is needed than what is implied by the questions in order that the junior high school student may find identity in the contemporary scene. Curriculum trends may not equate with those in *The Junior High School We Need,* the title of a report for the ASCD Commission on Secondary Education. Then, too, is the junior high school we need based on such problems as alienation, deprivation and other conditions which are associated with the youth and their quests for identity? Is there, instead, a tendency in much of the literature on the junior high school and its youth to regard this contingent of the educational continuum as a totality? In short, is there a marked disposition to make positive declarations about what the junior high school should be in terms

*Reprinted from *The High School Journal,* 50 (December 1966), 137-146, by permission of the publisher and Philo T. Pritzkau, University of Connecticut.

of a "system"? Let's look then at some of the curriculum trends and how they might relate to some of the questions indicated.

Some General Observations

That the junior high school is really a burning issue in American education becomes a reality when almost an entire issue of a major journal is devoted to it. In it Vars[1] editorializes about change and the junior high school, and suggests that junior high schools are changing and that the basic question remains the same: "What shall be the nature of education for young adolescents in today's society?" Wattenberg[2] emphasizes that today's younger adolescents are more dichotomized than any previous generation and then proceeds to indicate possible educational implications related to this condition. He emphasizes that a key educational task is "to devise arrangements under which every boy and girl can be a valued member of a continuing face-to-face group." He goes on by suggesting some of many ways in which this can be done such as building smaller schools, breaking big schools into house units, expanding the range of co-curricular activities and others. He ends the paragraph on a rather poignant reference when he suggests, "At the very least we can stare down the enthusiasts who think social problems can be solved by supermarket education dished out in monstrous educational parks."

Partin[3] re-emphasizes the importance of the original and, perhaps, continuing purpose of the junior high school which was to give exploratory experiences. He defines exploration as an activity within which the student does something to things and ideas and they, in turn, do something to him. He makes a distinction here between exploring as a comprehensive activity and sampling which is sometimes called exploratory. He stresses the fact that exploration is a search for meaning.

Johnson[4] pleads for greater respect and greater expectations of the adolescent's intellect. He would question the notion of prevocational preparation and would consider "... intellectual emphasis the most practical kind of preparation for both the vocational and the leisure-time realities of the future..."

Jones[5] re-emphasizes the importance of dealing with the many pressures

[1]The issue is *Educational Leadership,* Journal of the Association for Supervision and Curriculum Development. Washington, D.C. Dec. 1965.

[2]Association for Supervision and Curriculum Development, *Educational Leadership,* "Change and the Junior High School." Washington, D. C. Dec. 1965. P. 189.

[3]"Today's Junior High Students," p. 191-192. "To Sample—Or to Explore," p. 194-195.

[4]"The Adolescent Intellect," pp. 203-204.

[5]"Pressures and Adolescents," pp. 209-211.

which the junior high school youngster faces today. He discusses these pressures as parental, teacher, social, family conflict, homework and grades, socioeconomic and others. He further suggests that the pressures for high grades and accumulating knowledge so as to make high scores on college entrance examinations have moved from the senior high school to the junior high school. He recommends besides the improvement of teachers and teaching the early detection of problems of adolescents by the guidance counselor, the balancing of pressure of college preparation programs, and the mandatory study and practice of leadership and membership roles of students in the junior high school.

Perhaps the most revolutionary and, at the same time, one of the most rational discourses on the junior high schools, is by Hull.[6] He suggests that, in his opinion, the junior high school "may be America's greatest educational blunder." To paraphrase his discussion he deplores as a weakness the bland assumption that anything called a junior high school is the answer to early adolescent education. A junior high school is not a standard institution but exhibiting, instead, many shapes and forms of organization. Furthermore, according to Hull, the assumption that an appropriate grouping is seventh, eighth, and ninth grades together remains unexamined. In fact, it reveals an arbitrary arrangement which may approach the ridiculous when viewed in terms of interests of boys and girls of different ages. The gist of Hull's statements may be summed up by indicating that no real direction to education can be developed by thinking of the junior high school as an institution but by regarding schools as specific institutions having the characteristics which create a service rather than fashion a product.

Alexander and Williams[7] along with Hull seem to accentuate the refrain of increasing disenchantment with the schools for the middle school years. With rather impressive and elaborate documentation relative to this disenchantment they have proposed a model middle school which, no doubt, they and others hope may be reflected in the trend to middle school development. One could, perhaps, suggest that some specific schools already may have a curriculum plan and the organization for instruction which is proposed. Then we might just ask "Is this a school we need?"

Trends As Related to the Student

Perhaps one of the most noteworthy publications to stimulate an examination of the current curriculum practices was Planning for American Youth.[8] This publication prompted a study of adolescent needs which were

6"Are Junior High Schools the Answer?" pp. 213-216.

7"Schools for the Middle School Years," pp. 217-223.

8National Association of Secondary School Principals, *Planning for American Youth.* Washington, D. C., 1944.

spelled out in practices considered exemplary in the curriculum for youth. Bush[9] compared and participated in surveys based on the 10 Imperative Needs statement. Students of junior high schools, in roughly small communities, were asked to rank the needs in terms of their interest in 1947, in 1957 and in 1964. The ranking was made under two titles, "Things to Study About" and "Things to Do."

The table below reveals some shifting interests as among the three surveys.[10]

Need	*1947*		*1957*		*1964*	
	Study	*Doing*	*Study*	*Doing*	*Study*	*Doing*
1. Vocational preparation	4	8	4	8	2	3
2. Health	1	4	1	4	6	9
3. Citizenship	8	9	9	9	8	6
4. Family Relationship	5	1	8	1	1	2
5. Consumer Education	2	7	3	3	1	5
6. Science	9	3	2	6	9	7
7. Apprecation of Arts	10	5	5	5	10	8
8. Leisure	3	6	10	2	4	1
9. Cooperative Living–Values	7	10	6	7	5	4
10. Rational Thinking	6	2	7	10	7	10

As between 1947 and 1964, in particular, the shift in ranking seems to give greater priority in 1964 to vocational preparation, family relationship, leisure, and cooperative living-values. At the same time a lower ranking is given to rational thinking, appreciation of the arts, health and to some degree, in science. It should be noted that there appears to be a decided shift in science as between 1957 and 1964 giving a much lower estimation to this "survival" area. Perhaps the high ranking given to science in 1957 can be attributed to the national pressures for that area in that year.

Bush[11] indicates that the needs showing most increase in both studying and activity deal with the problem of searching for self. These adolescents express this searching in becoming used to themselves as individuals and developing independence from adults especially authority figures such as parents and teachers. They are beginning to reach decisions about their potential in the

[9]Phyllis I. Bush, "The Junior High School Student 1944-1964." *The Bulletin of the National Association of Secondary School Principals,* Washington, D. C., April 1965, pp. 50-55.

[10]*Ibid.,* p. 52.

[11]*Ibid.,* pp. 53-54.

vocational field. Bush further suggests that educators can understand this shift by noting that the community is meeting the needs expressed in the 1947 study and, thus, others become more imperative to youth. Furthermore, the importance of search for self is based upon fear of failure in the rapidly shifting society. A highly important observation made by Bush relative to the purposes of the junior high school is the following: "The adolescent has had no childhood during which freedom to explore his physical world would have provided a cognitive mass for future learning."

The reference to an implied desirability of a "cognitive mass" during childhood clearly suggests the moving down of the exploration period from junior high school to the upper grades in elementary school. It would appear that here is a rather vital indication of a hoped for trend toward an accentuation of the affective domain in the junior high school. In other words, exploration in the junior high school should tend toward doing that which would provide the student with a knowledge of self and an approach to individual identity.

Coming back to the shift of representation of the needs, several factors appear which are somewhat disturbing. These have to do with the drift away from rational thinking and appreciation of the arts. It would appear that any approach to identity on the part of youth could certainly not exclude an individual relating to the arts and rational thought. Is it possibly a fact that the practices in these areas in the junior high school have been of such a nature as to obscure an individual's relationship to them? Certainly the arts and rational thinking would be associated with values, leisure, and, to a considerable degree, family relationships. A factor which should be cause for disturbance also is the attitude which seems to suggest that self-orientation is located quite apart from the substance of subject matter. A real danger to the extension of existence on the part of young people is to explore the cognitive and affective domains of knowledge in a condition of compartmentalization. The attitude which seems to prevail here and which is incorporated into practice is that the search for self must be carried on under conditions which are immune from subject matter.

Another rather disturbing condition about much of the literature on the needs of junior high school youth is the priority placed on reality and practicality with the hidden suggestion that the theoretical may have depreciative effects. Furthermore, rarely if ever, is a distinction made between reality and the *Real.* As a result there develops a rather singular emphasis on reality as that which matters when, in fact, the identity of youth may be found in intensive inquiry into the *real*—the authentic.

Interpretations and Conclusions

A portion of the discussion below is based on a most comprehensive survey in practices in junior high school education throughout the United States conducted by William T. Gruhn and Harl R. Douglass in 1964.[12]

TRENDS WHICH MAY BE EXPECTED

There appears to be an expansion and intensification of the programs of mathematics for most students. Although general mathematics and arithmetic still command the most important place in the junior high school, modern mathematics is occupying an important place and gaining in respectability. Many of the principles underlying the rationale of modern mathematics are being incorporated into the programs which retain the traditional labels.

There is a definite shift downward from the senior high school to the junior high school in the inclusion of science and mathematics content in the curriculum. Some of this shift, however, has occurred in connection with the development of the modern mathematics programs. In the science area the programs of Earth Science and Physical Science have been developed. Traditional courses in mathematics which have, to a marked extent, been shifted downward from the high school are algebra and plane geometry in Grade 8. In science it has been biology. As one views some of the promising practices in science in junior high schools, however, it is apparent that some high level redevelopment of biology programs is taking place. The writer has observed both the development of content and practices relative to biology in some of the junior high schools and would say that the quality would rank above some of the better high school programs of a few years back.

An accompanying factor in the development and redevelopment of science programs in the junior high school is the vast strides which have been made by school systems in building science rooms and laboratories. Some of these would put many college facilities to shame. Of course, it should be recognized that this development dates largely from Sputnik and the pressures for science emanating from that event. Furthermore, through the tremendous efforts of the National Science Foundation in its federally subsidized Institute programs for teachers, there has been a great spurt in the development of science education in the junior high school.

Although the title, general science, and exploratory concept, is still retained for most science programs in Grade 7 and, to a lesser degree, in Grade 8, the content has, to a considerable extent, been redeveloped or "beefed up" to include elements of chemistry, physics, biology, geology and others. One might gather from this that the purpose of exploration has been intensified and focused.

Ever since Sputnik there has been a rather definite upward trend in

[12]This is an unpublished report which will be included in the Third Edition of William T. Gruhn and Harl R. Douglass', *The Junior High School,* N. Y. Roland Press. Permission for extractions from the report was granted by Dr. Wm. T. Gruhn, University of Connecticut.

offerings in the foreign languages in the junior high schools. This has been true in all three grades particularly in the 7th in which there were few, if any, offerings, several years ago. The rationale behind the expanded offerings continues to be(1)that knowledge of foreign languages will enhance American influence and promote greater understanding with other nations and(2)that such knowledge produces an over-all cultural polish of individuals.

Although it is not within the purpose of this article to pursue the extent of offerings in foreign languages in the grades below the 7th, Gruhn and Douglass revealed that perhaps, from one-fourth to one-half of the elementary schools offer one or more foreign language courses particularly in French. It would, therefore, be unheard of to fail to do at least as much in the junior high school grades.

What is certainly not surprising is that French and Spanish overwhelmingly dominate the foreign language offerings with German a poor third. Spanish seems to hold an edge over French in grades 7 and 8 which is, perhaps, due to greater attention to the southerly neighbors. The ninth grade has extended offerings in Latin.

English, of course, which has traditionally been a bulwark in the curriculum, continues to hold its dominant place in the school. There are, however, a few trends which deserve attention. One of these is the development of reading programs particularly in Grades 7 and 8. Many of these are remedial reading programs. Another trend is the struggle of linguistics to take the place of grammar. It is difficult to tell whether linguistics is winning out.

There are still a sizable number of schools where English is taught in core classes with Social Studies as the partner area. Although the Gruhn-Douglass survey shows core classes continuing about the same as they have been in the past few years, there appears to be a lack of that enthusiasm which prevailed at one time. Perhaps, they are viewed as suspect but, in the absence of a real alternative to a rather advantageous block scheduling, they are continued.

The status of the social studies in the junior high school poses a paradox. There are many offerings in the social studies as social studies particularly in Grades 7 and 8. These are usually required of most, if not all, students. In the ninth grade the social studies are mostly taught as separate subjects. Although the social studies seem to be retained as areas in the junior high school, little, if anything, is happening to intensify exploration or inquiry in depth in the field. Somehow the social studies and related areas appear to be in a state of continuing decay. Except in a few schools and, in comparison with other subjects such as in the area of science and mathematics, the social studies remain in a very static condition. In view of the importance of this area as verbalized from many sources and the rather passive universal attention given to it, a paradoxical condition is certainly evident—"the song is ended but the melody lingers on."

The purpose of exploration, and the so-called area of "needs" of junior high students, continues to be served in the continued adequate to rich offerings in industrial arts.

TRENDS WHICH MAY BE UNEXPECTED

At the time of Sputnik with the emphasis on science, mathematics, and foreign languages there was considerable concern about what areas in the junior high school would suffer as a result of this condition. No doubt, some areas did suffer but not the ones predicted such as the arts and humanities. Although these may have suffered at the beginning, the trend now seems to be toward slightly more emphasis in the arts and crafts and considerably more emphasis in music.

Programs for the gifted were pressured into being in a considerable segment of the high schools, but these have gradually shifted downward and have become more inclusive of students; they have also tended to upgrade the quality of substance of many areas. Furthermore, there has been increased emphasis in programs for the retarded, the emotionally disturbed and others more or less disadvantaged. Federal impetus has, of course, influenced this trend to a considerable extent.

As is true with the arts and music industrial arts areas have not suffered. This is also true in the areas of English.

Although it cannot be documented, it appears that the area which may have suffered largely by default is that of the social studies. Although the offerings in this area seem to be many, they at the same time, appear unexciting, uninspiring and in a state of erosion. The approach to social studies is analogous to the love of mother and country which everyone believes but which lacks the lustre of stimulating awareness to one's extended existence and the realities which have to be encountered. Perhaps, the whole area of the social studies should be cause for alarm on the part of the teachers, principals, and others in the junior high school.

A trend which may have been unexpected is the increasing disenchantment with the junior high school as the arrangement which relates to the problems of young adolescents. As a result there is more and more discussion and writing about other forms of groupings most of which are referred to as middle schools. Quite a number of plans different from the 6-3-3 are being attempted under the rationale that boys and girls group themselves quite differently in terms of interest than that associated with the 6-3-3. Many of these plans begin with organizational structure. A notable exception is the one indicated in the article by Alexander and Williams which sets no definite age or grade arrangement but which suggests criteria or guidelines for a *Model Middle School* along with a curriculum plan and organization for instruction.

Breakthrough Possibilities

The thinking about the junior high school reveals a sort of encapsulated condition. This condition suggests priorities which support unwittingly a more or less closed system when it comes to assessing the possibilities of the junior high school and the alternatives such as middle schools and other organizational groupings. The thinking proceeds largely on priorities which relate to organizational patterns rather than the approach to intensive programs of inquiry relative to knowledge. This condition poses some rather searching questions which need to be considered in an appraisal or reappraisal of the junior high school and its curriculum.

Conditions and questions which may suggest breakthrough possibilities through trends in the junior high school are the following:

Does a regrouping of children into "so-called" middle school arrangements constitute another form of organizational "bandwagonitis"?

May the flurry of rearrangements have the effect of placing people further into a state of out-of-awareness regarding areas of identity of youth with the pursuit of knowledge?

May the whole practice of segmentation of youth into age and grade groups in the educational continuum constitute a resignation to their further enculturation without providing the avenues to a recognition of the absurdities involved in this condition?

Is the pattern of cultural institutionalization becoming a form of encapsulated thinking?

As one appraises the programs in the junior high school do they not warrant a careful examination of the priorities associated with "orderation" designed for the facilitation of completion rather than the return to the pursuit of knowledge? In other words, is there a condition which unwittingly promotes the "death image" rather than the "life image" of the pupil?

Is there a danger that block scheduling, core classes and other arrangements become systems which may obscure the factors of alienation and identity which youth must confront?

To what degree has there generated thinking designed to affect the conditions for vertical as well as horizontal confrontation between the many societies of youth and teachers in the educational continuum?

A careful approach to these and other questions should promote the conditions for a greater sense of awareness on the part of youth and educators to a breakthrough to a greater identity with what is real and to develop many societies of youth with built-in systems of "openness" to dialogic encounter among them.